Cyberspace Law

This book explores what the American Civil Liberties Union calls the 'third era' in cyberspace, in which filters 'fundamentally alter the architectural structure of the Internet, with significant implications for free speech.' Although courts and nongovernmental organizations increasingly insist upon constitutional and other legal guarantees of a freewheeling Internet, multinational corporations compete to produce tools and strategies for making it more predictable. When Google attempted to improve our access to information contained in books and the World Wide Web, copyright litigation began to tie up the process of making content searchable. Just as the courts were insisting that using trademarks online to criticize their owners is protected by the First Amendment, corporations and trade associations accelerated their development of ways to make Internet companies liable for their users' infringing words and actions, potentially circumventing free speech rights. And as social networking and content-sharing sites have proliferated, so have the terms of service and content-detecting tools for finding, flagging, and deleting content that makes a corporation fear for its image or profits.

Cyberspace Law provides a legal history of Internet regulation since the mid-1990s, with a particular focus on freedom of speech, net neutrality, and efforts by patent, trademark, and copyright owners to compel Internet firms to monitor their online offerings and remove or pay for any violations of the rights of others.

This book will be of interest to students of law, communications, political science, government and policy, business, and economics, as well as anyone interested in free speech and commerce on the Internet.

Hannibal Travis has taught Internet Law at Florida International University and Villanova University. He is the author of numerous articles about the law and practice of Internet-related innovation, especially relating to blogs, digital libraries, and online videos. He is a graduate of Harvard Law School.

Cyberspace Law

Censorship and regulation of the Internet

Edited by

Hannibal Travis

Routledge
Taylor & Francis Group

LONDON AND NEW YORK

First published 2013
by Routledge
2 Park Square, Milton Park, Abingdon, Oxon OX14 4RN

Simultaneously published in the USA and Canada
by Routledge
711 Third Avenue, New York, NY 10017

Routledge is an imprint of the Taylor & Francis Group, an informa business

British Library Cataloguing in Publication Data
A catalogue record for this book is available from the British Library

Library of Congress Cataloguing in Publication Data
A catalog record for this book has been requested

ISBN 978-0-415-63030-6 (hbk)
ISBN 978-0-415-63031-3 (pbk)
ISBN 978-0-203-38475-6 (ebk)

Typeset in Garamond
by Cenveo Publisher Services

Printed and bound in the United States of America by Publishers Graphics, LLC on sustainably sourced paper.

For Merrill Travis, whose love of learning and contributions to the deployments of new technologies inspired his children to learn, teach, and write.

Contents

Illustrations

Figures

Tables

Preface

The views expressed in the chapters, as well as any errors, are the responsibility of the individual authors and of the various sources they cite or quote from, including many textual and Internet sources which could not be personally confirmed by the authors and editors due to limitations of time and resources. Views expressed in one chapter should not be attributed to the editor or to the other chapters' authors, or to the institutions and firms with which the individual authors and the editor are or may be affiliated.

Miami, Florida, October 2012

Acknowledgements

The editor would like to thank the individual authors for contributing creative, informative, and thought-provoking chapters to this volume. He thanks Dean Alex Acosta, Florida International University, and the people of the State of Florida for providing the sabbatical time during which this book was researched, prepared, and edited. He would also like to thank the current and former FIU College of Law students Vanessa Harlacher, Jessica Ciminero and Christian Sanchelima for their excellent research assistance.

List of contributors

Jasmine Abdel-khalik is the author of the chapter entitled, "Is eBay counterfeiting?," and is an Associate Professor of Law at the University of Missouri-Kansas City School of Law. She teaches Intellectual Property, Contract Law, Business Torts, Advanced Trademark, and Commercial Transactions. She is the author of 'To Live in In-"Fame"-Y: Reconceiving Scandalous Marks as Analogous to Famous Marks,' *Cardozo Arts & Entertainment Law Journal*, 25 (2007), and 'Is a Rose by Any Other Image Still a Rose? Disconnecting Dilution's Similarity Test from Traditional Trademark Concepts,' *University of Toledo Law Review*, 39 (2008). She practiced intellectual property litigation at Baker & McKenzie LLP and Freeborn & Peters, LLP.

Margreth Barrett is the author of Chapter 1, entitled "Claiming Web addresses as property." She is a Professor of Law at the University of California, Hastings. She is the author of several casebooks on intellectual property law, as well as 'Domain Names, Trademarks, and the First Amendment: Searching for Meaningful Boundaries,' *Connecticut Law Review* 39:973 (2007) (reprinted in *Trademark Reporter* 97:848 (2007)), and 'A Cause of Action for "passing Off"/Associational Marketing', *I.P. Theory* 1:1 (2010), 'Consolidating the Diffuse Paths to Trade Dress Functionality: Encountering TrafFix on the way to Sears,' *Washington and Lee Law Review* 61:79 (2004), and 'Trade Dress Protection for Product Configurations and the Federal Right to Copy,' *Hastings Communications and Entertainment Law Journal* 20:471 (1998).

Ann Bartow is the author of the chapter entitled, "Bad Samaritanism: *Barnes v. Yahoo!* and Section 230 ISP immunity." She is a Professor of Law at Pace Law School, and taught previously at the University of South Carolina School of Law. She teaches Intellectual Property Law, Copyright Law, Trademarks and Unfair Competition Law, Patent Law and Cyberspace Law. She is the author of, among many other works, 'A Feeling of Unease About Privacy Law,' *University of Pennsylvania Law Review* 154 (2006), 'Internet Defamation as Profit Center: The Monetization of Online

Harassment,' *Harvard Journal of Law and Gender* 32 (2009), and 'A Portrait of the Internet as a Young Man,' *Michigan Law Review* 108 (2010). She practiced law at McCutchen, Doyle, Brown & Enersen from 1990 to 1992.

Raphael Cohen-Almagor is the author of the chapter entitled, "Internet responsibility, geographic boundaries and business ethics." He is the Chair in Politics at the University of Hull, and Director of the Middle East Study Group. He teaches Internet regulation, Freedom of Expression, Media Ethics, Medical Ethics, Political Theory, and Internet Studies. He is the author of *Speech, Media and Ethics: The Limits of Free Expression* (2005), 2nd edn, New York: Palgrave Macmillan, 'Hate in the Classroom: Free Expression, Holocaust Denial, and Liberal Education,' *American Journal of Education* 114:215 (2008), and 'In Internet's Way,' *in Ethics and Evil in the Public Sphere: Media, Universal Values and Global Development* (2010), Creskill, NY: Hampton Press, and the editor of *Liberal Democracy and the Limits of Tolerance* (2000), Ann Arbor, MI: University of Michigan Press. Raphael is also the editor or co-editor of eight other books and the author of dozens of articles in the fields of philosophy, political science, law, media studies, sociology, ethics, history and education. He was Fulbright Visiting Professor at UCLA School of Law (1999–2000), Visiting Professor at Johns Hopkins University (2003–2004), Founder and Director of the Center for Democratic Studies, University of Haifa, Israel (2003–2007), and Fellow at the Woodrow Wilson International Center for Scholars (2007–2008).

Johanna K.P. Dennis is the author of the chapter entitled, "Owning methods of conducting business in cyberspace," and is an Associate Professor of Law at Southern University Law Center. She teaches Intellectual Property Law, Patent Law: Special Topics, and Immigration Law, and is a Registered Patent Attorney with the U.S. Patent and Trademark Office. She is the author of 'Divergence in Patent Systems: A Discussion of Biotechnology Transgenic Animal Patentability and US Patent System Reform,' *International Journal of Private Law* 1:268 (2008), and 'The "Process" of Patenting: Why Should We Care About a Potential U.S. Supreme Court Decision in *Bilski v. Doll?*,' *Computer Law & Security Review*, 25 (2009).

Amir Hassanabadi is the author of the chapter entitled, "Red flags of 'piracy' online." He is a graduate of the Boalt Hall School of Law at the University of California, Berkeley, and during the summer of 2012, practiced intellectual property and Internet law at Fenwick & West in Silicon Valley, California. He is the author of 'Viacom v. YouTube—All Eyes Blind: The Limits of the DMCA in a Web 2.0 World,' *Berkeley Technology Law Journal* 26:405 (2011).

Lateef Mtima is the author of the chapter entitled, "The promise of information justice." He is a Professor of Law and the Founder and Director of the

Institute for Intellectual Property and Social Justice at the Howard University School of Law. He teaches Introduction to Intellectual Property, Computer Law, Sales and Secured Transactions, and Torts. He is a member of the Advisory Board for the *BNA Patent, Trademark, and Copyright Journal*. He is the author of 'Fulfilling the Copyright Social Justice Promise: Digitized Textual Information,' *New York Law School Law Review* 55 (2010) (with Steven Jamar), 'The Centrality of Social Justice for an Academic Intellectual Property Institute,' *Southern Methodist University Law Review* 64:1127 (2011) (with Steven Jamar), 'Tasini and Its Progeny: The New Exclusive Right or Fair Use on the Electronic Publishing Frontier?,' *Fordham Intellectual Property, Media & Entertainment Law Journal* 14:369 (2004), and 'So Dark the CON(TU) of Man: The Quest for a Software Derivative Work Right in Section 117,' *University of Pittsburgh Law Review* 69:1 (2007). He has practiced law with Coudert Brothers in New York and San Francisco.

Hannibal Travis is the volume editor and wrote the Introduction as well as the chapters on "The 'monster' that ate social networking?" and "Neutralizing the open Internet," and the subchapter on "Who 'controls' the Internet?" He has taught Internet Law, Intellectual Property, Antitrust, International and Comparative Law, and Business Law at Florida International University in Miami, FL. He is the author of, among other works, 'YouTube from Afghanistan to Zimbabwe: Censor Locally, Tyrannize Globally,' in *Transnational Culture in the Internet Age* (2012), Cheltenham, England: Edward Elgar, 'The FCC's New Theory of the First Amendment,' *Santa Clara Law Review* 51:417 (2011), 'The Future According to Google: Technology Policy from the Standpoint of America's Fastest-Growing Technology Company,' *Yale Journal of Law and Technology* 11:209 (2009), 'Opting Out of the Internet in the United States and European Union: Copyright, Safe Harbors, and International Law,' *Notre Dame Law Review* 84:331 (2008), 'Of Blogs, eBooks, and Broadband: Access to Digital Media as a First Amendment Right,' *Hofstra Law Review* 35:1519 (2007), and 'Google Book Search and Fair Use: iTunes for Authors, or Napster for Books?,' *Miami Law Review* 61:87 (2006). From 1999 to 2000 and 2001 to 2004, he practiced intellectual property and Internet litigation at O'Melveny & Myers and Debevoise & Plimpton, respectively. His articles on Google and intellectual property and on software copyrights and licensing were selected by Thomson Reuters as among the best articles relating to intellectual property law published in 2008 and 2010, respectively.

Table of authorities

Constitutional Provisions

Statutes and E.C. Directives

5 U.S.C. § 551 et seq.
15 U.S.C. § 1114(1)(a)
15 U.S.C. § 1125(a)
15 U.S.C. § 1125(c)
15 U.S.C. § 1125(d)
15 U.S.C. § 1127 9,
17 U.S.C. § 512 (c)
17 U.S.C. § 512 (d)
18 U.S.C. § 2702
35 U.S.C. § 101
35 U.S.C. § 102
35 U.S.C. § 103
35 U.S.C. § 112
35 U.S.C. § 321
47 U.S.C. § 153(52)
47 U.S.C. § 154(i)
47 U.S.C. § 230
47 U.S.C. § 521

Advanced Telecommunications and Opportunity Reform Act (US), H.R. 5252 (2006)

America Invents Act (US) § 18(d)(1) (2011)

Cable Television Consumer Protection and Competition Act (US), § 2(a)(6), Pub. L. 102-385, 106 Stat. 1460, 1461 (Oct. 5, 1992), codified at 47 U.S.C. § 521

Communications Act (US) (1934)

Copyright Act (US) (1976), Pub. L. No. 94-553, 90 Stat. 2541 20, 22, 87

Criminal Code (Neth.) (1994) 192

Directive 2009/140/EC on a common regulatory framework for electronic communications and services (European Communities). Online. Available at: <http://eur-lex.europa.eu/LexUriServ/LexUriServ.do?uri=CELEX:32009L0140:EN:NOT>.

Electronic Communications Privacy Act

Freedom of the Press Act (Sweden) (1949), Article 4 192

Internet Freedom and Nondiscrimination Act (US), H.R. 5417 (2006)

Patent Act (US) (1793), 1 Stat. 318, 319, § 1

Patent Act (US) (1952)

Penal Code (Pakistan) (1960)

Public Order Act (UK) (1936)

Public Order Act (UK) (1986)

Race Relations Act (UK) (1976)

Race Relations (Amendment) Act (UK) (2000)

Stored Communications Act

U.S. House of Representatives, Advanced Telecommunications and Opportunity Reform Act, Report No. 109-470, H.R. 5252, 109th Cong. (2006).

U.S. House of Representatives, Digital Millennium Copyright Act, Report No. 105-551, Part 2, H.R. 2281, 105th Cong. (1998)

U.S. House of Representatives, Internet Freedom and Nondiscrimination Act, House Report No. 109-541, H.R. 5417, 109th Cong. (2006).

U.S. Senate, Digital Millennium Copyright Act, Senate Report No. 105-190, S. 2037, 105th Cong. (1998).

Introduction

Cyberspace as a product of public-private censorship

Hannibal Travis[1]

Cyberspace networks the globe. Its "bright lattices of logic" simulate and transcend the world in a "cage of neon" (Gibson, 1984, 5–10). Yet attempts to restrict it are at the center of some of the key legal battles of our time. Copyright owners seek to impose copyright filters on YouTube, possibly censoring thousands of channels and millions of videos in a way that television has never been regulated (Viacom, 2012). Trademark owners' complaints shape the content of eBay and other online shopping sites, and copyright holders have shut down some software services using arguably antiquated notions of "encouraging" illegality (Tiffany, 2010, 104). The American Civil Liberties Union has warned that patents are being issued by the U.S. government for inventions implicating methods of speech or thought implemented by computer (ACLU, 2008).

Public-private censorship is a subtle, arguably postmodern technique of watching and restricting the exercise of the freedoms of expression and association by seemingly nonviolent incentives and influences communicated by governments to private corporations and persons (Travis, 2011). This chapter explores a few important developments in the application of postmodern censorship from the mid-1990s to the early 2010s.

The Internet versus the State?

Although the U.S. government pioneered computers as early as the 1940s and the precursor to the Internet starting in the late 1960s, members of the public only began to adopt these technologies in large numbers in the 1980s

---

1 Associate Professor of Law, Florida International University College of Law. Portions of this Introduction were previously published in the articles 'Opting Out of the Internet in the United States and European Union: Copyright, Safe Harbors, and International Law,' *Notre Dame Law Review*, 84 (2008): 331, 'Of Blogs, eBooks, and Broadband: Access to Digital Media as a First Amendment Right,' *Hofstra Law Review*, 35:1519 (2007), and 'The Battle for Mindshare: The Emerging Consensus that the First Amendment Protects Corporate Criticism and Parody on the Internet,' *Virginia Journal of Law & Technology*, 10:3 (2005).

(*ACLU v. Reno*, 1996, 841; Hafner and Lyon, 1998, 54–62). Starting in about 1991, the World Wide Web opened up the Internet to a wider universe of readers (Berners-Lee, 2000, 15, 28–9, 55; Mills, 1996, A15), and politicians became more active in underwriting popular access to an "information super-highway" of electronic resources and federally-collected information (Richards, 1989, F1). The Web doubled in size every year in the 1990s (*MTV Networks v. Curry*, 1994, 203), as tens of millions of Americans subscribed to the Internet on America Online and other providers of Internet connectivity (Cha, 1999, E01), and began to utilize Web hosting services like Geocities, portals like Yahoo!, search engines like Altavista, social networking sites like Classmates.com, and other Internet service providers.

The early years of scholarly and popular discussion of the Internet involved a great deal of what James Boyle called "digital libertarianism" (Boyle, 1997). A libertarian framework concerning online speech commonly sees the individual's freedom to speak as being ideally unlimited. Inequalities in access to computers and Internet services were often ignored, perhaps on the assumption that the cost of any digital technology is reduced dramatically over time by mass production and increased competition. "Information wants to be free," John Perry Barlow reminded us. "Anybody can set up a Web site," the *New York Times* quoted the publisher of *High Times* as saying (Wren, 1997, A1). John Perry Barlow's influential *Declaration of the Independence of Cyberspace*, mirrored on 20 sites from Romania to Denmark by 1998, proclaimed that on the Internet, "whatever the human mind may create can be reproduced and distributed infinitely at no cost." For these reasons, Barlow predicted, the denizens of cyberspace would make "a world that all may enter without privilege or prejudice accorded by race, economic power, military force, or station of birth" (Barlow, 1997).

Some digital libertarians downplayed the threat of censorship on the assumption that "the thick fingers of Leviathan are too clumsy" to pose a threat to our cyberliberties (Boyle, 1997). Digital libertarians often reminded those concerned with the regulation of cyberspace that: "The Net interprets censorship as damage and routes around it" (Boyle, 1997). Indeed, the U.S. government built the early Internet as a means of decentralizing communications, so as to prevent disruption at a central node in time of war, as Iraqi and Yugoslav communications were disrupted by U.S. bombs (McWilliams, 2003). The Declaration mocked government with the point that it lacked "any methods of enforcement we have true reason to fear." As Boyle put it, the hope was that the "state is too big, too slow, too geographically and technically limited to regulate a global citizenry's fleeting interactions over a mercurial medium" (Boyle, 1997).

The tendencies of digital libertarianism found expression in such "cyber-zines" as *CNET*, *Wired*, *Slate*, and *Salon*. The Internet's victory over the State, according to the most effusive versions of digital libertarianism, would usher us into a free marketplace of ideas, in which the truth would prevail because there would no longer be any censors between it and "the people."

The State strikes back: Indirect regulation and mobilized private power

The late 1990s saw a series of coordinated pushes for the U.S. federal government to assert greater control over Internet content, but in accordance with the principle of privatization and corporate leadership within the National Information Infrastructure. In what follows, I explain three domains in which legislative reform efforts bore fruit during this time frame: indecency, copyright, and trademark. The results were the Communications Decency Act, the Digital Millennium Copyright Act (DMCA), and the Anti-cybersquatting Consumer Protection Act.

The primary function of the Communications Decency Act, or the CDA,[2] may not have been to actually punish and deter indecent speech through sporadically imposed fines and imprisonment after the fact, but rather to induce a scheme of private surveillance/deletion of, and hard-wired restrictions on, indecency. After all, a criminal-law strategy would be another attempt to frighten geographically dispersed individuals away from trading information in an environment highly resistant to centralized control, with an expectation of success somewhere in the order of the war on drugs. But there is another hypothesis. Lawrence Lessig stated it well: "Rather than regulating behavior directly, government will regulate indirectly. Rather than making rules that apply to constrain individuals directly, government will make rules that require a change in code … the architecture of the net" (Lessig, 1997, 184).

When one considers the widely shared interpretation of the CDA as criminalizing the role of Internet service providers (ISPs) in making indecent material available to minors,[3] the CDA would have induced private initiatives to "zone" Internet content using passwords, and to continually monitor the content on the Web for indecent sites available to the public without screening, for potential removal (this process could have been automated

---

2 The CDA prohibited the "knowing transmission of obscene or indecent messages to any recipient under 18 years of age" and the "knowing sending or displaying of patently offensive messages in a manner that is available to a person that is under 18 years of age." *Reno v. American Civil Liberties Union*, 521 U.S. 844 (1997). The Act provided two defenses, or "safe harbor" provisions: one, that a person has taken "good faith, reasonable, effective and appropriate actions under the circumstances to restrict or prevent access by minors … including any method which is feasible under available technology"; and two, that a person "has restricted access to such communication by requiring use of a verified credit card, debit account, adult access code, or adult personal identification number."

3 As Brock Meeks observed: "[T]he bill would slap criminal liabilities on all Internet service providers, commercial online services, bulletin board systems and even electronic mail providers whenever their services are used to transmit any material that's considered 'obscene, lewd, lascivious, filthy, or indecent.' Oh yeah, the person actually responsible for sending the message gets hammered as well, with up to US$100,000 in fines and two years behind bars." (Meeks, 1998).

within a relatively short period of time). The result would quite likely have been a considerably more universal and precise means of getting unscreened indecency off the Internet than a regime that merely attempted to punish individual speakers after the fact. The CDA attempted to exploit the advantages of "law as code" in terms of programming a system over traditional "law" as punishment for violation of a rule:

> Code is an efficient means of regulation. But its perfection makes it something different. One obeys these laws as code not because one should; one obeys these laws as code because one can do nothing else. There is no choice about whether to yield to the demand for a password; one complies if one wants to enter the system. In the well implemented system, there is no civil disobedience. Law as code is a start to the perfect technology of justice.
>
> (Lessig, 1996, 1408)

This meant that those who saw censorship exclusively in terms of brute force might be vulnerable to the efficient privatized implementation of the regulation of Internet indecency.

In order to understand what is at stake in regulatory schemes like the CDA, one must be attuned to indirect state action designed to induce private surveillance, to the possibility of "retail" precision control of content, to invisible ISP-level deletion of files, and to the danger of an increase in the Internet's economic productivity (in the push for more expensive-to-administer, credit-card-operated, increasingly commercial sites) coupled with the decrease in its diversity. As a zoning scheme achieved through password-protected hypertext code, the CDA would enjoy the lower administrative and political costs characteristic of a regime of surveillance.

There was a rather complex relationship between government threats and private initiatives in the debate over filtering software. Filtering software, or "User Empowerment Technologies" as they were somewhat euphemistically referred to in the 1990s (including by U.S. President Bill Clinton), came in two varieties (Weitzner, 1998). First, "Listener-centered" blocking software, such as Cyber-Sitter, Net-Nanny, and their progeny, typically blocked access to a list of forbidden sites while simultaneously automatically refusing to load documents containing "forbidden strings of words" (Boyle, 1997). Second, "Speaker-centered" rating systems, including the Platform for Internet Content Selection (PICS), allowed the embedding of rating information in the "meta-file" information provided in the programming language in which Web pages are written (Boyle, 1997). These systems were touted as promoting value-neutral user-based control over content, as diverse filtering regimes might emerge from which users could choose. With one click, users could render their browser incapable of accessing indecent, blasphemous, or racist sites, based on their own preferences.

The political reaction to these systems was considerably more restrained than that directed at the CDA, and understandably so; no one was being fined, or going to jail, or having their sites removed from the Internet. Proponents of such systems proclaimed, in effect, "Use this system, otherwise the government will pass laws to put you in jail." (Finkelstein, 1998). Indeed, the development of PICS was initiated by computer scientists and software engineers concerned with government censorship, as a means of forestalling such action (Resnick, 1998). However, some analysts expressed alarm at the prospects of censorship pursued with subtler means than direct government action. One objection to systems like PICS was that they might not remain voluntary for very long. Without a government mandate, third-party labeling and rating systems seem incapable of rating sufficient numbers of the vast and growing world of the Web. Although tens of thousands of sites were rated, this constituted only 2–4% of total Web sites as of 1998 (Resnick, 1998). This, of course, increased the attractiveness of a self-rating mandate, with two caveats: one, insufficient incentives to rate may warrant a requirement that "web browsers be configured to block access to all unrated sites" (Weitzner, 1998); and two, "[w]ithout a penalty system for mis-rating, the entire concept of a self-ratings system breaks down" (ACLU, 1997). Legislation introducing penalties for mis-rating sites was proposed (ACLU, 1997).

Even in the absence of a Web-ratings mandate, large private Internet concerns found it in their interest to make the Internet more "accessible," "family-friendly," and profitable. America Online embodied, in voluminous and murky "Terms of Service" and an entire bureaucracy of "Guides," a corporate policy along these lines (AOLSucks.org, 1998). Microsoft included PICS features in Internet Explorer, and Netscape pledged to do the same, bringing PICS to more than 90% of the browser market. The ACLU pointed to a disturbing potential for censorship:

> Unrated speech on the Internet is effectively blocked by these defaults. Search engines refuse to report on the existence of unrated or "unacceptably" rated sites.
>
> (ACLU, 1997)

This is a system even more indirect than was the CDA's envisioned public-private collaboration on surveillance and control. The detection and blocking of indecent sites by PICS could be automatic, hard-wired into the Web technologies of browsers and search engines. The precision of the regulation would be unprecedented, precluding any holes in the filtering software's lists of forbidden sites and search terms. Lessig advanced the following critique:

> The problem is that the filter can be imposed at the level of the individual user, the corporation, the proxy server, the Internet service provider,

or the national government. This is disastrous, because you can have invisible filtering done at any level of the distribution chain.

The invisible filtering would be likely be characterized by the wide scope of censorship now found in private filtering software, reaching gay sites; sexual education; reportage on violence from crime to war; and the occasional moment of profanity or objectionable content found in much art, political commentary, and human communication in all its forms.[4]

PICS might have led to a system of regulation of indecency arguably even more precise and expansive than the CDA would have been. Not the least of concerns was that the minimal government role and sweeping private roles could make an end-run around the constitutional concerns that meant the end of the CDA (Lessig, 1996, 894). We find, to an extent unmatched even by the CDA, that with "terms of service," backed by threats of government regulation of cyberspace, censorship has been privatized. This increases the extent and automaticity of the surveillance; the pinpoint accuracy of the control; and the invisible, apolitical, "merely technological" nature of the day-to-day regulation. The ACLU framed the threat that PICS posed as follows: "mandatory Internet self-rating could easily turn the most participatory communications medium the world has yet seen into a bland, homogenized, medium dominated by powerful American corporate speakers" (ACLU, 1997).

What, then, might really be at stake in Internet content regulation for obscenity or indecency in an age of widespread and readily accessible commercial pornography? The key to understanding the push for laws like the CDA can be found in Judge Dalzell's observation about the law's exception for commercial pornographers. What provisions such as the CDA and mandatory ratings schemes aimed for was an ordering and zoning of the Internet, a fixing of the multiplicity of its anarchic, and often indecent, streams of communication among users (Lessig, 1996). By making indecency increasingly unspeakable for noncommercial speakers who did not necessarily have the resources to verify the age of their listeners (*ACLU v. Reno*, 1997), or rate every digital utterance, the regulation of indecency would reduce the diversity of speech.

Fortunately for cyberspace, the United States Supreme Court, in *ACLU v. Reno*, condemned the CDA for seeking to confer "broad powers of censorship, in the form of a 'heckler's veto,' upon any opponent of indecent speech" (*ACLU v. Reno*, 1997, 880).

4 J.D. Lasica posed this question: "Consider one image, the Pulitzer Prizewinning photo of a young, naked, terrified Vietnamese girl whose village was napalmed by an American jet. Surely, that would have scored high on the violence and nudity rating scales." J.D. Lasica, 'X-Rated Ratings? (Newspapers and Rating of Internet Contents),' *Am. Journalism Review*, Oct, 1, 1997, p. 42.

The State as champion of copyrights against "piracy"

Governments' initial efforts to expand the rights of content owners culminated in the World Intellectual Property Organization's Copyright Treaty and the Clinton Administration's "White Paper" on intellectual property rights online. The Report of the Commerce Department's Working Group on Intellectual Property Rights advocated the privatization of copyright enforcement, with cyberspace's intermediaries being deputized to search out and delete infringing expressive or informational works (U.S. Department of Commerce, 1995). Legislation and a treaty designed to implement this regime was introduced soon after its release (NII Copyright Protection Act, 1995; WIPO Act, 1996).

Boyle summed up the effort: "On-line providers – America Online, for example – will become strictly liable for violations of copyright by their members, making it necessary for them to monitor what their users are doing" (Boyle, 1995). The proposals drafted Internet service providers such as Yahoo! and AOL into "copyright police", compelled to monitor use for infringement and facilitate the development of "documents [that] spy" on users (Samuelson, 1996). The White Paper referred to this regime for "managing rights in protected works" as a "combination of file- and system-based access controls" (U.S. Department of Commerce, 1995). The other major elements, such as labeling the temporary display of a document (i.e. Web browsing) as an infringement of the exclusive right to "reproduce" copies under the Copyright Act, terming digital transmissions as infringing "distributions" of copies under the Act, and dramatically reining in the fair use and first sale rights of consumers, had "negative synerg[ies]" with ISP strict liability and documents that spy on their users (Samuelson, 1996). After all, the very characteristics that induced the federal government to develop the Internet and that cyberlibertarians claim ensures its freedom would make any law outlawing the display of a work, or its fair use, or its resale, toothless in the absence of more sophisticated enforcement strategies. Even groups among the most prominent critics of the Department of Commerce and its legislative proposals supported legislation that encouraged private entities to control Internet users' freedoms in the name of fighting copyright violations (Digital Future Coalition, 1997).

Just as the CDA would have enlisted ISPs to control and monitor when and how indecent material would be made available online, the White Paper made ISPs the arbiters of how much one Internet user copied from or imitated the style of another user, or took from the content or style of printed or audiovisual work. The Commerce Department Working Group reasoned that ISPs must be liable for copyright infringement because "only they – are in a position to know the identity and activities of their subscribers and to stop unlawful activities" and "piracy" (1995). The ISPs, in performing the gatekeeper function, would be able, and needed to be incentivized, to perform the day-to-day function of searching for and deleting infringing speech. Their surveillance would be pervasive, rather than discontinuous, their control would err on the side of caution, rather than laxity, their remedial action would be far less visible than a series of FBI raids or massive jury verdicts, and the system as a whole would be far more profitable than would one of sporadic and expensive civil and criminal proceedings against individual offenders. Thus, ISP liability was different in important respects from a traditional system of due process in which injured parties must initiate litigation against individual infringers or otherwise bring in the authorities, once infringement inflicts harm.

James Boyle mentioned another advantage of enlisting ISPs as "private police": their indifference to the constitutional and statutory restraints faced by government actors (Boyle, 1997). By adopting disciplinary techniques, the federal government would be able to escape the "legal limitations of a sovereign-citizen relationship" (ibid.). If the ISPs could suffer civil liability every so often, or see their brethren suffer as much, it is difficult to imagine why they would not act quickly to eliminate this cost of doing business by searching their machines for borderline content and getting rid of it. By this simple mechanism, violations of privacy, "automatic scrutiny of e-mail, curtailing of fair use rights so as to make sure that no illicit content was being carried," and so on would occur automatically, far from legal scrutiny (ibid.).

Perhaps with enough time, compliance software would be developed, and channels of regular communication between content providers, governments, and ISPs established, so that the process of surveillance and control could take place at less cost and with more precision. Companies, and particularly the holders of vast "content portfolios," would establish positions or departments devoted to searching the Web or other Internet communications to find arguably infringing content. ISPs, in turn, would appoint departments to search for infringements using software that automatically scanned for the names of artists, labels, publishers, studios, or stations, and reported their presence, for the deletion of any quotations of or commentaries by ordinary Internet users on the works of the vast entertainment and media conglomerates. By 1998, this framework for privatizing enforcement was codified under U.S. law under the rubric of requirements that ISPs implement "a policy that provides for the termination in appropriate circumstances of subscribers and account holders of the service provider's system or network who are repeat infringers," and "accommodate and not interfere with ... standard technical measures ... used by copyright owners to identify or protect copyrighted works" (U.S. Code, 2011). Such attempts to deploy techniques of surveillance and retail control may give the lie to the claim that "the Net interprets censorship as damage and routes around it."

Turning to "file-based" access controls, the White Paper envisaged schemes to enable and reinforce "technological protection." These technological controls on the quotation of others' speech, as outlined in the White Paper, included encryption, digital signatures, and steganography. Encryption scrambles digital content so that only users authorized by the content provider to access the information will be able to decrypt it (i.e. through a password). Digital signatures put a "seal" on digital content so that "one will be able to identify from whom a particular file originated as well as verify that the contents of that file have not been altered from the contents as originally distributed." Steganography, sometimes called "digital fingerprinting" or "digital watermarking," uses "attributes that cannot be disassociated from the file that contains that information" (which, the White Paper implies, is not the case for digital signatures). At some points, the White Paper notes that such information may eventually be incorporated into files at lower levels, all the way down to the operating system level (U.S. Department of Commerce, 1995).

Two problems hinder the effectiveness of such file- or operating-system-based controls of copying. First, once a file has been decrypted as authorized it may be threatened with redistribution in that form without need for further authorization. Second, technologically-sophisticated users may either distribute versions of works for which the protections have been circumvented or develop and disseminate software itself designed to circumvent these protections. The White Paper addressed both problems: the first through ISP liability as noted above, and the second through its anti-circumvention and copyright management information provisions. The anti-circumvention provision contemplated civil liability for the manufacture, importation or distribution of "devices, products, components," and the performance of services, "that defeat technological methods of preventing unauthorized use" (U.S. Department of Commerce, 1995, Appendix 1, 6 (proposed 17 U.S.C. § 1201)). The copyright management information provision created civil liability for knowingly removing the information (basically the name of the author and copyright owner, the terms of use, and related information) or providing or distributing false information (ibid., Appendix 1, 6–7 (proposed 17 U.S.C. § 1202)). These proposals became law in 1998, and have figured in a number of cases in which artists and news sites have been sued, and one online video site driven bankrupt (Travis, 2012).

With technological protection, perpetual tracking replaces discontinuous intervention. As one Web-based provider of digital watermarking services proclaimed in the late 1990s:

> Our MarcSpider crawls the Web looking for your watermarked images and reports its findings to you … Think about it. You can discover exactly where your images are on the Web. And, anyone on the Internet can contact you through your images! In a sense, your digital watermark gives you a two-way communication tool; leverage it any way you wish.
>
> (Digimarc, 1998)

When these systems are able to control the use and reuse of content at the operating system level, many user freedoms, including fair use, will be threatened with decimation or elimination.

What anti-circumvention and copyright management laws do is encourage private attempts to monitor and control where intellectual content goes, and who sees it, by authorizing government intervention at precisely the point where private industry's control over the process might break down. Just as in the case of PICS, where proposed legislation would have mobilized the power of government to mandate private self-rating of Web sites, "copyright management" laws mobilize the power of government to punish individuals who attempt to side-step the strategies by which the distribution of digital content is restricted. Lessig describes the process as follows: "in the very near future, software will be able to control, perfectly, the use and distribution of intellectual property ... [The law must then] punish people who interfere with such software. [The idea is] that we use law to protect code" (Lessig, 1996–1997, 9–10).

The conscription of private coders by law expands governments' ability to control access to and use of copyrighted material on the Internet, while mini-mizing the political costs of this endeavor in terms of the visibility of state action and the policy-based limitations ordinarily placed upon the rights of copyright holders (Lessig, 1996–1997, 10). In this way, judges' observation that "the content on the Internet is as diverse as human thought" (*Reno v. ACLU*, 1996, 842) gives way to the Department of Commerce's demand that cyberspace helps "U.S. firms to compete and succeed in the global economy" (Department of Commerce, 1995, 10). Despite an awareness that copyright liability threatened to slow "investment" in the "speed and capacity of the Internet," and the improvement of "the variety and quality of services on the Internet" (Hatch, 1998, S4884–4886), Congress decided to make search engines and directories of information available on the Internet potentially liable for connecting users to information (U.S.C. §§ 512(c)–512(d), 512(j)(1)(A)). Among other things, they could be liable for the hosting or storing of material with "actual knowledge that the material or an activity using the material on the system or network is infringing," or an awareness "of facts or circumstances from which infringing activity is apparent," or a failure to remove the infringing speech "upon obtaining such knowledge or awareness" of it (ibid., §§ 512(c)(1), 512(d)(1)).

The State takes on "cybersquatters" and "cyberpiracy"

With the CDA rendered inoperative to censor indecency on the Internet, judges and litigants turned their gaze on copyright and trademark infringe-ment online. The late 1990s saw a surprising "explosion of Internet-related litigation arising out of trademark disputes" (Burk, 1998, 695–6). The Supreme Court prepared the ground for this "explosion" by being less recep-tive to assertions that reference to copyrighted or trademarked material could be just as important to conveying an idea as indecency. Despite rejecting "censorship" of indecent Internet speech in 1997, it has upheld statutes prohibiting the use of the word "Olympics" or corporate trademarks, despite appeals that such prohibitions could restrict "dissemination of a message for which there is no adequate translation" (San Francisco Arts and Athletics, 1987, 569–70). During two decades following the Court's major pronouncement on the relationship between trademarks and the First Amendment, trademark owners frequently turned to the courts to clamp down on Internet speech, including efforts by consumers, political activists, and small businesses to use the Internet to voice their complaints about unfair or unlawful corporate conduct. The owners of the "mega-brands" fired off cease-and-desist letters against small Web site owners with increasing frequency. Given its ever-expanding reach, trademark law had the potential to operate as perhaps the most powerful instrument, other than copyright law, of public or private censorship of the Internet.

With the exception of the controversies over unauthorized transmission of books, music, and movies over the Internet, trademark disputes became the dominating theme of cyberlaw. The cybersquatting controversy began in about 1994 with news stories about corporations registering each other's names as Internet addresses (Lewis, 1993, 3–10; Quittner, 1994). Tens of thousands of visitors accessed sites containing prominent trademarks such as mtv.com. MTV promptly filed suit, and obtained mtv.com back from former video jockey Adam Curry (*MTV v. Curry*, 1994, 202; Stevens & Woo, 1994, B1). Most of these early disputes were resolved without extensive litigation, and therefore contributed little to the development of the law (Zaitlen & Victor, 1996, 12). The suits' publicity, however, reinforced the "Gold Rush" mentality surrounding the possibility of claiming prime "real estate" on the Web (Quittner, 1994).

In trademark cases, courts shifted the focus from whether consumers would be confused as to the source of the products they buy, to whether their enthusiasm for a manufacturer could be somehow dampened. The claims of trademark owners began to move beyond objecting to blatant targeting of famous trademarks, to encompass broader claims to exclusive rights to the commercial use of English words in cyberspace. Sun Microsystems obtained an injunction against another company using the word "Sun" on any "World Wide Web pages and links, Internet domain names, or any other company material regardless of media" (Sun Microsystems, 1995, 1266). Congress passed an anti-"dilution" law for trademark owners in 1996, at which time some members of Congress expressed the hope that it would "'help stem the use of deceptive Internet addresses taken by those who are choosing marks that are associated with the products and reputations of others.'" (*Intermatic v. Toeppen*, 1996, 128, quoting Leahy, 1995, S19312). One court held that "'[b]ecause Internet communications transmit instantaneously on a worldwide basis there is little question that the 'in commerce' requirement would be met in a typical Internet message, be it trademark infringement or false advertising'" (ibid., 1239, quoting Gilson, 1996, 5–234). Other courts began restricting seemingly noncommercial expression on the Internet by focusing on the commercial impact on the plaintiff's business, rather than the defendant's noncommercial use of the trademark, or by examining for commercial activity not only the defendant's Web site, but any other sites to which it referred. On this basis the Second Circuit, in *Planned Parenthood v. Bucci*, upheld an injunction against an anti-abortion activist who used the domain name plannedparenthood.com to publicize his anti-abortion views (*Planned Parenthood Federation of America v. Bucci*, 1998, 920). The district court had ruled that although the defendant engaged in neither the advertising nor the sale of any services, the court held his use of the Internet in connection with the plaintiff's trademark occurred in the stream of commerce because Internet users may access his Web site "everywhere" (ibid., 1434 n. 7). Addressing the Lanham Act's anti-dilution provision, the court held that the defendant's Web site, which praised an anti-abortion book authored by someone other than the defendant (ibid., 1434), was engaging in commercial competition with Planned Parenthood in the market for "informational services," specifically "the distribution of those services over the Internet." The court dismissed the defendant's arguments that he did not receive any money from his Web site and was simply voicing his opinion on a matter of intense public concern in a way that the First Amendment protects (ibid, 1435–6).

Courts began to enjoin the "dissemination of … purely ideological information" over the Internet when the trademarks of prominent corporations or other organizations were implicated (*PETA v. Doughney*, 2000, 919). For example, in *People for the Ethical Treatment of Animals, Inc. v. Doughney*, the Fourth Circuit sustained such an injunction (2001, 359), concluding that the defendant engaged in a commercial use of the PETA mark in connection with the sale of goods or services by using the domain name peta.org to set up a Web site called "People Eating Tasty Animals" as a parody of the non-profit corporation People for the Ethical Treatment of Animals (ibid., 362–3). (See Figure I.1). Even though the defendant did not sell or advertise any products on his Web site, the court found the requisite connection to commercial activity in the bare possibility that the site would attract some Internet users who were initially searching for PETA's own site, coupled with the site's hyperlinks to 30 "meat, fur, leather, hunting, animal research, and other organizations, all of which held views generally antithetical to PETA's views" (ibid., 363, 365).

Injunctive relief against such "cybergripers" soon swept far beyond domain names to reach virtually any reference to a trademark in cyberspace (*OBH, Inc. v. Spotlight Magazine, Inc.*, 2000, 176). A small businessman in competition with the *Buffalo News* set up a Web site to complain about its allegedly unfair business practices. Although it was located at thebuffalonews.com, the site featured a prominent disclaimer of any relationship with the Buffalo News, and announced that it was designed to air "gripe[s]" and "parody" of the Buffalo News, and act as a "forum for discussion" of the Buffalo News by those desiring to exercise their "first amendment rights" (ibid., 181–3). The court held that even though his site's disclaimers removed all possible confusion as to whether it was affiliated with or endorsed by the Buffalo

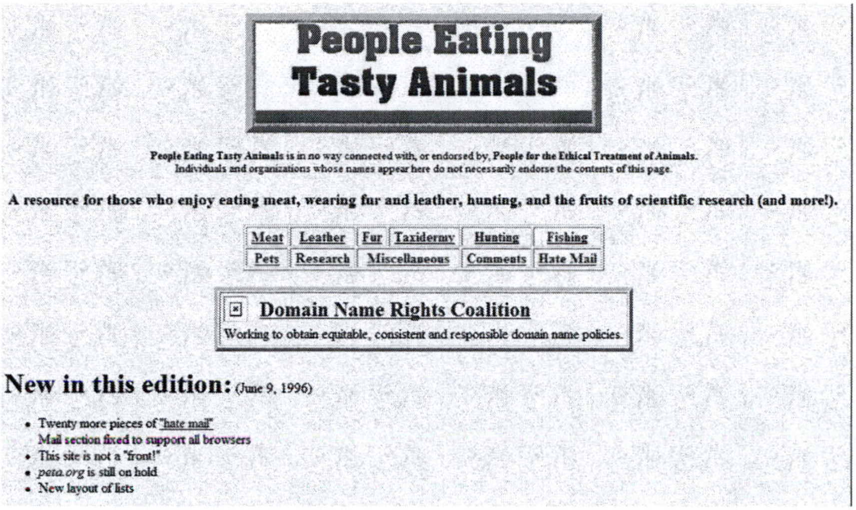

Figure I.1 Screenshot of content posted to peta.org, circa 2000.

News, the "momentar[y] ... initial interest confusion" violated the plaintiff's trademark (ibid., 190–91). Another court enjoined a Web site that disparaged the Starbucks Coffee trademark and mermaid logo as a symbol of excessive consumerism, even though the judge indicated that the site was a lawful parody under copyright and trademark infringement law *(Starbucks Corp. v. Dwyer*, 2000). "Critical commentary" was directly caught up in such lawsuits (Nissan, 2002, 980).

In 1999, Congress took additional action against the scourge of "cyberpirates" (U.S. House of Representatives, 1999, 5–6). The resulting legislation, called the Anti-cybersquatting Consumer Protection Act (ACPA), authorized injunctive relief and damages awards against any domain name holder who, with a "bad faith intent to profit" from a trademark, "registers, traffics in, or uses a domain name" that is "identical or confusingly similar" to the mark (U.S. Code, 1999, section 1125). The ACPA reached even further by allowing a trademark owner to sue the owner of a domain name that is "dilutive" of, but not similar to, its famous trademark (ibid.). In a series of cases, its sweeping language allowed trademark owners to restrain cybergripers (Travis, 2005, 69–70).

The business method patent explosion

Patent law threatened to require the reprogramming of some e-commerce sites in a case that made it to the U.S. Supreme Court in 2006. Complaints alleging the violation of patents online proliferated, and implicated the world's leading technology companies such as Amazon, Apple, eBay, Facebook, Google, Intel, and Microsoft. A key focus in the early stages of this struggle was the dispute between eBay and the owner of a patent on Internet auction listings at a fixed price about who owns this "method." eBay argued that this method of doing business online had been around since 1994, with the Web sites "Automatrix, Internet Plaza and Oslonett.no, [which] were electronic markets in that they were computerized systems that allowed participating buyers and sellers to exchange information about prices and product offerings" (*MercExchange v. eBay, Inc.*, 2002, 795–6). Indeed, one of the MercExchange patents most similar to these early sites proved to be invalid upon further proceedings (*MercExchange v. eBay, Inc.*, 2006, 1326). A jury, however, found one of MercExchange's other patents to be valid and willfully infringed (MercExchange, 2003, 698–9).

The Supreme Court ruled that MercExchange could potentially obtain a court order stopping eBay's violation of the auction patent (*eBay v. MercExchange*, 2006, 388). MercExchange argued that eBay became the dominant online auction site, at least in part by infringing one of MercExchange's patents (*MercExchange, L.L.C.*, 2007, 2). eBay fought the case for years, and a coalition of companies supporting eBay including Amazon.com and Google argued to the Supreme Court that the high-technology field was drowning in large numbers of patents that proved difficult to avoid in making complex inventions, with the number of patents issued annually doubling from 77,400 in 1985 to 157,900 in 2005 (*Time Warner et al.*, 2006, 9, citing USPTO, 2005). Yet the Supreme Court refused to rule out an injunction completely (*eBay v. MercExchange*, 2006, 394). On remand from the appeal, the district court refused an injunction, reasoning that damages for ongoing infringement could compensate the firm (*MercExchange, L.L.C.*, 2007, 6).

The Supreme Court's opinion in the eBay dispute has made it less likely that patent owners not engaged in active commercialization of the invention or competition with the infringer will obtain injunctive relief against leading technology or Internet companies (*Ellis et al.*, 2008, 442). Moreover, the Federal Circuit and the Supreme Court have reined in certain patents involving "abstract" methods, as Chapter 3 points out. The Federal Circuit has also taken a very broad and flexible view of the rule that patents should not issue on "obvious" inventions, applying it to conclude that a patent on uploading images to a social network was obvious in light of another Internet image service (*MySpace v. GraphOn*, 2012, 1262–4).

Other prominent disputes have involved patents on electronic commerce, Web searching, social networks, and smartphones. As described in Chapter 3, Amazon.com has obtained one of the most famous business method patents, on one-click Internet shopping, as well as patents on sending gifts and other e-commerce functionalities. Google settled a multi-million dollar patent challenge from Yahoo! on the cusp of its initial public offering (Gaither, 2004). As noted in Chapter 10, Facebook and Yahoo! are struggling over patents related to online advertising, news feeds, tagging photographs, and making recommendations to users. Apple has attempted to secure patent protection over the "look" of a smartphone or tablet with rounded corners, as well as over the ability to zoom in on photos and Web pages using pinches of the finger and thumb (Apple, 2012; Associated Press, 2012).

The Internet ascendant, as the First Amendment prevails

The First Amendment voids unclear "indecency" laws. The Supreme Court struck down the CDA as an overbroad and vague attempt to reduce the Internet to a kindergarten classroom (*ACLU v. Reno*, 1997, 849–50). It also invalidated the Child Online Protection Act (COPA) because, among other reasons, Internet users "may self-censor" rather than hazard stiff penalties for inadvertently displaying online materials that are harmful or indecent to minors (*Ashcroft*, 2004, 665–7, 670–73). The Court reasoned that COPA placed a burden on adults' Internet use, which the federal government conceded to be the case (ibid., 665). Parental filtering of their children's Internet use presented a much less restrictive means of ensuring decency than COPA, which required those who wanted to communicate in ways indecent or harmful to minors to migrate to platforms where ages and identities were confirmed by credit cards (ibid., 665–7).

Since the DMCA was passed, courts have also grown more sophisticated about protecting the Internet and its leading companies' operations from excessive copyright liability. As explained in more detail in Chapters 4 and 5, courts have limited the liability of search engines and storage sites to cases in which they author information rather than route it along in a transient way over Internet, do not implement a reasonable policy for dealing with repeat copyright infringers or interfere with a copyright owner's reasonable efforts to police the Web sites in question for possible infringements (*Kelly v. Arriba Soft Corp.*, 2003, 815–24). The courts reached similar results when a magazine sued ISPs, Web hosting companies, and credit card processing services for facilitating the infringement by Web sites of the magazine's photographs, holding that as long as the sites developed reasonable policies for responding to infringement of specific files, they were protected by the DMCA and other copyright defenses and limitations (*Perfect 10 v. Visa*, 2007, 796–8).

The tide also began to turn in favor of the independent Web speaker, and against overreaching corporations, when courts concluded that a Web site is not necessarily a form of commercial competition for purposes of the Lanham Act, and that it may deserve protection from censorship as a "consumer commentary" (*Bally Total Fitness v. Farber*, 1998, 1164). The Sixth Circuit, in *Taubman Co. v. Webfeats*, established clear binding authority that under the First Amendment, online criticism of companies cannot be censored as a result of overbroad trademark doctrines (2003, 770). The Sixth Circuit was addressing a case in which the defendant had established an informational

Web site concerning a shopping mall about to be erected near his home in Texas. After the mall developer sued him for trademark infringement, the defendant set up a number of additional Web sites criticizing the company and its lawyers, including taubmansucks.com (ibid., 772). The lower court issued an injunction as to both the informational and the complaint sites of the defendant, but the Sixth Circuit overturned it (ibid., 777). The court announced much more speech-protective principles of Internet trademark law that would set the tone for later cases:

> We find that [defendant's] use of Taubman's mark in the domain name "taubmansucks.com" is purely an exhibition of Free Speech, and the Lanham Act is not invoked. And although economic damage might be an intended effect of [defendant's] expression, the First Amendment protects critical commentary when there is no confusion as to source, even when it involves the criticism of a business. Such use is not subject to scrutiny under the Lanham Act. In fact, Taubman concedes that [defendant] is "free to shout 'Taubman Sucks!' from the rooftops...." Essentially, this is what he has done in his domain name. The rooftops of our past have evolved into the internet domain names of our present. We find that the domain name is a type of public expression, no different in scope than a billboard or a pulpit, and [defendant] has a First Amendment right to express his opinion about Taubman, and as long as his speech is not commercially misleading, the Lanham Act cannot be summoned to prevent it.
>
> (ibid., 777)

Later cases extended this reasoning to dilution suits (*TMI, Inc. v. Maxwell*, 2004, 433), uses of trademarks in subdomains (*Devere Group v. Opinion Corp.*, 2012, 3–5), and domain names without "sucks" in them (*Lamparello v. Falwell*, 2005, 309; *Nissan Motor v. Nissan Computer*, 2004, 1009).

Theories of Internet regulation

Two principal rationales for regulating communication on the Internet are the protection of physical and intellectual property rights, and promoting the efficiency of various markets. Although the First Amendment prohibits restraints on communication which are justified by its content (Mosley, 1972, 95–6), the moral right to receive a reward for one's own expression by restricting its unauthorized duplication and circulation has been called "content-neutral" (*Eldred v. Ashcroft*, 2003, 221). In other words, regardless of the content of his or her works, an author has the right to restrict distribution of them, or of the brand names and logos used in connection with them, or of the patented inventions they describe (Hughes, 1988, 287–366). The deservingness of an author or inventor to receive the profits attributable to his or her work grounds copyright and patent law, as well as trademark and trade secret law to an arguably lesser extent (ibid.).

A related but distinct version of the "moral desert" rationale for physical and intellectual property laws involves the potential of such rules to promote the full realization of individual and communal personalities and communities (Fisher, 1999; Waldron, 1993, 841–87). This "personality" or human capacities/self-realization approach also serves to justify tort laws protecting individual and intimate relationship privacy (Fisher, 1999). On the other hand, a person's interest in articulating his or her beliefs and perspectives free of interference lies behind some justifications for the freedom of speech (Tribe, 1988, 785).

The other prominent theory of regulations of the Internet and other forms of commerce invokes the hypothesis that the law is attempting to achieve economic efficiency (Landes and Posner, 1987, 265–6). Free-riding on intellectual property impairs efficiency by resulting in suboptimal investment in projects in which high fixed or average costs are expected, and with respect to which competitors may enter the market with knock-offs that have a low marginal cost to produce (Travis, 2005, 53). On the other hand, excessive protection of intellectual property deters the creation and commercialization of transformative or "fair use" works, including comparative advertising, parody, and criticism (ibid.). Net neutrality debates feature analogous arguments about potential efficiencies (Telecommunications Reports, 2008). Permitting broadband Internet service providers to discriminate against applications or videos that consume large amounts of bandwidth may improve the experience of the average or below-average user in terms of bandwidth, while deterring the invention and popularization of new types of applications or sites such as bitTorrent, YouTube, or Flickr, as discussed in Chapter 9.

Although these theories are beyond the scope of a lengthy exposition or critique in this Introduction, they will inform the chapters to follow, where appropriate.

The focus of this book

This book offers engaging and timely accounts of some of the key developments in the commercialization of cyberspace since 2005. These debates include whether Internet companies like eBay or Yahoo! have to take down pages offering counterfeit products or damaging to personal reputations, whether Google is allowed to scan and make a search engine of mostly out-of-print books in American libraries, whether Google and YouTube have to filter out unauthorized clips of pirated movies and TV shows or pay billions of dollars in damages, and whether entire methods of doing business on the Internet may be patented. Also, the book describes the lawsuit between Comcast and the US Federal Communications Commission (FCC) about the authority of the federal government to enact "net neutrality" rules making cyberspace freely accessible to all types of users. The broadband firms, which would like to censor offensive sites and videos, are invoking property rights in Internet infrastructure.

The book's thesis is that the rules of the road for Internet users have evolved to reflect a balance between the untrammeled freedom to communicate sought by many users, and the demands of governments, parents, other users, corporations, and associations of equipment and intellectual property owners for greater control, particularly control over the property that makes up the Internet's physical and virtual layers. The balance is being eroded, however, by new technological tools for spying on, shaping, and censoring communications over the Internet to an unprecedented degree. As techniques such as automated content matching (for YouTube) or surveillance "backdoors" (for Facebook) are perfected, the freedoms and privacy we enjoy on the Internet are being eroded. As governments and Internet corporations deploy them, tracking and blocking communications has become much easier than these activities were a decade ago. The ability to share information and opinions may thus be confined to a smaller zone of acceptable Internet use. Self-censorship is taking place, both in terms of what users search for and read on the Internet, and what they post and circulate online. Spying and threats have trampled on user freedoms.

The book addresses the regulation of Internet communication as the medium of free speech and commerce alike. It touches on important debates concerning Internet freedom, social networking and the law, protecting intellectual property, and regulating online economic activity. It covers a number of developments in online commerce and communication between 2005 and 2012 in particular. During the half-decade between about 2006 and 2011, a series of blockbuster disputes about policing cyberspace attracted wide coverage in the press, and prompted hundreds of affected companies and trade associations to file legal briefs and distribute press releases. The Internet industry accounts for trillions of dollars' worth of economic activity. Internet companies like YouTube and Yahoo! have been sold, or offered for sale, for billions of dollars.

Unfortunately, out of considerations of space and avoiding retreading issues reviewed in depth elsewhere, this book had to ignore some important issues of cyberspace regulation. Matters of Internet governance, including the role of the United Nations, are not discussed (Working Group on Internet Governance, 2005, paras. 15, 29, 52–6). The adaptation of the traditional doctrines of contract law, and their harmonization to promote electronic commerce across national borders, could not be addressed in detail (Overby, 1999, 219; Winn and Webber, 2006, 209). A number of important debates regarding the application of criminal and tort laws to Internet communication could not be surveyed or expanded upon in this book (Koenig and Rustad, 2005).

Although the globalization of cyberspace law has become apparent over the course of the past decade, the focus of this book is on the law of the United States. That being said, Chapter 8 on Yahoo!'s run-in with the French courts regarding Nazi memorabilia touches on aspects of European law that vary from the law of the United States. Today, most of the users of services like Google, Yahoo!, Facebook, and YouTube live outside of the United States. Yet these services claim that U.S. law governs many of their operations, and many of the frequent disputes about content hosted by them are resolved in U.S. courts. At the same time, the laws of Europe, China, and other nations as regards cyberspace have already received detailed coverage in published books and articles. Due to considerations of space and comprehensibility, this book does not attempt to summarize, paraphrase, or rehash their findings and conclusions.

Topical overview

The main theme of this book is that technological controls are satisfying corporations' and governments' demands for greater predictability in Internet usage, even as the courts fight to guarantee minimum freedoms and privacy guarantees online. As the American Civil Liberties Union (ACLU) points out, the installation of filters for copyrighted material could signal that "we are beginning to see the emergence of a third era—what we might call the 'filtering era,' which could fundamentally alter the architectural structure of the Internet, with significant implications for free speech as well as the nation's economy" (ACLU, 2010, 14).

The somewhat antiquated definitions and provisions of U.S. law enable some fast-developing technologies to outpace the law's attempts to "port" the Constitution to cyberspace. Although U.S. courts insist upon constitutional and other legal guarantees of a freewheeling Internet, multi-national corporations compete to produce tools and strategies for making it more predictable. As the Audible Magic Corporation maintained in reference to software for copyright "filtering," YouTube and more than 20 other Web 2.0 sites have opted to use such software to automate the process of flagging videos or audio tracks as matching copyrighted works, so as to consider deleting them (*Audible Magic Corp.*, 2012, 6, 11, 13, 17). As courts and Congress attempt to rein in Internet patents and make them harder to get, corporations overwhelm the patent office with new applications, and deluge Internet firms with complaints of infringement. Just as the courts were insisting that using trademarks online to criticize their owners is First Amendment-protected, corporations and trade associations accelerated their development of ways to make Internet companies liable for their users' infringing words and actions, potentially opening up an end run around the courts (see Chapter 6). And as social networking and content-sharing sites have proliferated, so have the terms of service and content-detecting tools for detecting, flagging, and deleting content that makes one or another corporation or trade association fear for its image or profits (see Chapters 4–5).

Although the laws have been calibrated over the years to address the emerging conflicts between communication and property in cyberspace, recent reforms and new technologies interact in sometimes unpredictable ways with earlier laws such as the Copyright Act of 1976 or the Patent Act of 1952. Frequently, the common-law heritage of the United States interacts with federal statutes to reach sometimes surprising conclusions. Therefore, a Web site proprietor like Yahoo! Inc. has no duty to take down defamatory statements about or characterizations of a person, but it may be sued for reneging on its promises to take such damaging material down. Yet as the courts stand up for free speech, sites like Facebook insidiously limit it. Scholars criticize this trend as an unfortunate consequence of applying judicial precedents on the right of property owners to expel political speakers to the rather different environment of cyberspace.

The book pursues its thesis across several domains of Internet law. "Owning Cyberspace" is the first topic, and groups together the chapters about exploiting brand names in new ways through the Internet, patenting methods of doing business over the Internet, and the social justice potential of fair uses of copyrighted works on the Internet. "Policing Cyberspace" is the next topic, and relates to efforts by patent, trademark, and copyright owners to enforce their rights online, and to compel Internet firms to monitor their online offerings and remove or pay for any infringements of others' rights. "Regulating Cyberspace" is the final topic, and deals with the ability of the law to require Internet companies to comply with a specific model of cyberspace, whether it be a "decent" and respectful one, or a neutral and universal Net.

Owning cyberspace

Part 1 of the book begins with the concept of censoring cyberspace by owning ideas. Courts and Congress have not allowed abstract ideas like laws of nature or basic ways of doing business to be owned by any one person or company. They have, however, granted patents on methods, processes, and machines that have specific results in industry or commerce. The first Part, entitled "Owning Cyberspace," surveys the debate regarding intellectual property online.

Chapter 1 is about "Claiming Web Addresses as Property." Courts and lawmakers have struggled with a number of analogies in resolving public policy debates about the ownership of Web addresses like www.mtv.com. The earliest analogy was probably to telephone numbers, with other analogies including vanity license plates, street signs, billboards, and even rooftops. A more appropriate analogy might be to a picket line outside of a business or factory. Picket lines publicize a communicative message by getting very close to the target's physical location. Similarly, a Web address or Facebook group containing a corporate trademark is a strategy often used to get as close as possible to the corporation's online location. This chapter details the legal problems that arise when one sets up a Web site with an Internet address that imitates the brand name or trademark of a big company or even a government. Corporations frequently argue that such addresses are illegal piracy of trademarks, but courts have found them to be entitled to a high level of First Amendment protection. Traditional doctrines of trademark law may ultimately clarify the law in this area. Among other things, a Web site that does not directly or indirectly compete with the trademark owner in markets important to the owner may be legal.

The second chapter ("The Promise of Information Justice") describes the ongoing struggle between authors, publishers, and proprietors of digital libraries and bookstores. The primary debate in this area has been between groups of authors and select publishers and Google, which scanned and made searchable millions of books from research libraries. After Google made peace with authors' and publishers' representatives in the United States, the struggle shifted to one between Google and its rivals in the Web advertising and sales space. The chapter details the intervention of authors' and publishers' societies, foreign countries, the U.S. government, Internet companies, and prominent law professors into a proposed settlement that would allow Google to sell online access to many copyrighted books. The settlement, endorsed by plaintiffs the Authors Guild and Association of American Publishers, as well as several nonprofit organizations, drew the ire of the Department of Justice and Google's competitors for potentially creating a book-download monopoly owned by Google. Germany and France attacked the deal for harming European authors and conflicting with European law. The settlement's many controversial provisions prompted the trial court judge to reject it, urging Google to allow authors to opt in rather than opt out of the settlement. The judge argued that although Google's universal digital library would be a boon to readers, the Department of Justice and others had persuaded him Google's monopoly could be a danger. This chapter handicaps the chances that Google will dominate eBooks as it does Web search results.

The third chapter reveals that neither Congress nor the Supreme Court has provided particularly clear or consistent answers to the question of when patents may issue on methods of Internet communication. The Patent Act of 1952, as modified over the years, has consistently been interpreted as allowing "business methods" to be patented, albeit not those that are pure ideas in the sense of not having technical elements. The Supreme Court concluded that business methods are patentable, and that an application to material objects or significant non-mathematical steps is required. The chapter describes the context of the decision in the remarkable rise of business method patents, particularly those involving the Internet, since the 1990s, in cases often involving e-commerce. It also traces the controversies in lower courts and the U.S. patent office since the decision in *Bilski*, as the vague standards set by the Supreme Court are applied to new inventions, and result in some patents arguably even more outlandish than Bilski's being issued. The future of business in cyberspace hangs in the balance.

Policing cyberspace

Part 2 reviews several recent debates about the duty to police illegal Internet content. From "stolen" content to fake online profiles to counterfeit auctions, who has the power and the responsibility to ensure legal compliance on the Internet? Copyright and trademark owners would like Internet companies to take the initiative in monitoring their offerings for unlicensed content, and delete it before it becomes visible. Web firms claim that this would cost too much and is not required by law. Courts have focused on the Internet companies' own knowledge and actions in responding to complaints, and have been very careful about not ordering a level of compliance that would slow down the innovation and usefulness of Internet-based platforms for information and business.

The fourth chapter, on "Red Flags of 'Piracy' Online," describes the high-stakes battle to make Web firms like Google responsible for the copyright infringements of their users in cyberspace. After key cases against *Napster* and *Grokster* failed to create clear rules in this area, a case brought by Viacom International against YouTube and its owner Google promised to clear the waters. The case involves thousands of Comedy Central, Cartoon Network, and other Viacom videos posted by users to YouTube without Viacom's permission. In a federal case filed in 2007, the media conglomerate formed of the merger of Paramount, MTV Networks, and Dreamworks SKG sought statutory or actual damages in excess of a billion dollars from Google under the Copyright Act of 1976. Further lawsuits sought class-action status on behalf of thousands of copyright holders in videos posted to YouTube. In 2010, the district court concluded that the plaintiffs failed to show that YouTube disregarded complaints as to specific videos, and in fact concluded that YouTube had removed every one of the thousands of videos it had received sufficiently detailed complaints about. Google praised the decision as a victory for Internet users as a whole, who look to platforms like YouTube to express themselves and connect with other users. Viacom and the other plaintiffs argued on appeal that discovering that specific users are posting multiple infringing videos, and that the site is becoming a haven for illicit content, should give rise to heightened obligations to monitor for and delete illicit content before it can do harm. The future of online video may hang in the balance.

The fifth chapter extends the analysis of online video's copyright problems by describing the decision by a U.S. appellate court in the YouTube case. The opinion raises provocative questions concerning the meaning of the term "control" under U.S. law, which helps divide companies that are not liable for the content that they store or index, from those that are.

The sixth chapter, on the question, "Is eBay Counterfeiting?," details the struggle between eBay and a coalition of brand owners including Tiffany and the Council of Fashion Designers of America regarding the sales of unauthorized copies of fashion items on auction sites. Tiffany filed suit in 2004, arguing that the vast majority of supposed eBay listings for Tiffany were for counterfeit items. By way of a response, eBay claimed that it had a trust and safety team dedicated to receiving complaints from brand owners, and resolving them quickly by deleting listings. The court sided with eBay, finding that eBay was not required to proactively seek out potential infringement, considering the large number of legitimate used items sold by far-flung sellers on its site. The case has become a lodestar for lawyers and companies who are enforcing trademarks online.

Chapter 7 delves into the topic of Internet companies' responsibility for their users' offensive behavior. This chapter illustrates the stakes involved in such disputes with the tragic personal story of a woman whose ex-boyfriend posted fake online profiles offering sexual intercourse. Yahoo!'s offices, whose site the profile had been posted to, promised the woman that they would take it down. After a two month delay, the woman filed suit against Yahoo! for negligence and violation of its promise to her to take the profile down. A court found that Yahoo! did not have to take down the profiles submitted by its user, but when it promised to take the profile down, it should have done so. The decision came on the heels of another controversial case in which Roommates.com was found responsible for encouraging users to submit discriminatory listings for apartment rentals and sublets, targeted by race and gender. Politicians and scholars have also criticized the source of the immunity for Web companies, the Communications Decency Act of 1996, for making it too difficult to protect privacy and reputation online. The ultimate question remains: to what extent should courts and Congress intervene as corporations regulate the content and appearance of cyberspace? The power of Facebook to take down many pages and entire groups of users designed for political and cultural speech underlines the relative marginality of laws and courts online.

Regulating cyberspace

Part 3 focuses on the constitutional and international law of regulating cyberspace. The central tension in cyberspace is between the First Amendment as interpreted in the United States, and a host of laws that not only Congress and the states but the rest of the countries in the world have passed regulating Internet content. Several possible solutions to this tension have emerged: distinguishing between narrowly targeted and excessively vague regulations, requiring a real risk of particularized harm before stepping in to limit free speech, and limiting regulations' ability to cross borders and disregard local constitutional and statutory protections. With three case studies on famous disputes at the intersection of freedom of speech and democratic governance of the Internet, this section explores the scope of cyberspace's key problem, and ways of solving it.

The eighth chapter, entitled "Internet Responsibility, Geographic Boundaries, and Business Ethics," involved an attempt to preempt enforcement of a French court's orders sanctioning Yahoo! for allowing access to material that could glorify or trivialize Nazi crimes or the Holocaust. Yahoo! sued the civil society organizations who had asked the French courts to enforce French law against glorifying or trivializing Nazi crimes or the Holocaust with respect to Yahoo!'s auctions. Yahoo! took down the material pursuant to its own anti-racism policies, but argued that potential enforcement of the French judgment in the United States entitled it to a declaration that the First Amendment would prohibit such enforcement, on account of French law's ambiguous application to works of history or literature. A California court disposed of the case on the rather narrow ground that the French civil society organizations had not had enough contact with Yahoo! in the United States to subject themselves to litigation there. The case illustrates some of the issues with enforcing national laws on offensive speech against global Web firms. As other nations apply censorious laws to the Internet, Web corporations have started buckling to their demands, applying foreign laws to U.S.-based sites and videos.

Chapter 9, on "Neutralizing the Open Internet," analyzes which agencies of the federal government may have the authority to regulate Internet service providers as they influence the content and applications that are available to Internet users. The FCC's decision that Comcast could be sanctioned for violating net neutrality principles adopted by the agency generated an outpouring of commentary and activism in Congress, academia, and industry. The D.C. Circuit's rebuking of the FCC for failure to respect principles of administrative law in announcing the principles in 2005 prompted extensive new proceedings in the FCC, and several attempts by the U.S. House of Representatives to defund enforcement of the principles. This chapter details the conflict of First Amendment interests represented by the case, especially those of Internet users in making communications and employing applications of their choice, and those of Internet service providers in adapting their networks to corporate visions of efficiency, legal compliance, and consumer demand. The subtle shaping of Internet traffic by advanced software may leave censorious laws far behind in terms of having an impact on the volume, character, and originality of Web content and applications.

The final chapter is called "The 'Monster' that Ate Social Networking." It tells the story of how Facebook became the dominant social networking site, and came under the control of Mark Zuckerberg and his allies through a variety of legal tactics. It describes the debate about whether Facebook has become a near-monopoly that invades privacy, controls what users can do or say with their friends, and limits the ability of other social networks to compete. A particularly salient issue to users of Facebook is the portability of profiles to other social networks, especially in the aftermath of changes to Facebook's terms of service that many users view as gross invasions of privacy and violations of earlier promises. *The New York Times* describes the portability of contacts and profiles as the major front in the battle for users and advertisers between Google and Facebook. As profiles and networks of friends and photographs remain stubbornly difficult to move, Facebook expands its power to control the nature of Internet speech by setting its own rules.

The final chapter sets forth the tentative conclusions of this collection of studies.

Bibliography

American Civil Liberties Union (ACLU), 'Network Neutrality 101: Why the Government Must Act to Preserve the Free and Open Internet (Oct. 2010).' Online. Available at: <http://www.aclu.org/files/assets/NetNeutrality_report_20101019.pdf>.

ACLU, *Fahrenheit 451.2: Is Cyberspace Burning?* Online. Available at: http://www.aclu.org/issues/cyber/burning.html (visited Jan. 20, 2005).

ACLU v. Reno, 929 F. Supp. 824 (E.D. Pa. 1996), *aff'd sub nom.* Reno v. ACLU, 521 U.S. 844 (1997).

AOLSucks.org, *Censorship Enforcement* (1998) <http://www.aolsucks.org/censor/cens-enforce.html>.

Apple Computer, Trial Brief, *Apple v. Samsung,* No. 11-cv-01846-LHK (N.D. Cal. 2012), http://online.wsj.com/public/resources/documents/72312appletrialbrief.pdf

Ashcroft v. American Civil Liberties Union (2004) 542 U.S. 656 (Supreme Court).

Associated Press, 'How Does Ruling on Smartphone Affect Consumers?,' Pittsburgh Tribune Review, Aug. 29, 2012. Online. Available at: <http://web2.westlaw.com> (search for "2012 WLNR 18383277").

Audible Magic Corporation, Brief of Amicus Curiae in Support of Neither Party, *Viacom International v. YouTube, Inc.,* 676 F. 3d 19 (2nd Cir. 2012).

Bally Total Fitness Holding Corp. v. Faber, 29 F. Supp. 2d 1161, 1164 (C.D. Cal. 1998).

Barlow, John Perry. *A Declaration of the Independence of Cyberspace.* 1997. Online. Available at: <https://projects.eff.org/~barlow/Declaration-Final.html>.

Barlow, John Perry. *Selling Wine Without Bottles: The Economy of Mind on the Global Net,* WIRED 2.03 (1993). Online. Available at: <http://www.wired.com/wired/archive/2.03/economy.ideas_pr.html> (accessed Aug. 15, 2012) (crediting Stewart Brand with the phrase).

Berners-Lee, Tim. *Weaving the Web: The Original Design and Ultimate Destiny of the World Wide Web* (2000).

Boyle, James. 'Foucault in Cyberspace: Surveillance, Sovereignty, and Hard-Wired Censors,' *University of Cincinnati Law Review* 66 (1997): 186, <http://www.wcl.american.edu/pub/faculty/boyle/foucault.htm>.

Boyle, James. 'Overregulating the Internet,' *The Washington Times*, Nov. 14, 1995, p. A17.

Burk, Dan L. 'Trademark Doctrines for Global Electronic Commerce,' *Southern California Law Review*, 49: 695–6 (1998).

Cha, Ariana Eunjung. '*AOL 5.0 Unplugs Other Internet Providers,*' *Wash. Post*, Dec. 24, 1999, at E01.

Devere Group GmbH v. Opinion Corp., — F.Supp.2d —, 2012 WL 2884986 (E.D.N.Y. July 13, 2012).

Digimarc Corp., *About Digital Watermarks*. Online. Available at: <http://web.archive.org/web/19971221015929/http://digimarc.com/about_wm.html> (visited Feb. 2, 2012).

Digital Future Coalition, *H.R. 3048 – Digital Era Copyright Enhancement Act, Section-By-Section Analysis* <http://www.ari.net/dfc/docs/sbsbou.htm> (accessed Jan. 20, 1998).

eBay v. Mercexchange, L.L.C., 547 U.S. 388 (2006).

Eldred v. Ashcroft, 537 U.S. 186 (2003).

Ellis, Douglas et al., 'The Economic Implications (and Uncertainties) of Obtaining Permanent Injunctive Relief After *eBay v. MercExchange*,' *Federal Circuit Bar Journal*, 17: 437 (2008).

Finkelstein, Seth. *Internet Blocking Programs and Privatized Censorship*. Online. Available at: <http://www.mit.edu/activities/safe/labeling/summary.html> (visited Jan. 20, 2003).

Fisher, William, Theories of Intellectual Property (1999). Harvard Law School. Online. Available at: <http://www.law.harvard.edu/faculty/tfisher/iptheory.html> (accessed Jan. 1, 2007).

Gaither, Chris, 'Google Settles Yahoo Patent Suit in Anticipation of IPO,' *Los Angeles Times*, Aug. 10, 2004, <http://articles.latimes.com/2004/aug/10/business/fi-google10>.

Gibson, William, *Neuromancer*. New York, ACE Books, 1984.

Gilson, Jerome, *Trademark Protection and Practice*, vol. 1 (1996): § 5.11[2] (1996).

Hafner, Katie & M. Lyon, *Where Wizards Stay Up Late: The Origins of the Internet* (1998).

Hatch, Sen. Orrin, 'Statement,' *Congressional Record* 144: §§ 4884–S4885 (1998).

Hughes, Justin, 'The Philosophy of Intellectual Property,' *Georgetown Law Journal*, 77: 287–366 (1988).

Intermatic Inc. v. Toeppen, 947 F. Supp. 1227 (N.D. Ill. 1996).

Jones, Ashby, 'The Apple-Samsung Trial: What Apple Will Attempt to Prove,' Wall Street Journal Digits Blog, July 24, 2012, <http://blogs.wsj.com/digits/2012/07/24/the-apple-samsung-trial-what-apple-will-attempt-to-prove/>.

Kelly v. Arriba Soft Corporation (2003) 336 F. 3d 811 (United States Court of Appeals for the Ninth Circuit).

Koenig, Thomas & Michael Rustad, 'Harmonizing Cybertort Law for Europe and America,' *Suffolk University Journal of High Technology Law*, Vol. 5 (2005). Online. Available at: <http://papers.ssrn.com/sol3/papers.cfm?abstract_id=935092>.

Lamparello v. Falwell, 420 F. 3d 309 (4th Cir. 2005).

Landes, William M. and Richard Posner, 'Trademark Law: An Economic Perspective,' *Journal of Law and Economics*, 30: 265 (1987).

Leahy, Sen. Patrick, 'Remarks of December 29, 1995,' *Congressional Record* 144: S19312 (104th Cong. 1995).

Lessig, Lawrence, 'Constitution and Code,' *Cumberland Law Review*, 27: 1–32 (1996–97).

Lessig, Lawrence, 'The Constitution of Code: Limitations on Choice-Based Critiques of Cyberspace Regulation,' *Commlaw Conspectus*, 5: 184 (1997).

Lessig, Lawrence, 'The Zones of Cyberspace,' *Stanford Law Review* 48: 1403 (1996).

Lewis, Peter H. 'He Ventured Into Cyberspace – Then Got MTV to Follow,' *The New York Times* (Dec. 19, 1993), pp. 3–10.

McWilliams, Brian, 'Iraq's Crash Course in Cyberwar,' *Wired* (May 22, 2003). Online. Available at: http://www.wired.com/politics/law/news/2003/05/58901?currentPage=2.

Meeks, Brock N. 'The Obscenity of Decency.' *Wired*. Online. Available at: <http://www.hotwired.com/clipper/exon.privacy.html> (accessed Feb. 15, 2004).

Mercexchange, L.L.C., Brief of Appellant *MercExchange, L.L.C. v. Ebay, Inc.*, No. 2007-1531 (Fed. Cir. Oct. 29, 2007).

MercExchange, L.L.C. v. eBay, Inc., 275 F. Supp. 2d 695 (E.D. Va. 2003).

MercExchange, L.L.C. v. eBay, Inc., 401 F. 3d 1323 (Fed. Cir. 2005).

Mills, M. 'Scientist's Brainchild Grows Into a Global Phenomenon,' *The Washington Post*, June 30, 1996, p. A15.

MTV Networks v. Curry, 867 F. Supp. 202 (S.D.N.Y. 1994).

MySpace, Inc. v. GraphOn Corp., 672 F. 3d 1250 (Fed. Cir. 2012).

NII Copyright Protection Act of 1995, S. 1284, 104th Cong. (1995), H.R. 2441, 104th Cong. (1995).

Nissan Motor Co. v. Nissan Computer Corp., 231 F. Supp. 2d 977 (C.D. Cal. 2002).

Nissan Motor Co. v. Nissan Computer Corp., 378 F. 3d 1002 (9th Cir. 2004).

OBH, Inc. v. Spotlight Magazine, Inc., 86 F. Supp. 2d 176 (N.D.N.Y. 2000).

Overby, A. Brooke, 'Will Cyberlaw Be Uniform: An Introduction to the UNCITRAL Model Law on Electronic Commerce,' *Tulane Journal of International and Comparative Law*, 7: 219 (1999).

People for the Ethical Treatment of Animals, Inc. v. Doughney, 113 F. Supp. 2d 915 (E.D. Va. 2000), aff'd 263 F. 3d 359 (4th Cir. 2001).

Perfect 10, Inc. v. Visa Int'l Serv. Ass'n, 494 F. 3d 788 (9th Cir. 2007).

Planned Parenthood Federation of Am., Inc. v. Bucci, 152 F. 3d 920 (2nd Cir.), *cert. denied*, 525 U.S. 834 (1998).

Planned Parenthood Fed'n of Am., Inc. v. Bucci, 42 U.S.P.Q. 2d (BNA) 1430 (S.D.N.Y. 1997).

Police Department of City of Chicago v. Mosley, 408 U.S. 92 (1972).

Quittner, Joshua. 'Billions Registered,' *Wired* 2.10 (Oct. 1994). Online. Available at http://www.wired.com/wired/archive/2.10/mcdonalds.html.

Resnick, Paul. PICS, Censorship, & Intellectual Freedom FAQ (1998) http://papers.ssrn.com/sol3/papers.cfm?abstract_id=11471 (accessed Sept. 1, 2012).

Richards, Evelyn. 'Bush to Unveil High-Tech Initiative; $ 2 Billion Computing Project Would Include Data "Superhighway,"' *Washington Post*, Sept. 7, 1989, p. F1.

Samuelson, Pamela. 'The Copyright Grab,' *Wired* 4.01 (1996), http://scratch.catalogue.com/white.html.

San Francisco Arts & Athletics, Inc. v. U.S. Olympic Committee, 483 U.S. 522, 569–70 (1987) (Brennan, J., dissenting).

Starbucks Corp. v. Dwyer, No. 3:00-CV-1499 MMC (N.D. Cal. preliminary injunction granted June 13, 2000).

Stevens, Amy & Junda Woo, 'MTV Internet "Handle" Suit,' *Wall Street Journal*, May 9, 1994, B8.

Sun Microsystems v. Sunriver Corp., 36 U.S.P.Q. 2d (BNA) 1266 (N.D. Cal. 1995).

Taubman Co. v. Webfeats, 319 F. 3d 770 (6th Cir. 2003).

Telecommunications Reports International, 'Number of Online Users in U.S. Reaches 70.7 Million, But Changes Loom' (Aug. 8, 2001), <http://www.tr.com/newsletters/rec/troc2q_pr.htm>.

Telecommunications Reports International, 'Senate Commerce Committee Debates Need For Net Neutrality Bill; Martin Says FCC Can Act Now,' *Telecommunications Reports*, May 1, 2008. Online. Available at: <http://web2.westlaw.com> (search for "2008 WLNR 7603332").

Tiffany (NJ) Inc. and Tiffany and Company v. eBay, Inc. (2010), 600 F. 3d 93 (2nd Cir.). Online. Available at: <http://www.lexis.com> (accessed 16 July 2012).

Time Warner Inc., et al., Brief of Amici Curiae in Support of Petitioners, Mercexchange L.L.C. v. eBay, Inc., 547 U.S. 388 (2006).

TMI, Inc. v. Maxwell, 368 F.3d 433 (5th Cir. 2004).

Travis, Hannibal, 'The Battle for Mindshare: The Emerging Consensus That the First Amendment Protects Corporate Criticism and Parody on the Internet,' *Virginia Journal of Law & Technology*, 10: 3 (2005).

Travis, Hannibal (2011) 'Postmodern Censorship of Pacifist Content on Television and the Internet,' *Notre Dame Journal of Law, Ethics and Public Policy*, 25: 2. Online. Available at: <http://papers.ssrn.com/sol3/papers.cfm?abstract_id=1809103> (accessed Sept. 1, 2012).

Travis, Hannibal. 'Trading Away the Internet,' Prawfsblawg, July 1, 2012. Online. Available at: <http://prawfsblawg.blogs.com/prawfsblawg/2012/07/trading-away-the-internet.html> (accessed Sept. 1, 2012).

Tribe, Laurence. *American Constitutional Law*. 2nd ed. 1988.

U.S. Code, title 15, section 1125.

U.S. Department of Commerce, Information Infrastructure Task Force, Intellectual Property and the National Information Infrastructure: The Report of the Working Group on Intellectual Property Rights (Sept. 1995) (visited Jan. 20, 2004) <http://www.uspto.gov/web/offices/com/doc/ipnii>.

U.S. House of Representatives, House Report No. 106-412 (1999).

U.S. PTO, Performance and Accountability Report, Fiscal Year 2005, at Table 2 (2005), http://www.uspto.gov/web/offices/com/annual/2005/060402_table2.html.

Waldron, Jeremy. 'From Authors to Copiers: Individual Rights and Social Values in Intellectual Property,' *Chicago-Kent Law Review*, 68: 841–87 (1993).

Weitzner, Daniel J. *Blocking and Filtering Content on the Internet after the CDA: Empowering Users and Families Without Chilling the Free Flow of Information Online.* Center for Democracy and Technology. Online. Available at: <http://www.cdt.org/speech/rating_issues.html> (visited Oct. 15, 2003).

White, S. 'Harvard Opens Laboratory for Computation: Hopes to Use Mechanical Brain to Solve Problems of All Social Sciences,' *The New York Times*, Dec. 29, 1946.

Winn, Jane and Mark Webber, 'The Impact of EU Unfair Contract Terms Law on US Business-to-Consumer Internet Merchants,' *Business Lawyer*, 62: 209 (2006).

WIPO Treaties Implementation Act, S. 1121, 105th Cong. (1996), H.R. 2281, 105th Cong. (1996).

Working Group on Internet Governance of the United Nations, Report. 2005. Available at: <http://www.wgig.org/docs/WGIGREPORT.pdf> (accessed Feb. 1, 2012).

Wren, Christopher S. 'A Seductive Drug Culture Flourishes on the Internet,' *The New York Times*, Jun. 20, 1997, p. A1.

Zaitlen, Richard & David Victor, (1996) 'The New Internet Domain Name Guidelines: Still Winner-Take-All,' *Computer Law* 13: 12–13.

Part 1
Owning cyberspace

1 Claiming Web addresses as property

Margreth Barrett[1]

In contrast to the broad property rights provided through patents and copyrights, courts and legislative bodies have traditionally tailored rights in trademarks narrowly, only to perform the specific function for which they were created. Trademark rights promote an efficient, competitive marketplace: They enable merchants to adopt a particular word or symbol to identify their goods[2] and prevent other merchants from using a confusingly similar word or symbol to identify their own goods when doing so would create a likelihood of consumer confusion about product source, sponsorship or affiliation. These limited rights ensure that consumers can easily and quickly identify and distinguish the goods of competing producers and effectively exercise their purchasing preferences. Trademark law reduces consumer search costs and allows consumers to reward quality through repeat patronage. This, in turn, enables producers to recoup investments in product quality and thus encourages them to strive for quality. A narrowly tailored set of rights in trademarks clearly promotes a competitive marketplace, to the ultimate benefit of consumers.[3]

However, overprotection of marks can actually undercut marketplace competition and efficiency by enabling mark owners to interfere with the flow of useful marketplace information to consumers. Rights in marks should not prevent competing producers from effectively communicating the nature,

---

1 Professor of Law, University of California at Hastings School of Law. This chapter draws from several more in-depth articles that Professor Barrett has published in the past. Most directly, it draws from 'Internet Trademark Suits and the Demise of "Trademark Use,"' *University of California at Davis Law Review* 39: 371 (2006); 'Finding Trademark Use: The Historical Foundation for Limiting Infringement Liability to Uses "In the Manner of a Mark,"' *Wake Forest Law Review* 43: 893 (2008); and 'Reconciling Fair Use and Trademark Use', *Cardozo Arts & Entertainment Law Journal* 28: 953 (2010). See also, Margaret Barrett, 'Trademarks and Digital Technologies: "Use" on the Net,' *Journal of Internet Law* 13:1 (May 2010).

2 Marks may identify goods *or* services. The "trademark use" principles discussed in this chapter generally apply to service marks, as well as trademarks. However, for the sake of brevity, I will generally refer only to marks used to identify goods.

3 *Qualitex Co. v. Jacobson Prods. Co.*, Inc. (1995), 514 U.S. 159, 163–164; S. Rep. No. 79-1333, at 1–17 (1946).

qualities, and characteristics of their own products to interested consumers, or prevent competitors, consumers, or the media from engaging in critical product critiques and commentary. Rights in marks should not interfere unnecessarily in the development of new digital technologies that assist consumers and promote competition by enhancing or aggregating available product information. Moreover, rights in marks must not intrude impermissibly on the public's First Amendment interests in freedom of speech.[4]

The "trademark use" requirement is one of the key ways that the law historically has limited trademark rights to their proper, pro-competitive scope. Essentially, the "trademark use" requirement *limits infringement claims to situations in which the defendant has used a confusingly similar word or symbol to identify the source, sponsorship, or affiliation of products that it is advertising, distributing, or selling.* The trademark use requirement focuses the cause of action on the specific harm that the law is meant to address: actions that undercut consumers' ability to rely on marks for accurate information about product source. It prevents mark owners from asserting their trademark rights in anticompetitive ways: to prohibit unauthorized uses of their marks that are unlikely to undercut consumer reliance interests and that may be pro-competitive and beneficial from the overall societal standpoint. The trademark use requirement also works to keep trademark law consistent with the First Amendment by limiting the infringement cause of action to commercial speech in most instances.[5]

The first part of this chapter will briefly describe the historical development of the "trademark use" limitation, more fully discuss its purpose and justifications, and provide a fuller definition of "trademark use." The chapter will then explain how some courts have almost completely undercut the trademark use limitation in the Internet context and explore the implications of this development for the freedom of speech.

Trademark law and trademark use

As the United States developed a more expansive and sophisticated marketplace, pressure grew to modernize and expand federal trademark protection. Section § 32(a)(1) of the federal trademark act (the Lanham Act) requires that infringement defendants "*use in commerce*" a reproduction, counterfeit, copy, or

---

4 U.S. Const. Amend. I.
5 Commercial speech, defined as speech that does no more than propose a commercial transaction, is subject to a lower level of First Amendment protection than other forms of speech. For in-depth discussion of commercial speech and the relationship between trademark protection and the First Amendment, see Margreth Barrett (2007), 'Domain Names, Trademarks and the First Amendment: Searching for Meaningful Boundaries,' *Connecticut Law Review* 29: 973.

colorable imitation of a registered mark "*in connection with the sale, offering for sale, distribution or advertising of goods or services.*"[6] The Lanham Act's unregistered mark infringement provision employs similar language.[7] Lanham Act § 45 defines "use in commerce" as entailing two things: (1) an affixation or other close association of the mark with the defendant's goods, and (2) a connection with interstate commerce sufficient to give Congress the constitutional authority to regulate the use.[8]

As I have explained in greater depth elsewhere,[9] the Lanham Act's legislative history makes it clear that Congress intended this statutory definition to apply in the infringement context and to carry forward the 1905/1920 Acts' general "affixation or other close association" requirement. Indeed, during the years leading up to final enactment of the Lanham Act, as Congress drafted successive bills, it repeatedly *altered* the language of the definition specifically *to track alterations* in the language of the infringement provision. However, even if that express statutory language and the legislative history surrounding it were absent, the "affixation or other close association" ("trademark use") requirement still should be deemed applicable under the Lanham Act because it was a part of the common law, which Congress intended to codify in the Lanham Act.[10] Either way, past practices demonstrate that courts have some degree of flexibility in construing and applying the "affixation or other close association" requirement in order to accomplish its underlying purpose as new media and business models emerge.

There are three basic factors that modern courts should apply in order to anchor the trademark use limitation to its historical roots and purposes. First, consumers should be able to *perceive* the defendant's application of the allegedly confusing word or symbol. Requiring perceptibility as a precondition to actionable trademark use flows naturally and logically from the concept of trademark use itself: Imperceptible uses are unlikely to communicate source to consumers and thus are unlikely to result in the kind of harm (consumer

---

6 15 U.S.C. § 1114(1)(a). As originally drafted, § 32 used the language: "in commerce, use." Congress later amended it to "use in commerce," characterizing the change as non-substantive. See H.R. Rep. No. 87-1108, at 2 (1961); Barrett, 'Finding Trademark Use', above, 947–53.

7 15 U.S.C. § 1125(a). This statutory language differed when originally enacted, but Congress subsequently amended it "to codify the courts' interpretation" of the original version. S. Rep. No. 100-515, at 40 (1988).

8 15 U.S.C. § 1127.

9 Until 2009, no court undertook to review the Lanham Act's legislative history with regard to the "trademark use" requirement. A panel of the Second Circuit undertook a limited review in *Rescuecom Corp. v. Google, Inc.*, 562 F. 3d 123, 131–141 (2d Cir. 2009), in which it ultimately concluded that the § 45 definition applies in infringement actions, albeit through a line of reasoning that differs significantly from my own. Barrett, 'Finding Trademark Use.'

10 Barrett, 'Finding Trademark Use,' op. cit., 960–64.

confusion about source) that the trademark law is meant to prevent.[11] A perceptibility requirement also furthers important policy goals. It provides a measure of certainty and objectivity to the trademark infringement cause of action, thus reducing the chilling effects that threatened infringement claims might otherwise have on competition. It provides a rational means of limiting mark owners' ever-expanding assertions of trademark rights to those cases in which consumer confusion is likely to be material and detrimental from a societal standpoint. It also facilitates investment in new technologies that can, through internal, externally imperceptible references to marks, provide consumers with efficient, customized digital indexing, reference, and search services, and customized advertising, all of which may enhance and tailor the flow of useful marketplace information to consumers, lower consumer search costs, and thus enhance competition. While the common law and federal statutory provisions historically contemplated *visual* perceptibility (undoubtedly because most marks were used in that way), modern courts should have the flexibility to find that other forms of sensory perception suffice. The key is that consumers be confronted with the mark in a manner that they are capable of perceiving through their senses.

Second, the defendant should *closely, directly associate* the allegedly infringing word or symbol with goods or services that it is advertising, selling, or otherwise disseminating. The common law and federal statutory "affixation or other close association" requirement primarily stressed physical proximity or connection. However, courts need not adhere literally to a physical proximity rule or even to the specific forms of association listed in Lanham Act § 45. Courts have historically enjoyed the flexibility to find actionable trademark use, as long as doing so is *consistent with the purposes* underlying the trademark use limitation, and the defendant's use has the same likely effect as the forms of use listed in the statutory language. For example, courts have readily found actionable trademark use when defendants used marks in advertisements for their goods, even though neither the 1905 Act nor the Lanham Act's § 45 definition of "use in commerce" for goods refers specifically to advertising use. In the absence of physical proximity, courts should consider whether the defendant clearly, directly associated the allegedly infringing mark with its own goods, for example, by using the word or symbol specifically to refer to its goods. The historical purpose of the early "affixation" and "affixation or other close association" requirements was to ensure that there was a close enough association of mark with goods to assume that consumers will

---

11 Hidden use of a mark may constitute a *step* toward creating a likelihood of confusion, for example, a step in the process of creating a misleading screen display. But it is not the hidden use, itself, that misleads consumers. Any liability should turn on the screen design itself rather than on the hidden use of the mark and should arise from another deceit-based theory of unfair competition, rather than from the law of trademark infringement. Ibid., 929–32.

mentally connect the mark to the defendant's products and be likely to infer that the mark indicates the products' source.

Finally, the defendant's use of the allegedly infringing word or symbol should make a "separate commercial impression" on the consumers who are exposed to it. While neither the common law nor the federal statutes explicitly stated this requirement, it seems clear that the use must be likely to come to consumers' attention in order to communicate product source. Relevant considerations might include where and how the word or symbol appears on the defendant's marketing materials and whether the use of the mark stands out. If the mark is used aurally, one might ask whether it is emphasized in some way.

It is clear from pre-Internet case law that the trademark use requirement prevents recognition of trademark rights "in gross." Courts have often stressed that the legal significance of words and symbols comprising marks lies in their *relationship* to a particular product, in their role in communicating the product's source.[12] A mark owner may only prevent uses of confusingly similar words or symbols to identify the source of others' products. Outside of the narrow confines of trademark use, words and symbols are the common property of all. Moreover, a line of non-Internet cases makes it clear that a *defendant's intent to benefit from the plaintiff's business goodwill* cannot substitute for a showing of "trademark use."[13] The trademark use requirement turns on consumers' likely perceptions. The defendant's intent to free ride is irrelevant to this inquiry. Trademark law was never meant to prevent all forms of free riding on a plaintiff's business goodwill. Indeed, we have long recognized that, in many instances, free riding can be pro-competitive.[14]

Requiring infringement plaintiffs to demonstrate the defendant's "trademark use" serves a screening or gate-keeping function, limiting assertions of trademark rights to those cases in which potential consumer confusion is likely to be material and detrimental from a societal standpoint. The relatively objective factors (perceptibility; close, direct association with the defendant's goods or services; separate commercial impression) together provide some assurance that consumers may look to the contested word or symbol for information about the source of the defendant's goods. The factors thus serve as a *proxy* for more fact-intensive, case-by-case findings regarding actual consumer perception. They enable courts efficiently to identify cases in which potential consumer confusion costs are unlikely to justify the societal costs of protracted litigation and dispose of them early in the litigation process.

---

12 *See, e.g., United Drug Co. v. Theodore Rectanus Co.* (1918), 248 U.S. 90, 97; *Interactive Products Corp. v. A2Z Mobile Office Solutions, Inc.* (6th Cir. 2003), 326 F. 3d 695.

13 *See, e.g., Holiday Inns, Inc. v. 800 Reservation, Inc.* (6th Cir. 1996), 86 F. 3d 619; *DaimlerChrysler AG v. Bloom* (8th Cir. 2003), 315 F. 3d 932.

14 *See, e.g., Smith v. Chanel, Inc.* (9th Cir. 1968), 402 F. 2d 562; *Societe Comptoir de L'Industrie Cotonniere Establissements Boussac v. Alexamder's Dep't Stores, Inc.* (2d Cir. 1962), 299 F. 2d 33, 36. An intent to free-ride is not necessarily an intent to confuse consumers.

The plaintiff's initial burden to demonstrate the defendant's "trademark use" thus promotes judicial efficiency and limits the chilling effects that threats of protracted, expensive infringement litigation may have on marketplace actors seeking to make socially beneficial (albeit unauthorized) uses of marks or words or symbols resembling marks. Requiring plaintiffs to demonstrate "trademark use" also promotes First Amendment interests by limiting infringement claims, in most cases, to a defendant's commercial speech, where the interest in preventing consumer confusion will more likely outweigh interests in unfettered uses of language. It protects marketplace efficiency by accommodating an unhampered flow of useful product information and critiques to consumers and helps to prevent assertion of trademark rights in a range of anti-competitive ways. Particularly in the digital context, the trademark use requirement may prevent trademark interests from unnecessarily chilling the development of new media and new business models that can benefit consumers—new technologies that (through novel or hidden references to marks) provide consumers with efficient, customized digital indexing, reference, and search services, as well as customized advertising tailored to individual consumer interests (all of which may lower consumer search costs and thus enhance competition).

"Trademark use" and the Internet

The Internet has provided a host of innovative ways for businesses and individuals to promote their own agendas through unauthorized use of other's marks: to divert online customers; to free-ride on the mark owner's business goodwill; to notify consumers that their products or services are comparable to, compatible with, or second-hand versions of the mark owner's product; to gripe about the mark owner's product or service; or to parody, criticize or argue with the mark owner's social, political, or religious views. The resulting avalanche of infringement suits threatens to undermine years of careful judicial and legislative efforts to balance the competing interests that come to bear in trademark infringement cases. Courts faced with new, unfamiliar technologies have too often lost sight of the important limiting function that the trademark use requirement should play.

Allegations that these new, unorthodox kinds of uses infringe are especially problematic because the scope of actionable "likelihood of consumer confusion" has also expanded—from consumer confusion about product source at the point of sale to confusion about sponsorship or affiliation, post-sale confusion, pre-sale (or "initial interest") confusion, and even to non-confusion, where the impact on the mark owner is similar to the impact that consumer confusion might have.[15] Given these expanded notions of actionable confusion,

---

15 For a famous example of the latter, *see Brookfield Communications, Inc. v. West Coast Entertainment Corp.* (9th Cir. 1999), 174 F. 3d 1036.

the requirement that plaintiffs demonstrate "a likelihood of consumer confusion," by itself, is inadequate to prevent trademark owners from asserting (and prevailing in) anticompetitive and potentially unconstitutional infringement claims. The limiting role of the trademark use requirement is more important than ever but, as will be discussed later, has been largely undermined in many jurisdictions.

The rest of this chapter will discuss four categories of Internet infringement cases: (1) "classic cybersquatting," (2) "forum site domain names," (3) "metatags," and (4) "contextual advertising," explaining how, in each category, courts have departed from the trademark use limitation and discussing the implications.

Classic "cybersquatting"

In the 1990s, a number of enterprising individuals registered multiple domain names consisting of others' marks followed by .com or another generic top-level domain, hoping later to sell the registrations at a profit to the trademark owners. When trademark owners brought suit against these "cybersquatters," the courts generally rejected the proposition that registering the plaintiff's mark as a domain name, by itself, constituted an infringing (or diluting) use of the mark, either on the part of the domain name registrant or the registering agency.[16] Likewise, courts found that the mere act of "warehousing" such domain names or "activating" them failed to constitute infringing or diluting use.[17] These findings clearly are correct, in light of the trademark use requirement: The defendants did not employ the marks to identify the source of goods or services, in even the most liberal sense.

However, a line of cases did find that registering a mark-encompassing domain name constituted an actionable Lanham Act use *when coupled with an intent to sell or license the registration* to the trademark owner. The Ninth Circuit's reasoning in *Panavision International, L.P. v. Toeppen*[18] is illustrative. In that case, the district court had specifically found that defendant Toeppen

---

16 *See, e.g., Panavision Int'l, L.P. v. Toeppen* (C.D. Cal. 1996), 945 F. Supp. 1296, 1303, *aff'd* (9th Cir. 1998), 141 F. 3d 1316; *Lockheed Martin Corp. v. Network Solutions, Inc.* (C.D. Ca. 1997), 985 F. Supp. 949, 957, *aff'd* (9th Cir. 1999),194 F. 3d 980.

17 *HQM, Ltd. v. Hatfield* (D. Md. 1999), 71 F. Supp. 2d 500, 508.

18 *Panavision International, L.P. v. Toeppen* (9th Cir. 1998), 141 F. 3d 1316. This particular case involved a dilution claim, but as I have explained elsewhere, courts uniformly construed the "commercial use in commerce" requirement of federal dilution law as essentially synonymous with infringement law's "trademark use" requirement. 15 U.S.C. §1125(c); *see* Barrett, 'Internet Trademark Suits', op. cit., 393–5. As amended by the Trademark Dilution Revision Act of 2006, Lanham Act § 43(c) expressly requires trademark use as a prerequisite for dilution relief. *See* Stacey L. Dogan & Mark A. Lemley (2007–08), 'The Trademark Use Requirement in Dilution Cases,' *Santa Clara Computer & High Technology Law Journal* 24: 541.

never used the contested *Panavision.com* domain name to identify goods or services. Nonetheless, the Ninth Circuit found actionable use by reasoning that Toeppen's "business" was to register trademarks as domain names and sell the registrations to the trademark owners. This was a *commercial use* of the marks.[19] Moreover, Toeppen *intended to trade on the value of the marks, in their capacity as marks*: he intended to sell to mark owners the value of exploiting the mark-encompassing domain name *as a* mark in the Internet context. The Ninth Circuit explained:

> Toeppen made a commercial use of Panavision's trademarks. It does not matter that he did not attach the marks to a product. Toeppen's commercial use was his attempt to sell the trademarks themselves.[20]

A number of other courts followed the Ninth Circuit's lead in finding that cybersquatting constituted actionable Lanham Act use.[21]

However, this line of decisions incorrectly equated "commercial" use with trademark use and found that an intent to trade on a word or symbol's value as a mark could substitute for use of the mark as a trademark to indicate the source of goods or services. These cases disassociated marks from their role in identifying the source of goods or services, which had long been deemed their *only* legally significant role, and effectively gave their owners a form of right in gross in words and symbols.[22]

As noted earlier, the infringement cause of action was not intended to penalize persons who seek to profit from the goodwill of others' marks, *per se*. Rather, Congress intended the cause of action to prevent unauthorized uses of marks that interfere with consumers' ability to rely on them for information about product source, sponsorship, or affiliation. None of the acts involved in the classic cybersquatting cases—registering the mark as a domain name, intending to profit by offering the registration for sale to the trademark owner, or actually offering to sell it—entail presenting the mark to consumers in a manner that permits them to determine the source, sponsorship, or affiliation of products. The fact that the word or symbol may indicate source to consumers *in other contexts* and have value for that reason does not convert

---

19 *Panavision*, op. cit., 1325.

20 *Id.*

21 *E.g.*, *Virtual Works, Inc. v. Network Solutions, Inc.* (E.D. Va. 2000), 106 F. Supp. 2d 845, 847, *aff'd* (4th Cir. 2001), 238 F. 3d 264; *Toys "R" Us, Inc. v. Abir* (S.D.N.Y. Feb. 10, 1999), No. 97 Civ. 8673 JGK, 1999 WL 61817, at 1; *Minnesota Mining & Manufacturing Co. v. Taylor* (D. Minn. 1998), 21 F. Supp. 2d 1003, 1005.

22 In *Panavision*, the Ninth Circuit relied on *Boston Professional Hockey Association, Inc. v. Dallas Cap & Emblem Manufacturing, Inc.* (5th Cir. 1994), 510 F. 2d 1004, 1011, for the proposition that sale of a mark by itself—in gross—is actionable. *Panavision*, op. cit., 1326 n.5. However, *Boston Professional* does not stand for that proposition. Barrett, 'Internet Trademark Suits,' op. cit., 387–9.

the defendant's particular action into a potentially infringing trademark use. None of the cybersquatting defendants' acts threatened to undercut the ability of consumers to rely on the plaintiffs' marks for information about the source, sponsorship, or affiliation of goods or services.

While arguments can be made in favor of prohibiting cybersquatting as a matter of policy, Congress did not do so in the Lanham Act infringement provisions. Congress has since enacted legislation that is specifically tailored to combat classic cybersquatting in Lanham Act § 43(d).[23] Courts have subsequently suggested that classic cybersquatting claims are better adjudicated under this new cause of action.[24] However, the reasoning in the *Panavision* line of cases, which focuses on the defendant's predatory intent and recognizes rights in a mark in gross, continues to serve as very problematic precedent for courts in evaluating the trademark use requirement in other Internet contexts.

The forum site domain name cases

Using a mark in a domain name to identify a working Web site *can* constitute the requisite trademark use for purposes of an infringement claim. If the defendant offers goods or services on the Web site, the incorporation of the plaintiff's mark into the domain name *may* closely, directly associate the mark with those goods or services and lead consumers to rely on the mark for information about their source, sponsorship, or affiliation. However, a number of courts have extended the infringement cause of action well beyond situations in which the defendant offers goods or services on a Web site identified by a mark-encompassing domain name. They have found actionable use when the defendant conducts *absolutely no meaningful commercial activity* on the denominated Web site. They have done this through one or more of the following lines of reasoning, each of which will be discussed later:

1. Stretching the meaning of "services" so that the defendant's expression of purely personal opinion is an "information service" and the challenged domain name can be characterized as identifying the source of that "service";
2. Relying on links from the defendant's Web site to "commercial" sites to hold that the defendant's site is also "commercial" (or to assume that consumers will understand the defendant's domain name to communicate the source of goods or services sold on the linked site);
3. Pairing the defendant's "use" of the mark with the plaintiff's marketing activities; and
4. Focusing on the defendant's "predatory intent" in lieu of trademark use.

---

23 15 U.S.C. § 1125(d).
24 *Porsche Cars N. Am., Inc. v. Porsche.net* (4th Cir. 2002), 302 F. 3d 248, 261; *Sporty's Farm L.L.C. v. Sportsman's Market, Inc.* (2nd Cir. 2000), 202 F. 3d 489, 497.

Expanding the meaning of "services"

In a number of cases, defendants have registered domain names consisting of the plaintiff's mark followed by a generic top-level domain, not to sell or distribute goods or services but to identify a forum Web site in which the defendant voices criticisms of the plaintiff or its product or contests the plaintiff's political, social, or religious views. For example, in *Planned Parenthood Federation of America, Inc. v. Bucci*,[25] plaintiff Planned Parenthood provided birth control counseling and abortion services. The defendant, an anti-abortion activist and devout Catholic, registered the domain name *planned-parenthood.com* and set up a personal Web site on which he stated his social and religious opposition to abortion and recommended a book that stated similar views. When Planned Parenthood sued, the court found actionable trademark use by reasoning that the defendant's statement of opposing religious views constituted a "service," the source of which he identified through use of the allegedly infringing domain name.[26] Likewise, in *People for the Ethical Treatment of Animals v. Doughney*, the Fourth Circuit reasoned that the term "services" should be "interpreted broadly, to include the dissemination of information, including purely ideological information."[27] On this reasoning, the court found that an individual's forum site ridicule of an animal rights organization constituted a Lanham Act "service," the source of which was identified by the defendant's domain name, which incorporated the animal rights organization's mark.

The Lanham Act does not define "services." However, the *Planned Parenthood* and *People for Ethical Treatment* courts' view of Lanham Act "services" is extraordinarily broad. To characterize a defendant's statement of personal opinion about social issues or religion as a Lanham Act "service" goes well beyond any established precedent and threatens to bring a wide array of fully protected First Amendment speech under the control of trademark owners. Since all Web sites provide some form of information or opinion, this construction would enable trademark owners to control *any* use of their marks as part of a domain name, even in connection with the most intensely personal, isolated statement of religious or political belief, rant, or product criticism on the Internet. It provides trademark owners significantly greater control of domain names than Congress was willing to do in its new anti-cybersquatting act.[28]

---

25 *Planned Parenthood Federation of America, Inc. v. Bucci* (S.D.N.Y. Mar. 24, 1997), No. 97 Civ. 0629, 1997 WL 133313, *aff'd* (2d Cir. 1997), 152 F. 3d 920.

26 Ibid., *4. The court characterized the defendant's "services" as "informational services for use in convincing people that certain activities, including the use of plaintiff's services, are morally wrong."

27 *People for the Ethical Treatment of Animals v. Doughney* (4th Cir. 2001), 263 F. 3d 359.

28 15 U.S.C. § 1125(d)(1)(B)(i)(IV).

Relying on links to commercial sites to find a trademark infringement

In other cases when non-commercial forum sites use mark-incorporating domain names, courts have relied on links from the forum site to find action-able trademark use. For example, in *Jews for Jesus v. Brodsky*,[29] Brodsky registered a domain name comprised of the plaintiff's "Jews for Jesus" mark and the .org top-level domain and used it to identify a Web site that stated his opposition to the plaintiff's religious message. That modest site provided a link to a site operated by Outreach Judaism, an organization that was also a vocal opponent of the religious views that the plaintiff promoted. The Outreach Judaism site offered additional criticisms of the plaintiff organization; information about its own, more traditional Jewish religious views; and some items for sale, such as audio tapes and books. When the Jews for Jesus organization sued Brodsky for infringement, the court relied on his site's link to the Outreach Judaism site (which the court deemed "commercial" due to its sale of religious books and tapes)[30] in finding actionable use, notwith-standing the defendant's express Web site disclaimer of any affiliation between himself and the linked organization.

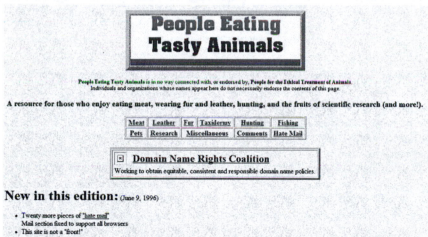

Figure 1.1 Screenshot of content posted to peta.org, circa 2000.

29 *Jews for Jesus v. Brodsky* (D.N.J. 1998), 993 F. Supp. 282, *aff'd* (3d Cir. 1998), 159 F. 3d 1351.
30 From the court's description of the Outreach Judaism site, it was unlikely that the site constituted commercial speech, even though it sold books and tapes. *See* Barrett, 'Domain Names, Trademarks, and the First Amendment,' op. cit., 1016–21.

In *People for the Ethical Treatment of Animals* ["PETA"] *v. Doughney*,[31] the plaintiff animal rights organization alleged infringement when the defendant registered the domain name *peta.org* and set up a site entitled "People Eating Tasty Animals," which ridiculed the plaintiff and its views. (See Figure 1.1). The defendant's site stated that it was a "resource for those who enjoy eating meat, wearing fur and leather, hunting, and the fruits of scientific research." While the defendant offered no goods or services on the site, he provided links to various meat, fur, leather, hunting, animal research, and other organizations, all of which held views or engaged in activities generally antithetical to the plaintiff's. There were no facts to suggest that the defendant had any financial or other connection with the linked sites. In finding the requisite trademark use, the court noted:

> To use PETA's mark "in connection with" goods or services, Doughney need not have actually sold or advertised goods or services on the www.peta.org website. Rather, Doughney need only have connected the website to others' goods or services.[32]

This line of cases may be understood in at least two different ways. First, the courts may simply be substituting "commercial use" for trademark use, as the Ninth Circuit did in the *Panavision* cybersquatter case, and reasoning that if a non-commercial forum site links to a commercial site, it becomes "commercial" itself, and any use of the mark on the forum site becomes actionable "commercial use" of the mark. This reasoning is problematic because trademark use is a more restrictive requirement than "commercial" use, which presumably includes any reference to a mark in a commercial context, regardless of whether it could be understood to identify the source of a defendant's goods or services. Many references to marks in a commercial context may constitute fully protected First Amendment speech and/or serve valuable, pro-competitive purposes. From the standpoint of First Amendment jurisprudence, it is highly doubtful that a mere link to a commercial site renders an otherwise clearly non-commercial forum site "commercial," too, and subjects it to the lower level of First-Amendment protection accorded to commercial speech.[33]

The "linking" cases might alternatively be understood to say that whenever a forum site links to sites that sell or advertise goods or services, consumers are likely to look to the forum site's domain name to identify the source of the products and services available on the linked sites. Certainly there may be instances in which it is unclear whether goods emanate from a linking site or a linked site, or whether the linked sites represent one or two separate entities.

31 Doughney, op. cit.
32 Ibid., 365.
33 Barrett, 'Domain Names, Trademarks, and the First Amendment,' op. cit., 1018–19.

That is by no means always the case, however, and the *Jews for Jesus/People for Ethical Treatment* line of cases apparently assumes that it is. It seems highly unlikely that Internet users routinely assume that a particular Web site's domain name designates the source of products and services available on all the various sites to which it links. Internet users are accustomed to encountering multiple links on the Web sites that they visit. There is no general expectation that linked and linking sites are part of a single or affiliated entity. Assuming otherwise undercuts the policies the trademark use doctrine should promote.

Links are beneficial to consumers and are a large part of the Internet's success. Grounding a finding of trademark use, and potential infringement liability, on the existence of a link on a noncommercial forum site simply discourages forum site defendants' operators from providing potentially relevant and useful links for their visitors and undercuts the effectiveness of the Internet to provide a wide range of information efficiently to users. Moreover, much like the "service" line of cases, the "link" cases give mark owners the means to censor a great deal of fully protected First Amendment expression on the Internet.[34] To avoid this, courts should carefully evaluate trademark use claims based on links and find links irrelevant unless the defendant's site does something (beyond providing links) to suggest a relationship between its domain name and the products or services offered on linked sites.[35]

Pairing the defendant's "use" with the plaintiff's goods and services

In evaluating actionable use on the Internet, a number of courts have focused not on the Lanham Act's requirement that the defendant make a "use in commerce" of the allegedly infringing word or symbol (and the § 45 definition of "use in commerce") but on the statutory language requiring that the

---

34 Use of the plaintiff's mark in the forum site domain name typically is a truthful, accurate description of the site's subject matter and contents because the site targets the plaintiff. Using the mark in the domain name enables the forum site operator to get his message to those who are most likely to be interested in it. To require the defendant to state his views without using the mark may effectively silence the defendant.

35 Some courts have hesitated to rely on links to establish actionable trademark use, suggesting that the connection between the defendant's domain name and the goods or services offered on a linked site is too attenuated and that the *Jews for Jesus/People for Ethical Treatment* approach gives trademark owners too much power to censor criticisms of their products, services, and ideological stances. See, e.g., *Bally Total Fitness Holding Corp. v. Faber* (C.D. Cal. 1998), 29 F. Supp. 2d 1161, 1168; *Voice-Tel Enterprises Inc. v. JOBA, Inc.* (N.D. Ga. 2003), 258 F. Supp. 2d 1353, 1363; *Ford Motor Co. v. 2600 Enterprises* (E.D. Mich. 2001), 177 F. Supp. 2d 661, 664. This response is more consistent with both the traditional scope of Lanham Act protection and the purposes underlying the trademark use limitation.

defendant use the mark "*in connection with*" goods or services.[36] Construed liberally and apart from the common-law tradition that it was meant to codify, this language may render a great many "non-trademark" uses actionable. A number of courts have relied on this language to find actionable use by forum site defendants who neither sell, distribute, nor advertise goods or services, and may not even link to sites that do. To do this, courts reason that the *defendant's use* of the plaintiff's mark in its domain name may negatively affect the *plaintiff's sales* of its own goods and services. In light of this potentially negative effect, the defendant's use of the mark can be deemed a use "in connection with" (*the plaintiff's*) goods or services. As the *Planned Parenthood* court explained:

> [D]efendant's use of plaintiff's mark [in its domain name] is "in connection with the distribution of services" because it is likely to prevent some Internet users from reaching plaintiff's own Internet website. Prospective users of plaintiff's services who mistakenly access defendant's website may fail to continue to search for plaintiff's own home page, due to anger, frustration, or the belief that plaintiff's home page does not exist. Therefore, defendant's action in appropriating plaintiff's mark has a connection to plaintiff's distribution of services.[37]

A number of other courts have followed the *Planned Parenthood* court's reasoning,[38] even though it amounts to little more than a play on the wording of the Lanham Act, and is foreign to the common law doctrine that the statutory language was meant to codify. This line of reasoning does nothing to ensure that the defendant's actions may lead to the kinds of harm that the trademark laws were meant to address: The defendant must use the allegedly infringing word or symbol in connection with goods or services *it is itself advertising, selling, or distributing* before the use can cause meaningful confusion about product or service source.

This line of reasoning also makes it possible for mark holders to censor non-commercial uses of their marks whenever the use could negatively affect their sales in some way. Since criticism of the plaintiff or its products is likely

---

36 15 U.S.C. § 1114(1)(a) (prohibiting use in commerce of "any reproduction, counterfeit, copy, or colorable imitation of a registered mark in connection with the sale, offering for sale, distribution, or advertising of any goods or services on or in connection with which such use is likely to cause confusion …"), § 1125(a) (prohibiting use in commerce "on or in connection with any goods or services, or any container for goods"). *See, e.g., Utah Lighthouse Ministry v. Foundation for Apologetic Information & Research* (10th Cir. 2008), 527 F. 3d 1045, 1054; *North American Medical Corp. v. Axiom Worldwide, Inc.* (11th Cir. 2008), 522 F. 3d 1211, 1220 n. 7.

37 *Planned Parenthood*, op. cit., *4.

38 *See, e.g., E. & J. Gallo Winery v. Spider Webs, Ltd.* (5th Cir. 2002), 286 F. 3d 270, 275; Doughney, op. cit., 365.

to negatively affect the plaintiff's sales, the plaintiff can silence the criticism by threatening protracted, costly litigation and potential liability against the critics. This clearly impairs, rather than facilitates, the free flow of useful marketplace information to consumers and impairs First Amendment freedoms as well.

While criticism, parody, or simply making the mark owner the butt of a joke may have a negative impact on the plaintiff's business goodwill, it is important to remember that the trademark laws were never intended to redress all injuries to a plaintiff's business goodwill or to prevent all free riding that might arise through a defendant's unauthorized reference to a plaintiff's mark. Thus, for example, a defendant's reference to the plaintiff's mark in comparative advertising may allow the defendant to free ride on the plaintiff's business goodwill and cause commercial loss to the plaintiff, but it is not actionable.[39] A defendant's retention of the plaintiff's mark in the course of selling plaintiff's goods secondhand may likewise take advantage of the plaintiff's business goodwill and cause the plaintiff commercial loss, but it is not actionable.[40] A dissatisfied consumer's reference to the plaintiff's mark in telling friends that the plaintiff's product is "lousy" may cause plaintiff to lose sales, too. That doesn't make it trademark infringement. In the same manner, incorporation of a plaintiff's mark into a domain name may cause the plaintiff to lose some potential customers who are distracted from their search for the plaintiff's Web site and enable the defendant to attract a greater audience for his own negative, non-commercial message about the plaintiff or its products. However, if the defendant's use of the mark does not signal the source of the defendant's goods or services to consumers, any commercial loss resulting from the use must be attributed to causes other than trademark infringement.[41]

Relying on the defendant's predatory intent

Finally, in finding infringement in forum site domain name cases, a number of courts have emphasized the defendant's apparent *intent to divert consumers* from their search for the plaintiff and expose them to the defendant's own conflicting religious, political, social, or consumer views. However, it is not clear why the defendant's predatory intent should be relevant in determining whether the defendant's actions constitute actionable trademark use.[42] One might argue that intent to harm should be viewed as circumstantial evidence of likely or actual harm, but harm to the plaintiff is not the appropriate

---

39 *Smith v. Chanel, Inc.* (9th Cir. 1968), 402 F.2d 562.
40 *Champion Spark Plug Co. v. Sanders* (1947), 331 U.S. 125.
41 Not all courts have accepted this line of reasoning. *See, e.g., Bosley Medical Institute, Inc. v. Kremer* (9th Cir. 2005), 403 F. 3d 672, 678–679; *Taubman Co. v. Webfeats* (6th Cir. 2003), 319 F. 3d 770, 777.
42 Barrett, 'Internet Trademark Suits,' 419 n. 204.

criteria for determining whether the defendant has made a Lanham Act trademark use. Trademark use turns on association of the plaintiff's mark with goods or services that do not come from the plaintiff, which creates the potential for consumer confusion about product source. A significant line of non-Internet cases have held that the defendant's intent cannot substitute for trademark use. There is no apparent reason why this rule should differ in the Internet context.[43]

The metatag cases

In addition to incorporating others' marks into domain names, Web site operators have incorporated others' marks in metatags—html code integrated into a Web site, which is generally invisible to Web site visitors but can be read by search engines. The metatags are meant to communicate Web site content to search engines. Search engines operate in different ways and continue to evolve. However, particularly during the late 1990s, search engines often relied on keywords in metatags to formulate and rank their search results. For example, X Co., the operator of a gardening Web site, might include the keyword "seeds" in its metatags. If an Internet user entered the term "seeds" as a search term, his search engine might find "seeds" in X Co.'s metatags and thus list X Co.'s Web site in the search result. Depending on the algorithm the search engine used for determining rankings, X Co. might get itself ranked higher in the search results (and thus increase the chances that the searcher would visit its Web site) by repeating the word "seeds" numerous times in its metatags. X Co. might likewise decide to include words constituting its competitor's mark in its metatags. This would land its Web site on the search result pages of Internet users who entered the competitor's mark as a search term.

Search engine designers have since moved away from heavy reliance on metatags in formulating search results. Nonetheless, during the period of heavier reliance, a number of lawsuits challenged defendants' use of marks in metatags. These suits resulted in a body of "metatagging" case law, which has served and will undoubtedly continue to serve as precedent in newly arising Internet contexts.

Assuming that the defendant sells goods or services on its Web site, does entering its competitor's mark into its Web site metatags constitute actionable trademark use? While courts frequently have found infringement in such cases, they have generally disregarded the whole question of trademark use. The Ninth Circuit's decision in *Brookfield Communications, Inc. v. West*

---

43 Bosley Med. Inst., 403 F. 3d 672, 679 (9th Cir. 2005); *Taubman Co. v. Webfeats*, 319 F. 3d 770, 775 (6th Cir. 2003); *Daimler Chrysler AG v. Bloom*, 315 F. 3d 932, 937–39 (8th Cir. 2003); *Holiday Inns, Inc. v. 800 Reservation, Inc.*, 86 F. 3d 619 (6th Cir. 1996); *Ford Motor Co. v. Greatdomains.com, Inc.*, 177 F. Supp. 2d, 635, 652 (E.D. Mich. 2001).

Coast Entertainment Corp.[44] has been the most influential of the metatagging decisions. In *Brookfield*, the defendant video rental chain set up a Web site (for purposes of evaluating the metatagging issue, the court assumed that its domain name was *Westcoastvideo.com*) and included the word "moviebuff" in its metatags. The Web site offered videos and other entertainment-related merchandise for sale or rent, along with a free searchable database of entertainment industry information. The plaintiff, which sold access to its own entertainment industry information database under the "MovieBuff" mark, alleged that this infringed its trademark. The Ninth Circuit held that the plaintiff was likely to succeed on the merits of its claim. The court did not expressly address the trademark use question but moved immediately into an evaluation of initial interest confusion. The court did, however, emphasize that the defendant's metatag use would divert Internet users looking for "Moviebuff" to its Web site, explaining:

> Using another's trademark in one's metatags is much like posting a sign with another's trademark in front of one's store. Suppose West Coast's competitor (let's call it "Blockbuster") puts up a billboard on a highway reading "West Coast Video: 2 miles ahead at Exit 7"—where West Coast is really located at Exit 8 but Blockbuster is located at Exit 7. Customers looking for West Coast's store will pull off at Exit 7 and drive around looking for it. Unable to locate West Coast, but seeing the Blockbuster store right by the highway entrance, they may simply rent there.[45]

If this analogy were correct, it might demonstrate trademark use. In the Ninth Circuit's scenario, the defendant's reference to the plaintiff's mark on the billboard directly associates the mark with goods located at a particular place (a store at Exit 7). Customers are exposed to the use and are invited to rely on it for information about the source of the goods in the referenced location.

The Ninth Circuit's analogy is inaccurate, however. Unlike in the billboard hypothetical, Internet users never perceive the defendant's reference to the plaintiff's mark in metatags. Thus, they do not (and cannot) rely on the presence of the mark to inform them about the source of goods or services located at the defendant's Web site. Moreover, unlike in the billboard situation, the defendant's actions do not take Internet users to the defendant's place of business. Rather, consumers are presented with a search result page that lists a number of Web sites by name. The only effect of the defendant's incorporation of the plaintiff's mark in metatags is to get the defendant's Web site listed on that search result page, along with the plaintiff's. Assuming that the defendant's domain name does not incorporate the plaintiff's mark (as the

---

44 *Brookfield Communications, Inc. v. West Coast Entertainment Corp.* (9th Cir. 1999), 174 F. 3d 1036.
45 Ibid., 1064.

Ninth Circuit assumed in *Brookfield*) and that the search results do not visibly reproduce site metatags (which they generally do not),[46] there is no occasion for consumer reliance or deception. Consumers are accustomed to receiving a range of listings on search result pages. They are unlikely to assume that the appearance of two sites on a search result page indicates that the sites or the goods or services they offer are related.

A better analogy is to a customer who walks into a restaurant and asks the waiter for a Coca-Cola. In response, the waiter hands the customer a menu of soft drink offerings, on which both Coca-Cola and Pepsi are clearly indicated, and asks the customer to make a selection. This action may invite the customer to *change her mind* and order a Pepsi, to the detriment of the Coca-Cola Company, but there is no consumer reliance on an unauthorized use of the plaintiff's mark and there is no interference with the ability of consumers to rely on the Coca-Cola mark for information about product source. Under the restaurant analogy, the metatagger's use of the plaintiff's mark just gets the metatagger on the menu (the search result page), along with the plaintiff and before the customer.

This introduction of choice between competing products undoubtedly will negatively affect the plaintiff's sales of its goods, but from a societal stand-point, the defendant's actions may be viewed as beneficial. Metatags may serve an important indexing function on the Internet. As the Ninth Circuit itself has noted, Web site operators have a legitimate interest in describing the contents of their sites, and the public has an important interest in their ability to do so.[47] To the extent that search engines rely on metatags, it may be useful for Web site operators to use others' marks in their metatags, for example, as a means of describing themselves or their products, as a means of comparing their products to those of their competitors, or as a means of notifying the public that they buy or sell new or used versions of the plaintiff's product or accessories that are compatible with it. Metatags that employ a plaintiff's mark may be an efficient way to notify persons searching for the plaintiff that the defendant's Web site has some information that may be relevant. Even when the defendant's sole purpose is to attract consumers to a product that directly competes with the plaintiff's, this may still serve the public interest. As others have explained, shoppers benefit from having a listing of other sites that they can opt to browse for alternatives to the plaintiff's product.[48] The ultimate purpose of trademark protection is to facilitate

---

46 In one reported case the metatag use apparently was visibly reflected in the search results. *North American Medical*, op. cit., 1220 n. 7.

47 *Playboy Enters., Inc. v. Welles* (9th Cir. 2002), 279 F. 3d 796, 803–804.

48 Consumers may use a mark as a form of shorthand for a particular product in formulating Web searches, hoping to obtain a listing of results well beyond the mark owner's Web site. Thomas F. Presson & James R. Barney (1998), 'Trademarks as Metatags: Infringement or Fair Use?,' AIPLA *Quarterly Journal* 26: 147–67.

the flow of useful marketplace information to consumers and to enhance marketplace efficiency. Trademark law should not be used to prohibit actions that promote these purposes but that do not interfere with consumer reliance interests. Search result listings that provide an array of information relevant to the product whose mark the consumer has entered, as well as to competing products, may be a highly valuable and efficient resource for consumers.

Metatagging is hard to distinguish from what routinely happens in brick-and-mortar stores. A consumer may go into a grocery store intending to buy a six-pack of Coca-Cola. However, approaching the soft drink shelves, she encounters a wide range of colas and other soft drink options sitting alongside the Coca-Cola. This exposure to multiple options may *divert her* and lead her to buy a different brand, but there is nothing in the store's decision to arrange similar goods together that asks the customer to rely on the plaintiff's mark for information about the source of the defendant's competing goods. And providing the opportunity for side-by-side comparison benefits the consumer.

Contextual advertising cases

In the most recent Internet trademark controversy, courts are again tending to ignore or construe away the trademark use requirement. Contextual advertising involves hidden references to marks to enable advertisers to target their most likely customers. There are two main varieties of contextual advertising: pop-ups and keying.

WhenU.Com, Inc.'s "SaveNow" software is an example of pop-ups. WhenU.Com installs the software onto users' computers with their consent. The SaveNow program tracks a computer user's activities on the Web, examining the search terms and Web site URLs that the user enters. It compares these terms and URLs to its directory, which lists a large number of Web addresses, keywords, and search terms categorized much as telephone directories categorize businesses. If it finds a match for the user's search term or URL, it identifies the relevant product or service category and causes an ad for a client in the same category to appear on the user's screen. For example, if the computer user is viewing the Wells Fargo Bank Web site at *www.wells-fargo.com*, the SaveNow program might find that URL in its directory and pop up an ad for the Chase Bank. The ads vary in their format and placement, but some of them partially obscure the window that the user has open at the time. The user must then either click the ad closed or click on the ad to visit the advertiser's Web site. The ads are displayed in separate, conspicuously labeled windows.

Keying allows advertisers to target consumers with certain interests by causing their banner advertisements or sponsored links to appear on the search result page whenever search engine users enter pre-identified search terms. Thus, for example, Wells Fargo Bank might pay a search engine to display its ads whenever its users enter the search term "mortgage" or "loan."

It might also have its ad keyed to another bank's mark, like Chase, so that each time an Internet user enters "Chase" as a search term, Wells Fargo's banner ad appears on the search result page. As in the case of the WhenU pop-ups, the banner ads or sponsored links generally include a link to the advertiser's Web site.

One can immediately see how a number of the Internet trademark use decisions discussed earlier might provide (and indeed have provided) a foundation for courts to find that sellers of contextual advertising services (or their clients) make actionable trademark use when they use marks to trigger pop-up or banner ads. For example, courts might draw a parallel to the cybersquatting decisions, reasoning that, much like cybersquatters offering to sell domain names that incorporate marks, contextual advertising services intentionally "trade on the value or good will" of the plaintiffs' marks, selling that value to advertisers who want to free ride on the plaintiffs' business goodwill. Courts might likewise analogize to the decisions finding placement of marks in metatags an actionable trademark use: In each instance the defendant makes a hidden reproduction of the plaintiff's mark as a means of getting its own products or services before Internet users who are seeking the plaintiff. Moreover, the forum site domain name decisions finding actionable use when the defendant's application of plaintiff's mark "affects" the plaintiff's sales would seem on point. The effect on the plaintiff's sales results from offering consumers additional choices, which may lead some who originally intended to purchase from the plaintiff to purchase elsewhere.

Following these precedents, however, takes the infringement cause of action even further from its limited purpose. Contextual advertising defendants do not engage in trademark use because they do not use marks as brands in a manner that is likely to communicate the source of their goods or services to consumers. Their use is strictly an internal, "machine linking" use to which consumers are never exposed.[49] Meaningful trademark use is likely to occur only if the contextual advertiser reproduces the plaintiff's mark in the ad itself.[50] Given the state of the "likelihood of consumer confusion" inquiry today, finding that hidden, internal uses of marks constitutes actionable use may effectively deter all such internal uses, which would deprive businesses and consumers alike of many potentially effective and beneficial digital marketing technologies. Barring infringement claims when there is no perceptible use of the plaintiff's mark does not necessarily preclude redress if

---

49 It follows that, "where the pure machine-linking function is the only use at issue, there is no trademark use and there can be no infringement." *U-Haul Int'l, Inc. v. WhenU.Com, Inc.* (E.D. Va. 2003), 279 F. Supp. 2d 734, 728.

50 While the search engine itself has been held a direct infringer in such cases, good arguments can be made that the advertising client should be deemed the direct infringer, if there is one, and that the search engine should be liable, if at all, under a theory of contributory infringement. Stacey L. Dogan (2010), 'Beyond Trademark Use,' *Journal of Telecommunications and High Technology Law* 8: 135.

the defendant's screen display is itself misleading: However, in such cases plaintiffs should rely on a different deceit-based unfair competition theory—one that rests only on the misleading nature of the screen display and does not expand the plaintiff's trademark rights by founding liability on the hidden use.[51]

Case decisions addressing contextual advertising have been decidedly mixed to date. Perhaps the most effective illustration of the range of court responses can be found in two recent Second Circuit decisions, where one panel adhered to the traditional understanding of trademark use and found that WhenU.Com's SaveNow pop-up advertising did not constitute actionable trademark use, and another panel essentially confined the first to its facts and held that Google's "Sponsored Link" keyword advertisement system constituted actionable use.

In the *WhenU.Com* case,[52] the Second Circuit rejected arguments that inclusion of the plaintiff's Web address (which consisted of its mark, "1-800 Contacts," coupled with the .com top-level domain) in the SaveNow directory constituted actionable trademark use. The court noted that:

> A company's internal utilization of a trademark in a way that does not communicate it to the public is analogous to an individual's private thoughts about a trademark. Such conduct simply does not violate the Lanham Act, which is concerned with the use of trademarks in connection with the sale of goods or services in a manner likely to lead to consumer confusion as to the source of such goods or services.[53]

The court also noted that the defendant had not actually used the plaintiff's mark in the directory as such. It had used only its very similar URL, again suggesting a non-trademark use—use as an address rather than use as a mark.

The *WhenU.Com* panel rejected arguments that the defendant's placement of pop-up ads over computer screens displaying the plaintiff's 1-800 Web site constituted an actionable "display" of the plaintiff's mark in connection with the advertised goods or services. First, the plaintiff itself placed the mark on its Web site, not the defendant. Moreover, the pop-up ads appeared on a separate window that was clearly labeled. The court stressed that computer users are accustomed to overlaid windows from different sources and were not likely, under the circumstances, to look to one window for information about the source of products displayed in the other.[54]

---

51 For discussion of alternative actions, *see* Barrett, 'Finding Trademark Use,' op. cit., 929–32. See also Margreth Barrett, 'A Cause of Action for "Passing Off"/Associational Marketing,' IP Theory 1:1 (2010).
52 *1-800 Contacts, Inc. v. WhenU.Com, Inc.* (2nd Cir. 2005), 414 F. 3d 400.
53 Ibid., 409.
54 Ibid., 410.

The *WhenU.Com* panel observed that the gist of the plaintiff's complaint was "WhenU's alleged effort to capitalize on a [computer] user's specific attempt to access the 1-800 website."[55] The court noted, however, that "[a]bsent improper use of 1-800's trademark," this form of free riding would not violate the Lanham Act.[56] Indeed, the panel likened WhenU's pop-ups to product placement in retail stores, when a store places its own house brands next to the trademarked products they emulate "in order to induce a customer who has specifically sought out the trademarked product to consider the store's less-expensive alternative."[57] The panel obviously believed that such product placement did not constitute actionable trademark use.

In closing, the *WhenU* court stressed that the plaintiff's survey evidence, which purported to indicate that computer users were confused about the source of pop-up ads, was irrelevant:

> [T]his rationale puts the cart before the horse. Not only are "use," "in commerce," and "likelihood of confusion" three distinct elements of a trademark infringement claim, but "use" must be decided as a threshold matter because, while any number of activities may be "in commerce" or create a likelihood of confusion, no such activity is actionable under the Lanham Act absent the "use" of a trademark.[58]

District Courts in the Second Circuit read the *WhenU* opinion to exonerate search engine keying from trademark infringement liability for lack of actionable trademark use. However, when the issue reached the Second Circuit in *Rescuecom Corp. v. Google, Inc.*,[59] the Second Circuit did an about-face. The *Google* panel distinguished *WhenU* on two grounds. First, the panel stressed that the *WhenU.Com* defendant did not use the plaintiff's mark, but its Web address, which consisted of its mark and .com. However, it is hard to see why this distinction should matter, since the same rule regarding "trademark use" applies regardless of whether the defendant allegedly used the plaintiff's exact mark or words or symbols that are confusingly similar to it, as the Web address surely was. Second, the *Google* panel stressed that WhenU did not sell the right to tie ads to specific marks but to *product and service categories* comprised of an array of relevant marks, Web addresses, and other keywords. WhenU's internal directory was proprietary and not shared with advertising clients. In contrast, Google sold rights to key ads to specific words and marks, and advertising clients were able to identify and see the mark to which they keyed their advertisements. The panel emphasized that

55 Ibid.
56 Ibid.
57 Ibid., 411.
58 Ibid., 412.
59 *Rescuecom Corp. v. Google, Inc.*, 562 F. 3d 123 (2d Cir. 2009).

"Google displays, offers, and sells Rescuecom's mark to Google's advertising customers when selling its advertising services."[60] This emphasis suggests that the panel adopted the reasoning in the early cybersquatting cases, which found trademark use because the defendant "*traded on the value of the plaintiff's mark as a mark*" and made it the basis of a commercial transaction. This reasoning essentially disassociates the mark from its role in identifying products and creates rights in gross in words and symbols.

The *Google* panel flatly rejected any rule that invisible, internal applications of marks could not result in trademark infringement. In the alternative, the court stressed that Google's use of the plaintiff's mark was not invisible: Google's *advertising clients were exposed to the mark* when they chose to key their ads to it. The problem with this argument, of course, is that the persons exposed to the mark (the advertising clients) were not the persons who were allegedly likely to be confused (consumers). Client exposure to the mark would thus seem irrelevant.

Finally, the *Google* panel rejected arguments that keying was analogous to product placement, not on the ground that product placement differed from keying but on the ground that *product placement constitutes actionable trademark use.*[61] If the *Google* opinion holds, the trademark use requirement would appear to be truly dead in the Second Circuit.[62]

Conclusion

Some commentators have argued that the trademark use requirement is "formalistic" and unnecessarily limits courts' ability to police misconduct on the Web.[63] But dispensing with this long-established limitation of trademark rights undercuts the common law's careful balance of competing interests. The current trend to ignore or trivialize the trademark use requirement in Internet contexts imposes serious costs to competition and First Amendment interests.

60 Ibid., 129.
61 The court stated: "It is not by reason of absence of a use of a mark in commerce that benign product placement escapes liability; it escapes liability because it is a benign practice which does not cause a likelihood of consumer confusion." Ibid., 130.
62 The Ninth Circuit has also adopted the Google panel's conclusion as to actionable trademark use. *Network Automation, Inc. v. Advanced Systems Concepts, Inc.*, 638 F. 3d 1137 (9th Cir. 2011).
63 Graeme B. Dinwoodie & Mark D. Janis (2007), 'Confusion Over Use: Contextualism in Trademark Law,' *Iowa Law Review* 92: 1597.

2 The promise of information justice

Lateef Mtima[1]

The prospect of the mass digitization of the world's storehouse of books presents the greatest boon to human culture and learning since the invention of the Gutenberg Press. The universal objectives of copyright and the stimulation of the creation, expression, compilation, and dissemination of information and knowledge, are all promoted and enhanced when libraries across the globe become available to all of humanity on an equitable basis. Through mass digitization the world's books can achieve their greatest potential to inform, inculcate, and inspire the widest possible audience, and level the global socio-economic and political playing fields in unprecedented and heretofore unimagined ways.

The Google Books Project, and the Google Books Settlement Agreement which would have allowed the Project to be realized, present the most comprehensive initiative to date to make mass digitization a reality. The Google Books Project effectively incorporates the benefits of digital information technology into the copyright regime. It provides solutions to some longstanding challenges to copyright social utility, such as the "orphan works" problem, and serves copyright social justice by including those who have been excluded in both analog and digital societies. Mass digitization, coupled with efficacious dissemination and accessibility, fulfills the copyright promise of knowledge and information justice.

But while mass digitization on a global scale is universally lauded as the epitome of copyright social utility, the implementation of the Google Books Project remains stalled in the courts and no equivalent initiative has emerged in its place. And in a display of irony that would baffle Icarus, it is copyright itself that has been used as the principal bulwark against the progress of mass digitization.

To understand this unlikely situation, and to ascertain the prospects for its resolution, one has to first appreciate how American copyright law and policy works, or perhaps more specifically, how it has been misinterpreted and

---

1 Associate Professor of Law, Howard University School of Law, and Director of the Institute for Intellectual Property and Social Justice.

misapplied in the digital information context. A key deficiency in contemporary copyright law and policy analysis has been its consistent failure to keep faith with the social utility and social justice mandates of copyright projection. The connection between this analytical myopia and the delay of mass-digitization becomes apparent when the Google Books Project, the arguments offered in support of and in opposition to its implementation, and the ultimate judicial rejection of the Google Books Settlement are considered.

The Google Books Project saga

In its original incarnation, the goals of the Google Books Project were somewhat limited in their social utility reach. Google sought to digitize the corpus of various elite libraries so that these books would be preserved in digital format, and then make useful "snippets" of their texts publically available, (Frosio 2011: 84–85; Samuelson 2011: 700) somewhat analogous to the creation and use of thumbnail images in connection with Internet search engine indices. Some copyright holders objected that such use of their works without their permission constituted copyright infringement and commenced litigation, which lawsuit was eventually granted class-action status (Authors Guild 2011: 670). After lengthy negotiations, Google and the class representatives agreed upon the terms of the Settlement Agreement: among other things, Google would be granted non-exclusive rights to digitize an expanded corpus of works and further, it would also be permitted to make their full texts (as opposed to merely snippets) publically available, in exchange for the payments of specific fees and royalties to participating copyright holders and/or a fiduciary trust. In addition, an "opt-out" provision preserved the right of any individual copyright holder to refuse to participate and withdraw her work from the Project (Hazard 2011: 2).

As a class action suit the Google Settlement required judicial approval. A wide variety of interested parties were permitted to submit amicus statements to the court, including authors and publishers societies, American and foreign governments, Internet companies, legal scholars, and various public interest and non-profit organizations. Among the arguments raised in support of the Settlement were that the Project would improve public and scholarly access to books, especially for underserved communities, including rural areas, and small colleges, as well as economically disadvantaged groups and the disabled, and that it would also improve the commercial market for many books and otherwise create new opportunities for rights holders to exploit their works. Among the arguments raised in opposition to the Settlement were that the Project contravened copyright property rights by requiring rights holders to affirmatively "opt-out" of the Project, and it would give Google an unfair advantage over competitors in the search, book-selling, or book scanning market, and that the Project did not provide adequate safeguards to protect the privacy of its users with regard to surveillance of their reading choices and interests. There were also objections extrinsic to the central goals of the Project, such as the arguments raised by some state governments that any unclaimed royalties generated by the Project should escheat to the state or be distributed to charitable organizations (Butler 2009).

In its assessment of the settlement, the court expressly acknowledged the social utility potential of the Google Book Project:

> The benefits of Google's book project are many. Books will become more accessible. Libraries, schools, researchers, and disadvantaged populations will gain access to far more books. Digitization will facilitate the conversion of books to Braille and audio formats, increasing access for individuals with disabilities. Authors and publishers will benefit as well, as new audiences will be generated and new sources of income created. Older books—particularly out-of-print books, many of which are falling apart buried in library stacks—will be preserved and given new life.
>
> (Authors Guild 2011: 670)

Nonetheless, the court ultimately rejected the Settlement, offering three principal bases for its decision. First, the court held that the Settlement was too broad in scope, resolving issues beyond the parties' original claims (i.e., the legal validity of disseminating text "snippets") which coupled with the opposition by some members of the class, rendered approval of the Settlement inappropriate given the representative nature of the class-action mechanism. Second, the court credited arguments proffered by the United States Department of Justice regarding potential antitrust impacts of the Google Books Project (U.S. Department of Justice 2010). Only the court's third basis, however, was directly related to copyright. The court held that permitting unauthorized digitization unless a rights holder affirmatively "opted-out" of the Project would be "incongruous with the purpose of the copyright laws [as it would] place the onus on copyright owners to come forward to protect their rights when Google copied their works without first seeking their permission" (Authors Guild 2011: 682).

The court's findings regarding the procedural propriety and potential antitrust effects of the settlement are debatable. Copyright disputes of this sort which involve myriad claim holders and interests have been resolved previously through judicially approved settlements and consent decrees arising in the context of class action litigation (Mtima & Jamar 2010: 98–100). Such decrees have also been upheld under the antitrust laws, absent even the non-exclusivity safeguards provided for in the settlement (Elhauge 2009: 6–8, 51–4). Moreover, the expressed antitrust concerns are somewhat speculative and may even be overblown (Hausman & Sidak 2009: 422–4, 431). The creation of a comprehensive digital corpus and a complementary book rights registry would create a digital market and actually increase competition for the use of many books. Consequently "[a] holding that [the s]ettlement violates antitrust law ... condemn[s] us all to zero output of [out-of-print] books and an effective price of infinity for new copies ..." (Elhauge 2009: 2–5, 18–23; *Harvard Law Review* 2012: 1277–80).

Despite questionable reasoning, the court's conclusions on these issues are apt to have a cautionary effect. To increase the chances of satisfying class action requirements and minimizing antitrust concerns, architects of future mass-digitization initiatives might construct and implement their projects incrementally, digitizing only a single class or species of works at a time. Antitrust precautions might also necessitate more collaborative ventures, with major entity participants undertaking more limited roles. For their part, rights holders who object to mass digitization of their works may become more strategic in structuring their infringement actions, possibly even avoiding the class action mechanism with an eye toward maximizing their control over the ultimate resolution of their claims.

It is the copyright prong of the court's decision, however, that is the most socially problematic and inimical to the progress of mass digitization. Although the court acknowledged the copyright social benefits of the Settlement, its allocation of dispositive weight to the copyright holder's prerogative to license (or to not license) her work effectively grants rights holders absolute dominion over mass digitization. This "commoditization" view of copyright eschews its social utility roots and social justice aspirations (Patry 2011: 139–40; Mtima 2012), which functions must be fully appreciated in order to place the court's decision, and the Google Book Project, into the proper socio-legal context.

Copyright social utility and social justice

American copyright law is based upon a broad directive of social utility. Article I of the Constitution prescribes that "Congress shall have the power ... to promote the Progress of Science and useful Arts, by securing for limited Times to Authors ... the exclusive Right to their Writings ..." Congress is thus empowered to incentivize authors by providing them with certain property rights in their works, such as the exclusive right to copy, display, or perform their works, thereby establishing a social engineering mechanism for advancing and shaping American culture. "The Supreme Court has often and consistently summarized the objectives of copyright law. [It] is not an inevitable, divine, or natural right that confers on authors the absolute ownership of their creations. It is designed rather to stimulate activity and progress in the arts for the intellectual enrichment of the public" (Leval 1990: 1107). "Congress thus seeks to define the rights included in copyright so as to serve the public welfare and not necessarily so as to maximize an author's control over his or her product" (Harper & Row 1985: 580). Thus, the overarching purpose of the copyright regime, including the grant of authors' property rights, is the furtherance of creative and artistic expression for the greater societal good.

Some legal scholars have questioned, however, whether copyright can fulfill its social utility function of cultural advancement unless it also achieves an adequate measure of cultural social justice (Aoki 2007: 721–3; Chon 2006: 2912). They posit whether a civilization or culture can genuinely advance if significant segments of its populace are deprived of the benefits of cultural progress and achievements. "No human domain should be immune from the claims of social justice. Intellectual property, like property law, structures social relations and has profound social effects" (Chander & Sunder 2007: 578; Wong 2012: 1). In this sense, social justice is part of the progress that copyright law intends to promote:

> The copyright law exists to further an enunciated social purpose, and much the same as when technological developments disrupt the copyright status quo and threaten to frustrate that purpose, where problems of copyright social injustice and inequity similarly impede copyright utility, affirmative legislative and judicial action is warranted. [E]valuating problems of copyright social injustice for their impact on copyright social utility can reveal a theory of copyright social justice firmly rooted in the [Constitution] itself ... This approach does not artificially transmogrify generic problems of social welfare into copyright dilemmas, but rather, acknowledges that certain social deficiencies gnaw at the very foundations of copyright protection. In such cases, it is not only appropriate to envision the copyright law as a tool for social justice, it is constitutionally mandated that the law be applied to correct social inequity in deference to the demands of copyright social utility.
>
> (Mtima 2009: 122, 135)

Where the interpretation and application of copyright law and policy excludes segments of society from full participation in the copyright regime, the social function of copyright is thwarted. Copyright protection must be available to protect the expressive works of all groups, communities, and subcultures in society, to ensure a bountiful intellectual and cultural cornucopia. Copyrighted works must be disseminated widely and equitably, to engender the broadest pedagogical and cultural impact and to stimulate the most diverse array of creative contributions in turn. And all authors and creators must enjoy equal protection of their attendant property rights, to promote universal faith and participation in the copyright system. Copyright social utility and copyright social justice are thus interdependent parts of the copyright social algorithm.

Congress and the courts employ various and specific mechanisms to ensure copyright social utility and to promote copyright social justice. One of the most important of these is the fair use doctrine, which employs a four-factor balance of interests test that permits the public to make use of copyrighted material for socially productive purposes without the permission of the copyright holder. "The social judgment in these cases is that ... these uses are not only so important but also so characteristically underfunded that they deserve a free ride ... These social judgments presuppose that the copyright owner will be able to earn returns in other markets that are sufficient to provide it with the incentives it needs to produce copyrighted works in the desired quantity and of the desired quality" (Goldstein 2010: §7.0.2, 7:7).

The four factors to be weighed are the purpose of the use, such as whether it is socially significant or will "transform" the work toward a new expressive purpose; the nature of the work to be used, that is whether it is a factual work such as a news article, which would receive less protection, or a fictional work, whose artistic elements warrant greater protection; the amount or the significance of the portion of the work to be used; and the effect on the commercial market for the work. The fair use doctrine thus assures that the authors' property right/secular incentive to create mechanism does not predominate over the social utility needs of society as a whole (Patry 2011: 215–16).

The fair use doctrine can be a pivotal social balancing tool when a new technological use for copyrighted works is introduced (Patry 2011: 225–7; Sag 2010: 27–9). New technologies can obscure the boundary between the authors' property rights and the rights and privileges allocated to the public. For instance, the act of using copyrighted photographs or artwork to create thumbnail images for Internet indexing and search engine use might be regarded simply as a kind of copying within the author's exclusive property rights or it might be considered conduct within the public's privilege to repurpose and otherwise build upon preexisting copyrighted material (Tushnet 2006: 994–6).

In light of the social importance of Internet search engines, resort to the fair use doctrine can resolve the matter. Assuming arguendo that digital thumbnail creation is merely a form of copying, applying the fair use four-factor test, two factors weigh in favor of allowing the use. Creating digital thumbnails for search indices is a socially transformative use which employs each image not as "art" but as an Internet "art-locator." Moreover, there is no negative impact on the commercial market for the images—thumbnails do not make good substitutes for full size reproductions. As to the third factor, where the nature of the use requires that the entire work be used, this factor is typically disregarded. Only one factor, the nature of the images, would militate against allowing the use where the images are aesthetic, such as paintings, as opposed to "factual," such as photographs of an historic or news-worthy event. Thus in the final weighing, the result is a two-to-one balance of the fair use factors in favor of allowing the use to proceed (Kelly 2003: 820–22; Perfect 10 2007: 725).

An even broader copyright social ordering mechanism is the compulsory copyright license. "A compulsory license is a statutory copyright licensing scheme whereby copyright owners are required to license their works to users at a government-fixed price ... Compulsory licenses are an exception to the copyright principle of exclusive ownership for authors of creative works, [implemented] when warranted by special circumstances" (U.S. Copyright Office 1997: http://www.copyright.gov/reports).

Congress most typically resorts to a compulsory license to address the introduction of a new technological use for copyrighted material which presents socially beneficial but legally complex opportunities for promoting cultural advancement. A compulsory license was implemented in connection with the proliferation of the technology that enables cable and satellite re-transmission of television broadcast signals, where the difficulty and expense of clearing all rights to copyrighted broadcasts was weighed against the benefit of making such broadcasts available to citizens in remote regions of the country (Mtima 2004: 406–8). Although Congress ultimately determined that broadcast copyright holders should profit from cable/satellite re-transmission, it also determined that given the social utilities at stake, rights holders should not possess the power to veto or control this activity. Instead, by enacting a compulsory license scheme, Congress effectively placed control over cable/satellite re-transmission in the hands of the public.

The obligation to consider copyright social utility and social justice extends to the digital information environment (Litman 1994: 33–4; Wong 2012: 33). Mass digitization of text through initiatives such as the Google Books Project would make vast numbers of books, including public domain and out-of-print books, available to essentially everyone with Internet access. Mass digitization thereby promotes copyright social utility and serves the inclusion and empowerment aims of copyright social justice. Moreover, the Google Books Project provides for payments to copyright holders as well as an "opt-out" provision, and thus the author property rights mechanism is also respected.

In granting undue weight to copyright holder autonomy the Google court's decision not only forestalls the Google Books Project, it jeopardizes the progress of mass digitization altogether. Nonetheless, the Google Books Project can still contribute to the advancement of mass digitization, both directly and as a model for other mass-digitization initiatives. Some examples of how the Project could be so harvested are explored next.

The Google Books Project and copyright social utility: Solving the problem of orphan works

There is no requirement that copyright transactions be publicly recorded. Consequently it can often be difficult, if not impossible, to ascertain who holds the legal rights to a copyrighted work at any given moment (Travis 2006: 805; Dahlberg 2011: 280–88; Berneman 2009: 292). Moreover, given that copyright protection continues for decades after the author of a work has died, unrecorded rights transfers that occurred both during the author's lifetime and subsequent to her death can control the commercial use of a work (Vuopala 2010: 17–21).

If all of the rights owners to a work cannot be identified it is not possible to make use of the work without risking suit for copyright infringement and the imposition of indeterminate damage awards. Consequently many such "orphan works" languish out of print and largely unavailable to the public. In light of the sheer volume of such works, the problem of orphan works may present the single greatest threat to copyright social utility. "[S]tudies estimate that, out of the 30 million books in U.S. libraries, between 2.8 and 5 million are orphans. [A] recent study published by the European Commission ... puts the number of orphan books in Europe at 3 million. However, others estimate that well over forty percent of all creative works in existence are orphaned" (Frosio 2011: 85–6; Vuopala 2010: 4–5).

The orphan works problem also has a deleterious impact on copyright social justice:

> Obtaining rights for works by disadvantaged groups tends to be especially difficult, particularly for ... "outsider" genres ... Typically, a copyright clearance search involves checking the Copyright Office's registry and other established rights databases ... When dealing with works by disadvantaged groups, however, these usual methods of locating rights holders are less likely to succeed ... [For example] [m]inority and poor white musicians were routinely excluded from performing rights organizations until the 1940s, and were less likely to register their copyrights ... Because of this, the orphan works problem disproportionately impacts access to cultural works by minorities, women, and other disadvantaged groups.
>
> (Dahlberg 2011: 276–7)

Works of special interest to members of marginalized communities often enjoy limited commercial markets to begin with. Where the prospective user of such a work cannot be certain that she has identified all of the work's rights holders, the added risk of copyright infringement litigation renders any use both commercially infeasible and legally unsound.

Efforts to promulgate legislative solutions to the orphan works problem have stalled for years. Various proposals before Congress have failed to garner sufficient support to be adopted (De La Durantaye 2010/11: 163). In the European Union, the European Commission has studied the problem and made various recommendations towards its redress, but little progress has been achieved. "Since its inception, Europeana ... has struggled in vain to find a way to include in-copyright works in its database and thereby avoid what the European Commission calls a "20th century black hole" in its collection" (De La Durantaye 2010/11: 161).

Legislative inability to solve the problem has left resolution of the orphan works dilemma to the private sector and the courts. A proper application of copyright social utility to the digital information context, however, helps to identify viable solutions. A social utility assessment of the Google Books Project would have enabled the court to approve the Settlement as a kind of "quasi-compulsory license" without encroaching upon Congress' legislative authority. Whereas only Congress can impose an actual compulsory license, the Google Books Project's "opt-out" provision preserves the rights of copyright holders to withdraw their works from the Project and instead negotiate individual licensing terms with any one at any time. In short, unlike a true compulsory license, under the Google Books Project copyright holders would retain the right to refuse to deal and thus maintain ultimate control over digital use of their works. At the same time, an immeasurable benefit to copyright social utility would be attained in connection with orphan works as well as the works of those authors who decide to participate in the Project.

Ironically, the pivotal objection to approval of the Settlement was that it contained the "opt-out" provision, because it could permit digitization of books without rights holders' prior consent. Critics argued that this would contravene the copyright holder's right to "sit back and do nothing" in so far as the licensing and dissemination of her work is concerned (Authors Guild 2011: 681). They contended that the law requires the use of an "opt-in" mechanism, whereby a book could only be digitized after the rights holder has *expressly* indicated her willingness to participate in the Project.

Application of the "opt-in" view of copyright to mass digitization ignores the social utility mandates of copyright law when considered in light of the technological realities of the digital information age. "The [author] consent rule was conceived in a time of primitive technological development in which it was immaterial whether we could use most of the available content ... Opt-out policies allow for the mass-aggregation of information whose trans-actional costs would be prohibitive under traditional copyright consent rules" (Frosio 2011: 96–7).

It is the societal benefit, not author property interests, that is given primacy under the copyright law. Where there is a conflict between serving the public interest and adhering to the author incentive mechanism the public interest takes precedence. "The copyright-patent clause is the only one of the enumerated powers of Congress that is prefaced by a statement of purpose: 'to promote the Progress of Science and useful Arts.' The clause does not say 'to maximize the returns to authors and inventors'" (Brown 1985: 592–3). If a copyright holder's right to receive compensation for her creative output would not be permitted to trump the demands of copyright social utility, then permitting her "right to sit back and do nothing" with her work to obstruct the progress of mass digitization is socially vacuous. Applying an "opt-in" rule to mass digitization makes no practical sense and contradicts sound copyright policy.

Indeed, insofar as orphan rights holders are concerned, it cannot truly be said that judicial approval of the Settlement's opt-out mechanism would violate their preferences. By definition, no one knows who these rights holders are, much less their views regarding the Google Books litigation. At best, the rejection of the Settlement rests on a *presumption* that orphan copyright holders would insist that until all the relevant rights holders can be identified, the ideas embodied within their works should receive no further exposure, and that no new royalties be generated on their behalf. Such a presumption, however, can only lead to results wholly inconsistent with any rational theory of copyright. "Anne Frank's diary was discovered by her father after the war. If Anne Frank's family members had not survived, no one may have obtained the rights to publish it" (Dahlberg 2011: 298). For orphan works, holding "the right to do nothing" sacrosanct undermines the social utility function of copyright, including the author incentive mechanism. Arguably, it is the preservation of such a "right" which traps orphan works in analog limbo, and not the Settlement's opt-out provision that should be deemed "incongruous with the purpose of the copyright laws."

Finally, an opt-out mechanism is not as antithetical to traditional copyright expectations as some critics would have it appear. In the absence of the Settlement, affected rights holders would retain the right to bring an action for copyright infringement where their works are used without their permission. They could therefore seek to recover money damages for any past use and also injunctive relief prohibiting any future use.

With regard to the injunctive remedy, the opt-out mechanism preserves it. Notice from a copyright holder indicating that she wishes to withdraw her work from the Project would legally preclude any further use of her work. As for the right to recover monetary damages, for an orphan work, actual damages are often difficult to establish because the work has not been licensed for some time and thus there is no benchmark for estimating lost revenues. In such cases, the law permits a complaining copyright holder to elect an award of statutory damages. Thus, application of the Settlement's "opt-out" provision to orphan copyright holders affects their rights in only one real way: instead of a statutory calculation of monetary damages, affected rights holders would be guaranteed the royalty fees provided for under the Settlement. Unsurprisingly, virtually all orphan works legislation proposals provide for similar liability limitation mechanisms (De La Durantaye 2010/11: 163). Given the social utilities at issue, this restriction upon remedies is not unduly injurious to author property expectations.

Accordingly, it seems likely that Congress and other legislative bodies will borrow from the structure of the Google Books Project in their efforts to construct orphan works' (and perhaps even compulsory digitization) legislation. First, there is a strong likelihood that Congress will simply convert the quasi-compulsory license framework of the Project into an outright compulsory digitization license. Indeed, many critics of the Settlement seemed to object more to what they perceived to be a usurpation of the legislative function than to substantive terms of the Settlement (Samuelson 2011: 697–8, 727). Thus, congressional implementation of the Project would likely be well received.

To the extent that a compulsory digitization license is not universally imposed, however, a Project-like "opt-out" licensing scheme will almost certainly be adopted for orphan works. Indeed, Congress has already recognized the need for "opt-out" mechanisms in the digital information context. In passing the Digital Millennium Copyright Act, Congress embraced an "opt-out" approach to the issue of Internet Service Provider (ISP) liability for unauthorized postings of copyrighted material. Although rights holders had urged the imposition of strict vicarious liability against ISPs for user infringement conduct (Religious Tech. Ctr. 1995: 1365–6), Congress instead placed the onus on copyright holders to police the Internet for unauthorized uses of their work and then to "opt-out" of such uses by instructing the ISP to take down their works. Congress appreciated that under an "opt-in" approach, even a simple email message could not be disseminated absent an absolute guarantee that anyone who might assert a copyright interest therein had expressly consented to its use on the Internet. Similarly, an "opt-in" approach to orphan works digitization traps virtually all such works in analog limbo.

Whether compulsory digitization is pervasively imposed or an "opt-out" mechanism is adopted only for orphan works, a rights registration mechanism such as the Books Rights Registry of the Project will be necessary. In a full compulsory scheme, a rights registry will be needed for directing license payments and for administering orphan royalties. In an opt-out system for orphan works, a rights registry would be needed to determine whether a work should be treated as an orphan work and to administer royalties, and would also help to prevent the creation of future orphans (Hausman & Sidak 2009: 428). In the European Union, the European Commission has already recommended to EU Member States the establishment of national Rights Clearance Centers similar to the Books Rights Registry (De La Durantaye 2010/11: 163) and various extended collective licensing systems are already in place in some Nordic countries (Samuelson 2011: 705–10).

Google Books and copyright social justice: Traversing the new digital divide and other social challenges

Many of the world's poor and marginalized people have limited access to civilization's storehouse of books. Entry to major libraries is typically available only to those who are privileged enough to attend or be employed by the elite research institutions which can afford to physically house such collections (Travis 2006: 762–3; Hausman & Sidak 2009: 421). Outside of research libraries, the commercial distribution of most books is dictated by the realities of commercial markets. Even where current rights holders can be identified, the transaction costs of finding them and licensing a work may exceed the anticipated commercial market value of the work (Travis 2006: 805–7). Nonetheless, many of the authors of these books would like their works to be widely accessible once again and segments of the public would like to read them. When it becomes commercially unfeasible to distribute these books, both authors and the public are underserved, and the central purpose of copyright, the advancement of knowledge and culture, is frustrated.

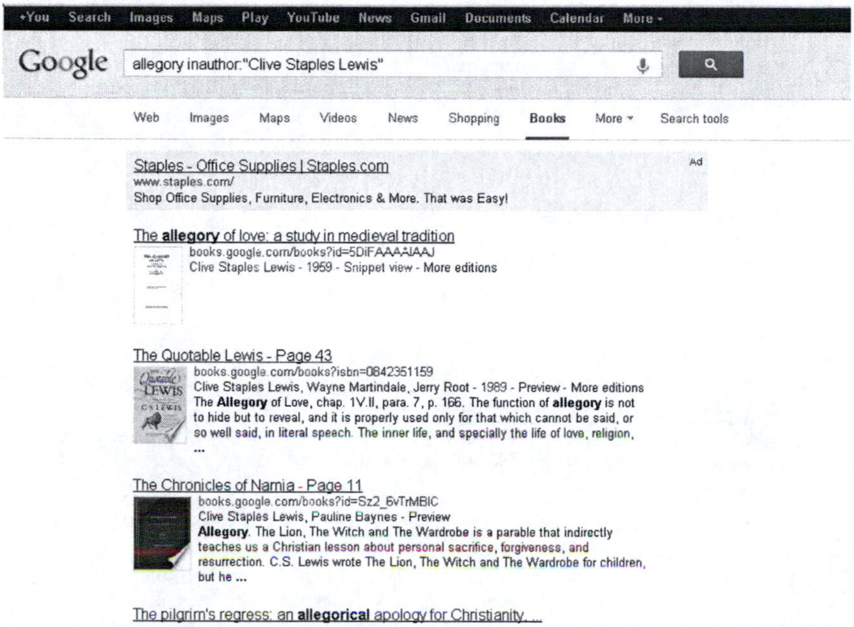

Figure 2.1 Screenshot of Google Book Search, circa 2012.

Source: Google Book Search, http://www.google.com/#hl=en&tbo=d&tbm
=bks&sclient=psy-ab&q=allegory+inauthor:%22Clive+Staples+Lewis%2
2&oq=allegory+inauthor:%22Clive+Staples+Lewis%22&gs_l=serp.
3...24247.25202.2.25390.9.9.0.0.0.1.84.531.9.9.0...0.0...1c.1.BRe1GqI
lBpU&pbx=1&bav=on.2,or.r_gc.r_pw.r_qf.&fp=f917e477de9f638d&biw
=1024&bih=612.

Additional copyright social deficiencies and inequities arise from the proliferation of digital information technology itself. While some people now enjoy
greater access to the global store of books, knowledge, and information, others
remain isolated from these advances due to their lack of access to information
technology and/or the skills to utilize such technology effectively (Edwards
2005: 585–6; Mills 2009: 385–8). Indeed, as digital formats become the dominant medium for development and dissemination of creative expression, access
to expressive works can actually *diminish* for many in marginalized communities (Wilhelm 2004: 19, 33–6). Works that are "born digital" do not easily
traverse the Digital Divide. Moreover, many books of particular interest to
marginalized groups do not enjoy a wide commercial audience, and given digitization transaction costs, are often passed over for digital conversion and
banished to analog oblivion (Brooks 2009: 125–32; Vuopala 2010: 5–6).

Collecting the world's store of printed knowledge into exhaustive digital
libraries accessible to everyone is an undeniable step towards leveling the

Palms - Volumes 1-3

books.google.com/books?id=_rcSAAAAIAAJ
1923 - Snippet view - More editions

We lift our voices: and other poems

books.google.com/books?id=EgYfAAAAIAAJ
Mae V. Cowdery, William Stanley Braithwaite - 1936 - Snippet view

The **Harlem** Group of Negro Writers

books.google.com/books?id=bFTmugAACAAJ
Melvin Beaunorus Tolson - 1940 - No preview - More editions

Rainbow round my shoulder: the blue trail of Black Ulysses - Page xx

books.google.com/books?isbn=0253218543
Howard Washington Odum, Steven Carl Tracy - 1928 - Preview - More editions
III The novels began to appear on the literary scene the year before "Black Friday"
was about to set the economy reeling, the **Harlem Renaissance** crashing, and
many literary artists careening to the Left, where the alliance of Communists, ...

Culture and Democracy in the United States - Page xliii

books.google.com/books?isbn=1560009667
Horace Meyer Kallen, Stephen J. Whitfield - 1924 - Preview - More editions
... discrimination, Kallen gave no seats in his orchestra to the indigenous Indians or
to Asian Americans.48 Nor did he defy the widespread denial of the value of black
participation in the nation's culture — even during the **Harlem Renaissance**.

‹ Goooooooooooooogle ›

Previous   1 2 3 **4** 5 6 7 **8** 9 10 11 12 13   **Next**

Figure 2.1 Continued.

> *Source*: Google Book Search, http://www.google.com/search?tbo
> =p&tbm=bks&q=%22harlem+renaissance%22&tbs=,cdr:1,cd_
> min:Jan+1_2+1920,cd_max:Dec+31_2+1950&num=10#q=
> %22harlem+renaissance%22&hl=en&tbo=d&tbas=0&tbs=cdr:1,cd_
> min:Jan+1_2+1920,cd_max:Dec+31_2+1950&tbm=bks&ei=2gdmUJO
> QEIXW9QSHqYHABw&start=30&sa=N&bav=on.2,or.r_gc.r_pw.r_qf.
> &fp=a7f4377fe713bceb&biw=1024&bih=655

world's educational and informational playing fields (Travis 2006: 762–4). It is also an unparalleled mechanism for scholarly cross-fertilization and artistic and informational exchange (Samuelson 2010: 1311–12, 1320). Efforts such as the Google Books Project are thus poised to fill the vacuum of governmental inaction to correct the copyright social utility deficiencies and injustices that endure and flourish in digital society. In addition to making millions of books available to those who don't enjoy the privilege of access to elite libraries, the Project would dramatically expand access to books for the blind and visually impaired through digital reproduction, manipulation, and vocalization of text (Courant 2009: 4). Under-developed communities and nations would encounter new vistas of innovation and self-determination (Jamar & Mtima 2012: 100–1).

As the gears of Congress grind excruciatingly slowly toward the full incor-poration of mass digitization into the copyright regime, incremental social progress may be achieved by applying the fair use doctrine to various aspects of the Google Books Project and similar initiatives. One such effort has been to assert fair use in connection with non-expressive uses of the Project corpus such as "data mining" (Sag 2010: 54–5). Data mining is the collective review of many works to discern factual constants and generalizations, and under-taking statistical analysis of a body of information (Sag 2012: 19–21; Samuelson 2010: 1324–5). For example, a person could read all of the fictional works published in America between 1900 and 1910, then read the same category of books published between 2000 and 2010, and compare both categories for depictions of racial discrimination. A human being could undertake this project without infringing upon any copyrights; however, it could take years to complete. Whereas a computer could accomplish such "data mining" in a fraction of the time, the books would first have to be digitized, i.e., copied; however, if the rights holders object to digitization, they could actually preclude this "reading" of their books (Nimmer 2009: § 8.02 [C]).

A social justice sensitive application of fair use should render unauthorized "data mining" legally permissible. Two fair use factors, the purpose of the use and its effect on the commercial market for the works, favor the use, given that this scholarly and educational use would not affect future sales of the works (Samuelson 2011: 718). With respect to the third factor, the amount of the work to be used, "data mining" requires that each entire work be digi-tized, and thus this factor would be disregarded. Only one factor, the nature of the works, tends to weigh against the use, because here the works to be used are fictional as opposed to factual works. Even this factor, however, may not weigh entirely against the use, to the extent that it is only factual data and not expressive material that is being "extracted."

Indeed, a federal court recently accepted many of these arguments (Authors Guild 2012: 14–22). A New York federal court ruled that data mining use of the Project corpus by university libraries constitutes a fair use, finding that such scholarly use does not negatively affect the market for the works and that it requires that the works be copied in their entirety. Moreover, the court further ruled that because data mining transforms the purpose of the works to one different than that intended by the works' authors, the nature of the works should be afforded little weight in the fair use analysis. The prospects for mass digitization would be most auspicious should this analysis be upheld on appeal.

Fair use could be similarly invoked to permit other digitization projects that address unique or compelling copyright social utility/justice needs. A project undertaken by the University of California at Santa Cruz to create a digital archive of artifacts and memorabilia of the rock band The Grateful Dead is illustrative (http://www.gdao.org/about). In some ways, this project is more ambitious than the Google Books Project, in that it is not limited to books but includes a wide variety of materials such as fan envelopes and letters, concert posters, professional and amateur photographs, tickets, backstage passes, laminates, "Fan Zines" and fan art, t-shirts, album covers, newspaper clippings, regalia, and video, audio, and digital content. Because each of these categories can involve different kinds of copyright protections, securing the rights to digitize such a diverse body of material is an ambitious undertaking.

To ensure that the Grateful Dead Archive (GDA) is compliant with copyright law, a fairly straightforward methodology was observed. First, an analysis as to whether specific material is still under copyright was undertaken. For in-copyright material, diligent attempts were made to ascertain the identity of the copyright holders, including use of known "Deadhead" community forums, and good faith efforts were made to obtain permission to digitize the material. Finally, where rights holders could not be identified a good-faith fair use analysis was undertaken (Hoon 2012: 752).

An important aspect of the GDA methodology is that it was not applied blunderbuss to the GDA corpus as a whole, but rather to discreet categories of the corpus. For example, concert posters were assessed as an individual category, independent of any analysis of other artifacts. As a threshold matter, some posters were determined to have passed into the public domain. For posters still under copyright, some were determined to be works for hire and the copyright holders were easily identified and permission to digitize the posters was obtained.

For many of the posters under copyright, however, copyright ownership could not be conclusively determined and consequently it was necessary to ascertain whether fair use would permit their use in the GDA. Similar to the analysis of data mining, the first two fair use factors favored the use. The GDA use transforms the purpose of the posters from publicizing concerts to that of completing an historical archive, and as thumbnail replicas, the digital images would have no impact on the commercial market for the posters (Kelly 2003: 820–22; Cambridge University 2012: 33–6). Once again the third factor was considered irrelevant, in that the use requires digitization of the entire works. Finally, the only factor that appears to weigh against the use is that of the nature of the works, the posters being artistic creations (although as discussed above, given that the use is transformative, a court might disregard this factor). Thus, here again there is at least a two-to-one fair use balance in favor of the digital archive use.

The GDA approach could be modified to accomplish a measure of copyright social justice in connection with sub-categories of books in the Google Books Project corpus. For example, some research indicates that African American works are often overlooked as candidates for commercial digitization and distribution (Brooks 2009: 125–32). In constructing a social justice-sensitive approach to this issue, a discrete and socially significant sub-category of such works would be identified, such as fictional works from the Harlem Renaissance Period. Next, a threshold copyright status analysis would likely reveal that some of these works have passed into the public domain while others are still within copyright, including some orphan works.

From a copyright social justice perspective, the Google Books' use of the orphan works and possibly even other works in this sub-category is a fair use. In assessing the purpose of the use, the public interest is a consideration (Frosio 2011: 98, 105; Mtima 2004: 436–8). Here the use could be considered socially transformative, or at least "socially resuscitative," in that it makes culturally significant and unique works available to the public, which works are otherwise largely unavailable even in analog formats (Sag 2012: 4). Moreover, courts could consider this factor in tandem with the atypical positive revenue and market impact (Perfect 10 2007: 720). Whereas a finding of fair use precludes the payment of compensation to the rights holder, inclusion in the Google Books Project generates royalties where there has been little or no revenue and the opt-out provision permits rights holders to pursue alternative licensing opportunities engendered by new interest in the work. "[A] use that has no demonstrable effect upon the potential market for ... the copyrighted work need not be prohibited in order to protect the author's incentive to create. The prohibition of such noncommercial uses would merely inhibit access to ideas without any countervailing benefit" (Sony 1984: 450–51). Although a commercial use, here the compelling social need, concomitant rights holder compensation, and positive "copyright resuscitation" would seem to favor the use (Bill Graham Archives 2006: 613–15).

As for the remaining two factors, the analysis is the same as that for data mining and the GDA. The entire works would have to be digitized, rendering the third factor null, and the fictional nature of the works would militate toward disallowing the use. Once again, a weighing of the fair use factors results in a two-to-one balance in favor of the use.

As society awaits legislative action, more progressive invocation of the fair use doctrine can spur incremental mass-digitization achievement (Aufderheide and Jaszi 2011: 9–11, 127–47; Brooks 2009: 134–5). Moreover, carefully delineated mass-digitization efforts also stand a better chance of assuaging antitrust and the other legal concerns which resulted in judicial rejection of the Google Settlement. While pervasive adoption of mass digitization into the copyright regime should remain the end-game, intermediate fair use initiatives can deliver immediate social justice benefits.

Fulfilling the promise of information justice

The functional compilation of the world's recorded knowledge is the ultimate fulfillment of the promise of copyright. We now possess the technology— what we need is the social commitment.

Throughout the past century, an "IP Commoditization Precept" dominated American intellectual property policy (Mtima 2012; Litman 1994: 33). Books and medicines were commoditized more like golf clubs and television sets than they were beneficially exploited and disseminated as befitting the bounty of human aspiration and ingenuity (Sunder 2012: 175–8). "In this country the laws have become so skewed toward the interests of present-day 'rights holders' that ... most of the recorded past has been locked up for generations to come—perhaps forever" (Brooks 2009: 125). The Google Books decision, however, may ultimately prove to be a watershed moment in the progressive evolution of copyright law and policy. Although the court rejected the Settlement, it nonetheless expressly acknowledged the Google Book Project's extraordinary copyright social utility/social justice value and thereby threw down the gauntlet to Congress to bring mass digitization to full fruition. This potent illustration of the tension between the copyright social function and undue deference to rights holder commoditization interests has heightened law and policy maker as well as public awareness of the importance of a socially balanced copyright regime (Wong 2012: 1–2).

The court's decision also provides some practical guidance for private entities as to how they might successfully construct and pursue their commercial digitization endeavors. Focused initiatives that withstand judicial scrutiny can increase and diversify available digitized content and eventually partner with existing archives to enhance their respective collections and/or expand their range of permitted digital applications. Acute social needs in underserved and marginalized communities can be targeted for immediate attention while simultaneously garnering public support for more pervasive mass-digitization undertakings. Pending decisive legislative action, private actors can thereby move mass digitization forward in socially significant, albeit incremental stages.

The forward momentum of mass digitization has perhaps been slowed but it has certainly not been halted. A rededication of legislative and judicial commitment to the social mandates of copyright protection will refuel its progress. After years of false starts and detours, copyright social utility and social justice demand that widespread mass digitization be achieved with all deliberate speed.

Bibliography

Aoki, K., (2007) 'Distributive and Syncretic Motives in Intellectual Property Law,' 40 *U.C. Davis L. Rev.* 717 (California).

Aufderheide, P. and Jaszi, P. (2011) *Reclaiming Fair Use* (University of Chicago Press, Chicago).

Berneman, B.A., (2009) 'Putting the Google Book Settlement in Perspective: Will Looking for a Book Ever Be the Same Again? (Patents, Copyrights, Trademarks, and Literary Property Course Handbook Series),' 972 PLI/Pat 289 (Practising Law Institute, New York).

Bill Graham Archives v. Dorling Kindersley Limited, 448 F. 3d 605 (2nd Cir. 2006).

Brooks, T., (2009) 'Only in America: The Unique Status of Sound Recordings under U.S. Copyright Law and How It Threatens Our Audio Heritage,' 27 *Am. Music* 125.

Brown, R.S., (1985) 'Eligibility for Copyright Protection: A Search for Principled Standards,' 70 *Minn. L. Rev.* 579, 592–3 (Minnesota).

Butler, B., (Sept. 28, 2009) 'The Google Book Settlement, Who Is Filing and What Are They Saying?' Association of Research Libraries. Online. http:// www.arl.org/ bm~doc/googlefilingcharts.pdf.

Cambridge University Press v. Becker, N.D. Ga., No. 1:08-cv-01425-ODE, 5/11/12, 2012 WL 1835696.

Chander, A. and Sunder, M., (2007) 'Is Nozick Kicking Rawls's Ass? Intellectual Property and Social Justice,' 40 *U.C. Davis L. Rev.* 563 (California).

Chon, M. (2006) 'Intellectual Property and the Development Divide,' *Cardozo Law Review* 27: 2821 (New York).

Courant, P., (Nov. 2, 2009) *Digitization and Accessibility*, Au Courant, http://paul-courant.net/?s=google+book.

Dahlberg, B., (2011) 'The Orphan Works Problem: Preserving Access to the Cultural History of Disadvantaged Groups,' 20 *S. Cal. Rev. L. & Soc. Just.* 275 (California).

De La Durantaye, K., (2010/11) *H Is for Harmonization: The Google Book Search Settlement and Orphan Works Legislation in the European Union*, 55 *N.Y.L. Sch. L. Rev.* 157 (New York).

Edwards, Y.D., (2005) *Looking Beyond the Digital Divide*, 57 *Fed. Comm.. L. J.* 585 (Washington, D.C.).

Elhauge, E., (2009) *Why the Google Books Settlement Is Procompetitive*, Harvard Law School Olin Center Law and Economics Working Paper Series. Online. Available at: <http://www.law.harvard.edu/programs/olin_center/>.

Frosio, G.F., (2011) 'Google Books Rejected: Taking the Orphans to the Digital Public Library of Alexandria,' *Santa Clara Computer & High Technology Law Journal* 28: 84–5 (California).

Glorioso, A., 'Google Books: An Orphan Works Solution,' 38 *Hofstra L. Rev.* 971, 992 (New York).

Goldstein, P., (2010) *Goldstein on Copyright* § 7.0.2, 3d ed.

Harper & Row Publishers, Inc. v. Nation Enterprises (1985) 471 U.S. 539 (United States Supreme Court).

Hausman, J.A. and Sidak, F.G., (2009), *Journal of Competition Law & Economics*, 5(3), 411.

Harvard Law Review (2012) 'Southern District of New York Rejects Proposed Google Books Settlement Agreement,' *Harvard Law Review*, 125: 1274.

Hazard, Jr., J.W., *Google Class Action Settlement*, § 9:36.50, Chapter 9, 1 Copyright Law in Business and Practice (rev. ed.) Database updated Oct. 2011.

Hoon, P.E. (2012) *The Elephant in the Room: Copyright and Mass Digitization Projects*, http://cipcommunity.org/s/1039/index.aspx?sid=1039&gid=1&pgid=752.

Jamar, S.D. and Mtima, L. (2012) 'A Social Justice Perspective on Intellectual Property, Innovation, and Entrepreneurship,' in Megan Carpenter (Ed.), *Entrepreneurship and Innovation in Evolving Economies*, Cheltenham: Edward Elgar, p. 78.

Kelly v. Arriba Soft Corporation (2003) 336 F. 3d 811 (United States Court of Appeals for the Ninth Circuit).

Leval, P.N., (1990) 'Toward a Fair Use Standard,' *Harvard Law Review*, 103: 1105 (Cambridge, MA).

Litman, J. (1994) 'The Exclusive Right to Read,' *Cardozo Arts & Entertainment Law Journal* 13: 29 (New York).

Mills, G.M., (2009) 'The Digital Divide: Left Behind on the Other Side,' *University of La Verne Law Review* 30: 381.

Mtima, L. (2012) 'What's Mine is Mine But What's Yours Is Ours: IP Imperialism, the Right of Publicity, and Intellectual Property Social Justice in the Digital Information Age,' *Arizona State Sports & Entertainment Law Journal* 2: 35.

Mtima, L., (2009) 'Copyright Social Utility and Social Justice Interdependence: A Paradigm for Intellectual Property Empowerment and Digital Entrepreneurship,' 112 *W. Va. L. Rev.* 97 (West Virginia).

Mtima, L., (2004) '*Tasini* and Its Progeny: The New Exclusive Right or Fair Use on the Electronic Publishing Frontier?,' *Fordham Intellectual Property, Media & Entertainment Law Journal*, 14: 369.

Mtima, L. and Jamar, S.D., (2010) 'Fulfilling the Copyright Social Justice Promise: Digitizing Textual Information,' *New York Law School Law Review*, 55: 77.

Nimmer, M.B. and Nimmer, D., *Nimmer on Copyright*, 8:8.02[C].

Patry, W., (2011) *How to Fix Copyright*, New York: Oxford University Press.

Perfect 10 v. Google, Inc., 487 F. 3d 701 (9th Cir. 2007).

Religious Tech. Ctr. vs. Netcom On-line Communication Servs., 907 F. Supp. 1361 (N.D. Cal. 1995).

Sag, M., (2010) *The Google Book Settlement & the Fair Use Counterfactual*, 55 N.Y.L. Sch. L. Rev. 19, 73 (New York).

Sag, M., (2012 forthcoming) 'Orphan Works as Grist for the Data Mill,' *Berkeley Technology Journal* (California).

Samuelson, P., (2011) 'Legislative Alternatives to the Google Book Settlement,' *Columbia Journal of Law and the Arts* 34: 697.

Samuelson, P., (2010) *Google Book Search and the Future of Books in Cyberspace*, 94 Minn. L. Rev. 1308 (Minnesota).

Sony Corporation of America v. Universal Studios, Inc., 464 U.S. 417 (1984).

Sunder, M., (2012) *From Goods to a Good Life: Intellectual Property and Global Justice* (Yale UP).

The Authors Guild v. Hathi Trust, 11 CV 6351 (HB) (S.D.N.Y. 2012).

Travis, H., (2006) 'Building Universal Digital Libraries: An Agenda for Copyright Reform,' *Pepperdine Law Review*, 33: 761.

Tushnet, R. (2006) 'My Library: Copyright and the Role of Institutions in a Peer-to-Peer World,' *UCLA Law Review* 53: 977.

U.S. Copyright Office, A Review of the Copyright Licensing Regimes Covering Retransmission of Broadcast Signals (1997). Online. Available at: <http://www.copyright.gov/reports/> (last visited Jan. 26, 2004).

U.S. Department of Justice, *Statement of Internet of the United States, The Authors Guild, Inc. v. Google*, Case No. 05-08136 (S.D.N.Y. 2010), http://www.justice.gov/atr/cases/f255000/255012.pdf.

U.S. Department of Justice Statement of Interest Regarding Proposed Amended Settlement Agreement, http://www.justice.gov/atr/cases/f255000/255012.pdf.

Vuopala, A., (2010) *Assessment of the Orphan Works Issue and Costs for Rights Clearance*, European Commission DG Information Society and Media Unit E4 Access to Information.

Wilhelm, A.G., (2004) *Digital Nation: Toward an Inclusive Information Society*, Cambridge: Cambridge University Press.

Wong, T., 'Intellectual Property through the Lens of Human Development,' *Journal of Public Interest Intellectual Property.* Online. Available at: http://www.piipajournal.org/article/view/9782/6698.

3   Owning methods of conducting business in cyberspace

Johanna K.P. Dennis[1]

Introduction

This chapter addresses the state of patentability of "business methods" and e-commerce. Neither Congress nor the U.S. Supreme Court has provided particularly clear or consistent guidance as to patent protection in this arena. The Patent Act of 1952, as modified over the years, has consistently been interpreted as allowing business methods to be patented, albeit not those that are pure ideas in the sense of not having technical elements. Recently, the Supreme Court confirmed that business methods are patentable, and that an application to material objects or significant non-mathematical steps is not necessarily required, while leaving open the question of what is required. The chapter describes the context of the recent decisions in the rise of business method patents since the 1990s, in cases often involving e-commerce. It also traces the controversies in lower courts and the U.S. Patent and Trademark Office since the Supreme Court's recent decision on business method patentability, as the vague standards set by the Supreme Court are applied to new inventions.

The origins of U.S. patent law

In 1870, the existing patent laws were codified, and under the present day Patent Act, a patentable invention is one that is a new and useful process, machine, manufacture or composition of matter, or improvement thereof (35 U.S.C. § 101). The present examination process requires that the patent applicant satisfy several statutory requirements, namely substance, utility, novelty and non-obviousness (35 U.S.C. §§ 101, 102, 103, 112). After the signing of the Uruguay Round Agreements Act of 1994, the patent term was modified to twenty years from the earliest filing date (108 Stat. 4809, § 532).[2]

---

1 Associate Professor of Law, Southern University Law Center.
2 "For applications filed on or after June 8, 1995, ... the term of a patent begins on the date the patent issues and ends on the date that is twenty years from ... the filing date of the earliest [priority] application.... All patents that were in force on June 8, 1995, or that issued on an application that was filed before June 8, 1995, have a term that is the greater of the "twenty-year term" or seventeen years from the patent grant." Manual of Patent Examining Procedure (hereinafter M.P.E.P.) § 2701 (8th edn. 2001). See also U.S. Patent Act, 35 U.S.C. § 154 (a)(2)–(3).

The modern day patent system is an agency under the Department of Commerce, and has a Director at the helm.

Only three major changes have been made to the U.S.'s patent scheme since its modern inception. The first was the creation of the Court of Appeals for the Federal Circuit (CAFC) in 1982, which is charged with hearing appeals on all patent matters, instead of the former system wherein the twelve circuit courts of appeal each had jurisdiction. The second change began in the early 1990s with modifying the income base for the U.S. Patent and Trademark Office (USPTO) from one based on tax revenue to one based on patent fees.[3] The USPTO has actually become a "profit center" by generating more revenue in fees than it costs to run the agency.[4] The third change became effective starting in September 2012, by way of the Leahy-Smith America Invents Act (AIA) (16 Sept. 2011), P.L. 112-29, 125 Stat. 284. The most substantial changes resulting from the AIA were the creation of the Patent Trial and Appeal Board (PTAB) (to replace the Board of Patent Appeals and Interferences (BPAI)), which Board would be responsible for *inter partes* review and post-grant review, 35 U.S.C. § 321 (effective Sept. 16, 2012); the elimination of interference actions; and the transition from a first-to-invent to a first-to-file patent system (AIA: §§ 3, 6 & 7). While the changes in the 1980s and 1990s were described as merely procedural and administrative, they arguably have had the effect of broadening patent rights, increasing the likelihood of patentees' success in litigation, and making it easier to obtain a patent in the first place.[5] Also, these changes resulted in a patent explosion concomitant with the time period, as the number of patent grants and applications increased exponentially. By contrast, the more recent changes via the AIA are substantive in nature and stand to profoundly impact not only the way the patent system operates, but the value of patent portfolios and corporate intellectual property (IP) strategies.

Generally, patents were intended to be defenses and protections for the patentee, as a kind of fence preventing others from invading the sacred property.

---

3 Under the Omnibus Budget Reconciliation Act of 1990, the USPTO became a fully fee-funded agency. Fees payable to the USPTO include not only application fees, but also maintenance fees at periodic intervals (3.5, 7.5 and 11.5 years) after issuance. (See U.S. Patent & Trademark Office 2012a).

4 As compared to fiscal years 2007, 2008, and 2009, when the USPTO operated at a net cost, in fiscal years 2010 and 2011, the USPTO has generated net income of $94.7 million and $88.3 million, respectively, "due to the continued increase of maintenance fees received, offset by decreased revenue recognition of previously collected deferred revenue" (U.S. Patent & Trademark Office 2012b).

5 The CAFC has interpreted patent law to make it "eas[i]er to get patents, easier to enforce patents against others, easier to get large financial awards from such enforcement, and harder for those accused of infringing patents to challenge the patents' validity" (Jaffe and Lerner 2007: 2). The USPTO's relatively "new" reliance on patent fees causes the agency to be more focused on its consumer—the patent applicant—and less focused on whether the application truly merits grant. Revenues come from quick patent examination and numerous grants, not from precise, detailed, and lengthy examinations resulting in denial.

However, more recently many patentees—or, more accurately the industry company to which the rights are often assigned—have been exercising their patent rights in an affirmative manner. Companies often engage in the practice of sifting through an intellectual property portfolio to determine how patents can be affirmatively enforced to require licenses and royalties, including searching for the so called "Rembrandts in the Attic"[6] and strategies such as creating "patent thickets."[7]

Business methods patentable

The procedures and strategies associated with patenting a business method have been, at times, complex and obscure. The AIA's 2011 language defining "covered business method patent[s]," whose validity may be challenged using the Act's new transitional post-grant review rules, is instructive as to the present meaning of "business method." There, Congress defined a "covered business method patent" as "a patent that claims a method or corresponding apparatus for performing data processing or other operations used in the practice, administration, or management of a financial product or service, except that the term does not include patents for technological inventions" (AIA § 18(d)(1)). More broadly, the USPTO defines the "business method" class of inventions as "machines and their corresponding methods for performing data processing or calculation operations, where the machine or method is utilized in the 1) practice, administration, or management of an enterprise, or 2) processing of financial data, or 3) determination of the charge for goods or services" (U.S. Patent & Trademark Office 4 July 2009).

In obtaining a patent for a business method, one must navigate the interactions between key players in the U.S. patent system: inventors, specially licensed attorneys or agents, governmental agencies (notably the USPTO and BPAI/PTAB), and the judiciary (federal trial and appellate courts). The patenting process usually begins by the inventor hiring a registered patent attorney or agent to "undertake the process of applying to the patent office for a patent on his or her invention" (Hunt 2001: 6). The application for patent must contain, among other things, a "description of the invention, a discussion of any related inventions or techniques known to the inventor (what is called the prior art), and a set of proposed claims that will define the property rights he or she is seeking" (Hunt 2001: 6). Employees of the USPTO in the same technology center as the field of the invention (patent examiners) "review the application, conduct their own search of the prior art,

---

6 "Rembrandts in the Attic" are those patents that are dormant and not actively part of the company's incentive to create, yet used later as a tool wielded against competitors to generate revenue and force licensing (Jaffe and Lerner 2007: 57–9).
7 A "dense web of overlapping intellectual property rights that a company must hack its way through in order to actually commercialize new technology" (Shapiro 2001: 119–20).

decide whether to grant a patent, and if so, [whether] the precise language of the patent's claims" are too broad or require amendment (Hunt 2001: 6). The inventor, by way of the patent attorney or agent, and the patent examiner engage in a negotiation of the language that should be used to describe the invention and its scope. If the parties are able to reach an agreement and the requirements in the patent statute are met by the application, then a patent will issue.

The basis for business methods—subject matter patentability of processes

The ability to obtain a patent derives from the U.S. Constitution in the Copyright Clause, which delegates to Congress the power to promote the progress of the useful arts by securing for inventors for limited times the exclusive right to their discoveries (U.S. Const. art. I, § 8, cl. 8). According to the present day version of 35 U.S.C. § 101, "[w]hoever invents or discovers any new and useful process, machine, manufacture, or composition of matter, or any new and useful improvement thereof, may obtain a patent therefor, subject to the conditions and requirements of this title." Section 101 traces its origins to the Patent Act of 1793, which mentioned "arts" where the term "process" now stands (1 Stat. 318, 319, § 1 (1793)). In 1952, Congress amended section 101 to indicate "process" and added a definition for "process" in section 100(b). Such changes notwithstanding, the Supreme Court has stated that this change did not alter the meaning of the statute, because a process was "considered a form of 'art' as that term was used in the 1793 Act" (*Diamond v. Diehr*, 450 U.S. 175, 182 (1981)). Furthermore, "[w]hether a claim is drawn to patent-eligible subject matter under § 101 is a threshold inquiry, and any claim of an application failing the requirements of § 101 must be rejected even if it meets all of the other legal requirements of patentability," *In re Bilski*, 545 F. 3d 943, 950 (Fed. Cir. 2008) (citing *In re Comiskey*, 499 F. 3d 1365, 1371 (Fed. Cir. 2007)),[8] including the requirements for novelty, 35 U.S.C. § 102, non-obviousness (35 U.S.C. § 103), and disclosure (35 U.S.C. § 112). Thus, any analysis for patent eligibility necessarily starts with the statute.

The definition of "process" within the statute is not particularly helpful because it defines the term in a circuitous manner.[9] While the ordinary meaning

---

8 See also *Parker v. Flook*, 437 U.S. 584, 593 (1978) ("The obligation to determine what type of discovery is sought to be patented must precede the determination of whether that discovery is, in fact, new or obvious").

9 "The term 'process' means process, art, or method, and includes a new use of a known process, machine, manufacture, composition of matter, or material" (35 U.S.C. § 100(b)).

of "process" is broad,[10] the Court has held that the meaning of "process" in § 101 is other than its ordinary meaning (*Parker v. Flook*, 437 U.S. 584, 588–89 (1978)). The definition for patent purposes is not so broad as to encompass laws of nature, natural phenomena, or abstract ideas (*Diehr*, 450 U.S. at 185). To be patent-eligible subject matter, an abstract idea must involve an application to a practical use (*Bilski*, 545 F. 3d at 1013 (Rader, C.J., dissenting)). This is so not because "natural phenomena [cannot be] processes, but rather [because of] the more fundamental understanding that they are not the kind of 'discoveries' that the statute was enacted to protect" (*Flook*, 437 U.S. at 593).[11]

The "useful, concrete and tangible result"

In the early years following the 1952 Patent Act, the USPTO had published guidelines which rejected the idea that computer programs were patentable. See e.g., U.S. Patent & Trademark Office, 33 Fed. Reg. 15581, 15609–10 (1968). However, as technology developed, inventions had become less driven by industrial innovations and increasingly based on computers and their programs and developments that could not be seen by the human eye or touched by human hands. In response to the existing limiting principles regarding the scope of section 101, the CAFC's predecessor court determined that patentability principles should be more expansive, with an eye towards computer technology.[12] Later, in the midst of the Dot-com Bubble,[13] as companies fought for internet presence and ways to enhance their business productivity using new technologies and the Internet, the last barrier to business method patentability was abolished.

In 1998, the CAFC addressed the question of whether patents could be granted on methods of structuring or operating a business, such as a

---

10 The ordinary meaning of "process" at the time the word was added to Section 101, was "'[a] procedure ... [a] series of actions, motions, or operations definitely conducing to an end, whether voluntary or involuntary.'" *Bilski*, 545 F. 3d at 952 (citing *Webster's New International Dictionary of the English Language* 1972).

11 It is noted that the unpatentability of natural phenomena supports Dennis' theory that foundational technologies should not be patentable (See Dennis, 2008: 286–88). Mathematical algorithms are like genes; neither exists because of mankind, though he may have first revealed them to our eyes.

12 See *In re Tarczy-Hornoch*, 397 F. 2d 856 (C.C.P.A. 1968) (overruling the "function of a machine" doctrine); *In re Bernhart*, 417 F. 2d 1395 (C.C.P.A. 1969) (discussing patentability of a programmed computer); *In re Musgrave*, 431 F. 2d 882 (C.C.P.A. 1970) (analyzing process claims encompassing computer programs).

13 "[A] historic speculative bubble covering roughly 1995–2000 (with a climax on March 10, 2000, with the NASDAQ peaking at 5132.52 in intraday trading before closing at 5048.62) during which stock markets in industrialized nations saw their equity value rise rapidly from growth in the Internet sector and related fields." (Wikipedia 2012; Galbraith and Hale 2004).

"hub-and-spoke" model. In *State Street Bank & Trust Co. v. Signature Financial Group, Inc.*, 149 F. 3d 1368, 1369 (Fed. Cir. 1998), the patentee, a mutual funds administrator and accounting agent, sought and obtained patent protection for "a data processing system ... for implementing an investment structure," wherein various "mutual funds ([s]pokes) pool their assets in an investment portfolio ([h]ub) organized as a partnership." The major benefits of such a system were the administrator (patentee) could easily "monitor and record the financial information flow and make all calculations necessary for maintaining a partner fund financial services configuration," consolidated "costs of administering the fund," and "the tax advantages of a partnership" (*Id.* at 1371). Subsequently, a licensee of the patent asserted that the patent was invalid and unenforceable for failing to claim patent eligible subject matter under section 101 (*Id.* at 1369). The court construed the claims of the patent as a machine consisting of means-plus-function elements (*Id.* at 1372).

In rejecting the licensee's claim that business methods could never be patent eligible subject matter, the CAFC indicated that unlike laws of nature, natural phenomena, and abstract ideas (including mathematical algorithms), business methods were not an exception to patentability.[14] In so doing, the court developed the so-called "useful, concrete and tangible result" test for patentability, which was particularly useful in evaluating business methods. In explaining the difference between mere mathematical algorithms and business methods incorporating them, the court stated "[u]npatentable mathematical algorithms are identifiable by showing they are merely abstract ideas constituting disembodied concepts or truths that are not 'useful.' From a practical standpoint, this means that to be patentable an algorithm must be applied in a 'useful' way" (*Id.* at 1373). On the other hand, a business method could be patentable when it involved the "transformation of data, representing discrete dollar amounts, by a machine through a series of mathematical calculations into a final share price," because it "constitutes a practical application of a mathematical algorithm, formula, or calculation, [by] produc[ing] 'a useful, concrete and tangible result'" (*Id.*). This "useful, concrete and tangible result" test focused on the transformation of raw data or signals by way of mathematical algorithms, formula or calculations into a different state or thing—a "smooth waveform" displayed on a monitor as in *In re Alappat*,

---

14 The court rejected the preexisting "business method" exception, that "merely represented the application of some general, but no longer applicable legal principle, perhaps arising out of the 'requirement for invention'—which was eliminated by § 103. Since the 1952 Patent Act, business methods have been, and should have been, subject to the same legal requirements for patentability as applied to any other process or method" (*State Street Bank*, 149 F. 3d at 1375). Thus, as long as the business method satisfies the statutory requirements for patentability, the court indicated that a patent could issue. By contrast, even when a mathematical algorithm fell into one of the four categories of patent eligible subject matter in section 101 and satisfied the other statutory requirements, it constituted an abstract idea which is never patentable since such ideas constitute an exception to patentability.

33 F. 3d 1526, 1544 (Fed. Cir. 1994) (*en banc*), information about the "condition of a patient's heart" as in *Arrhythmia Research Technology Inc. v. Corazonix
Corp.*, 958 F. 2d 1053 (Fed. Cir. 1992), and a "final share price momentarily
fixed for recording and reporting" as in *State Street Bank*, 149 F. 3d at 1373.

Later, in *AT&T Corp. v. Excel Communications, Inc.*, 172 F. 3d 1352, 1353,
1355 (Fed. Cir. 1999), an inventor sought a patent to a method of enhancing
a long-distance telephone call message record for billing purposes by "adding
a primary interexchange carrier (PIC) indicator," which correlates to data
about the subscriber and call recipient's long-distance carriers. The patent was
challenged as invalid on section 101 grounds because it "implicitly recite[d]
a mathematical algorithm." In upholding the patent's validity, the CAFC
affirmed the application of the "useful, concrete and tangible result" test as the
means by which use of a mathematical algorithm in a specific way could be
patentable without offending the judicial exceptions to patentability, so long
as such use does not "preempt[] other uses of the mathematical principle" (*Id.*
at 1358). Thus the "useful, concrete and tangible result" test was established
as the linchpin to patentability for business methods whether the patent
application read to a machine (as in *State Street Bank*) or a process (as in *AT&T*).

The growth of business methods

The CAFC's removal of the last obstacle to business method patenting
resulted in a swell of such patents being granted. As of August 7, 2012,
142,122 of 159,516 patents had issued over the fourteen year span since *State
Street Bank* in the five patent classification Classes most relevant to business
methods, e-commerce, and the Internet (Classes 705, 707, 709, 710 and
902), and 32,228 of 34,596 patents had issued over the same period in the
Class considered by the USPTO as the "business method class" (see Table 3.1
and Figure 3.1) (U.S. Patent & Trademark Office 2012c; 2012d; 2012e).
Further, the number of "business method class" filings and issued patents has
been steadily increasing over the past decade (see Table 3.2).

Some notable patents include the foundation for PayPal—eBay's secure
"electronic [funds] transfer system" which enables customers to purchase
items from merchants[15] using its "electronic catalog"[16]; the so-called original
six degrees of separation patent which formed the foundation for LinkedIn—"a
networking database in which the records of registered individuals are linked
by defined relationships" to the records of other individuals;[17] and Amazon.
com's system and method of "automated gifting" where the gift giver
preselects certain criteria and the system selects and sends an appropriate gift

---

15 U.S. Patent No. 5,870,473 (issued 9 February 1999) (Classes 380, 705 & 713).
16 U.S. Patent No. 6,029,142 (issued 22 February 2000) (Class 705).
17 U.S. Patent No. 6,175,831 (issued 16 January 2001) (Class 707). See also Friendster's
    patent, U.S. Patent No. 7,069,308 (issued 27 June 2006) (Classes 705, 707 & 709).

Table 3.1 Growth of business method patents after *State Street Bank*

Class	Total # of patents issued (as of August 7, 2012)[1]	# of patents issued after State Street Bank (July 23, 1998)	# of patents issued after Bilski (June 28, 2010)
Class 705: Data Processing: Financial, Business Practice, Management, or Cost/Price Determination	34,596	32,228 (93.2%)	12,293 (35.5%)
Class 707: Data Processing: Database and File Management or Data Structures	50,044	45,885 (91.7%)	12,191 (24.4%)
Class 709: Electrical computers and digital processing systems: multicomputer data transferring	61,609	58,574 (95.1%)	18,193 (29.5%)
Class 710: Electrical computers and digital data processing systems: input/ output	31,150	24,101 (77.4%)	4,616 (14.8%)
Class 902: Electronic funds transfer	2,079	839 (40.4%)	136 (6.5%)
Total # of patents	159,516	142,122 (89.1%)	43,475 (27.3%)

[1] Dating back to 1790.
* The total in each column does not add up to the total number of patents, because many patents and patent applications are classified in more than one class. E.g. U.S. Patent No. 8, 365, 267 is classified in classes 707, 709 and 710. Thus, the total in the last row represents the total number of unique patents.

to the recipient, solving the problem of lack of time or forgetfulness.[18] Other examples of e-commerce and Internet business method patents include: a method of "objectively characterizing quality of the social relationship" between two members of a social network based on monitoring patterns in and purposes of their discussions;[19] a system for "providing notice of patent and other legal rights" which allows the user to view the text of patents before accepting the acknowledgement (a form of click-through agreement);[20]

18 U.S. Patent No. 8,234,177 (issued 31 July 2012) (Class 705).
19 U.S. Patent No. 7,366,759 (issued 29 April 2008) (Class 709).
20 U.S. Patent No. 8,239,935 (issued 7 August 2012) (Classes 705 & 726).

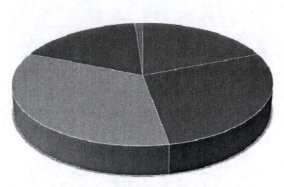

Class 705: Data Processing: Financial, Business Practice, Management, or Cost/Price Determination

Class 707: Data Processing: Database and File Management or Data Structures

Class 709: Electrical computers and digital processing systems: multicomputer data transferring

Class 710: Electrical computers and digital data processing systems: input/output

Class 902: Electronic funds transfer

Figure 3.1 Relative proportion of classes of business method patents issued (across five most relevant class codes), since 1790.

Table 3.2 Class 705 application filing and patents issued data

Fiscal Year	Class 705 Total Filings	Class 705 Issues
2002	7,400	494
2003	7,697	486
2004	8,412	291
2005	9,032	711
2006	10,884	1,195
2007	12,778	1,333
2008	14,527	1,643
2009	15,389	1,725
2010	17,231	3,649

Source: (U.S. Patent & Trademark Office 2012f).

a method of providing a life calendar that "automatically populate[s] with the user's life events and financial transactions so that the user can easily view and keep track of his life and financial situation over time;"[21] an "[o]nline loan application system using borrower profile information;"[22] and a "[m]ethod and system for delivering [and] redeeming dynamically and adaptively characterized promotional incentives" and rewards to customers.[23]

21 U.S. Patent No. 8,234,194 (issued 31 July 2012) (Class 705).
22 U.S. Patent No. 7,620,597 (issued 17 November 2009) (Class 705).
23 U.S. Patent No. 6,915,271 (issued 5 July 2005) (Class 705). See also U.S. Patent No. 7,054,830 (issued 30 May 2006) (Class 705).

A mere five months after the CAFC's *AT&T* decision, Amazon.com's 1-Click patent, one of the most well-known business method patents, was issued (Geist 27 January 2000).[24] The patent discloses the method and system wherein a customer can make an Internet purchase using a single click, thus bypassing the shopping cart, since payment and shipping information were previously entered by the customer and stored in a database.[25]

In February 2006, the USPTO received a request for reexamination of the 1-Click patent citing prior e-commerce and Digicash electronic cash references (U.S. Patent & Trademark Office 16 February 2006). On May 12, 2006, the Office ordered reexamination and on October 9, 2007, it issued a non-final Office Action rejecting claims 1–5 and 11–26 and confirming the patentability of claims 6–10 (U.S. Patent & Trademark Office 12 May 2006; 9 October 2007). Amazon.com responded by amending the two independent claims that were rejected to restrict them to an e-commerce "shopping cart model" (U.S. Patent & Trademark Office 29 November 2007), along with submitting several hundred prior art references. The USPTO accepted the amended claims in March 2010, and a reexamination certificate was subsequently issued (U.S. Patent & Trademark Office 2 March 2010; 13 July 2010).

In October 2010, the Federal Court of Canada held that Amazon.com's 1-Click patent could not be rejected in Canada simply because it was a business method, and the court ordered reexamination of the patent application.[26] However, Amazon.com's attempts to patent 1-Click and related technology in Europe have been less successful: 1-Click never received patent protection in Europe and the European patent to the "automated gifting" version of 1-Click was revoked after an opposition hearing for failing to satisfy the "inventive step" requirement in Article 56 of the European Patent Convention (EPC) (European Patent Office 12 July 2001). Amazon.com's "automated gifting" patent, which failed in Europe, was issued a U.S. patent on July 31, 2012.[27]

Despite its booming growth, not all parties in the software, Internet, e-commerce, and financial industries welcomed business method patenting with open arms. In October 2000, the Business Method Patent Improvement Act of 2000 (U.S. House of Representatives, 2000) was introduced to address "whether, and under what conditions, the government should be issuing 'business method' patents," and to "stimulate discussion regarding a solution to the perceived business method patent crisis" (U.S. Government Printing Office 3 October 2000; 4 October 2000). It was reintroduced in April 2001 (Govtrack.us 3 April 2001), but the bill twice died in committee (Govtrack. us 3 October 2000; 3 April 2001).

---

24 U.S. Patent No. 5,960,411 (issued 28 September 1999) (Class 705).
25 *Id.*
26 *Amazon.com, Inc. and The Attorney General of Canada and The Commissioner of Patents*, 2010 FC 1011, 14 October 2010.
27 '177 Patent.

Figure 3.2 Screenshot of Amazon.com's "1-Click" method of doing business online. By clicking the 1-Click checkout button, the user's default payment method will be charged for the item displayed on the page, and the item will be sent to the user at a pre-defined address via a pre-selected shipping speed.

Source: Amazon.com.

Later, between February and November 2002, the U.S. Federal Trade Commission (FTC) and the Antitrust Division of the U.S. Department of Justice held hearings regarding the antitrust implications of patents and the scope and type of patents being issued by the USPTO (U.S. Federal Trade Commission 20 November 2001; 2007a). In the Notice of Public Hearing, the FTC specifically identified business method patents and their effect on competition as an issue to be considered (U.S. Federal Trade Commission 20 November 2001). In response to the November 2001 Notice of Public Hearing and Opportunity for Comment, the FTC and Department of Justice received over 100 written submissions from over 60 entities or individuals (U.S. Federal Trade Commission 2007b). A substantial portion of these comments focused on the need for business method intellectual property protection (Kuester & Thompson 2001: 674–77), the value of business methods in innovation in the Internet era (Kuester & Thompson 2001: 687), the positive impact of business method patents on the economy,[28] and the expected growth in the areas of e-commerce and Internet-based financial transactions.[29] Meanwhile, others challenged the expanding scope of patentability and the patenting of things that should not have been patented (League for Programming Freedom 28 February 1991, 1–2, 6), and criticized business method patents as preventing use of the fundamental "'screws and nails' of the software industry" (Casamento 20 February 2002; League for Programming Freedom 28 February 1991, 8; Riches n.d., 1). The hearings resulted in two reports concluding that there was a delicate balance between promoting competition and permitting patents to technologies, and that in most cases, when properly applied, IP was a useful means of promoting innovation (U.S. Federal Trade Commission October 2003; U.S. Department of Justice and the Federal Trade Commission April 2007).

The impact of patents on free speech and communication in cyberspace

While the removal of obstacles to business method patenting has been lauded as a valuable means of "enabl[ing] the United States to maintain and increase its leadership in information technology" (Taylor 11 July 2002, 7), as was clear from the comments the FTC received in 2002, there were just as many concerns about the negative effects of patents in terms of deterring innovation, "especially because so much of the innovation in those fields builds incrementally on preceding work" (FTC October 2003, 14–15). Predominantly concerns about patenting are raised in the context of the impact of patents on competition, innovation and commercial development, and the potential for patent thickets (U.S. Federal Trade Commission October 2003, 6, citing Shapiro 2001, 119–20). For example, "[s]ome Hearings participants claimed that patents on computer software and business methods [were] not necessary to spur the invention, commercial development, or public disclosure of software or business methods" (U.S. Federal Trade Commission October 2003, 6, 14–15).

28 "[B]usiness methods patents, once through the growing pains of infancy, should enable the United States to maintain and increase its leadership in information technology" (Taylor 11 July 2002, 7).

29 "While e-commerce account[ed] for only a small share of economic activity [in 2001], it [was] growing many times faster than the bricks-and-mortar economy …. Internet banking and electronic bill payment are predicted to grow rapidly over the next decade" (Hunt 2001: 5).

However, there is another less obvious concern about expanding the scope of patentability, which is of paramount importance in terms of technology and communication in the online forum. That is, an increase in the number and scope of patents covering means of communication jeopardizes First Amendment freedom of speech and expression (U.S. Const. amend. I). For example, some of the patents to social networking sites are arguably so broad that they cover multiple means of interaction between individuals using an online system (e.g., '831 Patent, '308 Patent). Similarly, patents involving online components that we now recognize as being fundamental to the way the Internet functions, have been criticized as being overbroad. In *MySpace v. GraphOn*, 672 F. 3d 1250, 1265 (Fed. Cir. 2012) (Mayer, J., dissenting), GraphOn held patents to a means by which business and consumer users could "control the content and characterization of their own" entries in a search database, as opposed to such being controlled by the Internet search engine. The scope of the GraphOn patents was condemned as extending not only to "any online system in which users control the content and categorization of their own communications," but also to "most online advertising and social networking sites" (*Id.*) It is particularly telling when a claimed invention is "so 'widespread' that it 'approach[es] the level of a universal standard'." (*Id.*)

The effect of permitting patents and thereby ownership, monopolies and restrictions on free use of an invention that is fundamental in nature, is not only to quash competition, but especially in regards to the Internet, to silence communication and discourse. For example, in the business sense, GraphOn affirmatively leveraged its patents against major participants in the Internet and online arena, e.g., "Yahoo!, Google Inc., MySpace, Inc., Fox Audience Network, Inc., craigslist, Inc., AutoTrader.com, and eHarmony.com," and it used its patent portfolio to bully others into agreeing to "lump-sum licensing agreements worth nearly $10 million for use of its claimed system." (*Id.*). But in another sense, GraphOn's patents would prevent users from controlling their own entries in the online version of a "publically-accessible bulletin board." (*Id.* at 1265) (Mayer, J., dissenting), since any Internet database operator that allowed such control would be infringing the patents unless it agreed to pay GraphOn for the right to give the user control over their own entry. The effect here is that the means of communication (the Internet) and the actual dialogue (websites, search results, discussion boards, user profile "walls")[30] between individuals and business entities would be subject to "ownership" by a private entity, which raises First Amendment concerns about "the right to impose broad restrictions on the free flow of ideas and information over the Internet." (*Id.* at 1266 n.1.)

---

30 The dialogue is controlled by an outside entity if the users engaging in it have no control over removing, updating or modifying their own speech.

The First Amendment operates to limit the scope of monopolies permitted by both the Patent Act and the Copyright Act. *Eldred v. Ashcroft*, 537 U.S. 201 (2003). Because the Copyright Clause, U.S. Const. art. I, § 8, cl. 8, which enables both patents and copyrights, and the First Amendment, U.S. Const. amend. I, were adopted in close proximity, the Court has stated that it was the intention of the Framers of the Constitution that the "limited monopolies" afforded patents and copyrights be compatible with "free speech principles." (*Id.* at 219). More specifically, it has been argued that "because the First Amendment post-dates the [Copyright] clause in Article I, it modifies the [Copyright] clause" (Brief for Amicus Curiae American Civil Liberties Union for Affirmance In Support of Appellee 2008, 3). Further, "the presence of a limiting principle is even more necessary with respect to patent law than with respect to copyright, because ... 'the grant of a patent ... prevent[s] *full use* by others of the inventor's knowledge'" (Brief of the Software Freedom Law Center as Amicus Curiae in Support of Respondent 2009, 12 quoting *Eldred*, 537 U.S. at 217) (emphasis and alteration in original). As such, the balance between the First Amendment and the Patent Act is struck by exempting abstract ideas, laws of nature and natural phenomena from patentability. Since the "free and unrestricted Internet communication has become a staple of contemporary life," (*MySpace*, 672 F. 3d at 1265 (Mayer, J., dissenting), there should be no patent or claims of ownership restricting such communications, nor the use of any other innovation which forms the basis of development in the technological age.[31]

Therefore, just as fundamental principles in the industrial age were unpatentable (e.g., laws of nature, natural phenomena, abstract ideas), fundamental developments impacting the way business is done and interactions are had in the online context should be likewise unpatentable.[32] As such, if the "real world" version of the claimed method of communication would be unpatentable as an abstract idea or mental step, then the online or computer-based

---

31 Computer program source code is foundational technology, such that without a specific application or execution it remains "[i]n its unprocessed source code form" as "merely the expression of abstract ideas in human language" (Brief for Amicus Curiae American Civil Liberties Union for Affirmance in Support of Appellee 2008, 12–14).

32 "[I]solated DNA, whether small segments or whole genes," constitutes foundational research and to allow patents on such "violate[s] the First Amendment because they block scientific inquiry into the patented DNA," by "prevent[ing] access to each person's individual genetic information and depriv[ing] others from examining the ... genes and engaging in fundamental scientific work .... Because the patents grant control over a body of knowledge and over pure information, they violate the First Amendment" (Association for Molecular Pathology et al., Petition for Writ of Certiorari 2011, 30 citing *Ashcroft v. Free Speech Coal.*, 535 U.S. 234, 253 (2002) ("First Amendment freedoms are most in danger when the government seeks to control thought or to justify its laws for that impermissible end. The right to think is the beginning of freedom ...")).

correlation should also fail patentability for the same reasons.[33] To do otherwise would be to allow a patent to thought or speech protected by the First Amendment (Brief for Amicus Curiae American Civil Liberties Union for Affirmance In Support of Appellee 2008, 5–7).

Bilski v. Kappos: Shaking the foundation of business methods

USPTO and BPAI

Just as industries had come to rely on and expect business method patentability, their worlds, business models, and patent portfolios threatened to come crashing down. *Bilski v. Kappos* made its way to the U.S. Supreme Court via the patent applicants' petition for certiorari[34] appealing the CAFC's rejection of the application as unpatentable subject matter. The '892 application for a U.S. Patent[35] titled "Energy Risk Management Method," contained eleven claims, the most general of which claimed a method of determining and balancing risk, such as weather-related risks, in commodities trading. *Bilski*, 545 F. 3d at 949. More specifically, the idea embodied in the '892 application was that since consumers (such as coal power plants) need to purchase coal to produce electricity, and market participants (such as coal mining companies) produce coal to be sold, there was a particular method for insulating consumers from a price increase and market participants from a price decrease through use of an intermediary. On one hand, consumers want to avoid a sudden or drastic increase in the demand for coal because as demand increases price and costs to the consumer increase. On the other hand, market participants seek to avoid a drop in demand because this would decrease their revenue and further depress prices. The patent applicants sought protection for this method of addressing these complementary needs.

As such the '892 application described a method involving an intermediary, the "commodity provider," which party arranges either to sell coal to the

---

33 Circuit Judge Mayer compared GraphOn's patents to the claimed invention in *Bilski*, by stating that in *Bilski*, "the Supreme Court noted that '[h]edging is a fundamental economic practice long prevalent in our system of commerce and taught in any introductory finance class'," (*MySpace*, 672 F. 3d at 1265 (Mayer, J., dissenting) (quoting *Bilski v. Kappos*, 130 S. Ct. 3218, 3231 (2010) (citations and internal quotation marks omitted)). He continued: "The GraphOn patents were likewise directed to a fundamental and widely understood concept. The idea that information can be stored in a computer database by one person and then accessed, in an unedited form, by another person is a fundamental tenet of network computing and one that is likely to be taught in any basic computer science course." *Id*. See also *Flook*, 437 U.S. at 593 n. 15 (explaining that "in granting patent rights, the public must not be deprived of any rights that it theretofore freely enjoyed" (citations and internal quotation marks omitted)).

34 *Bilski v. Doll*, 129 S. Ct 2735 (2009).

35 U.S. Patent App. Serial No. 08/833,892 (10 April 1997).

power plant, or to provide the power plant with an option to buy coal at a fixed price. The consumer thus has been insulated from "the possibility of a spike in demand increasing the price of coal above the fixed price." *Bilski*, 545 F. 3d at 950. The intermediary would obtain the coal to sell from the mining companies at another fixed price. By again arranging to either buy coal from the mining company, or providing the mining company with an option to sell coal at a fixed price, the mining company has the security of knowing that it is insulated from a decrease in demand and thus a drop in price. The intermediary benefits by "hedg[ing] its risk." *Id.* That is, if demand for the commodity increases (thus increasing the price of the commodity), no doubt the intermediary has sold the commodity to the consumer at a lower price than it would have been able to obtain. But, the same increase in price would have caused the intermediary to expend more to obtain the commodity from the market participant. The intermediary is protected from the effects of an increase in demand and costs by having set a fixed price which is below that dictated by the inflated market. Thus, in the event of a spike in demand, the intermediary is no worse off. While this example is an embodiment of the claims in the patent application, the application was not limited to actual commodities and, as explained above, permitted options to buy or sell the commodity indicated. The kinds of commodities described in the application included natural gas, electricity and coal (Petition for Writ of Certiorari 2009: 5).

The USPTO patent examiner had rejected all claims in the patent application, indicating that "'the invention is not directed to the technological arts'" because "'the invention is not implemented on a specific apparatus and merely manipulates [an] abstract idea and solves a purely mathematical problem without any limitation to a practical application,'" *Bilski*, 545 F. 3d at 950 (quoting *Ex parte Bilski*, 2006 WL 5738364 (B.P.A.I. Sept. 26, 2006), slip op. at 3), and the "claims are not limited to operation on a computer,… [nor] limited by any specific apparatus." *Id.* (citing *Ex parte Bilski*, slip op. 4). Applicants' appeal to the Board of Patent Appeals and Interferences (BPAI) was equally unsuccessful. In considering the exclusion of abstract ideas from patentability, the "useful, concrete, and tangible result" test, *State Street Bank*, 149 F. 3d 1368, the "transformation of physical subject matter" test, *Ex parte Lundgren*, 76 U.S.P.Q. 2d 1385, 2004 WL 3561262 (B.P.A.I. Apr. 20, 2004), and the PTO's Interim Guidelines for Examination of Patent Applications for Patent Subject Matter Eligibility (U.S. Patent & Trademark Office 22 November 2005), the BPAI held that the examiner erred in relying on a "technological arts" test and erred in requiring a specific apparatus since even a claim which fails to recite a specific apparatus may be "patent-eligible subject matter 'if there is a transformation of physical subject matter from one state to another.'" *Bilski*, 545 F. 3d at 950 (quoting *Ex parte Bilski*, slip op. at 42). In explaining the concept of an apparatus-absent claim, the BPAI stated: "'mixing' two elements or compounds to produce a chemical substance or mixture is clearly a statutory transformation although no apparatus is claimed to perform the step and although the step could be performed manually." *Id.* (quoting *Ex parte Bilski*, slip op. at 42). Despite its determinations regarding the examiner's reasoning, the BPAI nonetheless "concluded that [a]pplicants' claims d[id] not involve any patent-eligible transformation, holding that transformation of 'non-physical financial risks and legal liabilities of the commodity provider, the consumer, and the market participants' is not patent-eligible subject matter." *Id.* (quoting *Ex parte Bilski*, slip op. at 43). In addition, the BPAI determined that "[a]pplicants' claims 'preempt[] any and every possible way of performing the steps of the [claimed process], by human or by any kind of machine or by any combination thereof,' and thus concluded that they only claim an abstract idea ineligible for patent protection." *Id.* (quoting *Ex parte Bilski*, slip op. at 46–47). Finally, applicants' claimed process was determined to fail to "produce a 'useful, concrete and tangible result,'" which also renders it ineligible for patent. *Id.* (quoting *Ex parte Bilski*, slip op. at 49–50). Accordingly, the BPAI sustained the examiner's rejection of the claims in the patent application.

The Federal Circuit Court of Appeals' decision—the creation of the "machine or transformation" test

In applicants' appeal to the CAFC in 2008, the court's en banc review resulted in an affirmance of the Board's decision.[36] In determining the meaning of "process" in section 101, the majority in *In re Bilski* relied heavily on *Benson, Flook*, and *Diehr*.

The Supreme Court had first grappled with the "process" issue in *Gothschalk v. Benson*. There, the applicant sought to patent a "method for converting binary-coded decimal (BCD) numerals into pure binary numerals" (*Benson*, 409 U.S. at 64). The Court ascertained that the application essentially described an algorithm, which involved the "conver[sion] [of] signals from binary-coded decimal form into pure binary form" (*Id.* at 65). However, because the application was "not limited to any particular art or technology, to any particular apparatus or machinery, or to any particular end use," the Court sought to determine whether in fact it would be permissible to allow a patent which preempted "any use of the claimed method in a general-purpose digital computer of any type" (*Id.* at 64). As part of this inquiry and to compare the scope, limitations and breadth of other patent applications, the Court engaged in a historical discussion of previously allowed and disallowed

---

36 In coming to its decision, the Federal Circuit overruled *State Street Bank* and *AT&T*, to the extent that they had relied on a "useful, concrete, and tangible result" test as the requirement for patent eligibility under 35 U.S.C. § 101.

patent applications.[37] Yet in *Diamond v. Diehr*, the Court was asked to determine whether the applicants presented a successful process patent in the application based on a physical and chemical process for molding synthetic rubber products, starting with "raw, uncured synthetic rubber" and ending with "the opening of the press at the conclusion of the cure" to observe consistently cured rubber (*Diehr*, 450 U.S. at 184). The patent application essentially involved a means for curing rubber which overcame the common problem in the art of "overcuring" or "undercuring," and by use of a mathematical equation and a computer, the application "significantly lessen[ed]" the possibility of unsatisfactory curing (*Id.* at 187). The claimed process used a mathematical equation, but did "not seek to pre-empt the use of that equation. Rather, [the application] [sought] only to foreclose from others the use of that equation in conjunction with all of the other steps in the claimed process," the other steps involving the chemical and physical components of the cure process (*Id.*) Likening the claimed process to the industrial processes of the historic process patent cases, the Court explained that the process at bar was no less patentable simply because it involved "a mathematical equation and a programmed digital computer" (*Diehr*, 450 U.S. at 185). Unlike the unsuccessful patents to mathematical algorithms in *Benson* and *Flook*, the applicants in *Diehr* "d[id] not seek to patent a mathematical formula," but instead sought patent protection for the chemical and physical curing of synthetic rubber (*Id.* at 187).

Contrary to the CAFC's rationale in *Bilski*, *Diehr* did not enunciate a "machine-or-transformation" test based on *Benson* and *Flook*. The *Diehr* Court specifically acknowledged that "[o]ur recent holdings in [*Benson*] and [*Flook*], both of which are computer-related, stand for no more than these long-established principles," "these principles" being that the common law exclusions from the statutory language, "laws of nature, natural phenomena, and abstract ideas," cannot be patented (*Id.* at 185–86). This pronouncement by the Court was nothing more than a clarification that "all of the transformation and machine linkage explanations simply restated the abstractness rule." *Bilski*, 545 F. 3d at 1013 (Rader, J., dissenting). The Court contrasted the *Diehr* application with those in *Benson* and *Flook*, noting that the former application sought "patent protection for a process of curing synthetic rubber," whereas the latter applications sought "to patent a mathematical formula" (*Diehr*, 450 U.S. at 187). The most significant factor in *Diehr* was that the claimed process was so much like the historically patentable chemical innovations that there was no need to create a new test narrowing the field of

---

37 The *Benson* Court discussed several process patent cases, including a few which were discussed in *Bilski*. Relied on in *Benson* were: *Cochrane v. Deener*, 94 U.S. 780 (1877) (a process for manufacturing flour); *Tilghman v. Proctor*, 102 U.S. 707 (1881) (manufacturing of fat acids and glycerine from fatty bodies by action of water at high temperature and pressure); *Expanded Metal Co. v. Bradford*, 214 U.S. 366 (1909) (process of expanding metal involving mechanical operations); *Smith v. Snow*, 294 U.S. 1 (1935) (process for setting eggs in staged incubation); and *Waxham v. Smith*, 294 U.S. 20 (1935) (same).

patent eligible processes in order for the *Diehr* process to be patentable. In addition, the Court made it significantly clear that it distinguished the application in *Diehr* from those in the unpatentable subject matter prior cases because *Diehr* did not involve the pre-emption of a mathematical formula or a law of nature. *Id.* at 185–88. The process in *Diehr* involved "'a novel and useful structure created with the aid of knowledge of scientific truth,'" not simply the truth itself, *id.* at 188 (quoting *Mackay Radio & Telegraph Co. v. Radio Corp.*, 306 U.S. 86, 94 (1939), and the true essence of the Court's holding is that "Arrhenius' equation is not patentable in isolation, but when a process for curing rubber is devised which incorporates in it a more efficient solution of the equation, that process is at the very least not barred at the threshold by § 101." *Id.*

After discussing at length its primary reasons for its holding that the claimed process was eligible subject matter, and specifically after reinforcing the already existing limitations to patentability (laws of nature and mathematical equations, field-of-use limitations, and post-solution activity), the *Diehr* Court stated:

> To hold otherwise would allow a competent draftsman to evade the recognized limitations on the type of subject matter eligible for patent protection. On the other hand, when a claim containing a mathematical formula implements or applies that formula in a structure or process which, when considered as a whole, is performing a function which the patent laws were designed to protect (e.g., transforming or reducing an article to a different state or thing), then the claim satisfies the requirements of § 101. *Id.* at 192.

Bilski relied on this statement by the *Diehr* Court as supporting the "transformation" component of the "machine-or-transformation" test, claiming that by including the concept of a transformation parenthetically, the Court intended that only "machine-or-transformation" processes should be patentable. However, the Court's statement falls short of supporting that point. The parenthetical notation introduced by "e.g." was simply an example of *one* kind of patentable process, one which includes a transformation. Further, the Court's holding rests on its determination that the claimed process in the case was not merely to a mathematical equation, and this statement at the end of the Court's opinion is nothing more than a summary of the law and dicta at best. The *Diehr* process was patentable because it involved more than a mere mathematical equation, not because it satisfied a "machine-or-transformation" test.[38] Had *Diehr* intended to establish a

---

38 This is supported by the statement in *Diehr* immediately following that on which *Bilski* relied. "Because we do not view respondents' claims as an attempt to patent a mathematical formula, but rather to be drawn to an industrial process for the molding of rubber products, we affirm the judgment of the Court of Customs and Patent Appeals." *Diehr*, 450 U.S. at 192–93.

"machine-or-transformation" test limiting the scope of patent eligible subject matter beyond that enunciated by the legislature, there would have been no need for the *Bilski* court to draw inferences from what the Court meant or read inbetween the lines of *Diehr*.

The response to the "machine or transformation" test

When one evaluates *Benson*, *Flook* and *Diehr* as a whole, it is clear that there is no sole "machine-or-transformation" test originating from those three cases. Since the CAFC's opinion in *Bilski* made the contrary assertion, the decision was unsurprisingly met with much resistance and opposition, the fear being that the *Bilski* test would wreak havoc with the future of innovation. Many posited that the test created uncertainty. The CAFC had admitted that "future developments in technology and the sciences may present difficult challenges" if this test was used as the sole path to process patentability (*Bilski*, 545 F. 3d at 956). Among the questions that the CAFC left open in *Bilski* were:

> What form or amount of "transformation" suffices? When is a "representative" of a physical object sufficiently linked to that object to satisfy the transformation test?… What link to a machine is sufficient to invoke the "or machine" prong? Are the "specific" machines of *Benson* required, or can a general purpose computer qualify? What constitutes "extra-solution activity?" If a process may meet eligibility muster as a "machine," why does the Act "require" a machine link for a "process" to show eligibility?" *Id.* at 1015 (Rader, J., dissenting).

The CAFC left it to future cases to clarify and refine the meaning of the test and to answer the questions left unanswered (*Id.* at 962). Just as the patent process did not come to a halt, the Board continued to issue decisions on matters impacting process patents and interpreting the meaning of the "machine-or-transformation" test.[39] The CAFC test, which imposed a new and restrictive view of § 101 patentability, changed "the settled expectations of those who relied on the law as it existed," and created uncertainty in patent prosecution (*Bilski*, 545 F. 3d at 977 (Newman, J., dissenting)). Further, while the CAFC focused primarily on the transformation prong of the test, as there was admittedly no machine in Bilski's application, many so-called business method patents likely will not satisfy the transformation prong. These inventions would need to look to the machine prong of the test. On this matter, other than indicating that involvement of machine must not merely be insignificant extra-solution activity and that "use of a specific machine must impose meaningful limits on the claim's scope," there was little

---

39 As of October 3, 2009, one full year after the CAFC's decision in *Bilski*, there were 88 BPAI decisions referencing the case.

guidance provided by the court (*Id.* at 961–62 (American Law Institute-American Bar Association 2 December 2008)). Thus, the future of process patent prosecution was unclear.

Second, in using a strict "machine-or-transformation" test, "the CAFC essentially confined all process patents to manufacturing methods, using a test that may have been appropriate during the Industrial Age but no longer fit our modern information-based economy" (Petition for Writ of Certiorari 2009: 4). Some individuals and companies responded to the test by claiming that it would impede innovation, and that "[r]equiring processes to be tied to a machine or [transformation] limits the patent incentives available to breakthroughs at the forefront of technology in fields known (e.g., internet commerce, information technology, industrial engineering, bioinformatics) and unknown" (Petition for Writ of Certiorari 2009: 25–27). Also, arguments were made that this new "test call[ed] into question countless process patents issued before the PTO and Federal Circuit began applying this more restrictive" set of criteria and further, the U.S. Supreme "Court has more than once admonished that 'courts must be cautious before adopting changes that disrupt the settled expectations of the inventing community.'" (Petition for Writ of Certiorari 2009: 29 quoting *Festo Corp. v. Shoketsu Kinzoku Kogyo Kabushiki Co., Ltd.*, 535 U.S. 722, 739 (2002)).

Finally, the CAFC's decision jeopardized business methods patents that had previously relied on *State Street* and *AT&T*, on the basis that such methods of doing business were patentable so long as there was a "useful, concrete, and tangible result."[40] Since the CAFC overruled the *State Street Bank* test, it opened up all patents granted under that standard to uncertainty (Brief for Boston Patent Law Ass'n as Amicus Curiae Supporting Petitioners 2009: 24 n. 11). Some financial service innovations fall within the business method category, including credit card rewards programs, electronic banking, and trading systems (American Law Institute-American Bar Association 2 December 2008). Beyond process patents in the business arena, the CAFC's new test impacted both software and biotechnology processes. "Software patents that were examined and issued under a different standard for eligibility under § 101 [were] left vulnerable to attack" (Petition for Writ of Certiorari 2009: 30; Petitioner's Reply Brief 2009: 8 citing Sachs and Hulse 2009: *3),[41] and one of the software industry's primary concerns is ensuring adequate intellectual property protection (Petition for Writ of Certiorari 2009: 31).

40 See *CyberSource Corp. v. Retail Decisions, Inc.*, 2009 WL 815448, at *9 (N.D. Cal. Mar. 27, 2009) ("*Bilski's* holding suggests a perilous future for most business method patents."); (American Law Institute-American Bar Association 2 December 2008).

41 It was predicted that the first casualties of *In re Bilski* would likely involve "software patents, particularly those issued after *Alappat* and *State Street*, [that] were written without paying homage to the court's talismanic 'machine-or-transformation' test" (Sachs and Hulse 2009: *3). It was also predicted that *Bilski* would have "profound implications" for Google's patents and its search engine and other services (Travis 2009: 221–22).

In addition, the CAFC's decision in *Bilski* created the potential for invalidation of many business method patents.[42]

In terms of patent prosecution, confused patent practitioners were encouraged to use multiple claim formats to structure patent applications and not to rely on "process" claims as their primary avenue to intellectual property protection (American Law Institute-American Bar Association 2 December 2008). In continuing education programs and patent boot camps, practitioners were advised that broad process claims will fail under *Bilski* as preempting the principle, very narrow claims will likewise fail as attempts to create field-of-use limitations, and that the only way to satisfy the CAFC's test was to become an expert claim draftsman and somehow include the application of computer technology (American Law Institute-American Bar Association 2 December 2008).

Further, while *Beauregard* claims (claims covering a computer-readable storage device which contains instructions causing a computer to perform a process, under *In re Beauregard*, 53 F. 3d 1583 (Fed. Cir. 1995)) were previously characterized as articles of manufacture, just prior to *Bilski*, the BPAI had taken the position that *Beauregard* claims should not be treated differently than process claims, and that the alleged "machine-or-transformation" test applied equally. *Ex parte Langemyr*, 2008 WL 5206740 (B.P.A.I. May 28, 2008). Thus, there was also a concern in the patent arena that the CAFC's decision in *Bilski* would be applied outside business method claims (Brief for Boston Patent Law Ass'n as Amicus Curiae Supporting Petitioners 2009, 24 n. 11)[43] and potentially beyond all presently known process innovations. While all of these concerns brewed in the IP arena, the CAFC's decision was ultimately appealed to the Supreme Court, with the hope and expectation that the Court would resolve these issues.

The U.S. Supreme Court's unhelpful clarification

Oral Argument was held on November 9, 2009, and the Supreme Court's decision came out on the last day of the term in June 2010 (*Bilski v. Kappos*, 130 S. Ct 3218 (2010)). In a 9-0 decision with two separate concurrences, the Court affirmed the CAFC's judgment that the Bilski application was unpatentable subject matter as it constituted an abstract idea, violating the well-established rule against patenting of abstract ideas, laws of nature and natural phenomena (*Id.* at 3222, 3229–31). The Court further rejected the

---

42 See e.g., *DealerTrack, Inc. v. Huber*, 657 F. Supp. 2d 1152 (C.D. Cal. 2009), aff'd, 674 F. 3d 1315 (Fed. Cir. 2012) (granting motion for summary judgment of invalidity of patent to an automated credit application system).

43 About 46% of utility patents granted over the past seventeen years were process patents (Brief of Koninklijke Philips Electronics N.V. as Amicus Curiae Supporting Petitioners 2009: 11 n.6).

CAFC's conclusion that the "machine or transformation test" was the *only* path to process patentability (*id.* at 3221, 3225–227), while noting that because the application was unpatentable under an existing rule, there was no need to "define further what constitutes a patentable 'process,' beyond pointing to the definition of that term provided in § 100(b) and looking to the guideposts in *Benson, Flook,* and *Diehr*" (which cases had held that a "machine or transformation" was *a* clue, but not the *only* clue to process patentability– *Id.* at 3221–222, 3231). In addition, the Court held that the Patent Act does not categorically exclude business methods, and thus there is no need for a "business method exception" (*id.* at 3222, 3228–229),[44] although it expressly indicated that its decision was in no way an "endors[ement of] the Federal Circuit's past interpretations of § 101," including that in *State Street*'s test for business methods (*Id.* at 3222, 3228–229). Ultimately, the Court volleyed the ball back to the Federal Circuit, should it wish to "develop ... other limiting criteria that further the Patent Act's purposes," so long as those criteria "are not inconsistent with [the Patent Act's] text" (*Id.* at 3222–223, 3231).

At least one other country's jurisprudence has relied on the Court's decision in *Bilski* as supporting the patentability of business methods. In October 2010, the Federal Court of Canada held that business methods were in fact patentable so long as they satisfied the statutory requirements for patentability in section 2 of the Patent Act of Canada, R.S.C., 1985, c. P-4, and the Canadian three part test for patentable arts.[45] In referring to *Bilski*, the Canadian court stated that not all business methods would be patentable, but instead "they are subject to the same requirements as other inventions under the Act" (*Amazon.com, Inc. and The Attorney General of Canada and The Commissioner of Patents*, 2010 FC 1011, at * 65, 14 October 2010).

The approach in the USA, Australia,[46] and as it ought to be in Canada, makes an eminent amount of sense given the nature of our legislation.

---

44 The Court explained that "process" in § 100(b) of the statute should not be read as to exclude business methods, and that § 273 of the Patent Act "specifically contemplates" the existence of business methods as "simply one kind of 'method' that is, at least in some circumstances, eligible for patenting under § 101." *Bilski*, 130 S. Ct at 3228–229.

45 The "three important elements in the test for art [are] ... i) it must not be a disembodied idea but have a method of practical application; ii) it must be a new and inventive method of applying skill and knowledge; and iii) it must have a commercially useful result." *Amazon.com, Inc. and The Attorney General of Canada and The Commissioner of Patents*, 2010 FC 1011, at * 52, 14 October 2010 (citing *Progressive Games, Inc. v. Canada (Commissioner of Patents)*, 177 F.T.R. 241 (T.D.) at * 16, aff'd, (2000) 9 C.P.R. (4th) 479 (F.C.A.)).

46 See *Grant v. Commissioner of Patents* [2006] FCAFC 120, at * 47 (Australia) (The claimed "asset protection scheme is not unpatentable because it is a 'business method'. Whether the method is properly the subject of letters patent is assessed by applying the principles that have been developed for determining whether a method is a manner of manufacture, irrespective of the area of activity in which the method is to be applied.").

It allows business methods to be assessed pursuant to the general categories in s. 2 of the Patent Act, preserving the rarity of exceptions. It also
avoids the difficulties encountered in the UK and Europe in attempting
to define a "business method". There is no need to resort to such attempts
at categorization here (*Id.* at * 68).

Despite its usefulness in reaffirming the patentability of business methods,
the Court's *Bilski* decision has been criticized as failing to provide sufficient
clarity by which the Federal Circuit could devise an alternative operable
means of testing process patents (Patently-O Blog 28 June 2010).[47] Other
critics have suggested that the Court's lack of guidance will result in section
101 determinations being pushed to the background, versus being the
threshold inquiry (*Id.*)

Clarity or confusion in the wake of *Bilski?*

*Post-*Bilski *in the USPTO*

As of August 7, 2012, there were 43,475 issued patents after the Court's
decision in *Bilski* in the same five classification Classes as discussed above,
including two reissues, and 12,293 issued patents in the business method
Class (U.S. Patent & Trademark Office 2012g). As of the same date, there
were 24,778 pending published[48] patent applications in the five relevant
Classes, of which 10,068 are in the business method Class (U.S. Patent &
Trademark Office 2012h).

On July 28, 2010, the USPTO issued an Interim Guidance to supplement
the previously issued Interim Examination Instructions and the memorandum on to the Patent Examining Corps on the *Bilski* Supreme Court decision (U.S. Patent & Trademark Office 7 March 2011). In the July 2010
Guidance, the Office provided its personnel with "factors to consider in
determining whether a claim is directed to an abstract idea and is therefore
not patent-eligible under 35 U.S.C. § 101" (U.S. Patent & Trademark Office
27 July 2010: 1–3). The Office advised that "factors that weigh in favor of
patent-eligibility satisfy the criteria of the machine-or-transformation test or
provide evidence that the abstract idea has been practically applied, and
factors that weigh against patent-eligibility neither satisfy the criteria of the

---

47 "[T]he opinion offers no clarity or aid for those tasked with determining whether a particu-
    lar innovation falls within Section 101. The opinion provides no new lines to be avoided.
    Rather, the outcome from the decision might be best stated as 'business as usual.' ... By
    refusing to state any particular rule or categorical exclusion, the Court has almost certainly
    pushed Section 101 patent eligibility to the background in most patent prosecution and
    litigation" (Patently-O Blog 28 June 2010).
48 Most patent applications are published eighteen months after the earliest filing date from
    which the application benefits. See 35 U.S.C. § 122; M.P.E.P. § 1120.

machine-or-transformation test nor provide evidence that the abstract idea has been practically applied" (U.S. Patent & Trademark Office 27 July 2010: 1). Further, despite the Court's caution regarding use of the "machine or transformation" test, the Office advised its personnel to continue to use the test, stating that it "remains an investigative tool and is a useful starting point for determining whether a claimed invention is a patent-eligible process" (U.S. Patent & Trademark Office 27 July 2010: 1). USPTO examiners were instructed to start with the "machine or transformation" test, and to apply the identified list of factors in cases where the invention failed the test to determine whether they were patentable nonetheless (U.S. Patent & Trademark Office 27 July 2010: 1).

It is questionable whether this is what the Court meant when it said that the test was "a" clue to patentability—the Court did not indicate that its intention was for the test to be used as the starting point, and that other clues would only be assessed defensively (in response to a failure to meet the test). The Court's lack of concreteness in its discussion regarding how to evaluate processes for subject matter eligibility left open the opportunity for the USPTO and Federal Circuit to continue to use the "machine or transformation" test as their primary indicator in process patent cases, while simply operating under the guise of having considered other tests as well. It appears that the USPTO and CAFC have done exactly that.

Post-Bilski *in the courts*

In *Research Corp. Technologies, Inc. v. Microsoft Corp.*, 627 F. 3d 859 (Fed. Cir. 2010), left struggling without much guidance after *Bilski*, the CAFC found itself caught between the threshold nature of section 101 and the Supreme Court's reminder in *Bilski* that "section 101 eligibility should not become a substitute for a patentability analysis related to prior art, adequate disclosure, or the other conditions and requirements of Title 35" (*Id.* at 868 (citing *Bilski*, 130 S. Ct at 3238; Stevens, J., concurring)). The CAFC thus attempted to identify situations in which it was required to start with the difficult section 101 analysis, as opposed to focusing on other statutory requirements.

In side-stepping the "machine or transformation" test, the court started its evaluation of the six process patents at bar by addressing the three judicial exceptions to patentability: laws of nature, natural phenomena and abstract ideas. Regarding the interplay between abstractness and section 101, the court stated that it "will not presume to define 'abstract' beyond the recognition that this disqualifying characteristic should exhibit itself so manifestly as to override the broad statutory categories of eligible subject matter and the statutory context that directs primary attention on the patentability criteria of the rest of the Patent Act" (*Id.*) Thus, the court would only look first to section 101 where the patent appeared to be "manifestly abstract." However, recognizing that there would be inventions that were "not so manifestly abstract as to override the statutory language of section 101," but that "nonetheless lack sufficient concrete disclosure to warrant a patent," the court indicated that the requirements of section 112 would "provide[] [the] power-ful tools to weed out claims that may present a vague or indefinite disclosure of the invention. Thus, a patent that presents a process sufficient to pass the coarse eligibility filter may nonetheless be invalid as indefinite because the invention would 'not provide sufficient particularity and clarity to inform skilled artisans of the bounds of the claim'" (*Id.* at 869 (quoting *Star Scientific., Inc. v. R.J. Reynolds Tobacco Co.*, 537 F. 3d 1357, 1371; Fed. Cir. 2008)). Thus, just as predicted, the CAFC tried to ease the burden of grappling with section 101 by "pushing [it] to the background" (Patently-O Blog 28 June 2010), and by only directly addressing section 101 in cases where the invention appears "manifestly abstract."

The following year, in *Cybersource Corporation v. Retail Decisions, Inc.*, 654 F. 3d 1366 (Fed. Cir. 2011), a case involving the financial and e-commerce sectors, the CAFC was called to apply its post-*Bilski* rules about business method patents and reasoning in *Research Corp.* regarding where to start the patentability inquiry. The two claims at issue in the patent covered a method and system for detecting fraud in credit card transaction using "Internet address" information, which was of particular significance in purely online transactions (e.g., product purchased is downloadable content) between a consumer and merchant (*Id.* at 1367–368). However, instead of following its own earlier advice and only addressing section 101 in cases where the inven-tion appeared "manifestly abstract," the court attempted to tackle section 101 head on. In fact, it started its analysis of the two claims using the "machine or transformation" test, and thereafter discussed the judicial excep-tions for laws of nature, natural phenomena and abstract ideas.

In stating that claim 3, "which recites a method for verifying the validity of a credit card transaction over the Internet," failed the "machine or trans-formation" test, the CAFC reasoned that it "simply requires one to 'obtain and compare intangible data pertinent to business risks,'" and "[t]he mere collection and organization of data regarding credit card numbers and Internet addresses is insufficient to meet the transformation prong of the test, [while] the plain language of claim 3 does not require the method to be performed by a particular machine, or even a machine at all" (*Id.* at 1370). The court then turned its attention to whether the patent failed on other grounds. In discussing whether the claim was drawn to an "unpatentable mental process—a subcategory of unpatentable abstract ideas," the court stated that "'application of [only] human intelligence to the solution of prac-tical problems is no more than a claim to a fundamental principle'" and "methods which can be performed mentally, or which are the equivalent of human mental work are unpatentable abstract ideas" (*Id.* at 1371 (quoting *Bilski*, 545 F. 3d at 965, and citing *Benson*, 409 U.S. at 67)). The court concluded that claim 3 was an unpatentable mental step, since it "extend[ed] to essentially any method of detecting credit card fraud based on information relating past transactions to a particular 'Internet address,' even methods that [could] be performed in the human mind," and "[did] not limit its scope to any particular fraud detection algorithm and no algorithms are disclosed in the '154 patent's specification" (*Id.* at 1372).

Addressing claim 2, which was a *Beauregard* claim drawn to a "computer readable medium containing program instructions" causing the computer to perform the described method in claim 3. In rejecting Cybersource's argument that "coupling the unpatentable mental process recited in claim 3 with a manufacture or machine renders it patent-eligible" (*id.* at 1374), and that claim 2 recites a "manufacture" not a "process," the court indicated that regardless of the statutory category, it looks to the underlying invention to assess patent eligibility. Here, it was clear that the underlying invention for both claims was "a method for detecting credit card fraud, not a manufacture for storing computer-readable information" (*Id.*) Determining that claim 2 was a process, the court turned once again to the "machine or transformation" test. Cybersource's argument that the claim involved a transformation because the method involved using "Internet address" information to build a "'map' of credit card numbers" that had used that Internet address failed because "mere manipulation or reorganization of data ... does not satisfy the transformation prong" (*Id.* at 1375). Likewise, the court found that claim 2's use of a computer failed the machine prong. The machine prong requires that the "use of the machine ... 'impose[s] meaningful limits on the claim's scope'" (*Id.*, quoting *Bilski*, 545 F. 3d at 961), i.e., "the machine 'must play a significant part in permitting the claimed method to be performed'" (*Id.*, quoting *SiRF Tech., Inc. v. Int'l Trade Comm'n*, 601 F. 3d 1319, 1333 (Fed. Cir. 2010)). Thus, "merely claiming a software implementation of a purely mental process that could otherwise be performed without the use of a computer does not satisfy the machine prong of the machine-or-transformation test" (*Id.*) Thus, Cybersource's claim 2 was doomed once the court invalidated claim 3: "[i]f the software method is not patentable, then neither is the 'computer readable medium'" that uses it (Patently-O Blog 16 August 2011). Some critics have argued that *Beauregard* claims directed to a tangible medium should be presumed statutory eligible subject matter under section 101 after *State Street Bank* and after *Research Corp.* and only challenged on section 101 grounds where "manifestly abstract;" thus, *Cybersource* involved an improper application of section 101 to invalidate the patent (Wegner 18 August 2011).

The CAFC redeemed itself, in part, in 2012 when it affirmed the district court's invalidation of four patents on section 102 and 103 grounds, as opposed to section 101. In *MySpace, Inc. v. GraphOn Corp.*, the court claimed that since the district court held the patents invalid under sections 102 and 103, and that decision was the one on appeal, the court was constrained to address only the issues before it. Nonetheless, in light of a "vigorous" dissenting opinion advocating for the invalidity of the patents on section 101 grounds, the majority opinion humbly explained why it thought it prudent to avoid the "swamp of verbiage that is § 101," *MySpace*, 672 F. 3d at 1260, and referred to the "[o]ther voices [that] urge judicial restraint in the face of what has become a plethora of opinions adding to our § 101 jurisprudence" (*Id.* at 1258).

Recognizing that there is "support for [starting the inquiry with section 101], as the dissent notes, in the literature and in the language found in some cases," the court stated:

> The problem with addressing § 101 initially every time it is presented as a defense is that the answer in each case requires the search for a universal truth: in the broad sweep of modern innovative technologies, does this invention fall outside the breadth of human endeavor that possibly can be patented under § 101? (*Id.*)

Since the Supreme Court has held that Congress intended for the Patent Act to be given "wide scope," while the Court itself created three judicial exceptions, the majority opinion indicated that its task under section 101 was to assess whether any of the exceptions were met. While "dealing with 'laws of nature' and 'physical phenomena' [are] reasonably manageable" given cases "provid[ing] workable guidance," the CAFC admitted that "[i]n an attempt to explain what an abstract idea is (or is not) we tried the 'machine or transformation' formula—the Supreme Court was not impressed" (*Id.* at 1259). The court reasoned that instead of struggling with a section 101 inquiry, when given a "clear path [to] decid[e] the question of patent validity," it ought to take the road less cluttered. All issued patents carry a presumption of validity and "any ground specified in part II of [title 35] as a condition of patentability" (sections 102 and 103) or the "failure to comply with any requirement of sections 112 or 251" may be raised as a defense in an action involving the validity of a patent (*Id.* at 1259–60). As such, since the criteria for evaluating a patent's validity under sections 102, 103, and 112 are "well developed and generally well understood," courts should "exercis[e] their inherent power to control the processes of litigation ... and insist that litigants initially address patent invalidity issues in terms of the conditions of patentability defenses as the statute provides, specifically §§ 102, 103, and 112" (*Id.* at 1260). To do so, would "make patent litigation more efficient, conserve judicial resources, and bring a degree of certainty to the interests of both patentees and their competitors in the marketplace." (*Id.*)

The district courts have also been dealing with how to evaluate patentability in business methods cases after *Bilski*.[49] It is likely that the CAFC will have

---

49   Two of these cases involved computers or computer systems. Compare *Graff/Ross Holdings LLP v. Fed. Home Loan Mortgage Corp.*, 2010 WL 6274263 (D.D.C. Aug. 27, 2010) ("a process for generating a 'purchase price' for at least one component of property using a computer") and *CLS Bank Int'l v. Alice Corp. Pty. Ltd.*, 768 F. Supp. 2d 221 (D.D.C. 2011) ("methods [and] systems that help [to] lessen [the] settlement risk of trades of financial instruments using a computer system") with *Island Intellectual Property LLC v. Deutsche Bank AG*, 2012 WL 386282 (S.D.N.Y. Feb. 6, 2012) ("methods enabling financial institutions, such as banks or broker dealers, to 'sweep' their clients' (e.g., individual depositors') funds into external accounts at multiple deposit taking banks that earn interest and provide FDIC Insurance").

even more opportunities to exercise the judicial restraint and prudence it suggested in *MySpace* regarding where section 101 falls in the patentability analysis, and to continue to develop meaningful guideposts for evaluating the validity or patentability of business methods.

Conclusion: Looking forward

In response to the question of who owns cyberspace, the answer lies in part in who owns the patents and intellectual property. As the courts continue to determine what is and is not patentable after *Bilski*, Internet industry leaders such as Google, eBay, Facebook and Yahoo will likely continue to apply for as much patent protection as they can.[50] By strategically maximizing their intellectual property and patent portfolios,[51] companies engaged in e-commerce, finance and business via the Internet may be more able to defensively protect themselves against threats of infringement, create potential avenues for licensing and cross-licensing,[52] and wield their IP against competitors who threaten their markets.[53]

Bibliography

Act of March 2, 1861, 12 Stat. 246, 249, § 16.

In re Alappat, 33 F. 3d 1526 (Fed. Cir. 1994) (en banc).

Amazon.com, Inc. and The Attorney General of Canada and The Commissioner of Patents, 2010 FC 1011, 14 October 2010.

American Law Institute-American Bar Association (2 December 2008) "Transformers Wanted: *In Re Bilski* Cuts Back on Business Methods." Telephone Seminar/Audio Webcast. Available http: <www.ali-aba.org/TSPV12> (accessed 17 August 2012).

Aronson v. Quick Point Pencil Co., 440 U.S. 257 (1979).

Arrhythmia Research Technology Inc. v. Corazonix Corp., 958 F. 2d 1053 (Fed. Cir. 1992).

Association for Molecular Pathology et al., Petition for Writ of Certiorari (2011) *Association for Molecular Pathology v. Myriad Genetics, Inc.*, No. 11-725. Online. Available Westlaw: 2011 WL 6257250.

AT&T Corp. v. Excel Communications, Inc., 172 F. 3d 1352 (Fed. Cir. 1999).

In re Beauregard, 53 F. 3d 1583 (Fed. Cir. 1995).

50 According to their website, eBay's patent portfolio includes at least 171 U.S. Patents, and their corresponding foreign counterparts (eBay n.d.).

51 E.g., Friendster's patent portfolio consisted of seven patents and eleven patent applications (Gannes 4 August 2010). See also (Festa 11 November 2003).

52 "Everyone wants to protect themselves in whatever way they can, so when it comes time to start arguing, they have something" (Festa 11 November 2003). See also (Intellectual Property Owners Association 15 November 2012: 13–15).

53 "Most of the patenting is being done by large corporations which can afford to build up their patent portfolios. Most often these patents are used against small companies to force them to pay royalties or to put potential competitors out of business" (Casamento 20 February 2002). See also (Panzarino 13 March 2012).

In re Bernhart, 417 F. 2d 1395 (C.C.P.A. 1969).

Ex parte Bilski, 2006 WL 5738364 (B.P.A.I. Sept. 26, 2006).

In re Bilski, 545 F. 3d 943 (Fed. Cir. 2008).

Bilski v. Doll, 129 S. Ct 2735 (2009).

Bilski v. Kappos, 130 S. Ct 3218 (2010).

Brief for Amicus Curiae American Civil Liberties Union for Affirmance in Support of Appellee (2008) *In re Bilski*, No. 2007-1130. Online. Available at: http://web2. westlaw.com (search "2008 WL 1842266"). Online. Available at: <http://www.aclu. org/files/pdfs/freespeech/in_re_bilski_aclu_amicus.pdf> (accessed 16 August 2012).

Brief for Boston Patent Law Ass'n as Amicus Curiae Supporting Petitioners (2009) *Bilski v. Doll*, No. 08-964. Online. Available Westlaw: 2009 WL 559339.

Brief of Koninklijke Philips Electronics N.V. as Amicus Curiae Supporting Petitioners (2009) *Bilski v. Doll*, No. 08-964. Online. Available at: http://web2. westlaw.com (search for "2009 WL 559338").

Brief of the Software Freedom Law Center as Amicus Curiae in Support of Respondent (2009) *Bilski v. Kappos*, No. 08-964. Online. Available at: <http://web2.westlaw. com> (at "2009 WL 3167953").

Casamento, G.J. (20 February 2002) FTC Hearings on Competition and Intellectual Property: Email to FTC. Online. Available at: <http://www.ftc.gov/os/comments/ intelpropertycomments/johncasamentogregory.htm> (accessed 11 August 2012).

CLS Bank Int'l v. Alice Corp. Pty. Ltd., 768 F. Supp. 2d 221 (D.D.C. 2011).

Cochrane v. Deener, 94 U.S. 780 (1877).

In re Comiskey, 499 F. 3d 1365 (Fed. Cir. 2007).

In re Comiskey, 554 F. 3d 967 (Fed. Cir. 2009).

Cybersource Corporation v. Retail Decisions, Inc., 654 F. 3d 1366 (Fed. Cir. 2011).

DealerTrack, Inc. v. Huber, 657 F. Supp. 2d 1152 (C.D. Cal. 2009), aff'd, 674 F. 3d 1315 (Fed. Cir. 2012).

Dennis, J.K.P. (2008) 'Divergence in Patent Systems: A Discussion of Biotechnology Transgenic Animal Patentability and US Patent System Reform,' *International Journal of Private Law*, 1(3/4): 268–303.

Diamond v. Chakrabarty, 447 U.S. 303 (1980).

Diamond v. Diehr, 450 U.S. 175, 182 (1981).

eBay (n.d.) Using eBay's Intellectual Property. Online. Available <http://pages.ebay. com/help/policies/everyone-ebayipuse.html> (accessed 12 August 2012).

Eibel Process Co. v. Minnesota & Ontario Paper Co., 261 U.S. 45 (1923).

Eldred v. Ashcroft, 537 U.S. 186 (2003).

European Patent Office (12 July 2001) EPO revokes Amazon's "Gift Ordering" Patent After Opposition Hearing. Online. Available at: <http://web.archive.org/ web/20090604043421/http://www.epo.org/topics/news/2007/20071207.html> (accessed 11 August 2012).

Expanded Metal Co. v. Bradford, 214 U.S. 366 (1909).

Festa, P. (11 November 2003) 'Investors Snub Friendster in Patent Grab,' *CNet News*. Online. Available <http://news.cnet.com/2100-1032_3-5106136.html> (accessed 12 August 2012).

Festo Corp. v. Shoketsu Kinzoku Kogyo Kabushiki Co., Ltd., 535 U.S. 722 (2002).

Funk Bros. Seed Co. v. Kalo Co., 333 U.S. 127 (1948).

Galbraith, J.K. and Hale, T. (2004) *Income Distribution and the Information Technology Bubble*, University of Texas Inequality Project Working Paper. Online. Available <http://utip.gov.utexas.edu/papers/utip_27.pdf> (accessed 8 August 2012).

Gannes, L. (4 August 2010) 'Facebook Buys Friendster Patents for $40M,' *Gigaom*. Online. Available <http://gigaom.com/2010/08/04/facebook-buys-friendster-patents-for-40m/> (accessed 12 August 2012).

Geist, M. (27 January 2000) 'A Patently Obvious Threat to E-Commerce,' *Globe and Mail: Technology*. Online. Archived <http://www.michaelgeist.ca/resc/html_bkup/jan272000.html> (accessed 13 August 2012).

Gothschalk v. Benson, 409 U.S. 43 (1972).

Govtrack.us (3 October 2000) Bill Summary and Status for H.R.5364, 106th Congr., 2nd session. Online. Available at: <http://www.govtrack.us/congress/bills/107/hr5364> (accessed 14 August 2012).

Govtrack.us (3 April 2001) Bill Summary and Status for H.R. 1332, 107th Congr., 1st session. Online. Available at: <http://www.govtrack.us/congress/bills/107/hr1332> (accessed 14 August 2012).

Graff/Ross Holdings LLP v. Fed. Home Loan Mortgage Corp., No. 07–796, 2010 WL 6274263 (D.D.C. Aug. 27, 2010).

Grant v. Commissioner of Patents [2006] FCAFC 120 (Australia).

Grant v. Raymond, 31 U.S. 218, 219 (1832).

The House Report on the Patent Act of 1952, H.R. Rep. No. 82-1923.

Hunt, R.M. (2001) 'You Can Patent That? Are Patents on Computer Programs and Business Methods Good for the New Economy?,' *Business Review*, Q1, 5–15.

Intellectual Property Owners Association (15 November 2002) Comments on the Joint Hearings of the Federal Trade Commission and the Department of Justice Regarding Competition and Intellectual Property Law and Policy in the Knowledge-Based Economy. Online. Available at: <http://www.ftc.gov/os/comments/intelpropertycomments/ipo.pdf> (accessed 11 Aug. 2012).

Island Intellectual Property LLC v. Deutsche Bank AG, 2012 WL 386282 (S.D.N.Y. Feb. 6, 2012).

Jaffe, A.B. and Lerner, J. (2007) *Innovation and Its Discontents: How our Broken Patent System is Endangering Innovation and Progress, and What to Do About It*, 3rd edn, Princeton: Princeton University Press.

Kuester, J.R. and Thompson, L.E. (2001) 'Risks Associated With Restricting Business Method and E-Commerce Patents,' *Georgia State Law Review*, 17, 657–90.

Kursh, H. (1959) *Inside the U.S. Patent Office: The Story of the Men, the Laws, and the Procedures of the American Patent System*, New York: Norton.

Ex parte Langemyr, 2008 WL 5206740 (B.P.A.I. May 28, 2008).

League for Programming Freedom (28 February 1991) Against Software Patents. Online. Available <http://www.ftc.gov/os/comments/intelpropertycomments/lpf.pdf> (accessed 11 August 2012).

Leahy-Smith America Invents Act (AIA) (16 Sept. 2011), P.L. 112-29 [H.R. 1249], 125 Stat. 284, 112th Congr. 1st session, §§ 3, 6, 7, 18(d)(1).

Le Roy v. Tatham, 55 U.S. (14 How.) 156 (1852).

Ex parte Lundgren, 76 U.S.P.Q.2d 1385, 2004 WL 3561262 (B.P.A.I. Apr. 20, 2004).

Mackay Radio & Telegraph Co. v. Radio Corp., of Am., 306 U.S. 86 (1939).

Manual of Patent Examining Procedure §§ 1120, 2701 (8th edn 2001).

Mercoid Corp. v. Mid-Continent Inv. Co., 320 U.S. 661 (1944).

In re Musgrave, 431 F. 2d 882 (C.C.P.A. 1970).

MySpace v. GraphOn, 672 F. 3d 1250 (Fed. Cir. 2012).

Neilson v. Harford, Web. Pat. Cases 295 (1844).

Omnibus Budget Reconciliation Act of 1990, Pub. L. 101-508, 104 Stat. 138.

O'Reilly v. Morse, 15 How. 62 (1854).

Panzarino, M. (13 March 2012) Friendster founder: Yahoo copied Friendster, whose patents are now owned by Facebook, *The Next Web: Insider*. Online. Available <http://thenextweb.com/insider/2012/03/13/friendster-founder-yahoo-is-on-shaky-ground-because-facebook-has-our-old-social-media-patents/> (accessed 12 August 2012).

Parker v. Flook, 437 U.S. 584 (1978).

Patent Act of Canada, R.S.C., 1985, c. P-4.

Patently-O Blog (28 June 2010) *Bilski v. Kappos*. Online. Available <http://www.patentlyo.com/patent/2010/06/bilski-v-kappos-business-methods-out-software-still-patentable.html> (accessed 14 August 2012).

Patently-O Blog (16 August 2011) If the software method is not patentable, then neither is the "computer readable medium." Online. Available <http://www.patentlyo.com/patent/2011/08/if-the-software-method-is-not-patentable-then-neither-is-the-computer-readable-medium.html> (accessed 14 August 2012).

Petitioner's Reply Brief (2009) *Bilski v. Doll*, No. 08-964. Online. Available Westlaw: 2009 WL 1317892.

Petition for Writ of Certiorari (2009) *Bilski v. Doll*, No. 08-964. Online. Available Westlaw: 2009 WL 226501.

Progressive Games, Inc. v. Canada (Commissioner of Patents), 177 F.T.R. 241 (T.D.), aff'd, (2000) 9 C.P.R. (4th) 479 (F.C.A.).

Research Corp. Technologies, Inc. v. Microsoft Corp., 627 F. 3d 859 (Fed. Cir. 2010).

Riches, Jr, R.M. (n.d.) Comments Regarding Competition and Intellectual Property. Online. Available <http://www.ftc.gov/os/comments/intelpropertycomments/ipriches.pdf> (accessed 12 August 2012).

Sachs, R.R. and Hulse, R.A. (2009) 'On Shaky Ground: The (Near) Future of Patents After *Bilski*,' *E-Commerce Law Report*, 11(2), 8, *3.

The Senate Report on the Patent Act of 1952, S. Rep. No. 82-1979.

Shapiro, C. (2001), 'Navigating the Patent Thicket: Cross Licenses, Patent Pools, and Standard-Setting,' *Innovation Policy and The Economy*, 1, 119–20.

SiRF Tech., Inc. v. Int'l Trade Comm'n, 601 F. 3d 1319 (Fed. Cir. 2010).

Smith v. Snow, 294 U.S. 1 (1935).

Star Scientific., Inc. v. R.J. Reynolds Tobacco Co., 537 F. 3d 1357 (Fed. Cir. 2008).

State Street Bank & Trust Co. v. Signature Financial Group, Inc., 149 F. 3d 1368 (Fed. Cir. 1998).

In re Tarczy-Hornoch, 397 F. 2d 856 (C.C.P.A. 1968).

Taylor, R.P. (11 July 2002) Statement of Robert P. Taylor on Behalf of Section of Intellectual Property Law American Bar Association. Online. Available <http://www.ftc.gov/opp/intellect/020711robertptaylor.pdf> (accessed 11 August 2012).

Tilghman v. Proctor, 102 U.S. 707 (1881).

Travis, H. (2009) 'The Future According to Google: Technology Policy From the Standpoint of America's Fastest-Growing Technology Company,' *Yale Journal of Law and Technology*, 11, 209–27.

United States v. Dubilier Condenser Corp., 289 U.S. 178 (1933).

Uruguay Round Agreements Act of 1994, Pub. L. 103-465, 108 Stat. 4809, § 532.

U.S. Const. amend. I.

U.S. Const. art. I, § 8, cl. 8.

U.S. Department of Justice and the Federal Trade Commission (April 2007), Antitrust Enforcement and Intellectual Property Rights: Promoting Innovation and Competition. Online. Available <http://www.ftc.gov/reports/innovation/P040101PromotingInnovationandCompetitionrpt0704.pdf> (accessed 12 August 2012).

U.S. Federal Trade Commission (20 November 2001) Competition and Intellectual Property Law and Policy in the Knowledge-Based Economy, 66 Fed. Reg. 58146-02.

U.S. Federal Trade Commission (15 November 2001a) Notice of Public Hearings and Opportunity for Comment. Online. Available <http://www.ftc.gov/os/2001/11/ciphearingsfrn.htm> (accessed 10 August 2012)

U.S. Federal Trade Commission (15 November 2001b) Muris Announces Plans for Intellectual Property Hearings. Online. Available <http://www.ftc.gov/opa/2001/11/iprelease.shtm> (accessed 10 August 2012).

U.S. Federal Trade Commission (October 2003) To Promote Innovation: The Proper Balance of Competition and Patent Law and Policy. Online. Available <http://www.ftc.gov/os/2003/10/innovationrpt.pdf> (accessed 12 August 2012).

U.S. Federal Trade Commission (2007a) Competition and Intellectual Property Law and Policy in the Knowledge-Based Economy. Online. Available <http://www.ftc.gov/opp/intellect/> (accessed 10 August 2012).

U.S. Federal Trade Commission (2007b) Competition and Intellectual Property Law and Policy in the Knowledge-Based Economy: Notice of Public Hearings and Opportunity for Comment. Online. Available <http://www.ftc.gov/os/comments/intelpropertycomments> (accessed 10 August 2012).

U.S. Government Printing Office (3 October 2000) Statement of Rep. Rick Boucher on the Introduction of the Business Method Patent Improvement Act of 2000, 146 Cong. Rec. E1659-60. Online. Available <http://www.gpo.gov/fdsys/pkg/CREC-2000-10-03/pdf/CREC-2000-10-03-pt1-PgE1651-2.pdf> (accessed 15 August 2012).

U.S. Government Printing Office (4 October 2000) Statement of Rep. Howard Berman on the Introduction of the Business Method Patent Improvement Act of 2000, 146 Cong. Rec. E1659-60. Online. Available <http://www.gpo.gov/fdsys/pkg/CREC-2000-10-04/pdf/CREC-2000-10-04-pt1-PgE1659.pdf> (accessed 15 August 2012).

U.S. House of Representatives, Business Method Patent Improvement Act of 2000 [H.R. 5364], 106th Congr. 2nd session.

U.S. House of Representatives, Business Method Patent Improvement Act of 2001 [H.R. 1332], 107th Congr. 1st session.

U.S. Patent Act, 35 U.S.C. §§ 100(b), 101, 102, 103, 112, 122, 154(a)(2)–(3), 321 (2012).

U.S. Patent Act of 1793, 1 Stat. 318, 319 § 1.

U.S. Patent & Trademark Office, 33 Fed.Reg. 15581, 15609–10 (1968).

U.S. Patent & Trademark Office (22 November 2005) Interim Guidelines for Examination of Patent Applications for Patent Subject Matter Eligibility, Off. Gaz. Pat. & Trademark Office 1300, 142.

U.S. Patent & Trademark Office (16 February 2006) Receipt of Orig Ex Parte Request by Third Party, Image File Wrapper for '411 Patent, App. Serial No. 90/007,946, in Patent Application Information Retrieval. Online. Available <http://portal.uspto.gov/external/portal/pair> (accessed 10 August 2012).

U.S. Patent & Trademark Office (12 May 2006) Determination—Reexam Ordered, Image File Wrapper for '411 Patent, App. Serial No. 90/007,946, in Patent

Application Information Retrieval. Online. Available <http://portal.uspto.gov/external/portal/pair> (accessed 10 August 2012).

U.S. Patent & Trademark Office (9 October 2007) Reexam—Non-Final Action, Image File Wrapper for '411 Patent, App. Serial No. 90/007,946, in Patent Application Information Retrieval. Online. Available <http://portal.uspto.gov/external/portal/pair> (accessed 10 August 2012).

U.S. Patent & Trademark Office (29 November 2007) Claims, Image File Wrapper for '411 Patent, App. Serial No. 90/007,946, in Patent Application Information Retrieval. Online. Available <http://portal.uspto.gov/external/portal/pair> (accessed 10 August 2012).

U.S. Patent & Trademark Office (4 July 2009) USPTO White Paper—Automated Business Methods—Section III Class 705. Online. Available <http://www.uspto.gov/patents/resources/methods/afmdpm/class705.jsp> (accessed 12 Aug. 2012).

U.S. Patent & Trademark Office (2 March 2010) Notice of Intent to Issue a Reexam Certificate, Image File Wrapper for '411 Patent, App. Serial No. 90/007,946, in Patent Application Information Retrieval. Online. Available <http://portal.uspto.gov/external/portal/pair> (accessed 10 August 2012).

U.S. Patent & Trademark Office (13 July 2010) Reexamination Certificate Issued, Image File Wrapper for '411 Patent, App. Serial No. 90/007,946, in Patent Application Information Retrieval. Online. Available <http://portal.uspto.gov/external/portal/pair> (accessed 10 August 2012).

U.S. Patent & Trademark Office (27 July 2010) Interim Guidance for Determining Subject Matter Eligibility for Process Claims in View of *Bilski v. Kappos*. Online. Available <http://www.uspto.gov/patents/law/exam/bilski_guidance_27jul2010.pdf> (accessed 10 August 2012).

U.S. Patent & Trademark Office (7 March 2011) Interim Guidance for Determining Subject Matter Eligibility for Process Claims in View of *Bilski v. Kappos*. Online. Available <http://www.uspto.gov/patents/announce/bilski_guidance.jsp> (accessed 10 August 2012).

U.S. Patent & Trademark Office (2012a) Fee Schedule. Online. Available <http://www.uspto.gov/web/offices/ac/qs/ope/fee092611.htm> (accessed 15 Aug. 2012).

U.S. Patent & Trademark Office (2012b) Statement of Net Cost. Online. Available <http://www.uspto.gov/about/stratplan/ar/2011/mda_06_01_02.html> (accessed 15 August 2012).

U.S. Patent & Trademark Office (2012c) Patent Full-Text Databases. Online. Available <http://patft.uspto.gov/> (search PatFT:Patents for "(((((CCL/705/$ OR CCL/707/$) OR CCL/709/$) OR CCL/710/$) OR CCL/902/$) AND ISD/19980723->20120807)") (accessed 7 August 2012).

U.S. Patent & Trademark Office (2012d) Patent Full-Text Databases. Online. Available <http://patft.uspto.gov/> (search PatFT:Patents for "(CCL/705/$ AND ISD/19980723->20120807)") (accessed 7 August 2012).

U.S. Patent & Trademark Office (2012e) Patent Business Methods. Online. Available <http://www.uspto.gov/web/menu/busmethp/index.html> (accessed 12 August 2012).

U.S. Patent & Trademark Office (2012f) Class 705 Application Filing and Patents Issued Data. Online. Available <http://www.uspto.gov/patents/resources/methods/applicationfiling.jsp> (accessed 12 August 2012).

U.S. Patent & Trademark Office (2012g) Patent Full-Text Databases. Online. Available <http://patft.uspto.gov/> (search PatFT:Patents for "((((((CCL/705/$ OR

CCL/707/$) OR CCL/709/$) OR CCL/710/$) OR CCL/902/$) AND ISD/20100628->20120807)" and for "(CCL/705/$ AND ISD/20100628->20120807)") (accessed 7 August 2012).

U.S. Patent & Trademark Office (2012h) Patent Full-Text Databases. Online. Available <http://patft.uspto.gov/> (search AppFT:Applications for "(CCL/705/$ OR CCL/707/$ OR CCL/709/$ OR CCL/710/$ OR CCL/902/$) AND APD/20100628->20120807" and for "(CCL/705/$ AND APD/20100628->20120807)") (accessed 7 August 2012).

U.S. Patent App. Serial No. 08/833,892 (10 April 1997).

U.S. Patent No. 5,870,473 (issued 9 February 1999).

U.S. Patent No. 5,960,411 (issued 28 September 1999).

U.S. Patent No. 6,029,142 (issued 22 February 2000).

U.S. Patent No. 6,175,831 (issued 16 January 2001).

U.S. Patent No. 6,915,271 (issued 5 July 2005).

U.S. Patent No. 7,054,830 (issued 30 May 2006).

U.S. Patent No. 7,069,308 (issued 27 June 2006).

U.S. Patent No. 7,366,759 (issued 29 April 2008).

U.S. Patent No. 7,620,597 (issued 17 November 2009).

U.S. Patent No. 8,234,177 (issued 31 July 2012).

U.S. Patent No. 8,234,194 (issued 31 July 2012).

U.S. Patent No. 8,239,935 (issued 7 August 2012).

Waxham v. Smith, 294 U.S. 20 (1935).

Webster's New International Dictionary of the English Language 1972, 2nd edn, Springfield, MA: Merriam-Webster.

Wegner, H.C. (18 August 2011) 'Cybersource Conflict with Precedent,' *iP Frontline*. Online. Available <http://www.ipfrontline.com/depts/article.aspx?id=25676&deptid=7> (accessed 14 August 2012).

Wikipedia (2012) Dot-com bubble. Online. Available <en.wikipedia.org/wiki/Dot-com_bubble> (accessed 10 August 2012).

Part 2

Policing cyberspace

4   Red flags of "piracy" online

Amir Hassanabadi

A billion-dollar cyberlaw debate

One billion dollars.[1] That is what media giant Viacom demanded in damages in its lawsuit against YouTube and its parent company Google alleging copyright infringement over Viacom clips uploaded to YouTube.[2] For its part, Google spent more than $100 million in pre-trial legal fees to defend itself against Viacom.[3] Congress enacted the Digital Millennium Copyright Act (DMCA) over a decade ago unaware of such a future conflict.[4] Congress did not divine YouTube—a website that encourages users to "Broadcast Yourself,"[5] has as a main attraction a video of a dog riding a skateboard,[6] and enthralls more viewers than most cable channels.[7] Congress was blind to the future technology, change, and costs of our new digital age. *Viacom v. YouTube* is but a prelude, an example of a coming wave of lawsuits and hamstrung legal judgments caused by an aging DMCA and related statutory provisions that are slipping into irrelevancy. Though YouTube won the day,

---

1 This figure is close to the $1.65 billion Google paid to purchase YouTube. Viacom International, Inc. (2010) Compl. for Declaratory and Injunctive Relief and Damages, p. 8, *Viacom International, Inc., v. YouTube, Inc.*, 718 F. Supp. 2d 514 (S.D.N.Y. 2010) (No. 07-2103).

2 *Ibid.*, p. 5.

3 Erick Schonfeld (2010) *Google Spent $100 Million Defending Against Viacom's $1 Billion Lawsuit*, Tech Crunch (Nov. 30), http://techcrunch.com/2010/07/15/google-viacom-100-million-lawsuit.

4 U.S. Code, title 17, section 512, codifying Digital Millennium Copyright Act, Pub. L. No. 105-304, 112 Stat. 2860 (1998) [hereinafter DMCA].

5 YouTube, Inc. (2012) YouTube. Online. http://www.youtube.com (last visited Sept. 1, 2012).

6 This video had more than 14 million views by 2010. *Skateboarding Dog*, YouTube (Jan. 24, 2011, 1:44 AM), http://www.youtube.com/watch?v=CQzUsTFqtW0.

7 Leena Rao (2010) comScore: Facebook Passes Yahoo to Become the Second Largest Video Site in the U.S., *Tech Crunch* (Oct. 27). Online. http://techcrunch.com/2010/09/30/comscore-facebook-passes-yahoo-to-become-the-second-largest-video-site-in-the-u-s/.

the strained reasoning of the court may leave the service vulnerable on appeal. The legal analysis in *Viacom v. YouTube* demonstrates that the DMCA may be unprepared to handle the demands of today, and more importantly, the uncertainties of tomorrow.

Hyperbole was widespread on both sides of the lawsuit. Attorneys for YouTube argued that a Viacom victory would be a blow to free expression on the Internet.[8] YouTube argued that its services had connected politicians to their constituents, allowed reporters to bring news from far-off war zones, and provided tools to protesters to fight repressive regimes.[9] The liberation of peoples, after all, was more important than the liberation of business cycles. For its part, Viacom stoked fears that if YouTube continued allowing users to upload copyrighted content with reckless abandon, studio after studio would collapse in Hollywood.[10] It was not fair, Viacom argued, for copyright owners to have the burden of policing YouTube's site for copyright infringement.[11] Echoing the concerns of many copyright owners, Viacom argued that they were being forced to play a game of "whack-a-mole"—using DMCA take-down notices to remove content only to see it pop up somewhere else.[12]

Each side submitted thousands of pieces of evidence and spent millions litigating the case. The court provided a meager 30-page opinion, half of it directly quoting legislative history, and almost none of it touching on important factual issues raised by both sides.[13] The court granted summary judgment to YouTube, holding that YouTube was protected by the DMCA's safe harbor provision.[14] According to the court, YouTube removed content whenever it had "actual knowledge" or was "aware of facts and circumstances from which infringing activity [was] apparent" under § 512(c). YouTube was not liable for the infringement of its users because in responding to takedown

8 Michael H. Rubin (2010) Partner, Wilson Sonsini Goodrich & Rosati, Remarks at Berkeley School of Law: YouTube, A Look Back at Viacom v. YouTube & Beyond (Aug. 26).

9 YouTube, Inc. (2010) Mem. of Law in Support of Defendants' Motion for Summary Judgment, pp. 1–2, *Viacom International, Inc. v. YouTube, Inc.*, 718 F. Supp. 2d 514 (S.D.N.Y.).

10 Alex Pham (2010) 'Viacom, Google Trade Accusations Over YouTube,' *Los Angeles Times* (Nov. 11). Online. Available at: http://articles.latimes.com/2010/mar/19/business/la-fi-ct-viatube19-2010mar19 (accessed Jan. 15, 2011).

11 Viacom argued, in part, that: "Defendants refused to prevent illegal uploading and imposed the entire burden on Viacom and the other studios to search YouTube 24/7 for infringing clips while Defendants reaped the profits." Viacom International (2010) Memorandum of Law in Support of Motion for Partial Summary Judgment and Inapplicability of the Digital Millennium Copyright Act Safe Harbor Defense at 28, *Viacom v. YouTube*, 718 F. Supp. 2d 514 (S.D.N.Y.)).

12 Nate Anderson (2011) Rightsholders Tire of Takedown Whack-A-Mole, Seek Gov't Help, Arstechnica (Jan. 31). Online. http://arstechnica.com/tech-policy/news/2010/05/rightsholders-tire-of-takedown-whack-a-mole-seek-govt-help.ars.

13 *Viacom v. YouTube* (2010) 718 F. Supp. 2d 514 (S.D.N.Y.).

14 *Ibid.*, 529.

notices with these actions, YouTube had met the statutory requirements for safe harbor protection.

In some corners, the verdict was celebrated. Commentator Mike Masnick of *Tech Dirt* called it "a huge victory for common sense and the proper application of liability."[15] Farhad Manjoo of *Slate*, who originally sided with Viacom, changed his mind shortly before the ruling and said he wanted to "upload a video apology to YouTube."[16] Kent Walker, the Vice President and General Counsel of Google, hailed it as "an important victory not just for us, but also for the billions of people around the world who use the web to communicate and share experiences with each other."[17]

Viacom, by contrast, called the decision "fundamentally flawed."[18] Its many supporters were dismayed. The American Federation of Musicians warned that "YouTube is more than a widespread infringer of copyrights; it [is] a catalyst and engine for copyright infringement on a global scale, unleashing a Pandora's box of illegal activity that will continue to threaten the output of America's creative industries for years to come."[19] Viacom has since hired superstar attorney Theodore Olson of *Bush v. Gore* and *Perry v. Schwarzenegger* fame to handle their appeal, which they filed in December of 2010.[20] Microsoft, the MPAA, the Directors Guild of America, Screen Actors Guild, Electronic Arts, CBS, and the International Intellectual Property Institute have all filed amicus briefs in support of Viacom's appeal.[21]

While not nearly as dire as Viacom and its supporters make it out to be, the decision in *Viacom v. YouTube* makes clear that the DMCA is slipping into irrelevancy and may not be able to accurately hit the moving target of issues that the evolving Internet landscape raises. Pressed against the dual concerns of looming and massive statutory damages and the DMCA's inability to predict Web 2.0 technologies, the court took a sledgehammer to the delicate issues at stake, rather than use the scalpel those issues deserved. The court

15 Mike Masnick (2010) *Huge Victory: Court Rules for YouTube Against Viacom*, Techdirt (Oct. 26, 2010). Online. http://www.techdirt.com/articles/20100623/1333269937.shtml.

16 Farhad Manjoo (2010) *Police Your Own Damn Copyrights*, Slate (Oct. 27). Online. http://www.slate.com/id/2258086/pagenum/all/#p2.

17 Kent Walker (2010) *YouTube Wins Case Against Viacom*, Broadcasting Ourselves: The Official YouTube Blog (Oct. 27). Online. http://youtube-global.blogspot.com/2010/06/youtube-wins-case-against-viacom.html.

18 Miguel Helft (2010) 'Judge Sides With Google in Viacom Video Suit,' *The New York Times* (Oct. 27), http://www.nytimes.com/2010/06/24/technology/24google.html?_r=1.

19 American Federation of Musicians et al. (2010) Brief as Amici Curiae Supporting Plaintiffs, *Viacom International Inc. v. YouTube, Inc.*, p. 17, 718 F. Supp. 2d 514 (S.D.N.Y. 2010).

20 Eriq Gardner (2010) 'Viacom Hires Superstar Lawyer to Handle YouTube Appeal,' Hollywood Reporter (Oct. 27), http://www.hollywoodreporter.com/blogs/thr-esq/viacom-hires-superstar-lawyer-handle-31587.

21 Eriq Gardner (2010) 'Viacom Friends Back Appeal of YouTube Decision,' Hollywood Reporter (Dec. 14), http://www.hollywoodreporter.com/blogs/thr-esq/viacom-friends-appeal-youtube-decision-58856.

ignored instances of specific knowledge and dismissed evidence of possibly overwhelming amounts of infringement. In choosing DMCA takedown notices over content filtering as the method of choice for "red flag" notification, the court has chosen to enforce a blunt instrument rather than an elegant tool.

The mechanics of a safe harbor

The relevant safe harbor provision[22] in the *Viacom v. YouTube* case can be found in 17 U.S.C. § 512(c)(1).[23] It reads that a service provider shall not be liable for monetary relief if it:

> (A)(i) does not have actual knowledge that the material or an activity using the material on the system or network is infringing; (ii) in the absence of such actual knowledge, is not aware of facts or circumstances from which infringing activity is apparent; or (iii) upon obtaining such knowledge or awareness, acts expeditiously to remove, or disable access to, the material;
>
> (B) does not receive a financial benefit directly attributable to the infringing activity, in a case in which the service provider has the right and ability to control such activity; and
>
> (C) upon notification of claimed infringement ... responds expeditiously to remove, or disable access to, the material that is claimed to be infringing or to be the subject of infringing activity.[24]

The safe harbor provision requires Online Service Providers (OSPs) "not to interfere with standard technical measures used by copyright holders to identify or protect copyrighted works."[25] It also requires OSPs to "adopt and reasonably implement a policy of terminating in appropriate circumstances the accounts of subscribers who are repeat infringers."[26] Furthermore, it imposes on OSPs a "notice and takedown" procedure that requires OSPs to

22 17 U.S.C. § 512 (c) is the relevant provision because it applies to "Information Residing on Systems or Networks at Direction of Users." This is what the court in *Viacom v. YouTube* classified YouTube as.

23 Another, almost identical provision appears in 17 U.S.C. § 512 (d). This section refers to information location tools—arguably a feature of YouTube. Discussion of this clause and its legal ramifications on *Viacom International, Inc. v. YouTube, Inc.* are beyond the scope of this chapter.

24 U.S. Code, title 17, § 512.

25 *Ibid.*, § 512(i).

26 Debra Weinstein (2008) 'Defining Expeditious: Uncharted Territory of the DMCA Safe Harbor Provision,' *Cardozo Arts & Entertainment Law Journal* 26: 589–98.

remove infringing material upon formal notice from a copyright holder.[27] Service providers who satisfy all of the above conditions are "protected from liability for all monetary relief for direct, vicarious, and contributory infringement in circumstances in which the infringing or allegedly infringing content are contained in the system without the knowledge and involvement of the service provider."[28]

The knowledge standard and red flags

A key component of § 512(c) is the knowledge standard of § 512(c)(1)(A)(ii)—revoking immunity from liability if an OSP becomes "aware of facts or circumstances from which infringing activity is apparent." This knowledge standard, according to Congress, is best understood as a "red flag" test.[29] According to Congress:

> The "red flag" test has both a subjective and an objective element. In determining whether the service provider was aware of a "red flag," the subjective awareness of the service provider of the facts or circumstances in question must be determined. However, in deciding whether those facts or circumstances constitute a "red flag"—in other words, whether infringing activity would have been apparent to a reasonable person operating under the same or similar circumstances—an objective standard should be used.[30]

The red flag test, then, has two parts that an OSP must meet. First, a court must find the OSP to be subjectively aware of the circumstances relating to the infringement. Second, a court must also find that the infringement would have been apparent to a reasonable person operating under similar circumstances as the OSP. Congress devised this two-part structure for the red flag test "to ensure that an OSP is not burdened with the duty to monitor its services or to affirmatively investigate circumstances indicating infringing activity."[31]

Furthermore, examples given in the Congressional committee report "make clear that the red flag must signal to the provider not just that the

---

27 U.S. Code, title 17, § 512(c). See also Pamela Samuelson et al. (2010) 'The Copyright Principles Project: Directions for Reform,' *Berkeley Technology Law Journal*, 25: 20.

28 Weinstein, op. cit., at 597.

29 H.R. Rep. 105-551, Part 2, at 53.

30 *Ibid.*

31 Liliana Chang (2010) 'The Red Flag Test for Apparent Knowledge Under the DMCA § 512(c) Safe Harbors,' *Cardozo Arts & Entertainment Law Journal* 28: 202.

activity is occurring, but that the activity is infringing."[32] In the context of information location tools,[33] the committee clarified that:

> A directory provider would not be ... aware merely because it saw one or more photographs of a celebrity at a site devoted to that person. The provider could not be expected ... to determine whether the photograph was still protected by copyright or was in the public domain; if the photograph was still protected by copyright, whether the use was licensed; and if the use was not licensed, whether it was permitted under the fair use doctrine.[34]

Congress stressed that knowledge of infringement could be ascertained even if the content owner does not give formal notice, stating that "copyright owners are not obligated to give notification of claimed infringement in order to enforce their rights."[35] Congress also outlined that:

> Section 512 does not require the use of a notice and takedown procedure. A service provider wishing to benefit from the limitation on liability under subsection (c) must "take down" or disable access to infringing material residing on its system or network of which it has actual knowledge or that meets the "red flag" test, even if the copyright owner or its agent does not notify it of a claim of infringement.[36]

This section makes plain that a court may find red flag knowledge *independently* of a takedown notice.

A decade is forever in tech years—the impact of the DMCA and the challenges of Web 2.0

Since its passage in 1998, the DMCA has been tethered to the promulgation of online and digital media.[37] DMCA anti-circumvention laws have been heralded as the "*sine qua non* for technologies like the DVD."[38] Similarly, the various immunities for liability extended by the DMCA have been described

---

32 R. Anthony Reese (2009) 'The Relationship Between the ISP Safe Harbors and the Ordinary Rules of Copyright Liability,' *Columbia Journal of Law and the Arts* 32: 434.
33 Red flag analysis under § 512(c) is the same as under § 512(d).
34 H.R. Rep. No. 105-551 (1998) Part 2, pp. 57–8.
35 *Ibid.*, p. 54.
36 *Ibid.*, pp. 57–8.
37 Aaron Freedman (2010) 'The DMCA: 10 Years of the Good, Bad, and Ugly', MacUser (Dec. 15). Online. http://www.macuser.com/legal/the_dmca_10_years_of_the_good.php.
38 David Kravets (2010) '10 Years Later, Misunderstood DMCA is the Law That Saved the Web,' Wired Threat Level Blog (Dec. 15). Online. <http://www.wired.com/threatlevel/2008/10/ten-years-later>.

as "absolutely crucial for giving us the Internet today"—without those blogs, MySpace and AOL could not exist.[39] Other lucrative and popular technologies such as DRM, the iPod, and iTunes may credit their existence, at least in part, to the DMCA.[40]

While the DMCA has certainly had an impact on the digital ecosystem we live in today, it is inadequate to address many of the challenges posed by that ecosystem. Just eight months after the passing of the bill, Napster was born.[41] Napster and its peer-to-peer system,[42] like many other Internet inventions that followed, upended much of the "foresight" of Congress and the DMCA.[43] Some estimates found that within a year, users of Napster had likely "distributed more music than the entire record industry from its inception a century earlier."[44]

Napster was only the beginning. Congress failed to foresee the rise of Web 2.0—a network of websites and service providers that thrive on user participation and content. This new Internet was developing in stark contrast to the operator driven architecture and function of the Internet in 1998. Services we take for granted today—photo sharing, search engines, blogs, e-commerce, video sharing, and social networks—were at the time of the birth of the DMCA "unheard of, embryonic or not yet conceived."[45] These are the Facebooks and YouTubes of the world—the present and future of the Internet.

Of course, Web 2.0 is no runaway train—service providers provide and control the software that facilitates user expression and content.[46] A particularly important technological breakthrough in the world of Web 2.0 has been the advent of content scanning tools. These tools use an audio or video "fingerprint" to identify and filter infringing works posted or distributed over the Internet. They have become "increasingly smart" and "capable of determining ... how much of a copyrighted movie is contained in a given online file and even whether the file combines video or audio tracks from the movie with new material."[47] Effective filtering technology is not cheap; YouTube and Google claim that their own fingerprinting technology,

39 *Ibid.* (quoting Fred von Lohmann of the Electronic Frontier Foundation).
40 Freedman, op. cit.
41 Peter S. Menell (2010), 'In Search of Copyright's Lost Ark: Interpreting the Right to Distribute in the Internet Age,' *Journal of the Copyright Society of the U.S.A.*, 59: 1–67.
42 A peer-to-peer file-sharing system is a network where computer systems can share files between systems within the network.
43 *Ibid.* p. 31. University of California at Berkeley Olin Program in Law & Economics Working Paper Series, Paper No. 1602022. Online. <http://papers.ssrn.com/sol3/papers.cfm?abstract_id=1679514>.
44 *Ibid.*
45 Kravets, op. cit.
46 Brandon Brown (2008) 'Note, Fortifying the Safe Harbors: Reevaluating the DMCA in a Web 2.0 World,' *Berkeley Technology Law Journal* 23: 441.
47 Samuelson et al., op cit., p. 41.

Content ID, is the product of "approximately 50,000 man hours of engineering time and millions of dollars of research and development costs."[48] However, the technology can also be profitable—identified videos can be monetized through targeted advertisements.[49]

Viacom v. YouTube

Hot on the heels of the development of the DMCA, the rise of Web 2.0, and the court cases that shaped liability for OSPs, came YouTube. YouTube is a website that hosts user-generated videos that can easily be uploaded and disseminated. Videos can be shared with friends, and even "embedded" into sections of other websites—all for free.[50] Much like the other Web 2.0 prodigy, Facebook, YouTube grew fast. YouTube was started in February 2005 in order to share videos of a simple dinner party.[51] Less than a year later, YouTube was streaming more than thirty million videos a day.[52] By October 2006, tech giant Google purchased YouTube for $1.65 billion in a stock-for-stock transaction.[53] In the year 2007 alone, YouTube used as much bandwidth as the entirety of the Internet in the year 2000.[54] Today, YouTube has 146.3 million unique viewers a day—far surpassing viewership for any media company web portal.[55]

YouTube's size and success has brought with it both attention and derision, particularly from media powerhouse Viacom. Viacom owns a great number of television networks and movie studios, including Paramount Pictures, MTV, Comedy Central, and Nickelodeon.[56] Viacom has found much of its copyrighted content available on YouTube—clips of its most popular programming including "The Daily Show" and "The Colbert Report" are consistently on YouTube's homepage top watched list.[57] Figure 4.1 displays a screenshot of YouTube.com from around 2012, containing previews of videos from

48 *Viacom v. YouTube*, 718 F. Supp. 2d 514 (S.D.N.Y. 2010).

49 Claire Cain Miller, 'YouTube Ads Turn Videos Into Revenue', *N.Y. Times* (Oct, 26, 2010, 2:09 PM), available at http://www.nytimes.com/2010/09/03/technology/03youtube. html?_r=1&th&emc=th.

50 Kevin C. Hormann (2009) 'Comment, The Death of the DMCA? How Viacom v. YouTube May Define the Future of Digital Content,' *Houston Law Review*, 46: 1354.

51 Eugene C. Kim (2007) 'Note, YouTube: Testing the Safe Harbors of Digital Copyright Law,' *Southern California Interdisciplinary Law Journal* 17: 142.

52 *Ibid.*, p. 141.

53 Press Release, Google, Google to Acquire YouTube for $1.65 Billion in Stock (Oct. 9, 2006), http://www.google.com/intl/en/press/pressrel/google_ youtube.html.

54 Hormann op. cit., 1356.

55 Leena Rao (2010) *comScore: Facebook Passes Yahoo to Become the Second Largest Video Site in the U.S.*, Techcrunch (Oct. 27), http://techcrunch.com/2010/09/30/comscore-facebook-passes-yahoo-to-become-the-second-largest-video-site-in-the-u-s/.

56 Kim, op. cit., 139.

57 *Ibid.*, 143.

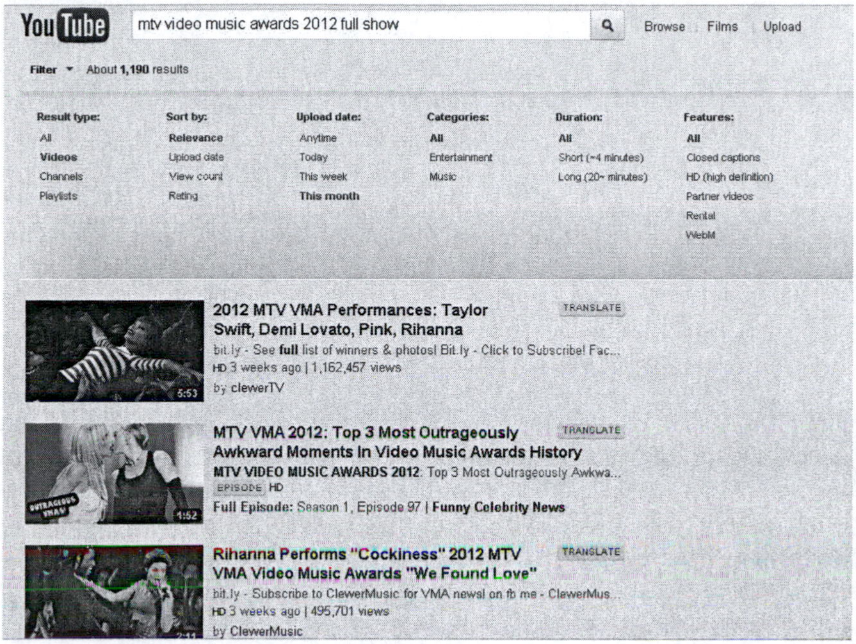

Figure 4.1 Screenshot of YouTube, circa 2012.

MTV, which have apparently been uploaded by persons or entities other than Viacom. While Figure 4.2 displays a similar screenshot from 2008. Viacom has identified YouTube as a threat—stealing its works and stymieing the development of Viacom's own possible web content portals.

Attempts at reconciling the two parties failed. Viacom and YouTube had originally negotiated an agreement in 2006 that would have allowed for YouTube to host Viacom's content on its site and split ad revenue through the Content ID system.[58] But the deal eventually fell through when YouTube refused to pay Viacom's demanded minimum payment guarantees that neared a billion dollars.[59] A frustrated Viacom next sent a takedown notice demanding more than 100,000 clips on YouTube be removed.[60] Viacom subsequently filed suit against YouTube and Google, claiming they were "liable for the

---

58 *Ibid.*, 169.
59 *Ibid.*, 143.
60 Michael Arrington (2010) *Google Slammed by Viacom Takedown Notice Demand*, Techcrunch (Dec. 21). Online. <http://techcrunch.com/2007/02/02/gootube-slammed-by-viacom-takedown-demand>.

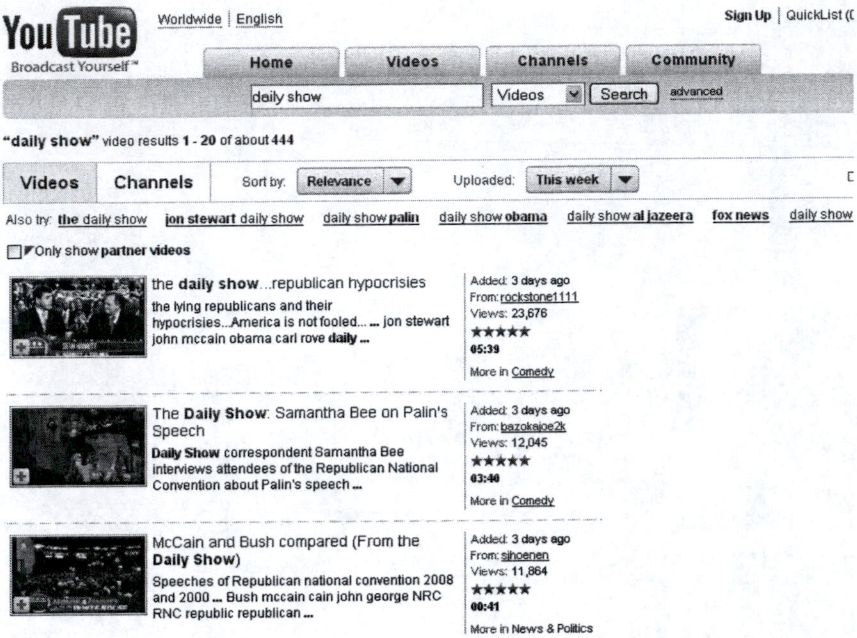

Figure 4.2 Screenshot of YouTube, circa 2008.

intentional infringement of thousands of Viacom's copyrighted works" under theories of direct and vicarious infringement.[61]

Viacom's argument

Viacom based its legal argument on what it believed was an "indisputable fact"—that "tens of thousands of videos on YouTube, resulting in hundreds of millions of views, were taken unlawfully from Viacom's copyrighted works without authorization."[62] In broad strokes, Viacom accused YouTube of "victimizing content owners."[63] Viacom alleged that the founders of YouTube had "single-mindedly focused on geometrically increasing the number of YouTube users to maximize its commercial value" and cast a "blind eye to ... the huge number of unauthorized copyrighted works posted on the site" to

---

61 *Viacom v. YouTube*, op. cit.
62 Viacom International, Memorandum, op. cit., p. 1.
63 *Ibid.*

achieve that end.[64] Viacom argued that Google and YouTube should be "liable for the rampant infringement they ... fostered and profited from."[65]

Viacom painted a picture of a young YouTube focused on garnering as many views as possible in order to quickly sell the company. To achieve this end, Viacom asserted, "YouTube implemented a policy of maintaining access to infringing videos unless and until it received a 'cease and desist' demand from the copyright owner."[66] Viacom argued that such a reading of the law would "render most of the statute enacted by Congress a nullity, for responding to takedown notices is only one of numerous preconditions to DMCA immunity."[67]

More specifically, Viacom posited that YouTube did not satisfy DMCA safe harbor provision § 512(c)(1)(A) because YouTube had "actual knowledge" and was "aware of facts or circumstances from which infringing activity [was] apparent," but failed to "act expeditiously" to stop it.[68] Viacom claimed that YouTube was, at a minimum, liable for contributory infringement based on its general knowledge and willful blindness of the pervasive infringement on the site.[69] General knowledge, according to Viacom, was achieved through the staggering amount of infringing material on the site, particularly in the early days of YouTube. YouTube also attained specific knowledge of various infringing works. Willful blindness stemmed from YouTube's refusal to use community flagging features and its selective application of content scanning technology. Ultimately,[70] Viacom moved for partial summary judgment, arguing that the defendants were not protected by the safe harbor provision.[71]

Viacom's evidence that YouTube was generally aware of facts or circumstances from which infringement was apparent

Viacom introduced evidence to support its claim that YouTube was generally aware of infringement. The evidence focused on estimates of the pervasiveness of infringement present on YouTube, particularly in its early days. For instance, Viacom presented an email from September 2005, wherein YouTube

---

64 *Ibid.*
65 *Ibid.*
66 Viacom International, Inc. (2011) Opening Brief for Plaintiffs-Appellants, p. 11, *Viacom v. YouTube*, No. 10-3270 (2nd Cir. Dec. 3, 2010).
67 Viacom International, Memorandum, op. cit., 3–4.
68 *Ibid.*, 11.
69 Daniel S. Schecter & Colin B. Vandell (2010) *Viacom v. YouTube: Safe Harbor Protection for Online Service Providers*, (Feb. 9), Latham & Watkins Client Alert. Online. Available at: <http://www.lw.com/upload/pubContent/_pdf/pub3638_1.pdf>.
70 Viacom made a number of other assertions and legal arguments that are outside the scope of this chapter.
71 *Viacom v. YouTube*, op. cit., 516.

cofounders Steven Chen and Jawed Karim discussed the implications of removing material that was "obviously infringing."[72] The group feared that the removal of the material would drop site traffic from "100,000 views a day down to about 20,000 views or maybe even lower."[73] That would mean that the founders of the site attributed 80% of its views to copyrighted material.

Viacom also presented instant message conversations that took place in late February 2006 between YouTube co-founder Steve Chen and YouTube product manager Maryrose Dunton.[74] Dunton reported the results of a "little exercise" she performed wherein she "went through all the most viewed/most discussed/top favorites/top rated to try and figure out what percentage is or has copyrighted material."[75] The number she reached "was over 70%."[76] In another instant message conversation in March of 2006, Dunton relayed to a co-worker that "the truth of the matter is, probably 75–80% of our views come from copyrighted material."[77]

Other evidence included the work of Google's due-diligence team that was assembled to analyze the percentage of professional content on YouTube's site before the acquisition. Storm Duncan, managing director of Credit Suisse and part of Google's YouTube acquisition due diligence team, assessed that 60% of the content on the site was premium/professional content.[78] In 2007, Credit Suisse estimated that only 10% of the video views of the premium content was authorized to be on YouTube.[79] Viacom argued that such pervasive infringement had to raise a red flag and signal that YouTube "*knew* of the infringing activity on its site and therefore had at least 'aware[ness] of facts or circumstances from which infringing activity is apparent.'"[80]

Viacom's evidence that YouTube was aware of specific instances of infringement

Viacom also introduced evidence that YouTube employees—and even founders—became aware of *specific* infringing clips. For instance, in August 2005, Jawed Karim and Chad Hurley agreed between each other to keep CNN

72 Hohengarten ¶ 233 & Ex. 215, JK00007416, at JK00007416.
73 *Ibid.*
74 Hohengarten ¶ 205 & Ex. 193, GOO001-00507535, at GOO001- 00507539.
75 *Ibid.*
76 *Ibid.*
77 Hohengarten ¶ 207 & Ex. 195, GOO001- 01931840, at GOO001-01931843.
78 Hohengarten ¶ 320 & Ex. 289, CSSU 001863, at CSSU 001957. Hohengarten ¶ 362 & Ex. 328 (Duncan 30(b)(6) Dep.) at 199:24-200:5, 207:25- 210:13.
79 Hohengarten ¶ 323 & Ex. 292, CSSU 004069, at CSSU 004071.
80 Viacom International, Opening Brief, op. cit., 24–5.

space shuttle footage on the site.[81] In September 2005, according to Viacom, Jawed Karim explicitly told his employees to keep known clips from Conan O'Brien and Jay Leno up on the site.[82] Viacom also introduced evidence of YouTube employees sharing playlist pages of material they believed to be infringed to their friends.[83] Several other employees were found to be sharing YouTube links showcasing clips from various Viacom properties such as the Daily Show, the Colbert Report, and South Park.[84] YouTube founder Jawed Karim shared at least seven infringing videos with a friend.[85]

Viacom's evidence of willful blindness

Viacom also suggested that YouTube had taken "affirmative steps to deprive itself of item-specific knowledge" in an effort to use the lack of such knowledge to qualify itself for DMCA safe harbor protection. Viacom pointed to a community-flagging feature that YouTube had initiated but abandoned. For a short period of time, YouTube allowed its users to flag videos that users identified as copyrighted work. YouTube swiftly abandoned the feature, explaining its removal was due to non-infringing content being flagged along

81 Viacom pointed out that: "On August 10, 2005, YouTube cofounder Jawed Karim responded to YouTube co-founder Chad Hurley ... 'lets remove stuff like movies/tv shows. lets keep short news clips for now. we can become stricter over time, just not overnight. like the CNN space shuttle clip, I like. we can remove it once we're bigger and better known, but for now that clip is fine.' Steve Chen replied, 'sounds good.'" Viacom International, Reply to Defendants' Counterstatement to Viacom's Statement of Undisputed Facts in Support of Its Motion for Partial Summary Judgment, *Viacom v. YouTube*, 718 F. Supp. 2d 514 (S.D.N.Y. 2010).

82 "In a September 1, 2005 email to YouTube co-founder Steve Chen and all YouTube employees, YouTube co-founder Jawed Karim stated, 'well, we SHOULD take down any: 1) movies 2) TV shows. We should KEEP: 1) news clips 2) comedy clips (Conan, Leno, etc) 3) music videos. In the future, I'd also reject these last three but not yet.'" *Ibid.*

83 "In a June 4, 2006 instant message conversation, YouTube product manager Matthew Liu (IM user name coda322) directed a friend to two YouTube profile playlist pages containing content that he recognized as infringing, stating, 'go watch some superman ... dont show other people though ... it can get taken off'; Liu's friend asked, 'why would it get taken off[?]'; Liu responded, 'cuz its copyrighted ... technically we shouldn't allow it ... but we're not going to take it off until the person that holds the copyright ... is like ... you shouldnt have that ... then we'll take it off.'" *Ibid.*

84 "In an August 24, 2006 email to other YouTube employees, YouTube systems administrator Paul Blair provided a link to a Daily Show clip on YouTube .... In an October 13, 2006 email to other Google employees, Google Video Product Manager Hunter Walk provided a link to a Colbert Report clip on YouTube ... . In a March 9, 2007 email to YouTube employees, a Google employee provided a link to a "Funny south park" video on YouTube .... In a March 23, 2007 email to other Google employees, a Google employee provided a link to a Daily Show clip on YouTube." *Ibid.*

85 *Viacom International v. YouTube, Inc.*, Docket #318, attachments #1–7.

with unlicensed copyrighted work.[86] Not so, according to Viacom. Viacom alleged that e-mails between Steven Chen and Jawed Karim made it clear that the decision to end the feature was motivated at least in part to avoid being served a notice that there was unlicensed material on the site—actively turning a blind eye to a possible red flag of infringement.[87]

Viacom also called YouTube's policies regarding video fingerprinting technology a form of turning a blind eye—going so far as to accuse YouTube of "high-tech extortion."[88] Viacom complained that "YouTube had the ability to forestall virtually all infringing activity during the upload process through the use of commercially available fingerprint filtering technology" but refused to do so until 2007.[89] Furthermore, when YouTube began filtering, only select content partners who had revenue sharing agreements were afforded such protection.[90] Viacom, of course, was not one of those partners.[91] Unlike registered content partners of YouTube, Viacom did not receive the benefit of the Content ID system that would have significantly reduced infringement for more than a year after negotiations broke down.[92]

Viacom accused YouTube of actively keeping this technology away from anyone who was not a content partner.[93] Viacom argued that it did not receive the benefit of the technology until May 2008—even though Viacom asked for it in February of 2007 after negotiations between the two companies broke down over content licensing deals.[94] Viacom did not receive notice of YouTube's plan to afford them the Content ID protection until the first status conference between the parties in litigation.[95] According to Viacom, it was a "deliberate business decision not to broadly deploy these techniques and instead … hold content owners hostage to Defendants' efforts to commercialize the site."[96] In effect, YouTube had "consciously blinded itself to …

86 YouTube Inc. (2010) Defendants' Opposition to Plaintiffs' Motions for Partial Summary Judgment, p. 19, *Viacom v. YouTube*, 718 F. Supp. 2d 514 (S.D.N.Y.).
87 "On September 23, 2005, YouTube cofounder Chad Hurley emailed YouTube cofounders Steve Chen and Jawed Karim, stating: 'can we remove the flagging link for 'copyrighted' today? we are starting to see complaints for this and basically if we don't remove them we could be held liable for being served a notice. it's actually better if we don't have the link there at all because then the copyright holder is responsible for serving us notice of the material and not the users. anyways, it would be good if we could remove this asap.'" Viacom International, Reply to Defendants' Counterstatement, op cit.
88 Viacom International, Memorandum, op. cit., 2.
89 Viacom International, Opening Brief, op. cit., 45.
90 Viacom International, Memorandum, op. cit., 2.
91 *Ibid*.
92 *Ibid*.
93 Viacom International, Reply to Defendants' Counterstatement, op. cit., para. 296.
94 *Ibid*.
95 *Ibid*., para. 314.
96 Viacom International, Memorandum, op. cit., 2.

specific knowledge of infringement by choosing to implement—but only selectively—commercially available digital fingerprint filtering technology."[97]

YouTube's defense

YouTube rejected all of Viacom's assertions. It painted itself as a service that was not just in full compliance with the DMCA, but also in line with the legislative intent behind it. YouTube touted itself as a service that achieved a "profound impact on culture, politics, and society in this country and around the world."[98] YouTube was valuable to a global society because it gave elected officials new ways to communicate with the American public, enabled reporting from conflicts around the globe, gave new means of exposure for rising artists, and even aided protestors in Iran in their struggle against the government.[99] These accomplishments were owed to the members of Congress who realized that Internet services would be valuable and revolutionary, and embedded safe harbor into the DMCA to protect services like YouTube. YouTube claimed that Viacom's lawsuit sought to "undo" all of these triumphs.[100]

YouTube defended its practice of waiting until receiving a takedown notice before removing content. According to YouTube, the "heart" of safe harbor provision was the notice-and-takedown procedure.[101] Thus YouTube's practice of "refraining from proactive monitoring for potential infringement is not only consistent with the DMCA, it makes perfect sense."[102] With the volume and complexity surrounding the rights associated with clips uploaded to YouTube, the burden was on the copyright holder, not the service provider, "to guess whether particular materials are or are not authorized."[103]

YouTube objected to Viacom's accusation that it was "willfully blind" to the content on its site.[104] YouTube claimed that § 512(c)'s knowledge requirement did not impose on it the need for any further inquiry or investigation—only to remove specific material known to be infringing through a DMCA takedown notice.[105] Such a reading of the DMCA, according to YouTube, was consistent with both case law and legislative intent.[106]

YouTube also moved for summary judgment, claiming that it was clearly entitled to DMCA safe-harbor protection. It argued that it met the threshold

97   Viacom International, Opening Brief, op. cit., 37.
98   YouTube, Inc., Memorandum in Support, op. cit., 2.
99   *Ibid.* at 2–3.
100 *Ibid.* at 2–3.
101 *Ibid.* at 2–3.
102 YouTube, Inc., Memorandum in Opposition, op. cit., 35.
103 *Ibid.*
104 *Ibid.*, 39.
105 *Ibid.*
106 *Ibid.* at 35.

qualifications: functioning as a "service provider," having a registered DMCA agent and appropriate repeat-infringer policy, and accommodating standard technical measures.[107] YouTube also claimed that it did not have actual or specific knowledge of the alleged infringements and responded expeditiously to any takedown notices.[108] YouTube, then, was entitled to the DMCA's safe harbor clause, thereby immune from all allegations of liability.[109]

YouTube's counterarguments to Viacom's evidence that YouTube was aware of facts or circumstances of infringement

YouTube attempted to debunk Viacom's evidence and assertions in two ways. The first was to challenge each piece of evidence that Viacom claimed to prove that YouTube was aware of pervasive or even specific infringement.[110] More generally, YouTube made the argument that it was impossible for any observer to ascertain what the exact percentage of material on the site was infringing because there was no way of knowing if the content was authorized by the owner or not.[111] The problem extended further than the percentage of all videos—in most instances, according to YouTube, it was impossible to know if *any* clip on YouTube was authorized.

YouTube blamed Viacom for much of this problem. YouTube pointed to Viacom's confusing uploading policy that included promotional uploads, stealth-marketing campaigns, and contradictory leave-up policies.[112] YouTube argued that Viacom's "widespread use of YouTube to market and promote

---

107 Viacom International, Memorandum in Support, 22.
108 *Ibid.*, 21–7.
109 *Viacom v. YouTube*, op. cit., 516.
110 For example, counsel for YouTube argued that the e-mail conversation between Steven Chen and Jawid Karim was taken out of context and that "Viacom's selective excerpt … distorts its meaning." Viacom International, Reply to Defendants' Counterstatement, op. cit. In regards to the instant message confirmation of March 2006, counsel for YouTube "disputed that the document provides any evidence of the percentage of copyrighted or infringing videos available on YouTube" (*id*). In response to the 60% figure, Duncan testified that someone else provided him with this information, but he did not recall who provided this information. YouTube, Inc., Schapiro Declaration (2009) Ex. 212, 199:22- 202:8. In regards to the 10% projection, counsel for YouTube argued that the "projection concerned only one category of authorized videos that could be monetized and reflects Google's plan to monetize only videos on YouTube subject to individually negotiated content-partnership agreements." *Ibid.*, 144:5–145:9.
111 YouTube argued that "A number of other factors—including the obscurity of much of the content posted on YouTube; the complex array of licensing and co-ownership issues attending much professional content; and fair use—make it even more difficult for YouTube to determine whether a given video is illegitimate." Def.'s Opp'n to Pls.' Motions for Partial Summary Judgment at 36, *Viacom v. YouTube*, 718 F. Supp. 2d 514 (S.D.N.Y. 2010), appeal docketed, No. 10-3270 (2nd Cir. Dec. 3, 2010) (No. 07-2103).
112 Viacom International, Memorandum, op. cit., 48.

their content—uses that continued even in the midst of this litigation" had defeated "any notion that the presence of [Viacom] material on YouTube create[d] a fact or circumstance from which infringing activity is apparent."[113] YouTube argued that Viacom's actions were important to the knowledge inquiry of the DMCA because it "significantly complicate[d] the task of distinguishing between authorized and unauthorized uploads" in two ways: "(1) the sheer number of authorized video clips that Viacom (and other media companies) ha[d] allowed to flood YouTube; and (2) the opaque manner in which those clips [were] frequently placed on YouTube."[114]

YouTube elaborated on the second point by presenting evidence that Viacom uploaded content to YouTube covertly, using an array of fake accounts and agents.[115] This was an effort to engage in "stealth marketing"—a technique that was designed to advertise to a savvy audience that disliked studio sponsored promotion by creating "the appearance of authentic grass-roots interest in the content being promoted."[116] Viacom partook in a campaign of concealing its connection to many of the videos it was responsible for uploading.[117] The general goal of this campaign was to make the uploaded content appear as though a "fan had created it and posted it."[118] Employees and agents would even go so far as to "rough up" the uploads with "time codes and other internal studio markings to make them seem illicit, even though the clips were actually part of a carefully crafted marketing initiative."[119] Even major celebrities, like Andy Samberg, were involved in the purposeful leaking of material.[120]

Making it more difficult to ascertain whether content on YouTube was authorized were Viacom's inconsistent and confusing uploading and take-down policies. YouTube presented evidence that Viacom would "come up with new rules every few days—sometimes even changing the rules within

113 *Ibid.*, 38.
114 *Ibid.*
115 *Ibid.*, 35.
116 *Ibid.*, 39.
117 Techniques included allegedly hiring an army of third-party marketing agents to upload clips on its behalf, creating and using YouTube accounts that lack any discernible connection to Viacom (such as "MysticalGirl8," "Demansr," "tesderiw," "GossipGirl40," "Snackboard," and "Keithhn"); deliberately using email addresses that "can't be traced to [Viacom]" when registering for YouTube accounts; having Viacom employees making special trips away from the company's premises (to places like Kinko's) to upload videos to YouTube from computers not traceable to Viacom; and altering its own videos to make them appear stolen, like "footage from the cutting room floor, so users feel they have found something unique." *Ibid.*, 40.
118 *Ibid.*, 39.
119 *Ibid.*
120 YouTube Inc. (2009) Rubin Declaration para. 226 & Ex. 25, *Viacom International v. YouTube*, Inc.

the same day."[121] Viacom would even allow material from programs that were central in the case—The Daily Show and the Colbert Report—to be uploaded, because "Jon Stewart and Stephen Colbert believed that their presence on YouTube was important for their ratings as well as for their relationship with their audience."[122]

Acts like these, with different uploading guidelines given to different companies and agents, created a maelstrom of confusion within Viacom over which uploads were actually authorized. This was evidenced by Viacom's confused and contradictory takedown notices and dropped clips from the lawsuit. In fact clips that Viacom initially included in its complaint—but subsequently dropped from the lawsuit—were posted by Viacom or one of its agents.[123] YouTube concluded that Viacom's uploading policy, "and the struggles of its own employees, agents, and lawyers to distinguish authorized from unauthorized clips," were "fatal to Viacom's claims about YouTube's knowledge ... of infringement."[124]

Court is in session

In his 30-page opinion, Judge Stanton rejected most of Viacom's arguments and granted summary judgment to YouTube. The court focused its analysis on whether or not YouTube was protected by the DMCA's safe harbor provision. The court bifurcated Viacom's principle safe harbor argument—that YouTube had "'actual knowledge' and [was] 'aware of facts and circumstances from which infringing activity [was] apparent,' but failed to 'act expeditiously' to stop it." The court rejected the assertion that YouTube failed to stop the infringement expeditiously, instead pointing out that when YouTube "received specific notice that a particular item infringed a copyright, [it] swiftly removed it." The court continued on to insist that all of the "clips in suit are off the YouTube website, most having been removed in response to DMCA takedown notices."[125]

The court then turned its attention to what it believed was the critical red flag question—whether the statutory phrases "'actual knowledge'" of infringement and awareness of "facts or circumstances from which infringing activity is apparent" refer to either "a general awareness that there are infringements" or rather "actual or constructive knowledge of specific and identifiable infringements."[126] The court concluded that the phrase referred

121　Viacom International, Memorandum, op. cit.
122　*Ibid.*, 48.
123　YouTube, Inc., Opposition Memorandum, op. cit.
124　*Ibid.* at 6.
125　*Viacom International v. YouTube, Inc.*, op. cit., 519.
126　*Viacom International v. YouTube, Inc.*, 718 F. Supp. 2d 514, 519, quoting U.S. Code, title 17, § 512(c).

to *actual and constructive knowledge*, not "mere knowledge of prevalence of such activity in general."[127]

The court concluded that when a service provider takes down infringing material upon receipt of a takedown notice it is given safe harbor under the DMCA, "even if otherwise he would be held as a contributory infringer under the general law."[128] Evidently, because YouTube removed material when it was given a takedown notice, it was protected "from liability for all monetary relief for direct, vicarious and contributory infringement."[129]

A legislative approach to safe harbor analysis

The court referred to legislative history to explain its decision. As it quoted broad swathes of excerpts from Committee Reports, the court concluded that the "tenor" of the reports along with an "instructive explanation of the need for specificity" made it clear that the legislation was intended to only hold service providers liable for infringing content about which the provider had specific knowledge.[130]

The court believed that its conclusion was "consistent with an area of the law devoted to protection of distinctive individual works, not of libraries."[131] The court read the legislative history as clearly putting the burden of finding infringing material on content providers, not service providers. The court agreed with YouTube and did not want to impose a "responsibility on service providers to discover which of their users' postings infringe a copyright" because that "would contravene the structure and operation of the DMCA."[132] The opinion leaned on prior case law to make this point, quoting the court in *Perfect 10, Inc. v. CCBill LLC* that refused to "shift a substantial burden from the copyright owner to the provider."[133]

The court validated its decision by stressing that the current DMCA structure was adequate. The court made much of the fact that the infringing works identified in the lawsuit may have only constituted "a small fraction of millions of works posted by others on the service's platform." The court felt that the current "DMCA notification regime works efficiently" because within one business day YouTube was able to remove all 100,000 videos that Viacom requested to be removed in a mass takedown.[134]

127 *Ibid.*, 523.
128 *Ibid.*, 526.
129 *Ibid.*
130 *Ibid.*, 519.
131 *Ibid.*
132 *Ibid.*, 523.
133 *Ibid.* (quoting *Perfect 10, Inc. v. CCBill LLC*, 488 F. 3d 1102, 1113 (9th Cir. 2007)).
134 *Ibid.*

Case law analysis of what triggers a red flag

In *UMG Recordings, Inc. v. Veoh Networks*, the district court applied the DMCA to a video-sharing service provider, concluding that the § 512(c) safe harbor protection applied.[135] The court further found that "UMG's 'evidence' f[ell] short of establishing actual knowledge within the meaning of the DMCA."[136] The court made clear "that merely hosting user-contributed material capable of copyright protection [was not] enough to impute actual knowledge to a service provider" because such a theory would render the "DMCA's notice-and-takedown provisions completely superfluous." Finally, the court also stated that UMG did not meet the "high bar for finding 'red flag' knowledge" as evidenced in *CCBill*—though it never gave an example of what would meet such a high bar.[137]

UMG's argument that Veoh was "ineligible for the safe harbor because its founders, employees, and investors knew that widespread infringement was occurring on the Veoh system" was also struck down. The court held that "there was no case holding that a provider's general awareness of infringement, without more, is enough to preclude application of § 512(c)."[138] Such general awareness was not enough to raise a red flag because it would be at odds with the safe harbor's purpose of "'facilitat[ing] the robust development and world-wide expansion of electronic commerce, communications … in the digital age.'"[139]

In the *YouTube* case, the court's analysis of prior case law focused on the mechanics of the "red flag" test. In its discussion of cases like *UMG Recordings, Inc. v. Veoh Networks, Inc.*, the court came to the conclusion that "awareness of pervasive copyright-infringing, however flagrant and blatant, does not impose liability on the service provider. It furnishes at most a statistical esti-mate of the chance any particular posting is infringing—and that is not a 'red flag' marking any particular work."[140] In other words, the court viewed case law to point towards a "red flag" test that can be triggered only by something more than "facts and circumstances" pointing to infringement.

According to the court, the only time a red flag can be triggered is when there is specific knowledge of infringement. The court relied on *Corbis Corp. v. Amazon.com*,[141] which found that Amazon would only have been notified by a red flag if they knew of infringement on a specific site, and not if they knew some sites were infringing in general.[142]

135 *UMG Recordings, Inc. v. Veoh Networks, Inc.*, 665 F. Supp. 2d 1099, 1108 (C.D. Cal. 2009).
136 *YouTube*, 718 F. Supp. 2d at 1109.
137 *Ibid.*, 1109, 1110.
138 *Ibid.*, 1111.
139 *Ibid.*, citing S. Rep. 105-190 (1998) 1–2; H.R. Rep. 105-551 (1998), Part 2, 21.
140 *Viacom International v. YouTube, Inc.*, op. cit., 524.
141 *Corbis Corp. v. Amazon.com, Inc.* (2004) 351 F. Supp. 2d 1090, 1108 (W.D. Wash.).
142 *Viacom International v. YouTube, Inc.*, op. cit., 523.

The argument that summary judgment should not have been granted

A copious amount of evidence was submitted to the court trying to prove whether or not YouTube had actual knowledge of infringement under DMCA § 512 (c). A reader would not be aware of such evidence when reading the opinion, however. The opinion glossed over or failed to mention most of the evidentiary back and forth between the parties. That was unfortunate, because this argument between the parties raised a genuine issue of material fact relating to YouTube's knowledge of infringement.[143] Viacom's argument was that summary judgment should not have been granted as a matter of law and the case should have gone to a jury.[144]

The opinion made it clear that as a matter of law the "mere knowledge of prevalence" of infringing activity was not enough to hold service providers like YouTube accountable for the infringement of its users.[145] The court required specific knowledge of specific work as a matter of law.

The opinion, however, never mentioned that Viacom submitted evidence that the founders of YouTube and their employees became aware of specific infringing clips.[146] The court may have been subtly referencing YouTube's defense to that accusation when it stated that a "provider cannot by inspection determine whether the use has been licensed by the owner, or whether its posting is a 'fair use' of the material."[147] But the veracity of either side's claims on specific knowledge is not a question of law; it is a question of fact. A jury should have decided whether or not YouTube employees and its founders were able to tell by inspection if the owner licensed the content in question.

The court also dismissed any statistical estimate of how much infringing material was present on YouTube. According to the court, such an estimate "furnishes at most a statistical estimate of the chance any particular posting is infringing—and that is not a 'red flag' marking any *particular* work."[148] The court stressed that "the infringing works in suit may be a small fraction of millions of works posted by others on the service's platform."[149]

---

143 The plaintiffs have since agreed with this point. See Opening Brief for Plaintiffs-Appellants, *Viacom v. YouTube*, 718 F. Supp. 2d 514 (S.D.N.Y. 2010), *appeal docketed*, No. 10-3270 (2nd Cir. Dec. 3, 2010) (No. 10-3270).

144 Summary judgment "should be rendered if the pleadings, the discovery and disclosure materials on file, and any affidavits show that there is no genuine issue as to any material fact and that the movant is entitled to judgment as a matter of law." Fed. R. Civ. P. 56(c).

145 *Viacom v. YouTube, Inc.*, op. cit., 523.

146 *Ibid.*, 516.

147 *Ibid.*, 524. YouTube made a similar argument in defense to Viacom's specific infringement claims. YouTube Inc., Defendants' Opposition, 36.

148 *Viacom v. YouTube, Inc.*, op. cit., 524 (emphasis added).

149 *Ibid.*, 524.

The court, however, underplayed *how much* of YouTube's material could have been infringing, particularly in its early days. Viacom presented evidence that at one point YouTube relied on infringing material for 80% of its site traffic. YouTube brought forth evidence countering that claim. But the court never mentioned the conflict over such key evidence. The "tenor" of the legislative history does not posit that Congress thought that as a matter of law a website that is *overwhelmingly* full of infringing material should continue to operate under DMCA protection. This disagreement over the prevalence of massive amounts of infringement represented a material factual dispute in the case.

The consequence of the court's reading of the DMCA is a notice and takedown *only* regime

The court's opinion implied that red flag knowledge can only be triggered with a notice and takedown, despite the clear distinction made in the DMCA. Though the court admitted that a service provider must remove content "if a service provider knows (from notice from the owner, *or* a "red flag") of specific instances of infringement,"[150] any logical inference from the court's holding suggests otherwise.

According to the court, awareness of "blatant" and "ubiquitous" infringement was not enough to trigger a red flag.[151] Despite arguments by Viacom and YouTube regarding the need for fingerprinting technologies, the court refused to place any such investigative duty on the service provider.[152] And the court's silence on the specific instances where YouTube employees and founders may have known about specific instances of infringement suggests that they too did not count as a red flag. The court simply provided no example of how one could possibly become "aware of facts or circumstances" that a specific item is infringing other than a notice from the true owner.

As the opinion itself suggested, this reading of the DMCA is inconsistent with legislative intent. As described earlier in this chapter, Congress made clear that red flag knowledge is attainable *independently* of a takedown notice.[153] Takedown notices were not meant to be the *only* way a service provider could become aware of red flags. The opinion makes Congress' intent on this matter impossible to achieve.

This portion of the ruling has already fostered unfair practices as opportunist companies are already attempting to hide behind this new takedown only regime. One such company is called Grooveshark—described by some as the

---

150 *Ibid.*, 525 (emphasis added).
151 *Ibid.*, 525, 528.
152 *Ibid.*, 529.
153 H.R. Rep. No. 105-551, Part 2, at 57–58 (1998).

"ugly" consequence of the decision.[154] Grooveshark scans a user's folder and uploads it to its server, calling it user-generated content. It then streams unlicensed music files for free. It will only take down the music when served a takedown notice. Grooveshark believes that this practice is legal because it comports to the safe harbor provision under the *Viacom* decision. Consequently Grooveshark has exasperated whack-a-mole costs and used it as leverage to "extract favorable licensing arrangements" from copyright owners. Thus Grooveshark "sees the lower court decision in *Viacom v. YouTube* as an invitation to cannibalize and leverage."[155] This troublesome development was certainly not Congress' intent.

Caught between a rock and a hard place—the court had few choices because of an antiquated DMCA

The district court's opinion seemed to be a result of the court attempting to satisfy the spirit of the DMCA, without the proper means under the DMCA to do so. In the decision the court repeatedly stressed that the purpose of the DMCA was to foster the development of the Internet. It must have seen its stringent red flag standards as the only way to achieve this goal in the face of mounting pressure from ramped up statutory damages on one hand, and the limited tools offered to monitor websites under the DMCA on the other.

If the court had not set its very stringent standard for red flag knowledge, then it would have been pressed against the ramped up statutory damage range for copyright infringement which allowed for Viacom's request of $1.65 billion dollars in damages. Surely, the court found this number unacceptable in the "absence of billion dollar harms."[156] Academics have called this issue the unsaid "elephant in the room" in the case.[157] To undercut this "elephant," the court returned again and again to legislative intent— Congress wanted to foster services like YouTube. In many ways, the statutory damages provisions make this impossible. Though the court never took up the subject, its decision comports with the logic that in a Web 2.0 world where a massive number of clips can be uploaded instantaneously, these damage provisions don't make sense.

The only way to protect YouTube and other Internet companies from such crippling liability was to limit acquired knowledge to the DMCA takedown notification system. The court stabbed YouTube's eye's blind to all other

---

154 Peter S. Menell (2010) 'Intellectual Property Issues: Assessing the DMCA Safe Harbors: The Good, the Bad, and the Ugly', Media Institute (Sep. 14). Online. http://www.mediain-stitute.org/new_site/IPI/2010/090110.php.

155 *Ibid.*

156 *Ibid.*

157 Peter S. Menell, 'Confronting the Elephant in the Room: Interpreting and Reforming Statutory Damages in the Internet Age' (Working Paper) (on file with author).

possible ways of becoming aware of infringement in order to protect it. The court venerated the DMCA notification system—praising it for working "efficiently."[158] It complimented YouTube on taking down more than 100,000 videos in one business day after Viacom sent a mass takedown notice.[159] Any lower standard for red flag knowledge would have put YouTube on the hook for billions in damages—which the court felt the safe harbor was designed to protect against.

Unfortunately, takedown notices are flawed and not at all "efficient." Examples of abuse abound, including magicians who have successfully sent takedown notices for videos debunking their tricks[160] and Twitter "tweets" unjustly removed due to DMCA takedown notices.[161] In the *Viacom* case alone, Viacom erroneously sent takedown notices of *other* content owner's work causing them to be removed and prompting annoyed copyright holders to complain about Viacom's "blatant abuse of the DMCA takedown statute."[162] Courts' too, have noted this problem. The district court in *Design Furnishings, Inc v. Zen Path LLC* recognized that the policy of immediately taking down material after receiving a takedown notice "essentially shift[s]" the burden off of copyright holders to prove copyright infringement.[163] Rather, takedown regimes "allow anyone to effectively shut down" a site held by a service provider "simply by filing the notice."[164]

It is clear that content filtering works more efficiently than a DMCA take-down only regime. Content filtering affords service providers actual know-ledge that a work is appearing unlicensed, and gives content providers a cheap, fast, and sometimes profitable way to identify infringing material. But there was no mention of filtering technology in the opinion. Most likely, the court felt restrained by prior precedent set by *Perfect 10, Inc. v. CCBill LLC*, which essentially refused to place any investigative burden on service providers to seek out infringed content. And of course content filtering is not in the DMCA—for obvious reasons it was not even a splinter in Congress' mind's eye.

The DMCA takedown system is a blunt instrument compared to the relatively elegant tool of content filtering. Indeed, YouTube's Content ID has essentially

---

158 *Viacom v. YouTube*, 718 F. Supp. 2d 514, 524 (S.D.N.Y. 2010), *appeal docketed*, No. 10-3270 (2nd Cir. Dec. 3, 2010).

159 *Ibid.*

160 Kravets, op. cit.

161 Jacqui Cheng (2010) *DMCA Abuse Extends to Twitter Posts*, ArsTechnica (Dec. 23). Online. http://arstechnica.com/tech-policy/news/2010/04/dmca-abuse-extends-to-twitter-posts.ars.

162 Viacom International, Memorandum, op. cit., 66.

163 *Design Furnishings, Inc. v. Zen Path LLC*, CIV. 2:10-02765, 2010 WL 4321568, at *5 (E.D. Cal. Oct. 21, 2010).

164 *Ibid.*

solved most future disputes between YouTube and content providers.[165] If the DMCA can be revised to have some kind of requirement for content filtering, courts will not have to cling to the takedown procedure as the only means to protect OSPs from crippling liability. This will force emerging companies to use filtering technology, and courts will not have to make hamstrung legal judgments to protect those companies from the mechanics of the DMCA.[166]

Conclusion

The district court's decision was appealed to the circuit court of appeals. In many ways, the abrupt reasoning of the court, and its possible overreaching (in terms of the law) to achieve a just social result, may end up hurting YouTube in the end. It was to be expected that the issues of specific infringements, pervasive knowledge of massive infringement, and DMCA takedown notices in lieu of other red flags would come up in the appellate court's opinion. It was also to be expected that the appellate court might similarly brush up against the issues of statutory damages and the DMCA's silence on content filtering. If the reasoning of the district court was not strong enough to withstand scrutiny, YouTube would still be at risk. These problems suggest that the DMCA requires reform to suit a Web 2.0 digital landscape. Only then will hamstrung decisions like *Viacom v. YouTube* be a thing of the past. The DMCA has lasted more than a decade because of the tools it has provided to content owners and service providers. In order to survive the next decade, the DMCA may need to sharpen its knives.

---

165 Menell, *Intellectual Property Issues*, op. cit.
166 Many commentators have advised against such a requirement. Brown, op. cit., 455; see also Hormann, op. cit., 1350. Others have tacitly accepted such a proposal. See Samuelson et al., op. cit., 20–21; see also Brett White (2010) 'Note, *Viacom v. YouTube*: A Proving Ground for DMCA Safe Harbors Against Secondary Liability,' *St John's Journal of Legal Commentary*, 24: 847.

5   Who controls the Internet?

The Second Circuit on YouTube

Hannibal Travis[1]

On appeal to the Second Circuit, Viacom attempted to distinguish YouTube and other "media" sites from Hotmail and other "private" storage sites (Viacom, 2011, 38). Viacom had also pointed out that YouTube was disqualified from asserting the Digital Millennium Copyright Act (DMCA) safe harbor because it obtained a direct financial benefit from users visiting the site to find unlicensed "premium" copyrighted material, and to view it without permission (Viacom, 2011, 25–34). Moreover, Viacom alleged that YouTube employees featured popular music or music videos on the site in order to maximize viewership, and targeted advertisements to unlicensed copyrighted videos (Viacom, 2011, 36). In their brief as amici curiae supporting Viacom, the Motion Picture Association of America (MPAA) and Independent Film & Television Alliance (IFTA) argued that YouTube should be found liable for copyright infringement because its founders encouraged the uploading of popular copyrighted video in order to become a destination site that could be sold at a high price to a larger company such as Google, that they were aware of patterns of infringement that they did nothing about, and they derived a direct financial benefit from these patterns of infringement (MPAA and IFTA, 2011, 1–31).

Furthermore, Viacom and the MPAA/IFTA appealed to the legislative history of the DMCA. Viacom maintained that Congress had intended site owners to respond on their own to infringements that would be "apparent to a reasonable person" (Viacom, 2011, 8, quoting U.S. House of Representatives, 1998, 53). Moreover, it said that Congress had envisioned that Web sites would be barred from protection under the safe harbor when either one file or page on them, or their entire site, was "obviously infringing," given the descriptions and advertisements used on the site (Viacom, 2011, 8, quoting U.S. House of Representatives, 1998, 58). In this way, and by mandating that sites not prevent copyright owners from finding infringements and complaining about them, Congress had tried to provide "strong incentives for service

---

1 Associate Professor of Law, Florida International University College of Law.

providers and copyright owners to cooperate to detect and deal with copyright infringement that takes place in the digital networked environment" (Viacom, 2011, 16, quoting U.S. House of Representatives, 1998, 49). The MPAA and IFTA argued that the Senate had intended that site owners as well as content owners "cooperate to detect and deal with copyright infringements that take place in the digital networked environment" (MPAA and IFTA, 2011, 3 quoting S. Rep. No. 105-190, at 20 (1998)). They also emphasized references to a "red flag" test in the legislative history, as setting forth a rule that Web site owners who ignore a "red flag" of infringing activity would be liable (MPAA and IFTA, 2011, 23, quoting U.S. Senate, 1998, 44; U.S. House of Representatives, 1998, 53).

The Second Circuit rejected Viacom's argument that YouTube's transcoding of user-supplied videos into the Adobe Flash format, or their streaming to other users, exceeded the DMCA safe harbor (Viacom, 2012, 40). The Second Circuit partially agreed with it that YouTube would not enjoy the safe harbor if it directly benefited from infringement it had the right and ability to control (Viacom, 2012, 38). It did not, however, find that Viacom had prevailed in arguing that because YouTube imposed detailed terms of service, it had enough control over the videos to be liable for their infringing content without the benefit of the DMCA's protection (Viacom, 2012, 37–8). This may have been because eBay, Facebook and other amici warned of the following potential consequences if the mere existence of terms of service allowing a site's operators to control its content made the DMCA inapplicable:

- "the suppression of some lawful, creative works and uses as a by-product of extra protection for other creative works and uses" (eBay et al., 2011, 28);
- threats to "many innovative Internet-based services, marketplaces, communities, and platforms, [which] have arisen or expanded due in substantial part to the safe harbor" (eBay et al., 2011, 9);
- "time sensitive videos making fair use of clips [may be] automatically blocked, their timeliness and impact [being] lost and they [will be] effectively censored" (Public Knowledge, 2011, 11);
- YouTube may rely on "automated content matching, with its thousands of false positives and inability to distinguish fair use, which will inevitably reduce the free flow of speech and expression online" (Public Knowledge, 2011, 11);
- "some 7,363 videos would be flagged for infringements [each year] when they did not even match a clip provided by cooperating copyright holders" as a result of "false positives" during "content matching" (Public Knowledge, 2011, 9–10);
- "flagging thousands of user videos as infringing [could] chill free speech and harm free expression" (Public Knowledge, 2011, 11);
- "broadcasters [have] sent DMCA takedown notices to remove political ads from a number of [political] campaigns without considering fair

use and ... such removal chilled political speech" (National Alliance for Media Art and Culture et al., 2011, 21–2);

- Congress noted in the legislative history "the *undesirability* of service-providers' monitoring (and functioning as private censors of) content their customers loaded" (Human Rights Watch et al., 2010, 24, citing S. Rep. 105-190 at 32); and
- "the prospect of billions of dollars in damages claims (and [YouTube's] reported litigation costs into the nine digits) is certain to deter firms that might otherwise enter the field to develop the next 'generation' of internet-based platforms and media, those that will make Facebook and YouTube seem dated," which will "drive smaller firms and non-profits to the side-lines" (Human Rights Watch et al., 2010, 20).

Ultimately, the Second Circuit struck a middle ground and left Internet entrepreneurs facing a great deal of uncertainty in the wake of its decision. The district court must make findings on a number of disputed elements of the DMCA safe harbor, on remand. These include: whether YouTube had knowledge or awareness of any specific instances of infringement of clips properly named by Viacom and the class action plaintiffs, so that a reasonable jury could rule that YouTube failed to take enough action to warrant the safe harbor; whether YouTube manifested a willful blindness as to specific instances of infringement on its site; whether YouTube had the right and ability to control the infringement—beyond having general control over when videos are removed—and derived a financial benefit from the scale of the infringement; and whether the "syndication" of YouTube videos to YouTube's commercial clients such as Verizon exceeded the scope of the user-directed "storage" safe harbor (Viacom, 2012, 41–2).

Commentators had varying reactions to the decision. Copyright and cyberlaw expert Eric Goldman remarked that the decision gave the plaintiffs a "superficial (but ultimately false) hope" of victory, "while remanding the case to an almost certain defense win (just at a much higher cost)" (Goldman, 2012). On the other hand, the chair of the Intellectual Property Law Section of the Federal Bar Association, Jack C. Schechter, observed that the Second Circuit "avoided an opportunity to provide some much needed clarity and, by and large, punted on this question" of what is sufficient "control" of users' content to make the safe harbor inapplicable (Schechter, 2012, 22). He described the decision as leaving online copyright law largely unchanged. In a similar vein, copyright expert Peter Menell viewed the Second Circuit's decision as absolving YouTube of any liability except in a few instances, in an act of judicial policymaking to avoid giving an unjust "windfall" to plaintiffs or imposing a disproportionate penalty on YouTube (Menell, 2012). James McQuivey, an analyst for Forrester Research, called the decision a victory for delay more than anything else, because more proceedings were needed after five years of copyright litigation that could take the Web "back to the stone age" (quoted in Stelter, 2012). At the other extreme, Richard Busch of

Forbes.com argued that the Second Circuit may have appreciably slowed the pace of infringement online, driving more sites to ask permission to post content (Busch, 2012). Likewise, Viacom hailed the decision as sending a clear message that "intentionally ignoring theft is not protected by the law" (quoted in Bray, 2012).

My own view is that the court could have struck a better balance between fidelity to the text and legislative history of the DMCA, and the goal of maximizing creative expression. It was right to confirm that the DMCA provides a defense to sites with knowledge of *any* infringement, or with control over which videos are removed for violation of the terms of service, or that provide streaming as well as storage functionality. The court should have provided more clarity, however, as to what degree of control is required before DMCA protection is lost.[2] And it was wrong to say that YouTube could be held liable for willful blindness, given the intention of Congress to make clear in the text and history of the DMCA that sites do not have a duty to proactively seek out and police infringement. As the court noted, § 512(m) of the DMCA states "that safe harbor protection shall not be conditioned on 'a service provider monitoring its service or affirmatively seeking facts indicating infringing activity, except to the extent consistent with a standard technical measure complying with the provisions of subsection (i)'" (Viacom, 2012, 35, quoting 17 U.S.C. § 512(m)(1)). Moreover, under another section, there is no obligation to develop or purchase content matching tools like AudibleMagic CopySense, which can flag (and possibly trigger the deletion of) lawful commentary or parody videos and a variety of other free speech activity.[3] Congress intended to relieve Web sites and their users of the burden of the sites' making "discriminating judgments about potential copyright infringement," a burden arguably reintroduced by the Second Circuit due to the brevity and lack of clarity of its decision (H.R. Rep. No. 105-551, pt 2,

2 The United States Court of Appeals for the Ninth Circuit and the United States District Court for the Central District of California have both, appropriately, ruled that "control" in the context of the DMCA means "control over specific infringing activity the provider knows about" and refuses to respond to, not control over its services in general, which every online service provider typically possesses: *UMG Recordings, Inc. v. Shelter Capital Partners LLC*, 667 F. 3d 1022, 1043 (9th Cir. 2011). Section 512(c), which was at issue in YouTube, applies on its face to "storage" of "material" on a "system" that is "controlled" by or for the service provider. *UMG Recordings, Inc. v. Veoh Networks Inc.*, 665 F. Supp. 2d 1099, 1113 (C.D. Cal. 2009). Nearly all Internet communication travels through networks and systems along which various providers are "transmitting, routing, or providing connections for, material through a system or network controlled or operated by or for the service provider," and Congress intended to shield most of this traffic from copyright liability in § 512 of the DMCA: 17 U.S.C. 512(a).

3 Section 512(i) recognizes the obligation of an online storage provider to "accommodate" and to "not interfere" with "standard technical measures," but defines them not as being bought or made by the providers, but as "technical measures that are used by copyright owners to identify or protect copyrighted works": 17 U.S.C. 512(i).

at 58 (1998)). Basic considerations of due process and legal precision dictate that an automatic copyright filter cannot replace the reasoned judgment of a court.

Bibliography

Bray, Chad (2012). 'Viacom Advances in YouTube Suit,' *The Wall Street Journal*, Apr. 5. Online. Available at: <http://online.wsj.com/article/SB100014240527023 03302504577325601224390774.html> (accessed Sept. 1, 2012).

Busch, Richard (2012). 'How the Second Circuit's Decision in Viacom May Change the Web,' *Forbes.com*. Online. Available at: <http://www.forbes.com/sites/ richardbusch/2012/05/30/how-the-second-circuits-decision-in-viacom-may-change-the-web/> (accessed Sept. 1, 2012).

Digital Millennium Copyright Act of 1998, House Report, H.R. Rep. No. 105–551 (1998).

Digital Millennium Copyright Act of 1998, Senate Report, S. Rep. 105–190 (1998).

eBay Inc.; Facebook, Inc.; IAC/InteractiveCorp; and Yahoo! Inc., Brief for Amici Curiae Supporting Defendants-Appellees and Urging Affirmance (2011) *Viacom International Inc. v. YouTube, Inc., YouTube, LLC and Google, Inc.*, 676 F. 3d 19 (2nd Cir. 2012) (No. 10-3270), (Apr. 14). Online. Available at: <web2.westlaw.com> (search for "2011 WL 1536815").

Goldman, Eric (2012). 'From Eric's Blog,' *Cyberspace Law*, 17: 21 (2012). Online. Available at: <http://www.lexis.com> (accessed 10 July 2012).

Human Rights Watch; Freedom House; Reporters without Borders; and Access, Brief for Amici Curiae in Support Defendants-Appellees (2010) *Viacom International Inc. v. YouTube, Inc., YouTube, LLC and Google, Inc.*, 676 F. 3d 19 (2nd Cir. 2012) (No. 10-3270). Online. Available at: <web2.westlaw.com> (search for "2010 WL 6510616").

Menell, Peter (2012). 'Judicial Regulation of Digital Copyright Windfalls: Making Interpretive and Policy Sense of *Viacom v. YouTube* and *UMG Recordings v. Shelter Capital Partners*.' 2012 IP Viewpoints. Online. Available at: <http://www.mediainstitute.org/IPI/2012/050212.php> (accessed Sept. 1, 2012).

MPAA and IFTA (2011) Brief as Amici Curiae Supporting Appellants, *Viacom International Inc. v. YouTube, Inc., YouTube, LLC and Google, Inc.*, 676 F. 3d 19 (2d Cir. 2012) (No. 10-3270) (Sept. 27). Online. Available at: <web2.westlaw.com> (search for "2011 WL 4541965").

National Alliance for Media Art and Culture and the Alliance for Community Media (2011) Brief of Amici Curiae in Support of Defendants-Appellees and in Support of Affirmance, *Viacom International Inc. v. YouTube, LLC and Google, Inc.*, 676 F. 3d 19 (2nd Cir. 2012) (No. 10-3270) (Apr. 7). Online. Available at: <web2.westlaw. com> (search for "2011 WL 1461433").

Public Knowledge, Brief as Amicus Curiae Supporting Defendants-Appellees and Urging Affirmance, *Viacom International Inc. v. YouTube, Inc., YouTube, LLC and Google, Inc.*, 676 F. 3d 19 (2nd Cir. 2012) (No. 10-3270), 2011 WL 4541968 (Sept. 27, 2011).

Schechter, Jack (2012). 'Is It Safe? The Digital Millennium Copyright Act's "Safe Harbor" in the Wake of *Viacom v. YouTube*,' *Federal Lawyer*, 59: 16–22.

Stelter, Brian (2012). 'Appeals Court Revives Viacom Suit Against YouTube,' *The New York Times Media Decoder Blog*, Apr. 5, Online. Available at: <http://mediadecoder.blogs.nytimes.com/2012/04/05/appeals-court-revives-viacom-suit-against-youtube/> (accessed Sept. 1, 2012).

U.S. House of Representatives (1998) H.R. Rep. No. 105–551, pt 2.

U.S. Senate (1998), Senate Report No. 105–190.

Viacom International, Reply Brief for Plaintiffs-Appellants (2011) *Viacom International Inc. v. YouTube, Inc., YouTube, LLC and Google, Inc.*, 676 F. 3d 19 (2nd Cir. 2012) (No. 10-3270) (Apr. 28). Online. Available at: <web2.westlaw.com> (search for "2011 WL 1747058").

Viacom International v. YouTube, Inc. (2012) 676 F. 3d 19 (2nd Cir.).

6 Is eBay counterfeiting?

Jasmine Abdel-khalik[1]

eBay is "the world's largest online marketplace, where practically anyone can buy and sell practically anything" (eBay, 2012). Rather than serve as a procurer and distributor of its own or others' products, eBay's business model is to use the Internet to facilitate individuals' sales of their own goods to buyers. It is the sellers that write the listings, possess the goods, and send the goods to the eventual buyers. eBay itself never has physical possession of the items sold. However, Tiffany (NJ) Inc. and Tiffany and Company (Tiffany) believe that many, if not most, of the eBay listings for TIFFANY-branded goods are, in fact, counterfeit. Accordingly, Tiffany sued eBay in 2004 based upon these third parties using eBay to sell counterfeit TIFFANY-branded goods.

Because eBay only provides a service for others to use, how could Tiffany allege that eBay is liable for counterfeiting marks on goods? The answer lies in both the nature of trademark protection and the expansion of trademark infringement actions beyond the direct infringer. But, as eBay ultimately was not held liable, the case raises the question of whether an Internet business model, interacting with real world goods, requires a change in our liability rules.

Trademarks and counterfeiting

Trademarks are used to identify the source of a product and are the repository of a company's goodwill, meaning the consumer's reaction to the product that may make him or her more (or less) likely to purchase the same product in the future. If a consumer buys a Coca-Cola drink and has a positive experience, then the engendered goodwill makes it more likely that the consumer will buy it in the future. And the consumer can use the trademark to identify that preferred good as coming from the same source. Therefore, trademarks

---

1 Associate Professor of Law, University of Missouri at Kansas City School of Law.

are effective tools to allow consumers to distinguish competing products and choose the products appropriate for their needs. Trademarks also encourage owners to invest in products that will engender the level of goodwill they seek. Because they encompass goodwill, trademarks are an essential part of most companies' intellectual property portfolio and overall asset value. For example, The Coca-Cola Company has identified its brand value at $71.9 billion, whereas its total asset value is nearly $80 billion (2012, p. 11). Although all companies do not have the same proportion of intangible to tangible asset value, trademarks are of significant importance for many businesses.

Protecting trademarks from infringement prevents other entities from obtaining the benefits of the trademark owners and, therefore, their consumers. To prevent this unfair competition, there are numerous ways to enforce trademark rights. Probably the most common form is a traditional likelihood of confusion claim, where the trademark owner proves that the purported infringer's mark is likely to create confusion as to source, sponsorship, affiliation, or endorsement. Although the traditional form of likelihood of confusion focuses on the consumer at the point of purchase, some courts have recognized other forms of confusion involving capturing the initial interest of consumers, even though they are no longer confused at the point of sale, or confusing people other than the consumer when they see the consumer with the product after the sale.

Another way that trademark owners protect their trademarks' value is to pursue counterfeiters. Counterfeiting occurs when an infringer intentionally reproduces an identical (or nearly identical) copy of another entity's trademarks on the infringer's products without permission from the trademark owner. To be an effective counterfeit product, the infringer generally uses the mark on a product similar in type to the trademark owner's products. For example, a stereotypical counterfeiting case may involve a counterfeiter selling a watch that looks like a ROLEX-brand watch but is sold under a BOLEX mark.

The harm caused by counterfeiting can be significant in one or more ways, particularly because counterfeiters often target luxury goods. Customers who buy counterfeit products may be lost customers of the trademark owner because the customers are purchasing the infringer's products rather than the trademark owner's product. On the other hand, one cannot simply assume that the counterfeiter's sales accurately reflect the trademark owner's loss as many of the counterfeiter's customers may not be financially able to afford the full-priced, luxury products. However, trademark owners also may lose customers because the lower quality counterfeit products cause a loss of goodwill (*Diane Von Furstenberg Studio*, 2007, p. 16). For example, even though the purchaser may be aware that he or she is purchasing a counterfeit good, those who see the consumer with the product now associate the (generally) lower-quality product with the trademark owner, diminishing the trademark owner's goodwill and potential sales (*Cartier*, 2005, p. 361).

These harms can be exponentially increased by the wide reach of the Internet (*Diane Von Furstenberg Studio*, 2007, pp. 16–17).

The origins of contributory liability in modern trademark infringement

Once any kind of trademark infringement is identified, most trademark litigation involves the trademark owner suing the direct infringer, the party selling the infringing goods or services. But there are occasions where suing the direct infringer is less useful for a number of reasons, including that a direct infringement suit may be less successful in ending the infringement, more harmful to business relationships, or less effective in incentivizing non-infringing behavior. For example, if someone other than the direct infringer has control over the direct infringer's actions, as in an employer-employee relationship, then perhaps a suit against the entity in control will be more effective in preventing future infringement. The question becomes what standards should guide the court in separating third parties who should be liable from those who should not be.

In 1982, the Supreme Court recognized contributory liability, a form of secondary liability, for modern trademark infringement in *Inwood Laboratories v. Ives Laboratories*. Ives sold the drug cyclandelate under the trademark CYCLOSPASMOL in either a blue capsule or a combination blue-red capsule depending on dosage. When Ives' patent on the drug expired, several competitors began to sell a generic version and utilized the same color coded packages to denote the dosages. Although the competitors clearly identified the origin of the products when selling their products to pharmacies, some pharmacists allegedly would dispense the generic pills under Ives trademark, CYCLOSPASMOL, rather than the drug's generic name. It is these pharmacists who could be subject to direct infringement claims, and there must be direct infringement before a contributory liability claim is viable. Instead of pursuing the direct infringers, Ives sued the generic pill competitors on the theory that the competitors "contributed to the infringing activities of pharmacists who mislabeled generic cyclandelate" through using the same color coding for the pills and promoting the generic medicine as equivalent to Ives' trademarked product (*Inwood*, 1982, p. 850). The Court recognized that the competitors could be contributorily liable if they (1) intentionally induced another to infringe or (2) continued to supply their goods to other entities when they knew or had reason to know that the other entities are directly infringing (*Inwood*, 1982, pp. 854, 860–61). The decision cemented the viability of contributory liability in modern trademark infringement cases and articulated a clear test. This is particularly notable because the Lanham Act, the federal statute providing for trademark protection in addition to common law protection, does not explicitly include secondary liability infringement. Instead, contributory liability is "a judicially created doctrine that derives from the common law of torts" (*Tiffany*, 2010, p. 103).

Evolving the second prong of contributory liability-facilitation

As an initial matter, there was some question post-*Inwood* as to whether contributory liability could be raised against service providers. As the Court in *Inwood* framed contributory liability, it applies in cases involving manufacturers or distributors of goods.

Contributory liability, however, has been extended to service providers. In a case involving a bricks-and-mortar analogy to eBay's Internet services, the Hard Rock Café Licensing Corporation (Hard Rock) sued Concession Services based upon two of its flea markets in the Chicago area, where an investigator had discovered obviously counterfeit goods. As such, Hard Rock's case was based on the services provided by Concession Services, which allowed vendors to sell their goods. In its 1992 decision, the Seventh Circuit Court of Appeals turned to common law tort principles, specifically those applicable to landlords or licensors, to determine that a flea market operator could be held liable under the same contributory liability standard as a manufacturer or distributor of counterfeit goods (*Hard Rock Café*, 1992, pp. 1148–9). Subsequently, courts routinely have found that contributory liability is as viable for services as it is for goods.

After the *Inwood* decision, perhaps the most heavily litigated aspect of contributory trademark liability is the appropriate scope of the second prong—continuing to supply goods to other entities when the purported infringer knew or had reason to know that the other entities are directly infringing. Specifically, there are two often contested issues: (1) although service providers can be liable, what kind should be and (2) what kind of knowledge do these service providers need to have to be liable.

First, with respect to the type of service entities subject to contributory liability, the Seventh Circuit in *Hard Rock Café* essentially used the landlord/licensor discussion to assess whether the operator of a flea market is more like a manufacturer/distributor, thus subject to liability, or more like a temporary help service, which should not be subject to liability. The implicit conflict sidestepped by the *Hard Rock Café* court is how to define the broader nature of service providers that should be subject to contributory liability. When addressing the same issue, the Ninth Circuit Court of Appeals in *Fonovisa, Inc. v. Cherry Auction, Inc.*, a similar swap meet case, adopted wholesale the Seventh Circuit's analogy to landlord liability (1996, p. 265). The Ninth Circuit found that there were sufficient facts for a contributory liability claim where the operator supplied parking, conducted advertising, retained the right to exclude any vendor for any reason, and received fees from customers. However, this still did not provide clear parameters to define when other types of service providers could be held liable.

The Ninth Circuit subsequently had the opportunity to address the appropriate, broader standard for policing trademark infringement in cyberspace in *Lockheed Martin Corporation v. Network Solutions (NSI), Inc.* Lockheed Martin sued NSI because of third parties registering domain names with NSI containing variations on a Lockheed Martin trademark, SKUNK WORKS. The Ninth Circuit stated that courts should "consider the extent of control exercised by the defendant over the third party's means of infringement[,]" specifically if the service provider has "direct control and monitoring of the instrumentality used by a third party" (*Lockheed Martin*, 1999, p. 984). And while leasing real estate allows for control and monitoring of direct infringers, NSI's service, routing domain name addresses to the registrant's IP address, does not. Prior to *Tiffany v. eBay*, district courts in Ohio, Michigan, and Maryland indicated a willingness to adopt the Ninth Circuit's direct control and monitoring standard for contributory trademark infringement by service providers (*Habeeba's Dance of the Arts*, 2006, p. 714; *Ford Motor Company*, 2001, pp. 646–7; *Fare Deals*, 2001, p. 689). Courts in the Seventh Circuit, however, have split on whether to utilize the direct control and monitoring standard (*Medline Industries*, 992, n.3).

Second, in addition to assessing whether a service provider is liable, the second prong of contributory liability requires that the purportedly infringing entity knows or has reason to know that the other entities are directly infringing. Addressing "reason to know" (also called constructive knowledge), the *Hard Rock Café* court defined it as requiring that the defendant "understand what a reasonably prudent person would understand" but also not imposing a duty to search for violations (1992, p. 1149). Few courts before *Tiffany v. eBay* wrestled with this particular requirement in detail.

Instead, courts focused on the parameters for demonstrating actual knowledge and the associated issue of willful blindness. In the *Hard Rock Café* case, Concession Services had minimal supervision of the vendors, did not keep records of the vendors' names and addresses, and had neither been asked to participate in nor voluntarily investigated past seizures of counterfeit goods, even though it had a policy of cooperating with trademark owners. These facts precluded arguing that Concession Services had actual knowledge of the vendors selling counterfeit goods.

However, the Seventh Circuit held that willful blindness is the equivalent of actual knowledge and could exist in this case. Despite the fact that there is no duty to preemptively investigate on the chance that some direct infringement may be happening, the purported contributory infringer also cannot bury its head in the sand because it fears that an investigation will reveal infringement. Thus, willful blindness is the equivalent of actual knowledge when the defendant "suspect[s] wrongdoing and deliberately fail[s] to investigate" (*Hard Rock Café*, 1992, p. 1149). In this case, there was some evidence that one of the managers may have suspected that there were counterfeit goods but did not further investigate. Having insufficient facts to assess whether there was willful blindness, the court could not decide the issue. Building on *Hard Rock Café*, the Ninth Circuit found in *Fonovisa* that there could be sufficient facts for a contributory liability claim in a swap market case where the local Sherriff's Department had successfully raided the swap meet for counterfeit goods and had sent a letter warning of on-going sales of infringing materials.

These cases confirm that actual and constructive knowledge is sufficient for the second prong and that willful blindness is the equivalent of actual knowledge. However, the facilitation prong continues to be the most litigated aspect of the contributory trademark liability standard, and these discussions continued in the next significant decision, *Tiffany v. eBay*.

The online marketplace and contributory liability

Tiffany's suit against eBay, while not the first decision to involve contributory trademark liability claims based on Internet services, is noteworthy because it not only further clarified contributory liability standards, but it did so in an Internet case with facts parallel to previously decided flea market cases. Thus, unlike some other Internet-based cases, *Tiffany v. eBay* involves the hybrid situation where the infringement overlaps the cyberworld and the real world.

As with many counterfeiting cases, Tiffany is a well established, luxury brand, specifically known for its high quality jewelry and other household goods sold under several Tiffany marks, and as is true for other luxury brands, maintaining its strong reputation is "critical to Tiffany's success ...." (*Tiffany*, 2008, pp. 471–2). Tiffany undertakes significant steps to ensure that its silver jewelry satisfies "Tiffany's exacting standards for, *inter alia*, composition, quality, shape, and polish of the metal, as well as the quality and integrity of the TIFFANY Marks appearing on the item" and "quality inspectors must be able to physically inspect each item" (*Tiffany*, 2008, p. 472). Moreover, Tiffany maintains tight control over its distribution chain. It sells its goods through official stores and its website and only sells discounted products to certain corporate accounts and international markets. There is, of course, the possibility that Tiffany customers would resell their purchases, demonstrating the need for a secondary market of legitimate Tiffany goods.

The court extensively discussed eBay's business model. To sell goods through eBay's service, third parties must register for an account and agree to the terms of the User Agreement. The User Agreement allows eBay to penalize sellers who violate any laws, eBay policies, or third party rights, up to and including suspending the user. After registering, sellers create their own listings and choose if they are going to sell their products through an auction, fixed price listings, or a hybrid between the two.[2] While eBay does not create the listings or have physical possession of the goods, it does provide services, marketing information, and support for its sellers to assist in increasing their sales on eBay and runs promotions, including ones to increase sales of luxury

---

2 Although eBay has a classified ad service as well, this service was not at issue.

brands. eBay's revenues come from an initial fee for each listing and, if the seller's goods are sold, a fee based upon the final price. Additional fees are charged for additional listing features, such as differentiating fonts, and PayPal, an eBay company, also charges a fee to process payment.

Recognizing the potential for third parties to sell counterfeit goods through its service, eBay has instituted a number of anti-counterfeiting measures. In addition to having a large group of customer service representatives, eBay, initially manually and then through software, searches listings for specific language that indicates problems, including indicia of counterfeiting. The software also evaluates other information that could suggest counterfeiting, such as prior issues associated with the seller's account. Any problem listings are flagged for review and resolution by customer service representatives. To facilitate gathering further information and eliminating problem listings, eBay created the VeRO program, where rights owners, like Tiffany, could report any potentially infringing listing they have identified using a "Notice of Claimed Infringement" (NOCI) form. eBay generally responds to NOCIs by removing the listing within twenty-four hours.

Despite these programs, Tiffany believed, and the trial court ultimately found, that "a significant portion [although not all] of the 'Tiffany' sterling silver jewelry" listed on eBay was actually counterfeit (*Tiffany*, 2008, p. 486). This belief was supported by numerous customer complaints based on purchases through eBay. After trying to pursue individual counterfeiters, Tiffany contacted eBay to demand that eBay take more proactive measures to prevent the listing and sale of counterfeit Tiffany branded goods on its website, such as banning listings selling five or more Tiffany goods. Tiffany also utilized the VeRO program to report over 284,000 listings in less than five years as containing potentially counterfeit Tiffany goods. While eBay would remove the listing after receiving a report, it would not automatically suspend the associated seller simply based on Tiffany's claims that the seller's listing seemed to contain counterfeit goods. eBay generally would suspend sellers under a "three strikes rule" although a seller could be suspended after the first violation if "the seller 'listed a number of infringing items,' and '[selling counterfeit merchandise] appears to be the only thing they've come to eBay to do'" (*Tiffany*, 2012, p. 100). eBay also undertook some additional steps, some implemented after litigation began, to identify listings containing counterfeit Tiffany goods.

The most difficult aspect of determining if a specific listing contains counterfeit Tiffany products is the inability to have the kind of physical inspection that occurred in earlier cases, such as *Hard Rock Café* and *Fonovisa*. While an eBay listing may contain a photograph of the product(s) to be sold, it is a paltry substitute for an in-person inspection.

For example, the below screenshots compare a product sold on eBay with the comparable product listed on Tiffany's website. Although the shape of the eBay item seems similar if not identical, the color is more green than the trademark Tiffany blue. That difference may be a function of the camera,

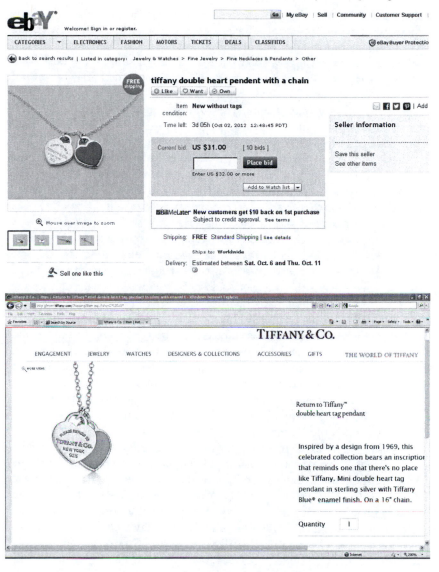

Figure 6.1 Screenshots of eBay.com and Tiffany.com, circa 2012.

lighting, or something else not related to the product itself. Without a physical inspection, it is difficult to know whether this is a counterfeit or genuine Tiffany product. The trial court recognized this problem when it found that, particularly with respect to products like those sold by Tiffany, "in many instances, determining whether an item is counterfeit will require a physical inspection of the item, and some degree of expertise on the part of the examiner" (*Tiffany*, 2008, p. 472 n.7). eBay never has physical possession of the products.

Tiffany cannot obtain physical possession without simply purchasing the products itself, not only creating a financial burden but effectively eliminating the secondary market for genuine Tiffany products. So, which entity should bear the burden of assessing whether listings contain counterfeit goods?

Believing that the burden should be on eBay, Tiffany sued eBay on several grounds, including contributory liability for counterfeit goods sold on eBay's website. Utilizing the *Inwood* standard, Tiffany argued that eBay continued to supply its services to direct infringers when it knew or had reason to know that the other entities were directly infringing due to the wide-spread sale of counterfeit products. Following the modern trend, the trial court found that the *Inwood* standard does applies to service providers and assessed whether eBay had sufficient control of the service so that it could be subject to liability.[3] Despite eBay's arguments to the contrary, the trial court found that eBay does exercise sufficient control and monitoring. eBay has control over its website (the medium used by the direct infringers), the transactions conducted through the website, and the listings on the website. eBay promotes the sale of Tiffany jewelry items and profits from the listing and sale of items. Based on these factors, eBay is the Internet analogy to flea markets and satisfies the first requirement for contributory liability under *Inwood*'s second prong.

However, Tiffany was ultimately unsuccessful in its contributory liability claim because it was unable to convince either the trial court or the Second Circuit Court of Appeals that eBay knew or had reason to know of the direct infringers' actions. For those listings specifically identified by Tiffany, eBay responded and, thus, could not be contributorily liable. For the rest of the listings, the trial court noted that there should be a high burden to establish knowledge. Adopting factors from an Eleventh Circuit Court of Appeals decision, a court should "'consider the nature and extent of the communication,' whether the defendant 'explicitly or implicitly encouraged the trademark violations,' 'the extent and nature of the violations being committed,' and whether there was a 'bad faith refusal to exercise a clear contractual power to halt the infringing activities ...'" (*Tiffany*, 2008, p. 508). Tiffany argued that, based upon its notice that there was a substantial amount of counterfeit goods on sale or taking the evidence "as a whole," eBay had sufficient knowledge to satisfy the contributory liability standard (*Tiffany*, 2010, p. 107). Finding that Tiffany provided "*generalized* notice that some portion of the Tiffany goods sold on its website might be counterfeit" both courts found the evidence insufficient (*Tiffany*, 2010, pp. 106, 109). eBay must have knowledge of (or reason to know about) specific listings that infringe. The fact that a listing *might* contain counterfeit goods is inadequate to impose liability on

---

3 Because the issue was not contested on appeal, the Second Circuit Court of Appeals, it assumed that *Inwood* applies to service providers without deciding it. Subsequent Second Circuit district courts have applied *Inwood* to service providers.

eBay, particularly when Tiffany cannot allege that all Tiffany goods sold through eBay are counterfeit.

The *Tiffany* courts also assessed whether eBay was willfully blind. The trial court equated willful blindness with constructive knowledge, and the Second Circuit equated willful blindness with actual knowledge, but both reached the same result. eBay was not willfully blind because it must suspect wrongdoing of specific individuals. Utilizing a narrower definition than used in *Hard Rock Café*, the *Tiffany* trial court held that willful blindness requires that "the defendant knew of a high probability of illegal conduct and purposefully contrived to avoid learning of it, for example, by failing to inquire further out of fear of the result of the inquiry" (*Tiffany*, 2008, p. 515). The appellate court did not specifically reference the trial court's high standard when it defined willful blindness; rather, it harkened back to previous courts' decisions by imposing liability when a service provider has "reason to suspect" infringement (*Tiffany*, 2010, pp. 109–10). Regardless, without receiving specific knowledge of individual infringers and failing to address it, eBay was not willfully blind. The *Tiffany* case appears to narrow contributory liability such that eBay's business model effectively avoids the possibility of contributory liability.

The consequences of *Tiffany v. eBay*

Following *Tiffany v. eBay*, courts continue to wrestle with the knowledge requirement for contributory liability's second prong. For example, a creative plaintiff argued that the accused contributory infringer had at least constructive knowledge ("reason to know") of the direct infringement because the trademark owner had a federal trademark registration (*GMA Accessories*, 2011, p. 466). Federal trademark registrations create constructive notice, meaning presumed notice to the world that an entity has claimed rights in a particular mark for a particular good or service. Of course, if the court were to agree that constructive notice based on registration is sufficient for contributory liability's constructive knowledge requirement, then it would essentially eliminate the knowledge requirement for all federally registered trademarks. Further, it would create great hardship for trademark owners who want to license their trademarks to third parties, who may find it difficult to sell their goods due to fear of potential liability when purchasing from anyone other than the trademark owners. Not surprisingly, the court refused to find constructive knowledge based upon the mere fact of a federal registration.

Perhaps reacting to the overbreadth of plaintiff's arguments, the court seems to suggest that the "reason to know" option is *only* satisfied by establishing willful blindness, which would limit the facilitation prong to either actual knowledge or willful blindness. Fortunately, not all post-*Tiffany* decisions have followed suit. For example, when considering if an executive is personally liable under a contributory infringement theory, a different court found that the executive would have reason to know of his furniture company's direct infringement based upon his substantive responsibilities and participation in the business, noting that he acquired actual knowledge later—after receiving a letter—and using willful blindness only as an alternative basis for the knowledge requirement (*Universal Furniture International*, 2011, pp. 47, 48 n.7). What these cases illustrate is the continuing struggle to define the contours of the knowledge requirement.

A potential additional consequence from the *Tiffany* decision could be a seismic shift to disposing quickly of any contributory infringement claims against Internet services based on the services' lack of knowledge. Certainly, that is the implication of the trial court's ruling in *Rosetta Stone v. Google, Inc.* Rosetta Stone sued Google because third parties were using the ROSETTA STONE mark as a keyword in Google's AdWord service, which meant that sellers of counterfeit Rosetta Stone products could pay to appear as a Sponsored Link when someone used the phrase Rosetta Stone in Google's search engine and also could use the trademark in their advertising text. At the summary judgment stage, Rosetta Stone's attorneys submitted a spreadsheet containing nearly 200 instances where Rosetta Stone provided specific notice of Sponsored Links advertising counterfeit products, purportedly without a sufficient response from Google (*Rosetta Stone*, 2012, p. 163). And yet, the trial court granted Google's summary judgment motion before trial at least partly because, relying on *Tiffany*, the court found that Google only had generalized knowledge of counterfeiting and could not determine which sellers were actually selling counterfeit Rosetta Stone products. In vacating this portion of the trial court's decision, the appellate court rightly attributed the pre-trial holding to an overextension on the *Tiffany* case (*Rosetta Stone*, 2012, p. 164). As of yet, however, there still is no determination whether Rosetta Stone will be successful in its claims.

One cannot say that all providers of Internet services are *per se* incapable of satisfying the knowledge requirement of contributory trademark liability simply by virtue of the fact that they provide Internet services. Some Internet services are far less attenuated from the evidence of counterfeiting. For example, a company that provided individual mentoring sessions and assistance in designing and building a website and registering the domain name copycatclubs.com for selling counterfeit and original golf clubs was liable for contributory trademark infringement (*Roger Cleveland Golf Company*, 2012, pp. 1–3, 5).

A purported contributory infringer is much more likely to be found knowledgeable of the direct infringement if the counterfeiting is prominently proclaimed or otherwise obviously intertwined with the service provided by the contributory infringer. In contrast, the *Rosetta Stone* case, much like the *Tiffany* dispute, involves a service that assists in selling a good, but the service is so attenuated from the product that the service provider could not see the physical object to assess whether it is counterfeit. The interesting issue resolved one way by *Tiffany* and not yet definitively answered in *Rosetta Stone* is how to determine liability when the reason why the entities have insufficient knowledge is the very business model created by these entities on the Internet. In other words, who should bear the burden of preventing counterfeit good sales when the service provider cannot assess the physical good sold by another because the service is provided on the Internet, and the other is careful to avoid labeling its goods as counterfeit?

Certainly, physical proximity increases control. In a recent bricks-and-mortar flea market case, the court reaffirmed that a flea market operator renting space to vendors, by its very physical proximity, has "substantially more control over potential direct infringers" than eBay or even the manufacturers in *Inwood* (*Coach*, 2011, pp. 20–21). Physical proximity also increases the likelihood of knowledge. Flea market operators, like the ones in *Hard Rock Café* and *Fonovisa*, have employees on site who can physically inspect vendors' merchandise and/or are aware of police raids or brand inspector assessments of the vendor's products. Such physical proximity is impossible on the Internet.

But what is true for the service provider is equally true, if not more so, for the trademark owner. It is difficult for companies to police unauthorized sales of goods when the sales occur on the Internet. The sheer magnitude of the Internet, and even the numerous listings that pop up in a single online marketplace, makes policing difficult for large companies like Tiffany and even more so for smaller companies without Tiffany's resources. As with Tiffany's own quality control rules, assessing the quality of a listed product in a secondary market would be easier with a physical inspection. But, for example, Tiffany cannot do so without purchasing every Tiffany brand product advertised, putting an untenable burden on the brand owners and depriving consumers of an Internet secondary market. And unlike the service providers, the brand owners have no control over the number of potential Internet marketplaces or how the marketplaces choose their customers, sell their products, or otherwise organize their business.

One might suggest that contributory liability is an unnecessary stick to prod service providers on the Internet, like eBay, to avoid offering services to counterfeit good sellers. As the trial court in *Tiffany* indicated, eBay has an interest in preventing counterfeiters from using its service in order to maintain eBay's reputation and avoid customer complaints (*Tiffany*, 2008, p.469). Despite that interest, eBay's very business model might allow it some latitude with customers, who are aware that eBay does not possess the physical products, as long as eBay is responsive to their immediate problems. The individual seller's reputation may suffer but perhaps customers' enthusiasm for using eBay's service may not be significantly diminished. And because eBay profits from each listing and transaction, "it has an incentive to permit such listings and sales to continue" (*Tiffany*, 2010, p. 109 n.13).

Unless a solution is found for this Internet created conflict, the cost of counterfeiting could be tremendous. Without an effective mechanism for ensuring trademark control, trademark owners may lose consumer goodwill because of the number of deceived consumers. Moreover, trademark owners may lose their incentive to create high quality products. Brand owners may start to believe that there is limited benefit to maintaining quality standards if customers do not feel that trademarks necessarily denote that quality. And in either instance, consumers lose.

There are two potential solutions to address the concerns raised by service providers on the Internet that are attenuated from the physical goods: soften the existing standards or change the standards. First, as courts continue to see Internet based contributory trademark infringement claims, it is possible that they will consider loosening the standard without actually changing the substantive requirements. In some ways, that liberalization may already be happening. In a pre-*Tiffany* case, the Ninth Circuit affirmed a motion to dismiss a contributory trademark infringement claim against credit card processing entities that processed payments on websites that were allegedly directly infringing on Perfect 10's copyrights and trademarks by selling Perfect 10's images. The court held that, because the defendants had no power to remove infringing material or directly stop their distribution over the Internet, control over the credit card processing system was insufficient to establish control over the "instrumentality" used to infringe. While refusing to process payments may have the practical effect of stopping or reducing the infringing activity, "[t]his, without more, does not constitute 'direct control'" (*Perfect 10*, 2007, p. 807).

One might think that a similar holding would occur when the direct infringement involved goods. But, in denying a motion to dismiss in a post-*Tiffany* case, another court reached a very different result for two of three contributory trademark defendants who provided credit card processing services for the sale of counterfeit goods. Keeping in mind that the control element is used to "exclude service providers that do not really contribute to the infringing conduct" and *liberally* citing the dissent from the *Perfect 10* decision, the court found that the "instrumentality" that must be controlled and monitored for contributory liability was a combination of the website offering and credit card processing (*Gucci*, 2010, pp. 250–52). The defendants could have refused to do business with the replica merchants, and given the prevalence of online credit card transactions, that refusal would have made the transactions significantly more difficult if not impossible. Notably, the court also found that the credit card transactions were more of an instrumentality in this case because the *Perfect 10* case involved infringing images. "[C]redit card services may not have been needed for a website to display infringing photographs," whereas payment is most definitely needed to sell counterfeit goods (*Gucci*, 2010, p. 253). Regardless, the *Gucci* court's decision indicates a willingness to broaden the contributory liability requirements to encompass an entity that it clearly believed was contributing to the infringement. Notably, the Ninth Circuit itself seemed to indicate a loosening of its standards when it held that web hosting entities were contributorily liable when some of its customers sold counterfeit goods through the websites. Because the contributory infringers controlled the websites, they "had direct control over the 'master switch' that kept the websites online and available" (*Louis Vuitton*, 2011, p. 943).

One could argue that this greater willingness to find sufficient "control" is a backlash against the unnecessarily stringent test created by the *Lockheed Martin* decision when it articulated the control and monitoring standard for service entities on the Internet. Although the court claimed that it was synthesizing prior decisions, none expressly discussed control and monitoring as the critical criteria for all contributory liability claims based on the facilitation prong. Alternatively, courts may reconsider what constitutes control and monitoring as they become more familiar with Internet business models. Thus, the liberalization may reflect a recognition that the control standard, either as articulated or as applied, is unnecessarily and unjustifiably narrow in the Internet context.

But liberalizing the existing standards can only carry contributory liability so far—particularly as the current loosening of standards appears focused only on the control aspect of the facilitation prong and not knowledge. For example, in the *Gucci* case, the defendants apparently sought out "replica" merchants as clients, were well aware that the direct infringers were in the replica business due to application and Internet information, and/or had resolved customer chargeback requests due to quality complaints. There was little doubt that the defendants knew of the direct infringers' activities. If catching bad actors is a motivation for liberalizing the control requirement, it is possible that courts may be similarly motivated to liberalize the knowledge standard as needed. On the other hand, knowledge may continue to be a high standard because courts are "reluctant to extend contributory trademark liability to defendants where there is some uncertainty as to the extent or the nature of the infringement" (*Tiffany*, 2008, p. 508).

Thus, without reconsideration, the current contributory liability standard may simply encourage Internet businesses to create business models that avoid obtaining sufficient information to trigger actual knowledge, constructive knowledge, or willful blindness. True, the *Tiffany* court seemed to be particularly impressed with eBay's anti-counterfeiting measures; but the business model created by eBay necessarily limits the knowledge that eBay could have and, thus, its effectiveness in preventing the sale of counterfeit goods. Should online marketplaces be able to avoid liability if their business models are what created the uncertainty as to infringement? Under the current law, it seems the answer will remain yes.

But one could easily argue that the answer should be no. eBay chose to set up a business where it does not have physical possession of the goods. It chooses what information a seller has to provide before it can register. It chooses what it will and will not know about the listings before they are posted. And, to a certain degree, eBay chooses what goods can be sold on its site. For example, eBay prohibits the sale of certain types of goods, such as firearms. And when one considers which entity is in the best position to minimize harm to the trademark owner by the sale of counterfeit goods with the least difficulty and cost, it is eBay—if it is incentivized to do so.

Thus, the second option is to change the contributory liability standard, perhaps particularly with respect to Internet services, to lower the burden on brand-owners and raise the obligations of the service providers. In so doing, one must be mindful that customers will also lose if the burden placed on online marketplaces is so large that it effectively eliminates their ability to do business. Striking the right balance may be difficult. Additionally, there may be some resistance, conceptually, to changing the contributory liability standard. Courts regularly say that the contributory trademark infringement standard derives from the common law of tort, which may suggest that, to some, it is immutably bound to its current form. And yet, contributory copyright liability, derived from the same common law of torts, has different parameters. Courts, including the Supreme Court, attribute the difference to the different scope of intellectual property rights encapsulated in trademark versus copyright. But it does suggest that the current contributory trademark infringement standard is malleable and can be changed to address new problems created by new technology.

Moreover, Mark McKenna has noted that the current contributory trademark infringement standard seems significantly attenuated from its common law tort roots and imposes a higher standard than used by tort law (2011, p. 2). He suggests that, rather than use secondary liability when generalized knowledge of harm is alleged, courts should assess the facts under a negligence claim, "evaluat[ing] ... whether the defendant's breach of duty owed to the plaintiff was the actual and proximate cause of the plaintiff mark owner's injuries" (McKenna, 2011, p. 26). Even by reconnecting trademark liability to the common law tort doctrine of negligence for generalized knowledge, the result in the *Tiffany* case may have been the same (McKenna, 2011, p. 45). The question then becomes if a negligence type claim would be sufficient to strike the right incentive balance without overly burdening either the Internet business or the brand owners.

David Bernstein and Michael Potenza suggest that the contributory trademark infringement standard should be changed to parallel § 27 of the Restatement (Third) of Unfair Competition Act, under which liability attaches if:

> (b) the actor fails to take reasonable precautions against the occurrence of the third person's infringing conduct in circumstances in which the infringing conduct can be reasonably anticipated.
>
> (American Law Institute (ALI), 2012;
> Bernstein and Potenza, 2011, p. 5)

Although the Restatement language limits itself to manufacturers and distributors, the proposal would extend the standard to service providers. Bernstein and Potenza suggest its flexibility better advances the underlying policies of trademarks, such as preventing consumer confusion and protecting the goodwill of the business by providing accurate information to consumers and reducing their search costs (2011, pp. 54–78). Although the Supreme Court rejected the "reasonable anticipation" standard in *Inwood*, it seemed to do so for the inducement prong, not facilitation, and it did so in a pre-Internet world. Further, the ALI stated that "the duty to take reasonable precautions … arises only when [there is] reason to anticipate that some substantial number of infringing sales will otherwise occur" (ALI, 2012 cmt. c). If this standard were applied, generalized knowledge of significant counterfeiting, as occurred in *Tiffany*, may be enough to trigger the duty for entities like eBay to take reasonable precautions. It seems possible that eBay would be more likely to be liable under this standard, but only to take "reasonable" precautions, which may strike the right balance between Internet businesses and brand owners.

Mark Bartholomew and Patrick McArdle have suggested importing a causation model used in epidemiology to assess global causal agents of disease to effectively distribute resources to combat diseases (2011, pp. 682–3). Alternatively, Connie Davis Powell has proposed adding a statutory safe harbor for online contributory trademark liability claims and a notice and takedown regime to balance counterfeiting concerns and encouraging new technology development for customers' benefit (2011/2012, pp. 17–21). Other commentators may suggest other creative solutions. These various proposals all indicate that contributory trademark infringement is still very much a doctrine in flux.

Conclusion

Ultimately, when weighing harm to the brand owner's goodwill, harm to fair competition, excessively burdening businesses utilizing new technology, or burdens on free speech, it is consumers who lose when the right balance is not struck in assessing liability. In the United States, it generally is the trademark owner's responsibility to police and protect its own brand. But, internet entities like eBay create attenuation between the service provider and the counterfeit goods and seem protected from liability in the United States under the current standard as long as the service entity is responsive to, rather than proactively gathering, knowledge of specific, potentially counterfeit products.

In contrast, some recent European decisions have rejected the current U.S. perspective, indicating that eBay should be held liable for "passively permitting counterfeit sales" (Weining et al., 2012, p. 14). For example, a French court found eBay liable for indirect infringement of Louis Vuitton's trademarks because eBay was necessary and active in the marketing and sales of infringing products (*SA Louis Vuitton*, 2008, p. 7–9, 11–12, 17). On the other hand, Directive 2000/31/EC of the European Parliament and of the Council of 8 June 2000, a directive on electronic commerce, provides liability exceptions for some Internet intermediaries. For example, three French decisions initially held Google liable due to its AdWords service, where companies (including counterfeiters) "purchase" keywords so that their advertisements appear as Sponsored Links when the keywords are entered in Google's internet search service (*Google France*, 2010, p. 9–11). Applying Directive 2000/31, the European Court of Justice (ECJ) held that an entity like Google may be exempt from liability as an intermediary service provider, assuming that its role "is neutral, in the sense that its conduct is merely technical, automatic and passive, pointing to a lack of knowledge or control of the data which it stores" (*Google France*, 2010, p. 6–9, 21–22). In a subsequent case involving eBay, the ECJ further stated that an entity is not neutral when it provides assistance, such as "optimising the presentation of the offers for sale in question or promoting those offers" (L'Oreal SA, 2011, 22). Moreover, even if a provider is a neutral entity, the liability exception will not apply if it had actual knowledge of "illegal activity or information" (ibid., 23). Thus, despite European courts' predilection for placing liability on Internet intermediaries, Directive 2000/31's liability exceptions may remove the policing burden from some Internet entities and return it to the trademark owner. As companies and courts struggle with policing infringement on the global Internet, the future holds the opportunity to see whether the current U.S. model or a broader infringement standard strikes the right balance.

Bibliography

Aitken, B. (2005), 'Keyword-Linked Advertising, Trademark Infringement, and Google's Contributory Liability,' *Duke Law & Technology Review* (21) 1. Online. Available at: <http://scholarship.law.duke.edu/dltr/vol4/iss1/20/>. (accessed 22 September 2012).

American Law Institute (2012), 'Contributory Infringement by Manufacturers and Distributors,' *Restatement of the Law, Third, Unfair Competition* §27. Online. Available at: <http://www.lexis.com> (accessed 8 September 2012).

Bartholomew, M. and McArdle, P. (2011), 'Causing Infringement,' *Vanderbilt Law Review* (64) 675. Online. Available at: <http://www.lexis.com> (accessed 10 July 2012).

Bernstein, D.H. and Potenza, M.R. (2011), 'Why the Reasonable Anticipation Standard Is the Reasonable Way to Access Contributory Trademark Liability in the Online Marketplace,' *Stanford Technology Law Review*, 9 (2011). Online. Available at: <http://www.lexis.com> (accessed 10 July 2012).

Cartier v. Symbolix, Inc. (2005), 386 F. Supp. 2d 354 (S.D.N.Y.). Online. Available at: <http://www.lexis.com> (accessed 16 July 2012).

Coach, Inc. v. Gata Corp. (2011), 2011 U.S. Dist. LEXIS 62317 (D.N.H. 9 June). Online. Available at: <http://www.lexis.com> (accessed 16 July 2012).

The Coca-Cola Company (2012), 2011 Annual Review. Online. Available at: <http://www.thecoca-colacompany.com/ourcompany/ar/> (accessed 14 August 2012).

Diane Von Furstenberg Studio v. Snyder (2007), 2007 U.S. Dist. LEXIS 78915 (E.D. Va. 23 Oct.). Online. Available at: <http://www.lexis.com> (accessed 16 July 2012).

eBay, Inc. (2012), Who We Are – eBay Inc. Online. Available at <http://www.ebayinc.com/who> (accessed 15 August 2012).

eBay, Inc. (2012), Tiffany Double Heart Pendent with a Chain. Online. Available at <http://www.ebay.com/itm/tiffany-double-heart-pendent-with-a-chain-/110955427459?pt=US_Fine_Necklaces_Pendants&hash=item19d5757683> (accessed 28 September 2012).

Fare Deals, Ltd. v. World Choice Travel.com, Inc. (2001), 180 F. Supp. 2d 678 (D.Md.). Online. Available at: <http://www.lexis.com> (accessed 16 July 2012).

Fonovisa, Inc. v. Cherry Auction, Inc. (1996), 76 F. 3d 259 (9th Cir.). Online. Available at: <http://www.lexis.com> (accessed 16 July 2012).

Ford Motor Company v. GreatDomains.com, Inc. (2001), 177 F. Supp. 2d 635 (E.D. Mich.). Online. Available at: <http://www.lexis.com> (accessed 2 September 2012).

GMA Accessories, Inc. v. Bop, Inc. (2011), 765 F. Supp. 2d 457 (S.D.N.Y.). Online. Available at: <http://www.lexis.com> (accessed 18 August 2012).

Google Fr. SARL v. Louis Vuitton Malletier SA (2010), C-236/08, C-237/08, C-238/08 (E.C.J.). Online. Available at: <http://curia.europa.eu/juris/recherche.jsf?language=en> (accessed 13 January 2013).

Gucci America, Inc. v. Frontline Processing Corp. (2010), 721 F. Supp. 2d 228 (S.D.N.Y.). Online. Available at: <http://www.lexis.com> (accessed 16 July 2012).

Habeeba's Dance of the Arts, Ltd. v. Knoblauch (2006), 420 F. Supp. 2d 709 (S.D. Ohio). Online. Available at: <http://www.lexis.com> (accessed 2 September 2012).

Hard Rock Café Licensing Corporation v. Concession Services, Incorporated (1992), 955 F. 2d 1143 (7th Cir.). Online. Available at: <http://www.lexis.com> (accessed 16 July 2012).

Inwood Laboratories v. Ives Laboratories (1982), 456 U.S. 844, 102 S. Ct. 2182. Online. Available at: <http://www.lexis.com> (accessed 16 July 2012).

Lockheed Martin Corporation v. Network Solutions, Inc. (1999), 194 F. 3d 980 (9th Cir.). Online. Available at: <http://www.lexis.com> (accessed 16 July 2012).

L'Oreal SA v. eBay International AG (2011), C-324/09 (E.C.J.). Online. Available at: <http://curia.europa.eu/juris/recherche.jsf?language=en> (accessed 15 January 2013).

Louis Vuitton Malletier, S.A. v. Akanoc Solutions, Inc. (2011), 658 F. 3d 936 (9th Cir.). Online. Available at: <http://www.lexis.com> (accessed 9 September 2012).

McKenna, M.P. (2011), 'Probabilistic Knowledge of Third-Party Trademark Infringement,' *Stanford Technology Law Review*, 2011 (10). Online. Available at: <http://www.lexis.com> (accessed 10 July 2012).

Medline Industries, Inc. v. Strategic Commercial Solutions, Inc. (2008), 553 F. Supp. 2d 979 (N.D. Ill.). Online. Available at: <http://www.lexis.com> (accessed 18 August 2012).

Perfect 10, Inc. v. Visa International Service Association (2007), 494 F. 3d 788 (9th Cir.). Online. Available at: <http://www.lexis.com> (accessed 16 July 2012).

Powell, C. (2011/2012), 'The eBay Exemption: Restructuring the Trademark Safe Harbor for Online Marketplaces,' *Santa Clara Computer & High Technology Law Journal*, 28: 1. Online. Available at <http://www.lexis.com> (accessed 22 September 2012).

Roger Cleveland Golf Company, Inc. v. Prince, 2012 U.S. Dist. LEXIS 46065 (D.S.C. 30 March). Online. Available at: <http://www.lexis.com> (accessed 18 August 2012).

Rosetta Stone, Ltd v. Google, Incorporated (2012), 676 F. 3d 144 (4th Cir.). Online. Available at: <http://www.lexis.com> (accessed 18 August 2012).

SA Louis Vuitton Malletier v. eBay, Inc. (2008), Tribunal de commerce {T. Com.} Commercial Court of Paris] Paris, RG 2006077799 (Fr.). Online. English translation available at <http://www.qbpc.org.cn/uploads/download/LVM%20vs%5B1%5D.%20eBay%20Paris%20Commercial%20Ct%20Decision.pdf> (accessed 3 January 2013).

Tiffany & Co. (2012), Return to Tiffany™ Double Heart Tag Pendant. Online. Available at <http://www.tiffany.com/Shopping/Item.aspx?sku=27125107> (accessed 28 September 2012).

Tiffany (NJ) Inc. and Tiffany and Company v. eBay, Inc. (2008), 576 F. Supp. 2d 463 (S.D.N.Y.). Online. Available at: <http://www.lexis.com> (accessed 16 July 2012).

Tiffany (NJ) Inc. and Tiffany and Company v. eBay, Inc. (2010), 600 F. 3d 93 (2nd Cir.). Online. Available at: <http://www.lexis.com> (accessed 16 July 2012).

Travis, Hannibal (2005), 'The Battle for Mindshare: The Emerging Consensus that the First Amendment Protects Corporate Criticism and Parody on the Internet,' *Virginia Journal of Law and Technology*, 10: 1. Online. Available at: <http://www.lexis.com> (accessed 22 September 2012).

Universal Furniture International, Inc. v. Frankel (2011), 835 F. Supp. 2d 35 (M.D.N.C.). Online. Available at: <http://www.lexis.com> (accessed 18 August 2012).

Weining, Z., Wang, L., and Faulkner, Y. (2012), 'Cyber-based Trademark Infringement,' *Intellectual Property Today*, 14. Online. Available at: <http://www.lexis.com> (accessed 22 September 2012).

7 Bad Samaritanism

Barnes v. Yahoo! and Section 230 ISP immunity

Ann Bartow[1]

Imagine that a local business has posters on its walls that feature naked photos of you, claim that you like violent romantic encounters with strangers, and disclose your name, work address, phone number and e-mail address. You find out about these posters when men unknown to you who have seen the posters show up at your place of employment and demand rough sex. You visit this local business and request that the posters be immediately removed. The business owners shrug and say they don't have to. Your next stop is the police department, where a sympathetic officer says she will arrest anyone who commits a crime against you, and that includes the person who put up the posters, if she can discover who it was. "Can't you just ask the proprietors of the local business?" you ask. "I can ask them," says the officer, "but they don't have to tell me. And they don't have to take the posters down, either." You find this completely incomprehensible. You return to the local business and with permission, you tear down the posters, ripping them into small pieces, hoping that this will end the matter. But the next day unknown men continue contacting you, and you discover this is because fresh copies of the posters are once again hanging on the walls of the local business. Because it seems clear that law enforcement officials will not help you solve the problem, you decide to consult an attorney. The lawyer you meet with says she would be happy to bring suit against the person who created and distributed the posters, but there isn't any way to hold the local business liable for the bad things that are happening as a consequence of the posters, or even to pressure the proprietors to take the posters down. This is because there is a law that grants immunity to businesses for anything posted on their walls by third parties. Businesses don't have any incentives under the law to police or remove posters placed on their walls by third parties, and in fact if the posters are drawing in paying customers, they may actually be motivated to encourage them.

---

1 Professor of Law, Pace Law School.

Sound preposterous? In real space it might be. It isn't, if we move the hypothetical situation online. Then it becomes very much like the *Barnes v. Yahoo!* dispute and many similar cases. Someone pretends to be you on the Internet, posting naked photos you didn't even know had been taken. They post your personal information in a context that encourages strangers to contact you at work and at home, expecting and demanding sex. This is terrifying, so you contact the police, providing the name of an ex-boyfriend you guess might be the perpetrator of this cruelty. You also contact the Internet service provider hosting the online venues where you are being impersonated, but that company refuses to help you in any way. It can profit from the disgusting acts of third parties any way it likes, and Congress has stripped you of any meaningful legal recourse when it passed Section 230 of the Communications Decency Act. "Decency," in this context, it turns out, means that Internet service providers (ISPs) don't have to show you any. You have been stripped of some of the legal tools the law might otherwise offer harassment victims.

Interpersonal harassing, bullying and stalking predate the Internet, but the networked world facilitates abusive acts from remote locations, with what can be a high degree of anonymity for technologically savvy perpetrators. Much of this violence occurs within families, or in the context of romantic relationships, current or past. The Internet offers angry people a variety of weapons that can be used to bring the kinds of suffering to other people that the legal system is often very reluctant to respond to.

It is indisputable that men can be subject to Internet harassment. The very first important case that judicially established the breathtaking scope of Section 230 immunity for online service providers involved the victimization of a man named Ken Zeran. The facts in this case, as recited by the Fourth Circuit Court of Appeals, are as follows:

> On April 25, 1995, an unidentified person posted a message on an AOL bulletin board advertising "Naughty Oklahoma T-Shirts." The posting described the sale of shirts featuring offensive and tasteless slogans related to the April 19, 1995, bombing of the Alfred P. Murrah Federal Building in Oklahoma City. Those interested in purchasing the shirts were instructed to call "Ken" at Zeran's home phone number in Seattle, Washington. As a result of this anonymously perpetrated prank, Zeran received a high volume of calls, comprised primarily of angry and derogatory messages, but also including death threats. Zeran could not change his phone number because he relied on its availability to the public in running his business out of his home. Later that day, Zeran called AOL and informed a company representative of his predicament. The employee assured Zeran that the posting would be removed from AOL's bulletin board but explained that as a matter of policy AOL would not post a retraction. The parties dispute the date that AOL removed this original posting from its bulletin board.

On April 26, the next day, an unknown person posted another message advertising additional shirts with new tasteless slogans related to the Oklahoma City bombing. Again, interested buyers were told to call Zeran's phone number, to ask for "Ken," and to "please call back if busy" due to high demand. The angry, threatening phone calls intensified. Over the next four days, an unidentified party continued to post messages on AOL's bulletin board, advertising additional items including bumper stickers and key chains with still more offensive slogans. During this time period, Zeran called AOL repeatedly and was told by company representatives that the individual account from which the messages were posted would soon be closed. Zeran also reported his case to Seattle FBI agents. By April 30, Zeran was receiving an abusive phone call approximately every two minutes.

Meanwhile, an announcer for Oklahoma City radio station KRXO received a copy of the first AOL posting. On May 1, the announcer related the message's contents on the air, attributed them to "Ken" at Zeran's phone number, and urged the listening audience to call the number. After this radio broadcast, Zeran was inundated with death threats and other violent calls from Oklahoma City residents. Over the next few days, Zeran talked to both KRXO and AOL representatives. He also spoke to his local police, who subsequently surveilled his home to protect his safety. By May 14, after an Oklahoma City newspaper published a story exposing the shirt advertisements as a hoax and after KRXO made an on-air apology, the number of calls to Zeran's residence finally subsided to fifteen per day.[2]

Zeran unsuccessfully argued that once he notified AOL of the unidentified third party's hoax, AOL had a duty to remove the defamatory posting promptly, to notify its subscribers of the message's false nature, and to effectively screen future defamatory material. Section 230, it was held, immunized AOL from liability for anything posted by "content providers" using its services. This effectively meant that AOL had no duty to do anything: to remove postings that were leading to death threats and other harms; to correct misinformation that was leading to death threats and other harms; to prevent future postings that would likely lead to death threats and other harms; nor to assist Zeran in identifying the culprit who was victimizing him. In 2011 Ken Zeran commented publicly for the first time about his ordeal. He said in part:

> The statute is paradoxical. Examine the term Congress chose to title Section 230—"The Good Samaritan Act." The Good Samaritan concept

---

2 Zeran v. America Online (1997) 129 F.3d 327 (4th Cir.).

in legal terms provides a safe haven to those who render aid on a voluntary basis. The term is derived from The Gospel According to St Luke.

"There was a scholar of the law who stood up to test him and said, 'Teacher, what must I do to inherit eternal life?' Jesus said to him, 'What is written in the law? How do you read it?' He said in reply, 'You shall love the Lord, your God, with all your heart, with all your being, with all your strength, and with all your mind, and your neighbor as yourself.' He replied to him, 'You have answered correctly; do this and you will live.' But because he wished to justify himself, he said to Jesus, 'And who is my neighbor?' Jesus replied, 'A man fell victim to robbers as he went down from Jerusalem to Jericho. They stripped and beat him and went off, leaving him half-dead. A priest happened to be going down that road, but when he saw him, he passed by on the opposite side. Likewise a Levite came to the place, and when he saw him, he passed by on the opposite side. But a Samaritan traveler who came upon him was moved with compassion at the sight. He approached the victim, poured oil and wine over his wounds and bandaged them. Then he lifted him up on his own animal, took him to an inn and cared for him. The next day he took out two silver coins and gave them to the innkeeper with the instruction, "Take care of him. If you spend more than what I have given you, I shall repay you on my way back." Which of these three, in your opinion, was neighbor to the robbers' victim?' He answered, 'The one who treated him with mercy.' Jesus said to him, 'Go and do likewise.'"

As the namesake, this gospel is instructive in viewing Section 230. It is indeed instructive to the very process itself in reviewing Section 230. Biblical scholars explain that Jesus was actually changing the law, also known as the "Great Reversal." The Levite and priest were bound by law not to touch the dying man. The parable actually negates the commonly held belief system and challenges followers to view the world in a different way. Jesus is asking those that question him to leave behind traditional law and embrace a compassionate way of living.

So in light of Congress using the "Good Samaritan" to explain its intent and purpose—think about the following:

Did Jesus mean that it is ok for the priest and Levite to either help the dying man or not? That they would not be liable for breaking the "new" law by failing to respond to the dying man? Is that the lesson?

In statements made in the landmark case *Zeran v. AOL*, The United States District Court's Opinion noted that "By AOL's lights, it is immune from state common law liability for any material on its network as long as that material was put online by a third party. And this is so, AOL's counsel contended, even if AOL knew of the defamatory nature of the material and made a decision not to remove it from the network based on a malicious desire to cause harm to the party defamed."

Is this what Jesus meant? Was Jesus focused on a third party who injured the man? Is this what Congress meant?

This is exactly what Section 230 says. One is NOT required to help the "dying man." AOL's counsel, in a courageous legal move, drove home the point. It also makes my case today. Section 230 has turned the parable and its own namesake upside down.

The paradox of *Zeran v. AOL* was referenced in *Blown to Bits, Your Life, Liberty, and Happiness after the Digital Explosion*—"Congress had given the ISP's a complete waiver of responsibility for the consequences of false and damaging statements, even when the ISP knew they were false. Had anyone in Congress thought through the implications of the Good Samaritan clause?"[3]

People who want to inflict misery upon others are facilitated by the Internet and ignored or even encouraged by online service providers who can profitably take advantage of the perversely named Good Samaritan Act. A person can understand the importance of anonymous speech and of the First Amendment and still recognize that under Section 230 the financial incentives for ISPs fall in favor of ignoring Internet harassment. Addressing it would cost money and resources. Both controversial news reports and sexy intriguing dating profiles, even when false, and generate logons, eyeballs, and browser clicks, all the things that lead to revenues.

Zeran lost badly in court due to Section 230. Things have played out slightly differently for Cecilia Barnes. First, the uncontested facts:[4] In December of 2004 a former boyfriend created Yahoo! accounts using her name, and made it look as though she was soliciting men for rough, anonymous sex. The account profiles contained nude photos of Barnes that had been taken without her knowledge, and disclosed her daytime contact information, including the address, e-mail address and telephone number of her place of employment. The ex-boyfriend also posed as Barnes in Yahoo! chat rooms, directing people to the false profiles and actively encouraged the belief that Barnes desired violent sexual contact with strangers. She leaned about the profile and the chats when men unknown to her began contacting her at work by phone and e-mail and appearing there in person, expecting to have sex with her. This not only put her job at risk, but also put her at risk for sexual assault by men who would claim the acts were consensual based on the Yahoo! facilitated communications. It was, as a judge later noted, "[A] dangerous, cruel, and highly indecent use of the internet for the apparent purpose of revenge."[5]

3 Kenneth Zeran (2011) 'The Cultural High Road Along the Internet Landscape in The Pursuit of Happiness': A Commentary. Online. Available at: <http://www.kennethzeran. com/zeran_sec_230_commentary.html> (accessed Sept. 1, 2012).
4 Yahoo! Inc. (2005) Notice of Removal, *Barnes v. Yahoo! Inc.*, Case No. 2005cv00926 (D. Or. complaint filed May 24), http://www.citmedialaw.org/sites/citmedialaw.org/files/2005-06-23-Yahoo%27s%20Notice%20of%20Removal.pdf.
5 *Barnes v. Yahoo!*, 570 F. 3d 1096 (9th Cir. 2009)

Barnes was probably very relieved to discover that Yahoo! had an online mechanism for dealing with this sort of problem. Following Yahoo!'s posted instructions, in January of 2005 Barnes mailed Yahoo! a copy of her photo identification and a signed statement explaining that the unauthorized profiles in her name had been posted by someone who was trying to punish and harm her, and asking that the false profiles be taken down. But there was no response from Yahoo! The frightening e-mails, calls and visits from strange men demanding sex continued, so Barnes again contacted Yahoo! in the Yahoo!-specified manner in February of 2005, and two more times in March of 2005. Still the profiles remained accessible, and contact by men who accessed them continued.

Cecilia Barnes took her plight to the media. When Yahoo! learned that a report critical of Yahoo!'s failure to respond to Barnes' requests for assistance was going to air on a Portland, Oregon news program, suddenly Yahoo! expressed a precipitous willingness to help. Barnes was contacted by Mary Osaka, Yahoo!'s Director of Communications, who asked for a faxed copy of the signed statements Barnes had previously mailed to Yahoo!, and promised that she would personally walk the statements over to the Yahoo! department charged with removing unauthorized profiles, and that Yahoo! would take down the profiles that were causing Barnes so much trauma. Barnes believed her, but unfortunately for Barnes there wasn't any follow-through by Yahoo!

For almost two months Barnes took no further action regarding the profiles and the trouble they had caused, expecting Yahoo! to honor its word. But through late May of 2005, the false profiles remained available through Yahoo!, and the communications continued.

In addition to giving Barnes an unwarranted sense of optimism and security, by lying to her Yahoo! had also headed off a negative news report about Barnes' plight by promising to take down the profiles that were causing men to show up at her place of employment and demanding to have sex with her. Yahoo! received a useful positive public relations benefit from making this representation but did not actually do anything it promised.

Finally, Cecelia Barnes filed a complaint against Yahoo! in an Oregon state court, asserting that once Yahoo! agreed to remove the deeply problematic profiles to protect Barnes from further contacts resulting from them, it had a duty to do so. Yahoo! immediately had the case removed to federal district court where Yahoo!'s characterization of the dispute was as follows:[6]

> According to the Complaint, this case arises out of a cruel and persistent hoax that was perpetuated on the Plaintiff Cecilia Barnes by her

---

6 Yahoo! Inc. (2005) Memorandum in Support of Motion to Dismiss the Complaint, *Barnes v. Yahoo! Inc.*, Case No. 2005cv00926 (D. Or. complaint filed May 24), http://docs.justia.com/cases/federal/district-courts/oregon/ordce/6:2005cv00926/74096/10/0.pdf?ts=1188586679.

ex-boyfriend. In particular, for reasons that are not alleged, the Plaintiff's ex-boyfriend allegedly engaged in a campaign to harass the Plaintiff using the Internet by setting up a series of online "profiles"—publicly available web pages on which a peson typically displays personal information about herself such as name, address, age, hobbies, pictures or other content—that contained information about the Plaintiff and falsely appeared to have been posted by her. These profiles included nude pictures of the Plaintiff and information about how to contact her at her workplace. Because the ex-boyfriend also allegedly impersonated the Plaintiff in discussions in online chat rooms, "soliciting" other men by directing them to the unauthorized profiles, the Plaintiff allegedly was visited and harassed at her office by unwanted suitors.

Rather than sue the ex-boyfriend who perpetrated this harassment, the Plaintiff has sued Yahoo! Inc. ("Yahoo!"), one of the world's largest and best known providers of interactive computer services. She has done so even though Yahoo! indisputably had no role in creating or developing any of the online profiles or the chat room conversations about which she complains. Instead, Yahoo!'s involvement in this case stems from the fact that the ex-boyfriend allegedly used Yahoo!'s Internet-based services to post the profiles and engage in the chat room conversations. Although the Plaintiff concedes that Yahoo! had "no initial responsibility to act" as a result of the ex-boyfriend's abuse, she claims that Yahoo! gratuitously assumed a legal duty to act when one of its employees allegedly told her that Yahoo! would "stop" the unauthorized profiles, and that thereafter Yahoo! negligently failed to fulfill that alleged duty.[7]

Here and in other parts of the Memorandum of Law, and in other filings as well, Yahoo! repeatedly raised questions about why Barnes didn't name the ex-boyfriend in her Complaint or pursue legal action against him. Was she too afraid of him to pursue legal action against him directly? Given his relentless and extreme methods of revenge he employed against her simply for breaking up with him, such fear might be understandable. Or had she settled her dispute with him in some way? Yahoo! wanted each judge to wonder about this, hinting not very subtly that perhaps all Barnes was really interested in was obtaining money from a well-resourced corporation.

Yahoo!'s position was that it had no direct responsibility for what it snidely characterized as an "unwanted suitor" problem, and no duty to help her solve it. Yahoo!'s legal response to Barnes' Complaint was a Motion to Dismiss,[8]

---

7 Ibid., p. 1.
8 Yahoo! Inc. (2005) Motion to Dismiss the Complaint, Reply in Support of Motion to Dismiss the Complaint, *Barnes v. Yahoo! Inc.*, Case No. 2005cv00926 (D. Or. complaint filed May 24, 2005), http://docs.justia.com/cases/federal/district-courts/oregon/ordce/6:2005cv00926/74096/9/0.pdf?ts=1188586665.

based on an assertion that Section 230 of the Communications Decency Act barred Barnes' claim.[9] Rather than denying that it had reneged on its promise to remove the profiles after the immediate danger of a wholly negative news report had passed, Yahoo! characterized Barnes' recitation of these facts as an effort to "artfully plead around Section 230."[10] Yahoo! argued that lies (characterized by Yahoo! as "broken promises") were not punishable, citing several cases in which other Internet service providers had also offered help to online harassment victims but ultimately declined to provide it. The judge agreed, and dismissed all of Barnes' claims.[11] Barnes rather intrepidly appealed.[12]

The Ninth Circuit concluded that Barnes potentially had a promissory estoppel based cause of action that was outside the scope of Section 230 immunity, and remanded the case back to the district court to determine whether or not she actually did.[13] One reaction to the Ninth Circuit's holding was that unless it is overruled, it will cause ISPs to issue directives to their employees not to promise to remove material or even to inquire into whether the material should be removed. Any inclinations to be Good Samaritans ISPs might have felt would be snuffed out, if indeed they had any, if promising to help but failing to follow through was legally actionable. But could this truly make the situation any worse for people in Barnes' situation? Yahoo! felt free not only to not take action, but to lie and say that it would take action for public relations purposes, and then not take any action at all. When the trial court said this was covered by Section 230 immunity, many legal commentators agreed.

When the dispute moved back again to the district court, Yahoo! was unable to get Barnes' complaint dismissed a second time. The court concluded that Barnes had alleged facts from which it could be inferred that she relied to her detriment on Yahoo!'s alleged promise, writing:

9 Yahoo! Inc. (2005) Memorandum in Support of Motion to Dismiss, op. cit. See also, Yahoo! Inc., Reply in Support of Motion to Dismiss the Complaint, *Barnes v. Yahoo! Inc.*, Case No. 2005cv00926 (D. Or. complaint filed May 24, 2005), http://docs.justia.com/cases/federal/district-courts/oregon/ordce/6:2005cv00926/74096/19/0.pdf?ts=1188586694.

10 Yahoo! Inc. (2005) Memorandum in Support of Motion to Dismiss, op. cit. See also, Yahoo! Inc., Reply in Support of Motion to Dismiss the Complaint, *Barnes v. Yahoo! Inc.*, Case No. 2005cv00926 (D. Or. complaint filed May 24, 2005), p. 4, http://docs.justia.com/cases/federal/district-courts/oregon/ordce/6:2005cv00926/74096/19/0.pdf?ts=1188586694.

11 *Barnes v. Yahoo! Inc.* (2005) Case No. 2005cv00926 (D. Or. complaint dismissed Nov. 8, 2005), http://docs.justia.com/cases/federal/district-courts/oregon/ordce/6:2005cv00926/74096/20/

12 Cecelia Barnes (2005) *Barnes v. Yahoo! Inc.*, Case No. 2005cv00926 (D. Or. notice of appeal filed Dec. 5), http://docs.justia.com/cases/federal/district-courts/oregon/ordce/6:2005cv00926/74096/22/0.pdf?ts=1188586698.

13 *Barnes v. Yahoo!, Inc.* (2009) 570 F. 3d 1096 (9th Cir.) (amending 565 F. 3d 560).

The amended complaint alleges plaintiff attempted, unsuccessfully, to convince defendant to remove the unauthorized profiles. These attempts occurred over the course of three months. Then, in March 2005, a reporter learned of plaintiff's plight and began to prepare a news story regarding "Yahoo!'s indifference to the dangers to which Plaintiff Barnes was exposed …". Coincidentally, on the exact day the reporter called defendant for a comment on the proposed news story, Osako, defendant's Director of Communication, telephoned plaintiff regarding the profiles. The logical inference is that the reporter, with one phone call, was able to succeed in calling attention to plaintiff's situation, when plaintiff, acting on her own, had failed to do so.

The amended complaint alleges that Osako asked plaintiff to fax her the documents plaintiff had previously mailed to defendant. Then plaintiff states: "Ms Osako told Plaintiff Barnes that she would person-ally walk the statements over to the division responsible for stopping unauthorized profiles and they would take care of it. Ms Osako assured Plaintiff Barnes that Defendant Yahoo! would put a stop to the unauthor-ized profiles?" Next, plaintiff called the reporter.

Although plaintiff does not specifically use the term "reliance," one can infer that plaintiff called the reporter, informing him defendant was indeed going to remove the profiles, in reliance on defendant's promise to plaintiff that it would remove the profiles. For the purpose of this motion, it is reasonable to conclude Osako's intention in calling the plaintiff was ultimately to have plaintiff call the reporter and, in effect, diffuse the story before it aired.[14]

Barnes claimed she thought help was coming, and so didn't take protective actions she otherwise might have taken. She asserted that the detrimental reliance made her worse off than she would have been if Yahoo! had just told her to go and pound sand when she asked for help, and the Ninth Circuit decided that Yahoo! should have to answer for this in court. This didn't mean that Yahoo! would necessarily be held liable for what it did or failed to do, just that Barnes gets a chance to prove that what Yahoo! did was wrong as a matter of law.

Whether Section 230 immunity extends to lies is a complicated question. In *Doe v. SexSearch.com* the defendants were the operators of a website that helps connect people who wish to hook up to have sex. Doe met Jane Roe, a user of the service who had posted a profile saying that she was 18 and wanted sex, through the website. After they met offline at Roe's home and had "consensual" sex it turned out that Roe was actually only 14, and Doe was arrested for felony statutory rape. Doe sued the site SexSearch.com for failing

---

14 *Barnes v. Yahoo! Inc.* Case No. 2005cv00926, 2009 U.S. Dist. LEXIS 116274 (D. Or. motion to dismiss denied Dec. 11, 2009).

to verify Roe's age, alleging that the website represented that all members were over 18.

The court concluded that because Roe supplied the specific content at issue, a false representation of her age, Section 230 immunized the website. The court concluded that "the mere fact SexSearch provided the questionnaire Jane Doe answered falsely is not enough to consider SexSearch the developer of the false profile." SexSearch.com's incorrect claims about the ages of all of its members may have given Doe a false sense of security about Roe being an adult, but according to the court it was Roe's dishonesty on her profile that proximately caused Doe's legal problems, and Section 230 meant that SexSearch.com could not be held responsible. The court also noted that "Plaintiff clearly had the ability to confirm Jane Roe's age when he met with her in person, before they had sex, yet failed to do so."

Relatedly, *Anthony v. Yahoo! Inc.* is a class action in which the named plaintiff was a user of Yahoo!'s dating subscription services. He alleged that Yahoo! creates false personal profiles and retains expired profiles to make the subscription service look more attractive to existing subscribers, thereby engaging in false and negligent misrepresentations and in deceptive and unfair trade practices. Because the complaint alleged that Yahoo! created false profiles, and sent false or expired profiles to subscribers, Yahoo! was the content provider of the information at the center of the dispute, and therefore was found to be acting outside of Section 230's immunities.[15]

Isolating "violence against women" as a distinct social problem has been controversial.[16] There is cultural resistance to the idea that "violence against women" is legitimately a category of crimes against persons, with unique and cognizable traits. Everything that is inflicted on women can be inflicted on men. And as a matter of sheer numbers, men are the victims of violent crimes more often than women are. Yet there are certain kinds of crimes that are disproportionately committed against women, by men, which lack inverse or parallel corollaries. Women are beaten and sexually assaulted by men in far greater numbers than men are similarly physically abused by women. Men are far more likely to be hit, wounded, raped and sodomized by other men than women, while women rarely suffer violent attacks, sexual or otherwise, by other women. And women are far more likely to be killed by men than the reverse.

---

15 *Anthony v. Yahoo! Inc.* (2006) 421 F. Supp. 2d 1257 (N.D. Cal. 2006).
16 Jennifer Bendery (2012) 'Violence Against Women Act Prompts Partisan Debate Among Female Lawmakers,' *The Huffington Post* (Apr. 25). Online. Available at: <http://www.huffingtonpost.com/2012/04/25/violence-against-women-act-female-lawmakers_n_1453890.html> (accessed Sept. 1, 2012); Janice Shaw Crouse et al. (2012) 'Should the Violence Against Women Act Be Reauthorized?' *U.S. News and World Report*. Online. Available at: <http://www.usnews.com/debate-club/should-the-violence-against-women-act-be-reauthorized> (accessed Sept. 1, 2012).

Women are constantly being monitored and judged. Consider the *contretemps* surrounding the topless photos of Kate Middleton. A common response was to censure her for taking her top off in what she thought was a private environment, and for having breasts generally. Coterminous with the 2012 Summer Olympics in London, *The New York Times* published a short article about the intersection of social media, and the almost real-time criticism of Olympic athletes. Entitled "Stronger, Faster, Nastier,"[17] it relayed the following:

> Thanks to the rise of social media, reverence for athletic achievement at the Olympics can now be measured in milliseconds. Even as Gabby Douglas was performing the routines that would earn her the all-around gold medal in gymnastics, a few Twitter users were criticizing her pony-tailed clipped coif.
>
> On Friday, Joe Scarborough ran a video clip of the American women's soccer team's gold-medal game, in which Carli Lloyd scored two goals for the team and went on to say: "When someone tells me I can't do something, I'm going to prove them wrong. That's what a champion is all about and that's what I am: a champion."
>
> Mr Scarborough and his cohorts then jumped on Ms Lloyd for using the first-person singular too much ("There's no 'I' in team"), questioning her chances for an endorsement deal ....
>
> But it was only the latest example in a week of sniping that included brutish commentary from Conan O'Brien and others about Holley Mangold, the American weight lifter and sister of the New York Jets center Nick Mangold. "I predict 350 lb weight lifter Holley Mangold will bring home the gold and 4 guys against their will," Mr O'Brien posted to his Twitter account.
>
> The British swimmer Rebecca Adlington's looks were criticized. "I worry that Rebecca Adlington will have an unfair advantage in the swimming by possessing a dolphin's face," wrote the comedian Frankie Boyle.
>
> Ms Adlington's American counterpart, Allison Schmitt, may have fared even worse. The Canton, Mich., native was said to look and sound "retarded" by a multitude of social media users, as the sports site Deadspin pointed out.[18]

The author of the piece never acknowledged that each one of the examples concerned harsh commentary about a *female* athlete. Similarly, a harassment case that has been described as establishing a constitutional right to stalk

---

17 Bee Shyuan Chang (2012) 'Stronger, Faster, Nastier,' The New York Times (Aug. 12). Online. Available at: <http://www.nytimes.com/2012/08/12/fashion/social-media-speeds-up-criticism-of-olympians-noted.html> (accessed Sept. 1, 2012).
18 Ibid.

and harass people on Twitter also featured a female victim, "privileg[ing] a cyberstalker William Lawrence Cassidy's right to free speech over a Buddhist leader Alyce Zeoli's right to be free from harassment. Cassidy had criticized Zeoli's looks, criticized Buddhism, described cinematic ways that Zeoli could die, and told her to commit suicide. A judge ruled that Zeoli was a public figure and that she could have avoided harassment by simply not looking at Cassidy's tweets."[19]

Gendered hate speech online is simply another manifestation of targeted violence against women. Driven by sexism and misogynistic beliefs about women, debilitating hate speech that interferes with women's participation in cyberspace occurs as men act out their needs for power and control. The architecture of the Internet facilitates the deployment of hate speech from remote locations, often behind a veil of anonymity. Online or off, verbal assaults are generally legal in the sense that they have First Amendment protection, as long as specific threats are not uttered. And the right to freely express hatred of women in particular is deeply instantiated within First Amendment jurisprudence.

Hate-fueled words and images are deployed to constrain women from full and equal online citizenship, and it may be that this is an unintended consequence of the laws and architecture of cyberspace. Technologically-facilitated anonymity, ISP immunity under Section 230 of the Communications Decency Act and robust theories of free speech are harnessed together into the service of preserving a culture of male dominance on the Internet.

Jeremy Waldron has written that:

> In a well-ordered society, where people are visibly impressed by signs of one another's commitment to justice, everyone can enjoy a certain assurance as they go about their business. They know that when they leave home in the morning they can reasonably count on not being discriminated against or humiliated or terrorized. They feel secure in the basic rights that justice defines; they can face social interactions without the elemental risks that interaction would involve if one could not count on others to act justly.[20]

19 Kashmir Hill (2012) 'You Have a Constitutional Right to Stalk and Harass People on Twitter,' Forbes.com. Online. Available at: <http://www.forbes.com/sites/kashmirhill/2011/12/16/you-have-a-constitutional-right-to-stalk-and-harass-people-on-twitter/> (accessed Sept. 1, 2012). See also Kashmir Hill (2012) 'Malicious Exes Are So Much More Horrible in the Internet Age,' Forbes.com. Online. Available at: <http://www.forbes.com/sites/kashmirhill/2012/05/23/malicious-ex-boyfriends-are-so-much-more-horrible-in-the-internet-age/> (accessed Sept. 1, 2012).
20 Jeremy Waldron (2009) What Does a Well-Ordered Society Look Like? New York University School of Law (Oct. 5–7). Online. Available at: <http://www.law.nyu.edu/news/ECM_PRO_063313> (accessed Sept. 1, 2012).

The Internet is not a well ordered society. One might conclude that Barnes got justice when she was able to move forward with her promissory estoppel claim against Yahoo!, but similarly situated women have not been as fortunate. There have been a number of cases in which romantic partners have broken up, and the scorned male sets up a fake dating profile saying that his former lover is looking for violent sex, and she is then harangued by strangers seeking the same. I use the male pronoun for the harasser and the female pronoun for the victim because that is the typical gender pattern. A related variation entails the use of fake personal ads designed to target an individual for unwanted inquiries. There is online publication of a mix of both true and false information (accurate contact information is paired with fictionalized sexual desires) deliberately designed to make the target suffer when strangers treat the published ads or profiles as legitimate.

Now consider some similar cases that illustrate the ongoing effects of Section 230. In *Carafano v. Metrosplash.com, Inc.*,[21] actor Christianne Carafano sued Matchmaker.com, an Internet dating site, after an anonymous individual created a Matchmaker.com profile under the name "Chase529." The profile listed Carafano's home address and e-mail address, and included four pictures of her. Among other things, the answers to the questionnaire indicated that the user was "looking for a one night stand" and "might be persuaded to have a homosexual experience."

Matchmaker.com is an Internet dating site that allows members to post their own profiles and search a database of other members' profiles. Members fill out a questionnaire, and their answers become part of their profile. Matchmaker.com does not seek to verify the identity of members or the accuracy of the profiles, but all members must agree to the Matchmaker Disclaimer, which prohibits users from putting their home address, e-mail address, or telephone number in their profile.

Carafano claims that she received obscene phone calls and e-mails as a result of the profile. After learning about the profile, Carafano contacted the police. Two days later, Carafano's website manager contacted Matchmaker. com. To its credit, Matchmaker.com removed Chase529's profile from its system. Efforts by Carafano to hold Matchmaker.com legally responsible for her suffering from its existence failed. The district court rejected Matchmaker. com's argument based on Section 230, finding that it was partly responsible for providing profile content. The court nevertheless granted summary judgment to the defendants because Carafano had failed to raise a genuine issue of fact for essential elements of her claims. The Ninth Circuit affirmed the district court's ruling, but on different grounds. It held that Section 230 did in fact immunize the defendant because Matchmaker could not be considered an "information content provider" under the statute as no profile had any content until a user actively created it.

21 *Carafano v. Metrosplash.com, Inc.* (2003) 339 F. 3d 1119 (9th Cir.).

In *Landry-Bell v. Various, Inc.*,[22] an ex-boyfriend was alleged to have created a user profile saying that Landry-Bell would like to engage in, as the court described it, "lewd and obscene acts of perversion." The profile was posted to Various' adultfriendfinder.com web service, the self-described "World's Largest Sex & Swinger Personals Site." Landry-Bell sued both the ex-boyfriend and Various, Inc. for invasion of privacy, defamation and intentional infliction of emotional distress. She tried to avoid dismissal under Section 230 by arguing that Various was a content originator because Various submitted the content to search engines, added descriptors, such as "horny," to the content, displayed titles, organized the content by geography, provided an internal search engine of profiles, provided a mechanism to input data, and asked questions that elicit information from users, and performed internal computer testing to "determining purity and compatibility scores." But she failed.

Doe v. Friendfinder Network, Inc.[23] involved yet another false user-supplied profile on adult dating/hook-up services. The Friendfinder case featured an allegation that when the plaintiff complained, the sites removed the profile but displayed the following message on the profile page: "Sorry, this member has removed his/her profile," which allegedly implied that the plaintiff in fact had authorized the page initially, and another that portions of the fake profile had been displayed on third-party sites as "teasers" to advertise the adult dating services. Neither was enough to avoid dismissal predicated upon Section 230 immunity.

Section 230 perpetuates Bad Samaritanism, which disproportionately burdens women. Yahoo!'s articulation of the "core policy goals" of Section 230 throughout the Barnes litigation went like this:

> Although Congress recognized that technologies that enable millions of citizens to engage in online speech inevitably will be abused sometimes by purveyors of unlawful and harmful information, it determined that the appropriate policy balance is to permit recourse against the actual wrongdoer—that is, the originator of the harmful information—while shielding service providers from liability. Congress struck this balance in order to avoid discouraging service providers from both developing and offering innovative platforms for vibrant and diverse free speech and from engaging in forms of voluntary self-regulation that would otherwise increase their risk of liability.[24]

Yahoo!'s description of Section 230 as some kind of balance, via which stakeholders are apportioned both benefits and burdens, is truly laughable. While it is true that Section 230 does not technically preclude "recourse against the actual wrongdoer," it does not vest ISPs with any obligation to disclose

---

22 Landry-Bell v. Various, Inc. (2005) 2005 US Dist LEXIS 38741 (W.D. La. Dec. 27).
23 Doe v. Friendfinder Network, Inc., 2008 WL 803947 (D.N.H. March 27, 2008)
24 Barnes v. Yahoo!, Memorandum in Support of Motion to Dismiss, op. cit., 17.

the identity of the bad actor, even though the ISP may be the only entity in possession of this information. Yahoo! is generally free to do anything or nothing at all, in terms of facilitating the publication and distribution of harmful information. (Figure 7.1 below displays an excerpt of Yahoo! Inc.'s "terms of service" addressing the posting of unlawful or harassing material.)

To the extent that ISPs make money when harmful information is posted but have to spend money to curtail its spread or its impact, Congress created only strong incentives for ISPs to encourage inflammatory speech; there is nothing in the legislation that serves as a counterweight.

The online harassment of Barnes and other women is also independently profitable if it draws plentiful online interactions from interested observers, which translates into advertising revenues ISPs want to continue to enjoy as well. Can anyone doubt for a second that harassing posts about women often trigger pornography ads, and that men interested in violent sex with women are also interested in porn?

You agree to not use the Yahoo! Services to:

    a. upload, post, email, transmit or otherwise make available any Content that is unlawful, harmful, threatening, abusive, harassing, tortious, defamatory, vulgar, obscene, libelous, invasive of another's privacy, hateful, or racially, ethnically or otherwise objectionable;

    b. harm minors in any way;

    c. impersonate any person or entity, including, but not limited to, a Yahoo! official, forum leader, guide or host, or falsely state or otherwise misrepresent your affiliation with a person or entity;

    d. forge headers or otherwise manipulate identifiers in order to disguise the origin of any Content transmitted through the Yahoo! Service;

    e. upload, post, email, transmit or otherwise make available any Content that you do not have a right to make available under any law or under contractual or fiduciary relationships (such as inside information, proprietary and confidential information learned or disclosed as part of employment relationships or under nondisclosure agreements);

    f. upload, post, email, transmit or otherwise make available any Content that infringes any patent, trademark, trade secret, copyright or other proprietary rights ("Rights") of any party;

Figure 7.1 Screenshot of Excerpt from Yahoo!'s Terms of Service.

    Source: Yahoo! Inc. (2008), Terms of Service (US). Online. http://info.yahoo. com/legal/us/yahoo/utos/utos-173.html.

Certainly, the approach to online speech that Section 230 of the Communications Decency Act promulgates makes sense in many contexts. Treating an ISP such as Yahoo! like a conventional publisher elides important differences between the process of publishing a book, magazine or newspaper, and the technological methods by which material is added to and distributed on the Internet. The sheer scale of Yahoo!'s Internet presence precludes the possibility of pre-screening posted material as a matter of logistics. To make ISPs like Yahoo! legally liable for content they did not generate and cannot effectively police would throttle the communicative capabilities of the Internet.

But that doesn't mean ISPs couldn't be required to offer assistance to people like Barnes. The ISPs have so much money and influence that the possibility that Section 230 will be amended to require ISPs to do anything helpful for women like Barnes, including simply not lie to them, is slim. But the almost absolute immunity enjoyed by ISPs could be ratcheted down a few notches. Section 230 doesn't provide ISP immunity from criminal laws related to child pornography. If Cecelia Barnes had been 17 years old when the reported events occurred, the nude photographs would have almost certainly been removed by Yahoo! once the company was made aware of it.

A more conditional ISP immunity would be framed by ISPs as logistically impossible, but the lessons of the Digital Millennium Copyright Act (DMCA) demonstrate that it would not be. Under the so called "notice and takedown" provisions of the DMCA, when an ISP takes down online information that a copyright holder alleges was not authorized, it is essentially immune from copyright based liability for distributing infringing materials. If it chooses not to respond to the copyright holder's demand, the ISP may later have to defend its decision not to on the merits.

Barnes asserted that the nude photos were taken without her knowledge. This perhaps exacerbates the perception of her level of victimization. She might have seemed less deserving of sympathy if she had instead noted that she had willingly posed for them. But if she held the copyright in the photos, and asked Yahoo! to remove them for that reason, Yahoo! almost certainly would have removed them with great alacrity. Section 230(e)(2)[25] specifically declaims any effect on intellectual property law, meaning online service providers are not immunized from liability related to the facilitation of copyright infringement. This point is illustrated quite powerfully by *Balsley v. LFP.*[26]

25 U.S. Code, title 47, section 230. Online. Available at: <http://codes.lp.findlaw.com/uscode/47/5/II/I/230> (accessed Sept. 1, 2012).

26 — F.3d —, 2012 WL 3517571 (6th Cir. 2012). Online. Available at: <http://law.justia.com/cases/federal/appellate-courts/ca6/11-3445/11-3445-2012-08-16.html> (accessed Sept. 1, 2012).

In March 2003 Catherine Bosley was a news anchor for a CBS television affiliate in Ohio. While on vacation in Florida, she entered a "wet t-shirt" contest at a bar and ultimately danced nude. An amateur photographer named Gontran Durocher took pictures of her and published them online. A few months later, Bosley lost her position as a news anchor when the story was publicly reported. Bosley then purchased the copyrights in the photographs from Durocher. After public interest in the photographs diminished, Bosley was able to secure new employment as a television reporter in another city.

Meanwhile, *Hustler Magazine* has a recurring "Hot News Babes" feature, which is a "contest" that invites Hustler readers to nominate young, attractive female news reporters; Hustler editors feature one reporter's picture in each edition, and the reader who nominates the chosen reporter receives a "prize pack." In August of 2005 a Hustler reader nominated Bosley as a "hot news babe," explaining that nude photographs of Bosley were available online and that Bosley lost a job over them. After Hustler published one of the photographs taken by Durocher for which she had purchased the copyright, Bosley was able to successfully bring a copyright infringement suit against Hustler. Her ownership of the copyrights in the photographs also entitles her to send "notice and take down" requests to online service providers that facilitate unauthorized publications of these photos, which the ISPs are very likely to comply with.[27]

Copyright law is not the only Section 230 circumventing claim that might be raised in a harassment situation. A federal Lanham Act false designation of origin claim with respect to the use of the false profile in the advertising teasers may also be an intellectual property claim that falls outside of Section 230 immunities. A false designation of origin claim, framed as false endorsement, may be equivalent to a right of publicity claim.[28] A right of publicity claim is an intellectual property claim that roots in privacy law, possibly monetizing invasion of privacy claims in a way that takes it outside the Section 230 immunity penumbra.

Turning to the police is one additional option for victims. It isn't particularly cost effective, though. In the situation Barnes faced, she would have had to call the police every time a man initiated unwanted contact and persisted after she asked him to leave her alone. When the nuisance perpetuated by men "innocently" responding to the false profiles would reach the threshold level at which the police would arrest individual perpetrators (who had after all been misled by the Yahoo! postings), must have been uncertain. In my experience advocating for online harassment victims, sometimes police officers

---

27 U.S. Code, title 17, section 512, http://www.copyright.gov/legislation/dmca.pdf
28 Eric Goldman (2008) 47 USC 230 Trifecta of Cases—Friendfinder, e360insight, iBrattleboro Technology and Marketing Blog (Apr. 28). Online. Available at: <http://blog.ericgoldman.org/archives/2008/04/47_usc_230_trifecta.htm> (accessed Sept. 1, 2012), citing Doe v. Friendfinder Network, Inc. (2008) 2008 WL 803947 (D.N.H. Mar. 27).

would refuse to act even when a victim was receiving death threats, simply admonishing women to "be more aware of their surroundings," or offering similarly useless advice.

Sometimes law enforcement will refuse to get involved until a crime has unambiguously occurred. A former Marine named Jebidiah James Stipe took revenge on his ex-girlfriend by posting a "rape fantasy ad" to Craigslist supposedly written by her which said: "Need a real aggressive man with no concern for woman." Presumably intrigued and aroused by this appeal, a man named Ty Oliver McDowell responded to the ad and communicated with the "woman" who posted the ad via e-mail. In reality it was Stipe setting up his ex-girlfriend for a violent sexual attack. McDowell obtained the victim's address, forcibly entered her home, tied her up, raped her at knifepoint, beat her severely and sexually penetrated her with a metal knife-sharpener. Both men eventually received identical sentences of 60 years to life, Stipe having pled guilty to sexual assault, aggravated kidnapping, and aggravated burglary.[29]

Barnes v. Yahoo! is a case that illustrates how laws and social norms leave the strikingly vulnerable victims of aggressive and sustained harassment campaigns. It has a bookend of sorts, but one that raises concerns as well as a bit of optimism. After Sean Sayer's girlfriend M.B. broke up with him in 2006, he began a lengthy and vicious Internet based campaign of terror that she could not stop even by moving thousands of miles away. According to one media report[30] Sayer was convicted of stalking M.B. and she was granted a protection from abuse order against him, which he was convicted of violating. Then he took his rage online. M.B. told investigators that a male stranger showed up at her South Portland, ME home in October 2008 who claimed he met her on the Internet and arranged to meet her for a sexual encounter. Several more men went to her house in the following days similarly looking for sexual encounters. Next, "M.B. discovered an advertisement in the 'casual encounters' section of the website Craigslist with a photo of herself, directions to her house and a list of sexual things she would do when interested individuals arrived, according to the affidavit."[31]

As a result of the harassment, M.B. legally changed her name and moved to Louisiana, but a male stranger showed up at her home in Louisiana and

---

29 Associated Press (2010) 'Ex-Marine Jebidiah James Stipe Gets 60 Years For Craigslist Rape Plot,' CBS News.com (June 29). Online. Available at: <http://www.cbsnews.com/8301-504083_162-20009162-504083.html>; Ben Neary (2010) 'Second Man Gets 60 Years in Wyoming Rape Case,' *Ventura County Star* (June 29). Online. Available at: <http://www.vcstar.com/news/2010/jun/29/2nd-man-gets-60-years-in-wyo-internet-rape-case/?print=1> (accessed Sept. 1, 2012).
30 Gilliam Graham, 'Man Faces Federal Cyberstalking Charge,' Biddeford-Saco-Old Orchard Beach Courier Blog Archive (July 22). Online. Available at: <http://blog.inthecourier.com/2011/07/22/man-faces-federal-cyberstalking-charge.aspx>.
31 Ibid.

called her by her new name a few months later. Like the others, the man claimed he had met her on the Internet and had come to her house for a sexual encounter.

After she sent a written complaint to the Maine Attorney General's Office, Detective Laurie Northrup of the computer crimes unit spoke with M.B. about sex videos she found of herself posted on adult websites. They had been consensually recorded, but M.B. had not expected nor desired them to become publicly accessible.

Detective Northrup learned that Sayer had created social networking accounts using M.B.'s name and birth date, and began seriously investigating Sayer's activities. According to a judge's order denying Sayer's attempt to suppress evidence in the case, this investigation unfolded as follows:

> The obvious digital detective work: issuing subpoenas to PayPal, Facebook, MySpace and Yahoo! to get identifying information and IP addresses for the person who had posted fake profiles, placed ads, and posted videos online. This led to an unhelpful trove of email addresses that had been created for the purpose of the postings. The IP addresses were more useful, showing the location of the networks from which the postings had been made, including many spots around the town in [of] Maine where Sayer lived, as well as few from the Netherlands.
>
> Law enforcement drove into Sayer's driveway, pretending they were pulling in to turn around, and then used a laptop to determine which wireless signals he could pick up from his house. The judge explains: "Part of the government's case is that the defendant used others' wireless access so that his actions could not be traced to him." For example, a Craigslist ad posting and a new Facebook account created on Sayer's ex-girlfriend's behalf were both linked back to the IP address of Richard Cook in Biddeford, Maine, "who lived across the street from the defendant and had an unsecure wireless internet connection." Tricky, but not tricky enough.
>
> Law enforcement installed a "live-feed video camera" at a neighbor's house, with the neighbor's permission. (They must not have been big fans of Sayer.) Law enforcement apparently wanted to use this to help track Sayer's offline movements and tie them to his online activity. It didn't seem to have been very helpful. In one example of its use, "the camera showed the defendant leaving his house at 1:45 p.m. on April 2, and at 6:37 p.m. a new Facebook account was created purporting to be the victim." It's unclear how that helps their case.
>
> In November 2009, the officers searched Sayer's home (with a search warrant). They found two desktop computers without hard drives, numerous computer components, a laptop case and a digital camera with a USB cable attached. Weirdly, no laptop and no hard drives. "The defendant explained that the laptop had gotten wet so he threw it away and the hard drives had been 'hacked' and were unusable."

In December 2009, Sayer's ex moved back to Maine from Louisiana. Shortly thereafter, "someone" welcomed her back by creating a new MySpace account for her which "linked to pornographic videos of the victim." After Detective Northrup obtained subscriber information and a connection log associated with the MySpace profile, she "learned that the profile was created and accessed by numerous IP addresses all registered to users in Saco, Maine. When Detective Northrup visited each of the addresses, she determined that all had unsecure wireless networks that would allow someone parked near the location to access the internet through their unsecure wireless connection."

In December 2009, they got a court order to put a GPS tracker on Sayer's green Ford Ranger pick-up truck.

More useful than the camera at the neighbor's house was the camera outside the Saco House of Pizza, which was pointed at the parking lot of a sweets shop with an open Wi-Fi network used by the perpetrator. From the judge's order: "The owner of Saco House of Pizza gave Detective Northrup the video surveillance tape from December 12, 2009, the date when Pepperell Sweets' wireless had been used to access the MySpace profile of the victim. The video shows a small green pickup truck pulling into a parking space in front of Pepperell Sweets minutes before the connection was made to the MySpace profile. The truck stayed parked for 21 minutes." Yes, they linked Sayer's truck with a MySpace posting made from the sweet shop's Wi-Fi network. Sweet indeed. The owner of Saco Pizza also later told an agent he saw a man typing on his laptop in the truck.

In January 2010, law enforcement actually installed the GPS tracker on the truck. "Over the next week, the defendant's pickup truck was detected driving and stopping for periods of time in areas corresponding to the IP addresses that accessed the fraudulent MySpace account for the victim."

In July 2010, they searched Sayer's house again. This time, they found a laptop. Once they examined it, they found evidence of 49 different Yahoo! profiles Sayer had created, including "luvmarriedmen29@yahoo. com." (Had the first 28 iterations of that already been claimed?) The account was often accessed from an Amsterdam-based IP address, leading the detective to suggest that Sayer was spoofing his IP address.[32]

Sayer's arrest illustrates what is possible when law enforcement agents dedicate substantial resources to investigating an online harassment situation. The perpetrator can be identified, and potentially brought to justice for

32 *United States v. Sayer,* Case No. 2:11-cr-113, slip op. (D. Me. motion to suppress/exclude denied June 13, 2012). Online. Available at: <http://www.med.uscourts.gov/Opinions/Hornby/2012/DBH_06132012_2-11cr113_U_S_V_SAYER.pdf>.

his crimes. But not all police officers are going to be willing to invest the necessary time or money. Some may view the harassment as "only words" that the First Amendment protects, or as incivility that is best handled as a civil matter. Others may feel that the victim has in some way brought the harassment on herself, and is therefore undeserving of assistance.

Conclusion

Ultimately, only a refashioning of Section 230 immunity will induce online service providers to find cost-effective ways to assist Internet harassment victims. They will not evolve into true Good Samaritans without powerful legal incentives to do so.

Part 3

Regulating cyberspace

8 Internet responsibility, geographic boundaries, and business ethics

Raphael Cohen-Almagor[1]

> The mind of the superior man is conversant with righteousness; the mind of the mean man is conversant with gain.
>
> Confucius (quoted in Tung 1921, p. 80)

Introduction

In his cyber law scholarship, Lawrence Lessig (1999, pp. 43–4) distinguishes between two claims. One is that, given its architecture, it is difficult for governments to *regulate behavior* on the Net. The other is that it is difficult for governments to *regulate the architecture of the Net*. The first claim is true. The second is not. It is not hard for governments to take steps to alter Net architecture, and in so doing, facilitate the regulation of Net behavior.

In the late 1990s, the Internet seemed a perfect medium for business: Supra-national, diffusive, with wide distribution and little regulation, offering enormous opportunities to investors. In his famous "Declaration of the Independence of Cyberspace," the Internet theorist John Perry Barlow wrote:

> Governments of the Industrial World, you weary giants of flesh and steel .... You have no sovereignty where we gather. You have no moral right to rule us nor do you possess any methods of enforcement we have true reason to fear. Cyberspace does not lie within your borders.[2]

Cases like *Yahoo!* mark the beginning of the end of the no-sovereignty illusion. They demonstrate that Internet Service Providers (ISPs) have to respect

---

1 Professor and Chair of Politics, University of Hull. The author of this chapter thanks Janet Spikes for her excellent research assistance. Gratitude is also expressed to Ann Bartow, Nikolaus Peifer, Joel R. Reidenberg, and Jack Hayward for their useful suggestions and incisive criticisms. A former version of this chapter was originally published by Springer. The chapter is published with kind permission from Springer Science+Business Media: *Journal of Business Ethics*, "Freedom of Expression, Internet Responsibility and Business Ethics: The Yahoo! Saga and Its Aftermath," Vol. 106, issue 3 (2012): 353–65, DOI: 10.1007/s10551-011-1001-z by Raphael Cohen-Almagor>.
2 "The Internet's new borders" (11 August 2001); Shea (15 January 2006, p. K4).

domestic state legislation in order to avoid legal risks. An ISP is a company or other organization that provides a gateway to the Internet, enabling users to establish contact with the public network. Many ISPs also provide e-mail service, storage capacity, proprietary chat rooms, and information regarding news, weather, finance, social and political events, travel and vacations. Some offer games to their subscribers and provide opportunities for shopping. Yahoo! is one of the most popular search engines and Websites in the world. The company also provides multiple other web services, including a directory (Yahoo! Directory), e-mail, news, maps, advertising, auction site and video sharing (Yahoo! Video) (<http://everything.yahoo.com/>; <http://uk.yahoo.com/?p=us> accessed 20 April 2012).

The Yahoo! controversy juxtaposes two contrasting views: Yahoo!'s Internet-separatist view that it can engage in commerce as it chooses notwithstanding national laws and morals, versus the view that countries have the right and ability to assert their sovereignty on the Net. This chapter argues for the adoption of standards of Corporate Social Responsibility (CSR), under which limits are placed upon free expression in the interest of furthering goals of social responsibility. CSR on the Internet, especially when it concerns ISPs, may require limiting some information deemed by sovereigns to be anti-social and offensive (Levmore and Nussbaum 2010).

In his seminal work, H.R. Bowen (1953, p. 6) defined corporate social responsibility as the obligations of business people to make decisions, to pursue policies or "to follow those lines of action which are desirable in terms of the objectives and values of our society." The Internet is international in character, but it is susceptible to the constraints of national laws. There is not one law for the Internet and another for all other forms of communication.

This chapter comprises four sections: First, the Yahoo! saga as it unfolded in France and the USA is described in detail. Next, a comparative legal dimension is provided, explaining how different countries address the challenge of hate and racist speech. Then it considers the business dimension of the Yahoo! affair. Finally, it discusses responsible terms of service Internet companies can employ that prohibit anti-social, violent content on their servers.

The Yahoo! saga

Sales of Nazi merchandise are against the law in France. Section R645-1 of the French Criminal Code strictly prohibits the selling or displaying of anything that incites racism. The French Criminal Code prohibits the display of Nazi symbols. The Yahoo! saga started in February of 2000 when Marc Knobel, director of the International League against Racism and Anti-Semitism (Ligue Internationale Contre le Racisme et l'Antisémitisme, LICRA) and a member of the Observatory of Antisemitism, went to the Yahoo! auction site and saw pages of Nazi-related paraphernalia. The site featured swastika arm-bands, SS daggers, concentration camp photos, striped uniforms once worn by Nazi camp prisoners, and replicas of the Zyklon B gas canisters (Crumm and Capeloto 11 December 2000, p. A1; Reuters 27 February 2002, p. C4). While sales of Nazi merchandise are against French law, Knobel acknowledged that the auctions might be legal in the United States, but believed them to be illegal within the borders of France.

In April of 2000, LICRA together with two other organizations, UEJF (Union des Étudiants Juifs de France) and MRAP (Mouvement contre le Racisme, l'Antisémitisme et pour la Paix), asked Yahoo! to either remove the Nazi memorabilia from its American websites or make all such auctions inaccessible to Web surfers in France and its territories such as Martinique and French Guyana in accordance with its own Terms of Service agreement, which prohibited Netusers from posting content that was "hateful, or racially, ethnically or otherwise objectionable" (<http://uk.docs.yahoo.com/info/terms.html> accessed 20 April 2012). If it did not, the organizations asked that the California-based company be fined $96,000 for each day of non-compliance. Ronald Katz, a lawyer representing the French groups, asserted: "There is this naïve idea that the Internet changes everything. It doesn't change everything. It doesn't change the laws in France" (Guernsey 15 March 2001).

Figure 8.1 Example of Nazi paraphernalia: Photograph of manufacturers' Zyklon B canister labels.

  Source: United States government.

Yahoo! did not respond to the demands and legal action commenced. At the first hearing in the Tribunal de Grande Instance de Paris on 15 May 2000 defending counsel Christophe Pecard noted that Yahoo! maintained a French-language website (Yahoo!.fr) that complied with French law. He argued that "Internet users who go to Yahoo.com undertake a virtual voyage to the US," so no offense could be said to take place in France (Le Menestrel, Hunter and de Bettignies 2002, pp. 135–44). In any case, he said, it would be technically impossible for Yahoo! to block all access to its sites from France. Yahoo! claimed that it had no power to identify the national origins of its customers and thus no control over where in the world its digital products went. Were Yahoo! forced to comply with French law, it would need to remove the Nazi items from all its servers, thereby depriving Yahoo! users everywhere from buying them, and making French law the effective rule for the world (Goldsmith and Wu 2006, p. 5). In response, the plaintiffs' lawyer, Stéphane Lilti, asserted that France had the sovereign right to prohibit the sale of Nazi merchandise within its borders, and argued that Yahoo! should not be exempt from French law (Le Menestrel, Hunter and de Bettignies 2002).

The French court orders

On 22 May 2000, Judge Jean-Jacques Gomez ruled that Yahoo!'s sales were "an offense to the collective memory of a nation profoundly wounded by the atrocities committed in the name of the Nazi criminal enterprise."[3] He rejected all of Yahoo! Inc.'s jurisdiction related arguments, holding that though the Yahoo!.com site was located on a server in California, and perhaps intended for an American audience, harm was suffered in French territory, and Yahoo! auctions were not protected in France by the United States' First Amendment. Judge Gomez ordered Yahoo! Inc. "to take all measures such as would dissuade and render impossible all consultations on yahoo.com of the service of auctioning of Nazi objects as well as any other site or service which constitute an apology of nazism or which contest the nazi crimes."[4] In other words, the French court said that there can be no apology for Nazi crime, and that it is impossible to contest or downplay the horrific magnitude of evil-doing that had happened. Nazi crimes should be condemned without

---

3 *LICRA v. Yahoo! Inc. and Yahoo! France* (Tribunal de Grande Instance de Paris, 22 May 2000), affirmed in *LICRA and UEJF v. Yahoo! Inc. and Yahoo! France* (Tribunal de Grande Instance de Paris, 20 November 2000).

4 *La Ligue Contre le Racisme at l'Antisémitisme (L.I.C.R.A.) and L'Union des Etudiants Juifs de France (U.E.J.F.) v. Yahoo! Inc. and Yahoo! France*, Interim Court Order, The County Court of Paris 6 (22 May 2000). The Superior Court of Paris reiterated this in its 20 November 2000 order. The original and English translation are provided in the Appendix to the Complaint for Declaratory Relief in *Yahoo! Inc. v. L.I.C.R.A. and U.E.J.F.*, 169 F. Supp. 2d 1181 (N.D. Cal. 2001) (No. 00-21275).

any reservation. Yahoo! Inc. was ordered to prevent access from French territory to the Nazi objects and hate speech sites in question, or face a penalty of 100,000 francs per day for non-compliance (Kohl 2007, pp. 201–2).

In reaction to this court judgment, Heather Killen, a Yahoo! vice president, commented (*San Jose Mercury News* 25 July 2000): "It's very difficult to do business if you have to wake up every day and say 'OK, whose laws do I follow? ... We have many countries and many laws and just one Internet." Yahoo! argued that even if French officials identified and blocked the offending offshore website, the same information could be posted on mirror sites outside France (Goldsmith and Wu 2006, p. 2), and to keep out the Nazi pages France would need to shut down every single Internet access point within its borders. Furthermore, even this would not be completely effective because determined users in France could access the Net by a telephone call to an Internet access provider in another country (Goldsmith and Wu 2006, p. 3). Yahoo! co-founder Jerry Yang did not believe that one country's laws should regulate the Internet in other parts of the world, and asserted that asking Yahoo! to filter access to its sites according to the nationality of Web surfers was "very naïve" (Love 11 August 2000, p. C6). Later it became clear that it was Yang who was naïve. France instantiated new legal standards for the Internet which came into conflict with Yahoo!'s business practices.

Marc Levy, who represented the International League Against Racism and Anti-Semitism, observed that "freedom of expression is not unlimited ... The law does not permit racism in writing, on television or on the radio, and I see no reason to have an exception for the Internet" (Dembart 29 May 2000). Yahoo!, he said, should not be exempt from laws in the countries where it does business. Levy expressed "great satisfaction" with the ruling, saying the judge had "rendered a service to the Internet," which otherwise ran the risk of becoming a "no-law zone" ("French court says Yahoo broke racial law" 23 May 2000).

Judge Gomez gave Yahoo! two months to figure out how to block French surfers from the disputed auction sites. During this interval, Cyril Houri, the founder of a fledgling American firm called Infosplit, contacted the plaintiff's lawyer, Stéphane Lilti, and told him that he had developed a new technology that could identify and screen Internet content on the basis of its geographical source (Method and Systems for Locating Geographical Locations of Online Users). Using this technology he learned the Yahoo! servers accessed by Netusers in France, which the firm had claimed were protected by the U.S. First Amendment to the U.S. Constitution, were actually located on a website in Stockholm, Sweden. Yahoo! placed constantly updated "mirror" copies of its U.S. site on servers in Sweden to make access to it in Europe faster (Goldsmith and Wu 2006, p. 7, quoting communication from Cyril Houri).

When the trial resumed on 24 July 2000, Yahoo! lawyers again asserted that it was technically impossible to identify and filter out French visitors to the firm's U.S.-based websites. "It's technically not in Yahoo!'s power to do this," said Armando Fox, a computer science professor at Stanford University. He added: "All Yahoo! sees is an IP address, and anyone can set up a tunneling proxy to change an IP address. There's no way to reliably map an incoming connection" ("Yahoo! Ruling Exposes Risks of Being Global" 1 July 2000). Attorneys for the company said they had pulled Third Reich paraphernalia from their France-based site, Yahoo.fr and added warnings to pages with sensitive material, alerting French Netusers that they risked breaking French law by viewing them (Associated Press 25 July 2000, p. A5).[5]

But this solution was not acceptable to the plaintiffs because it was still possible to buy the illegal items via the U.S. server. In addition, Lilti raised Houri's geo-location technology with the court, alleging that Yahoo! auctions in France were not in fact coming from American servers, and that the assumption that every web page was equally accessible to every Netuser everywhere in the world was simply wrong. If Yahoo! could target French users from Swedish servers, Lilti argued, it could potentially identify Netusers by geographic location and screen them out (Goldsmith and Wu 2006, p. 7).

In August 2000, Judge Gomez appointed three Internet experts—Vinton Cerf, considered to be the "father" of the Internet, Ben Laurie, a British Internet expert, and Francois Wallon, a French technologist—to assess the extent to which Yahoo! could block transmissions into France. The experts concluded that it was possible to locate 70% of Netusers, a figure that could be increased by 20% if Yahoo! asked the users who requested the illegal contents to declare their nationality.[6] The three experts also suggested that Netusers could be forced to declare their geographical location and to answer certain questions if they use key words such as "Nazi" in their searches. While Vinton Cerf expressed some philosophical reservations about the proposals, he admitted they were technically feasible (Cue 10 January 2001, p. 1).

In November 2000, Judge Gomez reaffirmed his 22 May order and ruled that Yahoo! was avoiding a moral and ethical exigency that all democratic societies share.[7] In his final ruling on 20 November, Gomez said Yahoo! had already prohibited the sale of human organs, cigarettes, live animals, drugs, and used underwear. He observed that it would cost the company very little to extend the list of banned goods to include Nazi symbols, and that doing so "would have the merit of satisfying an ethical and moral standard shared by all democratic societies" (Cue 10 January 2001, p. 1). He noted that Yahoo! welcomed French visitors to its U.S. website with French-language

---

5 However, while Yahoo! removed the items from the commercial auction site it still continued to allow them to be sold in chat rooms accessible worldwide. See Egelko (11 February 2005, p. C3).

6 Union des Etudiants Juifs de France, TGI Paris, Nov. 20, 2000, Ord. ref., J.C.P. 2000, Actu., 2219; Piazza (1 February 2001, p. 38).

7 Conclusions pour la Société Yahoo! Inc., A Monsieur le Président du Tribunal de Grande Instance de Paris, Audience de reféré du 15 mai 2000: 18.

advertisements, which showed that Yahoo! was tailoring content for France, and that it could, at least to some extent, identify and screen Netusers by geography.[8] Marc Knobel said in reaction: "The French justice system has heard us … It is no longer OK for online retailers to say they are not affected by existing laws." He maintained that if global Internet companies weren't willing to put "ethics and morals" first themselves, they would be forced to do so.[9]

Yahoo! Inc. was again directed to satisfy the terms of Judge Gomez's previous order within three months, or pay a fine of FF 100,000 (about $13,600) per day thereafter if they failed to comply with its legal obligations.[10] Yahoo! representatives responded by challenging the legitimacy of the proceedings and verdict (Associated Press 21 November 2000, p. 3D; Vick 2005, pp. 41–2).

Yahoo! knew it was violating French law. Its managers knew that Nazi paraphernalia was highly offensive to the French people, especially the Jews after the Holocaust. Yet Yahoo! preferred to behave as if American legal norms applied globally.

American salvation?

After realizing that Yahoo! could not win in France, the company directors decided to seek help on its home soil, thinking that an American court would decline to enforce the French judgment against the company and would grant Yahoo! permission to continue its unfettered business practices on the global Internet. Yahoo! filed suit against LICRA and UEJF in federal district court, seeking a declaratory judgment that the interim orders of the French court were not enforceable in the United States.[11] In January 2001,

---

8 *La Ligue Contre le Racisme at l'Antisémitisme (L.I.C.R.A.) and L'Union des Etudiants Juifs de France (U.E.J.F.) v. Yahoo! Inc. and Yahoo! France*, Interim Court Order, The County Court of Paris 6, 22 May 2000. For critical discussion, see Corn-Revere (2003).

9 *LICRA et UEJF v Yahoo! Inc*, Ordonnance Référé, TGI Paris (20 November 2000), Ord. ref., J.C.P. 2000, Actu., 2219; see also Essick (21 November 2000).

10 Two days after Judge Gomez decided the Yahoo! case another judge rendered his verdict on similar facts and issues against UEJF. In this case, Multimania hosted a website entitled "nsdap" (an acronym for the Nazi party) whose content related to Adolf Hitler, the Nazi ideology, Nazi texts, and symbols. Once on notice, Multimania removed access to the website. Multimania had also supervised the websites it hosted by use of a search engine and keywords relating to usual illegal content found on the Internet. But Multimania had not used the acronym "nsdap" for its search. The court found that Multimania acted reasonably and promptly given its competence and the technical means available to detect illegal content. Unlike Yahoo!, Multimania acted in good faith and the court held that it was not liable. See *Ass'n Union des Etudiants Juifs de France v. SA Multimania Prod.*, Tribunal de grande instance de Nanterre (24 May 2000); see also Amadei (November 2001/February 2002, p. 189).

11 Reidenberg (2005, p. 1959) argues that Yahoo! introduced a misleading translation of the French decision at the district court.

after both interim orders had been entered by the French court, and after Yahoo! had filed suit in federal district court, Yahoo! adopted a new policy prohibiting use of auctions or classified advertisements on Yahoo.com to offer or trade in items associated with groups principally known for hateful and violent positions directed at others, based on race or similar factors. Yahoo! pulled all Nazi, Ku Klux Klan and similar items associated with hatred and violence from its auction sites, announcing that it "will no longer allow items that are associated with groups which promoted or glorify hatred and violence, to be listed on any of Yahoo!'s commerce properties" (Editorial 13 January 2001, p. 22; Wolverton and Pelline 2 January 2001). Yahoo! also said it would start a new policy that included having trained representatives monitoring the site regularly. In addition, Yahoo! would use software to identify potentially objectionable items (Wolverton and Pelline 2 January 2001). Because of these actions that brought Yahoo! into substantial compliance with French law, the fines were not imposed.

In November 2001, the U.S. District Court for the Northern District of California considered the important differences between the French legal norms and the American First Amendment and ruled that the Yahoo! order could not be enforced in the United States. Judge Jeremy Fogel concluded that the French ruling was inconsistent with the First Amendment, and held that while France could regulate speech in its territory, "this court" would not enforce a foreign order that violated the protections granted under the United States Constitution. Yahoo! showed that the threat to its constitutional rights was real and immediate.[12]

The litigation culminated in January of 2006 with a lengthy and fractured opinion by an en banc panel of the U.S. Court of Appeals for the Ninth Circuit.[13] Eight of the eleven judges concluded that the District Court had personal jurisdiction over the French organizations but notwithstanding its view of the jurisdictional issue three of the eight judges also concluded that Yahoo!'s claim was not "ripe for adjudication" and should be dismissed on those grounds because LICRA and UEJF had not sought enforcement of the French court's orders in the USA, the French court may not impose a fine even if they do ask for one, and it is unlikely a U.S. court would enforce such a fine even if a French court imposed one. Enforcement is unlikely "not because of the First Amendment, but rather because of the general principle of comity under which American courts do not enforce monetary fines or penalties awarded by foreign courts" (*Yahoo! Inc. v. LICRA and UEJF*, 433 F 3d 1199, 9th Cir. 2006). Though five of those eight judges did think Yahoo!'s case was "ripe," three of the court's eleven judges concluded that the District Court did not have personal jurisdiction over the French organizations.

---

12 *Yahoo! Inc. v. La Ligue Contre le Racisme Yahoo! Inc.*, 169 F. Supp. 2d 1181; 2001 US Dist. Lexis 18378 (7 November 2001).
13 *Yahoo! Inc. v. LICRA and UEJF*, 433 F 3d 1199 (9th Cir. 2006). See also *Yahoo! Inc. v. LICRA and UEJF*, 379 F 3d 1120 (9th Cir. 2004).

Since a majority of judges (six of the eleven) voted to dismiss the case for one reason or another, dismissed it was. Yahoo! did not receive the judicial support it was hoping for.

Comparative legal dimension

As an American company Yahoo! relied in its business model upon a First Amendment view of freedom of expression. The First Amendment is enshrined in the American legal and political culture. It explicitly instructs: "Congress shall make no law respecting an establishment of religion, or prohibiting the free exercise thereof; or abridging the freedom of speech, or of the press; or the right of the people peaceably to assemble, and to petition the Government for a redress of grievances" (First Amendment—Religion and Expression). This is a sharp and uncompromising statement, leading American scholars and judges to argue that no law means no law (Dennis, Gillmor and Grey 1978; Konvitz 1963, pp. 393–506; Shapiro 1966, p. 87; Martin 1961, p. 109; Brown 22 March 2011). One of the preeminent American justices of the Supreme Court, Hugo L. Black (1960, p. 879) asserted in a classic article his belief that the Constitution "with its absolute guarantees of individual rights, is the best hope for the aspirations of freedom which men share everywhere." The First Amendment was designed to guarantee the freest interchange of ideas about all public matters. If the Constitution withdraws from Government all power over subject matter in areas such as speech, press, assembly, and petition, wrote Black (1960), "there is nothing over which authority may be exerted."

Another iconic legal authority, Alexander Meiklejohn (1965, p. 107), asserted that the First Amendment declares that with respect to belief, political discussion, political advocacy, political planning, the citizens are the sovereign, and the Congress is their subordinate agent. Meiklejohn (1965, p. 124) coined the saying that "to be afraid of any idea is to be unfit for self-government." According to this view, the public responsibilities of citizenship in the free world are in a vital sense beyond the reach of any legislative control. Consequently, freedom of expression in the American tradition occupies an especially protected normative position. Generally speaking, expression is perceived as doing less injury to other social goals than action. It has less immediate consequences, and is less irremediable in its impact (Emerson 1970, pp. 9, 292).[14] Only when expression might immediately translate to harmful action, when one is able to prove a clear link between

---

14 See also Black (1960, p. 879); Meiklejohn (1966, pp. 19–26); Emerson (1970); Baker (1992); BeVier (1978, pp. 299–358); Schauer (1982); Dworkin (1985); Bollinger (1986); Smolla (1993); Gates Jr et al. (1995); Fiss (2000, pp. 70–78); Newman (2010, pp. 119–23). For views that balance freedom of expression with other values such as privacy and the dignity of a person, see Matsuda et al. (1993); Tsesis (2002); Delgado and Stefancic (2004); Cohen-Almagor (1994, 2005, 2006, 2007).

the harmful speech and the resulting harmful action, is it possible to justify restrictions on freedom of expression. This approach sets a very high threshold to satisfy. Only in clear and exceptional cases are there grounds to limit expression. Hate speech, in its varied general manifestations, is protected speech in the United States (Cohen-Almagor 1993, pp. 453–70; Heyman 2008, esp. pp. 164–83; Lawrence 2006, http://papers.ssrn.com/sol3/papers.cfm?abstract_id=921923; Waldron 2010, pp. 1596–657). Only hate crimes are criminalized.

Other democracies in the western world are more willing to regulate hate speech. Most European countries, especially those that were under Nazi occupation or fought against Nazi Germany, are very cognizant of the harms of hate speech because the horrors of WWII are well remembered, and the power of hate propaganda is well appreciated. Hate speech led not only to the destruction of European Jewry but also to mass murders on a horrific scale of all "inferior races" and "undesired elements."[15] In consequence, many European nations have laws prohibiting hate speech. Spain passed legislation authorizing judges to shut down Spanish sites and block access to U.S. Web pages that do not comply with its national laws to address threats to its national defense and public order (Scheeres 9 November 2002; Ramasastry 6 February 2003). In the Netherlands, Section 137 of the Criminal Code makes it a criminal offense to "deliberately give public expression to views insulting to a group of persons on account of their race, religion or conviction or sexual preference" (Sadurski 1999, p. 179). In Sweden, the Freedom of the Press Act (Chap. 7, Art. 4) prohibits the expression of contempt for any population group "with allusion to its race, skin colour, national or ethnic origin, or religious faith" (Sadurski 1999, p. 179).

Britain has recognized dangers associated with the fascist uses of hate speech. Its earliest attempt to curb such speech was Article 5 of the Public Order Act (1936).[16] This legislation was intended to counter the verbal attacks on the Jewish community made by Oswald Mosley and his fellow members in the British Union of Fascists, which led to outbreaks of violence in Britain. The law was bolstered in 1965 with section 6 of the British Race

---

15 On the horrors of WWII, their root causes and justifications, see Hilberg (1985); Mosse (1997); Klee et al. (eds.) (1996); Sereny (1983); Burleigh and Wippermann (1993); Fings et al. (1997); Fings (1999); Aly, Heim, and Blunden (2003); Lusane (2002); Brustein (2003); Johnson and Reuband (2006); Ehrenreich, (2007); Browning (2007); Goldhagen (2009); Kershaw (2009); Nazi racism, <http://www.ushmm.org/outreach/en/article.php?ModuleId=10007679>; Racism: An Overview, <http://www.ushmm.org/wlc/en/article.php?ModuleId=10005184>; Wistrich (2010).

16 Public Order Act (1936), 1 Edw. 8 & 1 Geo. 6, c. 6, § 5 (U.K.). This legislation was later replaced by Public Order Act (1986).

Relations Act, making it an offense to stir up hatred against a racial group.[17] Section 17 of the Public Order Act of 1986 defines "racial hatred" as hatred against a group of persons by reference to color, race, nationality (including citizenship) or ethnic or national origins. Other European countries that have enacted laws penalizing the distribution of hate propaganda include Austria, Belgium, Cyprus, Hungary, Italy, and Switzerland (Jones 1998, pp. 189–224, 259–313; Tsesis 2002; 2002a, p. 5; 2009, esp. pp. 499–501; Cohen-Almagor 2010, pp. 125–32).[18]

The implications of the Yahoo! saga are particularly relevant for Germany, where many racist and hate groups post messages on American sites that are illegal in Germany. German radicals access the Internet for those purposes from Germany, in clear violation of German law. Children are targeted in an attempt to lure them to racist, radical ideologies. According to a recent study, the number of right-wing extremist contributions from Germany to Internet platforms aimed at school children or music fans—Facebook, YouTube, Twitter and other social networking tools—rose from 750 in 2007 to about 6,000 in 2010 (Hate Monitor Net, 26 August 2010). In July 2009, the then Justice Minister Brigitte Zypries said her office would appeal to foreign Internet providers to use their own terms of service as grounds for eliminating content promoting fascism. She called for ISPs in the U.S. and elsewhere to remove neo-Nazi images, text and other content that can be viewed inside the country in violation of laws forbidding any Nazi symbols (McGroarty 10 July 2009). It is doubtful, however, that U.S. companies have rushed to remove material that is protected under the First Amendment.[19]

---

17 Barendt (2007); Supperstone (1981, p. 15); Home Office, *Racial Discrimination*, White Paper (September 1975), Commd. 6234; Commission for Racial Equality, *Reviews of the Race Relations Act* (1985, 1992); *Race Relations Act* (1976); Her Majesty's Stationery Office, *Race Relations (Amendment) Act* 2000.

18 I asked the eminent historian, Saul Friedlander, how to explain the American attitude to hate speech as compared to the European. He answered (on 22 July 2011) that the striking difference is especially "between the situation in most of continental Europe, on the one hand, and in Great Britain, Sweden and Switzerland, on the other (who were not under German occupation). In the US, in my opinion, the first amendment is crucial."

19 In August 2000, the Düsseldorf District Authority President, Jurgen Bussow, wrote to four American ISPs, requesting that they prevent access to four websites containing racist, neo-Nazi material. This action was unsuccessful. See Akdeniz (2008, p. 236). On 8 February 2002, Jurgen Bussow ordered all ISPs in the German State of Nordrhein-Westfalen (North Rhine-Westphalia) to block user access to two specific U.S.-based hate sites, Stormfront and Nazi-Lauck (Press Release, *Bezirksregierung Düsseldorf erlässt Sperrungsverfügungen wegen rechtsextremischer Angebote im Internet*, 42/2002 8 Feb. 2002). More than 30 of the 76 ISPs in Nordrhein-Westfalen lost various court battles which may be found in Oberverwaltungsgericht Münster, 2003 *Multimedia und Recht* (MMR) 348; Verwaltungsgericht Düsseldorf 2003 MMR 305; *Verwaltungsgericht Arnsberg* 2003 *Zeitschrift für Urheber- und Medienrecht Rechtsprechungsreport* 222. However, this blocking directive is local and does not compel the other German landers (states), and it relates to only two hate sites. See Eberwine (2004).

Business dimension

The business dimension of the Yahoo! saga was implicitly acknowledged in November of 2000, when Yahoo!'s management decided that auctions would henceforth be a paying service, and Yahoo! would decide what could be properly sold. Yahoo! realized that it had assets in France including a French subsidiary that might be at risk of seizure if the company failed to comply with the French court's ruling. Shares of Yahoo! Inc. fell nearly 15 percent on New York's Nasdaq stock market after the Gomez verdict. This was their lowest level in two years (Reuters 21 November 2000, p. B1). Yahoo! was sensitive to the wishes of its foreign customers, because 40 percent of its traffic at that time was outside the USA. Analysts noted that legal issues facing the company were not likely to be the main cause of the stock's weakness, but feared that any additional successful suits could hurt international revenues (Reuters 22 November 2000, p. B5).

Sometimes there is tension between freedom of information, on the one hand, and moral and social responsibility, on the other, which can have significant business implications not only for the company at hand but for other information and communication companies in the future. In business, responsibility is defined in terms of obligations accepted by employers in relation to their employees and suppliers to customers and clients. There is often a basis in law, but many responsibilities are customary, subject to negotiation according to the interests and balance of power of the parties involved, and dictated by competitive necessities. The acceptance and fulfillment of responsibilities by business actors is mainly determined by considerations of long-term self-interest and maintaining good customer relations, although ethical principles may also play a part (McQuail 2003, p. 191).[20] CSR scholar Keith Davis (1973, p. 313) asserts that it is a firm's obligation to consider the effects of its decisions on society in a manner that will accomplish social benefits as well as traditional economic benefits. This means that "social responsibility begins where the law ends. A firm is not being socially responsible if it merely complies with the minimum requirements of the law, because this is what any good citizen would do."[21] Yahoo! focused on the legal aspects of its auction site by merely complying with the American requirements of the law which champions freedom of expression.

The main principles of CSR dictate integrated, sustainable decision-making which takes into consideration the positive and negative potential consequences of decisions; obligations on the part of corporations not only to consider different stakeholders and interests but also to incorporate them into the decision-making processes; transparency that is vital for ensuring accountability to stakeholders; liability for decisions and enactment of

---

20 For further discussion, see Horrigan (2010).
21 See also Kotler and Lee (2005).

remedial measures to redress harm inflicted as a result of conduct (Goodpaster 2010, pp. 126–57; Kerr, Janda and Pitts 2009; Werther and Chandler 2010). Archie Carroll (1979, pp. 497–505; 1981) articulated in his seminal work that beyond the obvious economic and legal obligations that a firm has, the social responsibility of businesses also encompasses ethical and discretionary responsibilities. Business is expected, by definition, to make a profit. Society expects business to obey the law. In addition, ethical responsibilities include adherence to ethical norms. By "ethical norms" Carroll means adherence to fairness, justice and due process. And finally, by discretionary responsibilities Carroll refers to philanthropic contributions and non-profit social welfare activities.[22] Carroll's pyramid of CSR depicted the economic category at the base and then built upward through legal, ethical and philanthropic categories. In his view, a company with good CSR practices should strive to make a profit while obeying the law and it should behave ethically as a good corporate citizen (Carroll September 1999, pp. 268–95; Carroll and Buchholtz 2011, esp. chaps. 2, 6).

According to Carroll's formulation, Yahoo! did not behave responsibly because its conduct lacked ethical perspective. Instead, the Yahoo! officials exhibited amoral management. "Amoral managers," Carroll explains (1991, pp. 39–48), "are neither immoral nor moral but are not sensitive to the fact that their everyday business decisions may have deleterious effects on others." In my assessment, the Yahoo! managers ignored the ethical dimension of their business because they were unresponsive to local laws and were inattentive to the implications of their conduct on stakeholders.

Corporate Social Responsibility carries a special meaning in the context of information and communication technologies (ICT). ICTs make humanity increasingly accountable, morally speaking, for the way information is transferred (Floridi and Sanders 2001, pp. 55–66). Members of these professions are trained to practice a core skill, requiring autonomous judgment as well as expertise. ICT professionals have an inviolable duty to abide by the terms of service and see that their clients are satisfied. Their work is based on knowledge and skill. Certain standards and qualifications are expected to be maintained.[23]

Corporate Social Responsibility on the Internet may prompt ICT professionals to adopt different modes of operation: The first is to follow the law of the land. The second is to do more than following the laws. I believe my analysis implies that multinational companies must do more than follow the laws in the home country of the head office; they need to integrate the laws of the host country into the decision-making process, for instance banning hate speech even where this is not required, as is the case in the United States.

---

22 See also Crane (September 2009).
23 Compare to the responsibilities of the press; see McQuail (2003, p. 191); Cohen-Almagor (2005, pp. 87–123).

And the third is to ignore the laws of the host country where the laws are manifestly unethical. This is the case, for instance, when the law aims to censor political speech or certain groups because of their race, culture or religion.

David Radin (2001, p. F3), the President of Radio Network, asserts that removing Nazi memorabilia from auction sites is the right business decision. First, removing the objectionable materials will probably not harm the company's sales dramatically, but will have a goodwill effect throughout the world, possibly attracting more users. Second, from a business standpoint, it is easier to implement restrictions worldwide than to create business and technical processes that treat citizens of different countries differently in order to universally stay on the right side of the law. Third, Radin rightly notes, it is the morally responsible thing to do.[24]

Although hate speech is legally tolerated in the US, Yahoo! Inc.'s commercial image would not have gained much if it were seen to be condoning the sale of Nazi memorabilia via its websites. Even in the absence of enforceability, factors such as market forces, moral beliefs, or a combination of them, may by themselves or in combination with legal measures compel legal compliance (Kohl 2007, p. 207).

Adopting norms of social responsibility could be beneficial for ISPs and Web Hosting Services. This ethical practice could contribute to each firm's reputation and marketing. Indeed, there is a significant positive relationship between CSR activities and consumers' purchasing decisions (Lee and Shin June 2010, pp. 193–5). Stewart Lewis (2003, pp. 356–94) argues that CSR, referring to practices that improve the workplace and benefit society beyond what companies are legally mandated to do, is established as a fundamental addition to stakeholders' criteria for judging companies, and calls for a reappraisal of companies' brand and reputation management. Upholding norms of CSR benefit both the firm and the societies in which it operates.

Responsible terms of service

Online intermediaries encompass conduits such as ISPs, platforms such as video sharing sites, social networking sites that allow Netusers to access online content and interact with each other, and Web hosting companies that provide space on servers they own for use by their clients as well as Internet connectivity. Some ISPs offer guidelines regarding prohibited Internet content and usage, terms of service cancellation, and even

---

24 See also Fannon (2003, pp. 93–103).

user responsibilities. ISPs may prohibit posting legally seditious or offensive content. For example,

Yahoo!'s rules state that it is prohibited to	"upload, post, transmit or otherwise make available any Content that is unlawful, harmful, threatening, abusive, harassing, tortuous, defamatory, vulgar, obscene, libelous, invasive of another's privacy, hateful, adult-oriented, or racially, ethnically or otherwise objectionable."[25]
Basic ISP's rules state that it is prohibited to	"Post or transmit any unlawful, threatening, abusive, libelous, defamatory, obscene, pornographic, profane, or otherwise objectionable information of any kind, including without limitation any transmissions constituting or encouraging conduct that would constitute a criminal offense, give rise to civil liability, or otherwise violate any local, state, national or international law …"[26]
DataPipe's rules state that it is prohibited to	"transmit, distribute or store material (a) in violation of any applicable law, (b) in a manner that will infringe the copyright, trademark, trade secret or other intellectual property rights of others or the privacy, publicity or other personal rights of others, or (c) that is obscene, threatening, abusive or hateful, including the advocating of terrorism and/or the killing of any individual or group."[27]

Several ISP associations have developed different codes concerning, among other things, the protection of minors.[28]

ISPs may choose to pre-screen and refuse any content that is available via their service. Yahoo! declares that it may or may not pre-screen and that it has "the right (but not the obligation) in their sole discretion to pre-screen, refuse, or remove any Content that is available via the Yahoo! Services. Without limiting the foregoing, Yahoo! and its designees shall have the right to remove any Content that violates the TOS or is otherwise objectionable."[29] Some ISPs assert the right to terminate service under any circumstances and without prior notice, especially if content violates the Terms of Service agreement or if law enforcement or other government agencies request the removal. Some ISPs reserve the right to remove information that does not

---

25 <http://docs.yahoo.com/info/terms/lfws/> (accessed 20 April 2012).
26 <http://www.basicisp.net/TOS/DSLTOS.aspx> (accessed 20 April 2012).
27 <http://www.datapipe.com/legal/acceptable_use_policy/> (accessed 20 April 2012).
28 For further discussion, see Organisation for Economic Co-operation and Development (2006); Price and Verhulst (2000).
29 <http://docs.yahoo.com/info/terms> (accessed 20 April 2012).

meet the standards they set.[30] However, if such content is not removed by the ISP, neither it nor its partners assume any liability. In this context, let me mention that the American Congress passed the "Good Samaritan provision," included in the 1996 Communication Decency Act (section 230-c-2) which protects ISPs that voluntarily take action to restrict access to problematic material: "No provider or user of an interactive computer service shall be held liable on account of—(A) any action voluntarily taken in good faith to restrict access to or availability of material that the provider or user considers to be obscene, lewd, lascivious, filthy, excessively violent, harassing, or otherwise objectionable, whether or not such material is constitutionally protected."[31]

Whatever responsible steps corporations take, it is imperative that these steps should be transparent, and communicated to the public. In 2002, Google, the world's most popular search engine, quietly deleted more than 100 controversial sites from some search result listings. It did so secretly, without public discussion or explanation and, as a result, was subjected to intense criticism. Most of the sites that were removed from Google.fr (France) and Google.de (Germany) were anti-Semitic, pro-Nazi or related to white supremacy (McCullagh 23 October 2002). However, the removed sites continue to appear in listings on the main Google.com site.

In 2005, Google spokesman Steve Langdon announced that Google News does not allow hate content. "If we are made aware of articles that contain hate content, we will remove them," he said (Kuchinskas 23 March 2005). Among the removed news was *National Vanguard*, a publication of the National Alliance, an organization for "people of European descent" aiming to achieve a new consciousness, a new order, and a new people. *The National Vanguard* describes itself as "fearless—uncompromising—brilliant—witty—educational. National Vanguard provides the information and the insights that White America's future leaders will need to guide our nation through the dangerous, revolutionary times ahead."[32] Indeed, news organizations have editorial discretion over what they run and do not run. Google made a conscious decision not to help in the spread of racism and bigotry. In this case, Google proactively adopted ethical norms of CSR.[33]

Economically speaking, some may raise the concern that enforcing liability on Internet intermediaries will significantly raise the costs of business. One way to offset the incurred costs might be higher subscription fees. As a result, some subscribers who will not be able to afford the service would leave

---

30 <http://legal.web.aol.com/aol/aolpol/comguide.html> (accessed 20 April 2012).
31 CDA 47 U.S.C. at <http://www4.law.cornell.edu/uscode/47/230.html> (accessed 20 April 2012). For further discussion, see chapter 7 in this volume.
32 <http://www.natvan.com/national-vanguard/> (accessed 20 April 2012).
33 For a critique of Google for its lax attitude on human rights in China, see Dann and Haddow (2008, pp. 219–34).

the market. There are several ways to address this concern. One is to suggest more advertising, or the same amount of advertising charging more money, accompanied with an explanation for the reason why the price has risen. Another is governmental tax incentives to Internet intermediaries based on the number of subscribers. A third way is to impose financial penalties against those who systematically violate their own terms and conditions of service, penalizing people who abuse the service for their misconduct.

To be sure, Internet intermediaries need to be careful in restricting speech. Adopting an extremely overzealous monitoring policy increases the likelihood of subscribers' being informed about such a policy, and thus might create a negative reputation for an ISP, which in turn would encourage its users to experiment with other service providers (Hamdani May 2002, pp. 929–30). What Internet intermediaries could certainly do is to provide a uniform channel for user complaints. Such a channel (which could be as simple as a link to the CyberTipline) could easily be placed on the complaints or customer service page of the service provider (Thornburgh and Lin 2002, p. 380).

Conclusion

The Internet has been perceived as an unfettered highway, and the way to combat problematic speech is said to be by more speech. Organizations and associations were set up to protect and promote freedom of expression, freedom of information and privacy on the Internet.[34] The Internet's design and *raison d'être* are open architecture, freedom of expression, and neutral network of networks. In the prevailing western liberal tradition, freedom of expression is perceived as a fundamental human right and censorship should not be allowed to inhibit the free flow of information. This is especially true for the Internet.

The aim of this chapter is to show that (1) ethically speaking, Yahoo! should not entertain Nazi material on its servers; (2) ethics and business go hand in hand as the decision not to entertain such material serves the company's best interests; and (3) international companies like Yahoo! should strive to respect the laws of the countries in which they operate. Although international in character, the medium of the Internet is not above the law.

France has pushed forward new legal standards for the Internet. The Yahoo! saga opened a renewed discussion about the national boundaries of

---

34 Among them are The Center for Democracy and Technology (CDT), <http://cdt.org/>; The Electronic Frontier Foundation (EFF), <http://www.eff.org/>; The Electronic Privacy Information Center (EPIC), <http://epic.org/>; The Global Internet Liberty Campaign (GILC), <http://gilc.org/>; The Internet Society, <http://www.isoc.org/>; The Association for Progressive Communication, <http://www.apc.org>; Save the Internet, <http://savethe internet.com/> (all sites accessed on 20 April 2012).

the Internet. The case urges us to reconsider the international aspects of the Internet as a global phenomenon, with an enhanced awareness of national sovereignty and national laws. International companies need to be cognizant of different state laws and are required to identify the appropriate approach when these laws come into conflict with their home-country laws.

When corporations violate national laws, nations can assert their regulatory authority. The threat of multiple regulatory exposures will not destroy the Internet. What is needed is a formal strategic planning effort which is positively linked to CSR (Galbreath June 2010, pp. 511–25). Firms may be required to filter content geographically to comply with national laws but only for a small fraction of their communications. This will impose extra costs on multinational intermediaries, but in light of the constantly innovative Internet, this cost will be trivial in the long run (Goldsmith and Wu 2006, pp. 160–61). We can and should expect business to adhere to some norms of social and corporate responsibility. And corporations should strive to respect and abide by domestic laws.

Lasting social change needs a combination of solid governmental support and committed corporate action. A comprehensive look at the movement for CSR shows that market forces often jumpstart responsibility. Consumer demand for responsibility may push companies to produce certain products and abandon others; actual (or threatened) consumer boycotts act to influence decision-making processes; "naming and shaming" practices by non-governmental organizations, pressure from socially responsible investors, and values held by employees and management are all influential. Yet there is no guarantee that a company will sustain its efforts past a marketing campaign if practices and standards are not enshrined in law. And corporations will only participate for the long-term in CSR if it is good for their bottom line. While profitability may not be the only reason corporations will or should behave virtuously, it has become the most influential reason. CSR is sustainable only if virtue pays off (Vogel 2005; Campbell and Miller 2004; Painter-Morland 2011). Thus what is needed to address the threat of hateful messages is to take legal action as France did, inspired by a strong tradition of sovereign state regulation and with confidence that its values were of universal validity.

Bibliography

Akdeniz, Y. (2008) *Internet Child Pornography and the Law* (Aldershot: Ashgate).

Aly, G., Heim, S. and Blunden, A.G. (2003) *Architects of Annihilation: Auschwitz and the Logic of Destruction* (NJ: Princeton University Press).

Amadei, X. (November 2001/February 2002) 'Note, Standards of Liability for Internet Service Providers: A Comparative Study of France and the United States with a Specific Focus on Copyright, Defamation, and Illicit Content,' *Cornell International L. J.* 35, 189, <http://www.highbeam.com/doc/1G1-87710965.html> (accessed on 20 April 2012).

Associated Press (25 July 2000) 'Groups sue Yahoo! over sale of Nazi objects in France,' *St. Louis Post-Dispatch* (Missouri), A5.

Associated Press (21 November 2000) 'Yahoo loses court ruling in France,' *Milwaukee Journal Sentinel* (Wisconsin), 3D.

Ass'n Union des Etudiants Juifs de France v. SA Multimania Prod. (24 May 2000) Tribunal de grande instance de Nanterre, <http://translate.google.co.uk/translate? hl=en&sl=fr&u=http://www.juriscom.net/txt/jurisfr/cti/tginanterre20000524. htm&sa=X&oi=translate&resnum=2&ct=result&prev=/search%3Fq%3DMultim ania%2Bnsdap%26hl%3Den%26rlz%3D1T4SKPB_enGB304GB304> (accessed on 20 April 2012).

Baker, C.E. (1992) *Human Liberty and Freedom of Speech* (NY: Oxford University Press).

Barendt, E. (2007) *Freedom of Speech* (New York: Oxford University Press).

BeVier, L.R. (1978) 'The First Amendment and Political Speech: An Inquiry into the Substance and Limits of Principle,' *Stanford L. Rev.* 30(2), 299–358.

Black, H.L. (1960) 'The Bill of Rights,' *NY University Law Review* 35, 865–81, <http://www.criminology.fsu.edu/faculty/gertz/hugoblack.htm> (accessed on 20 April 2012).

Bollinger, L.C. (1986) *The Tolerant Society* (Oxford: Clarendon Press).

Bowen, H.R. (1953) *Social Responsibilities of the Businessman* (NY: Harper and Row).

Brown, D. (22 March 2011) 'Opinion: "No law" means "no law" when it comes to protecting NPR and the First Amendment,' *First Amendment Coalition*, <http:// www.firstamendmentcoalition.org/2011/03/opinion-no-law-means-no-law-when-it-comes-to-protecting-npr-and-the-first-amendment/> (accessed on 20 April 2012).

Browning, C.R. (2007) *The Origins of the Final Solution: The Evolution of Nazi Jewish Policy, September 1939–March 1942* (Winnipeg: Bison Books).

Brustein, W.I. (2003) *Roots of Hate: Anti-Semitism in Europe Before the Holocaust* (Cambridge: Cambridge University Press).

Burleigh, M. and Wippermann, W. (1993) *The Racial State: Germany 1933–1945* (Cambridge: Cambridge University Press).

Campbell, T. and Miller, S. (eds.) (2004) *Human Rights and the Moral Responsibilities of Corporate and Public Sector Organizations* (Dordrecht: Kluwer).

Carroll, A.B. (1979) 'A Three-dimensional Conceptual Model of Corporate Social Performance,' *Academy of Management Review* 4, 497–505.

Carroll, A.B. (1981) *Business and Society: Managing Corporate Social Performance* (Boston: Little, Brown).

Carroll, A.B. (1991) 'The Pyramid of Corporate Social Responsibility: Toward the Moral Management of Organizational Stakeholders,' *Business Horizons* 34, 39–48.

Carroll, A.B. (September 1999) 'Corporate Social Responsibility,' *Business and Society* 38(3), 268–95.

Carroll, A.B. and Buchholtz, A.K. (2011) *Business and Society: Ethics and Stakeholder Management* (NY: South-Western College Publishing).

Cohen-Almagor, R. (1993) 'Harm Principle, Offence Principle, and the Skokie Affair,' *Political Studies* XLI(3), 453–70.

Cohen-Almagor, R. (1994) *The Boundaries of Liberty and Tolerance* (Gainesville, FL: The University Press of Florida).

Cohen-Almagor, R. (2005) *Speech, Media and Ethics* (Houndmills: Palgrave).

Cohen-Almagor, R. (2006) *The Scope of Tolerance* (London: Routledge).

Cohen-Almagor, R. (2007) *The Democratic 'Catch': Free Speech and Its Limits* (Tel Aviv: Maariv Publication House (Hebrew).

Cohen-Almagor, R. (2010) 'Countering Hate on the Internet—A Rejoinder,' *Amsterdam Law Forum* 2(2), 125–32.

Commission for Racial Equality, *Reviews of the Race Relations Act* (1985, 1992).

Corn-Revere, R. (2003) 'Caught in the Seamless Web: Does the Internet's Global Reach Justify Less Freedom of Speech?,' in Adam Thierer and Clyde Wayne Crews Jr. (eds.), *Who Rules the Net?* (Washington, DC: Cato Institute).

Crane, A. (ed.) (2009) *The Oxford Handbook of Corporate Social Responsibility* (Oxford: Handbooks Online).

Crumm, D. and Capeloto, A. (11 December 2000) 'Hate is up for bid on some web sites sellers hawk Hitler trinkets, KKK knives,' *Detroit Free Press*, A1.

Cue, E. (10 January 2001) 'National boundaries: latest frontier in cyberspace,' *Christian Science Monitor*, 1.

Dann, G.E. and Haddow, N. (2008) 'Just Doing Business or Doing Just Business: Google, Microsoft, Yahoo! and the Business of Censoring China's Internet,' *J. of Business Ethics* 79, 219–34.

Davis, K. (1973) 'The Case For and Against Business Assumption of Social Responsibilities,' *Academy of Management Journal*, 16: 312–22. Online. Available at: <http://uweb.txstate.edu/~ek10/socialresponsibility.pdf> (accessed 20 April 2012).

Delgado, R. and Stefancic, J. (2004) *Understanding Words That Wound* (Boulder, CO: Westview).

Dembart, L. (29 May 2000) 'Boundaries on Nazi Sites Remain Unsettled in Internet's Global Village,' *International Herald Tribune*, <http://www.iht.com/articles/2000/05/29/ttfrance.2.t.php> (accessed 20 April 2012).

Dennis, E.E., Gillmor, D.M. and Grey, D.L. (eds.) (1978) *Justice Hugo Black and the First Amendment: "'No Law" Means No Law'* (Ames, IA: Iowa State University Press).

Directorate for Science, Technology and Industry Committee for Information, Computer and Communications Policy (2006) *Working Party on the Information Economy*, <http://www.biac.org/members/iccp/mtg/2008-06-seoul-min/DSTI-ICCP-IE(2005)3-FINAL.pdf> (accessed on 20 April 2012).

Dworkin, R. (1985) *A Matter of Principle* (Cambridge, MA: Harvard University Press).

Eberwine, E.T. (2004) 'Sound and Fury Signifying Nothing: Jurgen Bussow's Battle against Hate-Speech on the Internet,' *New York Law Review*, 49: 353–410.

Editorial (13 January 2001) 'A Web of Thought Control,' *Chicago Tribune*, 22.

Egelko, B. (11 February 2005) 'Yahoo Getting New Hearing on Posting Nazi Items,' *The San Francisco Chronicle*, C3.

Ehrenreich, E. (2007) *The Nazi Ancestral Proof: Genealogy, Racial Science, and the Final Solution* (Bloomington, IN: Indiana University Press).

Emerson, T.I. (1970) *The System of Freedom of Expression* (NY: Random House).

Essick, K. (21 November 2000) 'Judge to Yahoo: Block Nazi Goods from French,' *PCWorld*, <http://www.pcworld.com/article/35419/judge_to_yahoo_block_nazi_goods_from_french.html> (accessed on 20 April 2012).

Fannon, I.L. (2003) *Working Within Two Kinds of Capitalism* (Portland, OR: Hart).

Fings, K. et al. (1997) *The Gypsies during the Second World War: Volume 1: From Race Science to the Camps* (Hatfield: University of Hertfordshire Press).

Fings, K. (1999) *In the Shadow of the Swastika: Volume 2: The Gypsies during the Second World War* (Hatfield: University of Hertfordshire Press).

First Amendment—Religion and Expression, <http://caselaw.lp.findlaw.com/data/constitution/amendment01/> (accessed on 20 April 2012).

Fiss, O. (2000) 'Freedom of Speech and Political Violence,' in R.Cohen-Almagor (ed.), *Liberal Democracy and the Limits of Tolerance* (Ann Arbor: University of Michigan Press), 70–78.

Floridi, L. and Sanders, J.W. (2001) 'Artificial Evil and the Foundation of Computer Ethics,' *Ethics and Information Technology* 3(1), 55–66.

'French court says Yahoo broke racial law' (23 May 2000) *New York Times*, <http://query.nytimes.com/gst/fullpage.html?res=9E00E2D61E3AF930A15756C0A966 9C8B63&n=Top/Reference/Times%20Topics/Subjects/A/Auctions> (accessed on 20 April 2012).

Galbreath, J. (June 2010) 'Drivers of Corporate Social Responsibility: The Role of Formal Strategic Planning and Firm Culture,' *British J. of Management* 21, 511–25.

Gates, H.L. Jr et al. (1995) *Speaking of Race, Speaking of Sex: Hate Speech, Civil Rights, and Civil Liberties* (NY: New York University Press).

Goldhagen, D.J. (2009) *Worse Than War: Genocide, Eliminationism, and the Ongoing Assault on Humanity* (NY: Public Affairs).

Goldsmith, J. and Wu, T. (2006) *Who Controls the Internet? Illusions of a Borderless World* (New York: Oxford University Press).

Goodpaster, K.E. (2010) 'Corporate Responsibility and Its Constituents,' in GeorgeG.Brenkert and TomL.Beauchamp (eds.), *The Oxford Handbook of Business Ethics* (NY: Oxford University Press), 126–57.

Guernsey, L. (15 March 2001) 'Welcome to the Web. Passport, Please?,' *New York Times*, <http://query.nytimes.com/gst/fullpage.html?res=9B01E7D71F3AF936A 25750C0A9679C8B6> (accessed on 20 April 2012).

Hamdani, A. (May 2002) 'Who's Liable for Cyberwrongs?,' *Cornell Law Review* 87, 901–57.

Hate Monitor Net, 'Internet extremism growing in Germany' (26 August 2010) *Hate Monitor Net*, <http://groups.google.com/group/hate-monitor-net/browse_ thread/thread/e73b32d616e6cb80> (accessed on 20 April 2012).

Heyman, S.J. (2008) *Free Speech and Human Dignity* (New Haven, CT: Yale University Press).

Hilberg, R. (1985) *The Destruction of the European Jews* (NY: Holmes and Meier).

Home Office (September 1975) *Racial Discrimination*, White Paper, Commd. 6234.

Horrigan, B. (2010) *Corporate Social Responsibility in the 21st Century: Debates, Models and Practices across Government, Law and Business* (Northampton, MA: Edward Elgar).

Johnson, E.A. and Reuband, K.-H. (2006) *What We Knew: Terror, Mass Murder, and Everyday Life in Nazi Germany* (NY: Basic Books).

Jones, T.D. (1998) *Human Rights: Group Defamation, Freedom of Expression and the Law of Nations* (Boston: Martinus Nijhoff).

Kerr, M., Janda, R. and Pitts, C. (2009) *Corporate Social Responsibility—A Legal Analysis* (Markham, Ontario: LexisNexis).

Kershaw, I. (2009) *Hitler, the Germans, and the Final Solution* (New Haven, CT: Yale University Press).

Klee, E. et al. (eds.) (1996) *The Good Old Days: The Holocaust as Seen by Its Perpetrators and Bystanders* (NY: William S. Konecky Associate).

Kohl, U. (2007) *Jurisdiction and the Internet: A Study of Regulatory Competence over Online Activity* (Cambridge: Cambridge University Press).

Konvitz, M.R. (1963) *First Amendment Freedoms* (Ithaca, NY: Cornell University Press).

Kotler, P. and Lee, N. (2005) *Corporate Social Responsibility: Doing the Most Good for Your Company and Your Cause* (Hoboken, NJ: John Wiley and Sons).

Kuchinskas, S. (23 March 2005) 'Google Axes Hate News,' *Internetnews.com*, <http://www.internetnews.com/xSP/article.php/3492361> (accessed on 20 April 2012).

La Ligue Contre le Racisme et l'Antisémitisme (L.I.C.R.A.) and L'Union des Etudiants Juifs de France (U.E.J.F.) v. Yahoo! Inc. and Yahoo! France (22 May 2000) Interim Court Order, The County Court of Paris 6, <http://www.juriscom.net/txt/jurisfr/cti/tgiparis20001120.htm> (accessed on 20 April 2012).

Lawrence, F.M. (2006) 'The Hate Crime Project and its Limitations: Evaluating the Societal Gains and Risk in Bias Crime Law Enforcement,' *GWU Law School Public Law Research Paper*, No. 216, <http://papers.ssrn.com/sol3/papers.cfm?abstract_id=921923> (accessed on 20 April 2012).

Lee, K.-H. and Shin, D. (June 2010) 'Consumers' Responses to CSR Activities: The Linkage between Increased Awareness and Purchase Intention,' *Public Relations Review* 36, 193–5.

Le Menestrel, M., Hunter, M. and de Bettignies, H.-C. (2002) 'Internet e-ethics in Confrontation with an Activists' Agenda: Yahoo! on Trial,' *Journal of Business Ethics* 39, 135–44.

Lessig, L. (1999) *Code and Other Laws of Cyberspace* (New York: Basic Books).

Levmore, S. and Nussbaum, M.C. (eds.) (2010) *The Offensive Internet: Speech, Privacy, and Reputation* (Cambridge, MA: Harvard University Press).

Lewis, S. (2003) 'Reputation and Corporate Responsibility,' *Journal of Communication Management* 7(4), 356–94.

LICRA v. Yahoo! Inc. and Yahoo! France (22 May 2000) Tribunal de Grande Instance de Paris.

LICRA and UEJF v. Yahoo! Inc. and Yahoo! France (20 November 2000) Tribunal de Grande Instance de Paris, <http://www.lapres.net/yahen11.html> and <http://www.foruminternet.org/actualities/lire.phtml?id=273> (accessed on 20 April 2012).

Love, B. (11 August 2000) 'Auctions of Nazi gear may yet cost Yahoo!,' *The Seattle Times*, C6.

Lusane, C. (2002) *Hitler's Black Victims: The Historical Experiences of European Blacks, Africans and African Americans During the Nazi Era* (NY: Routledge).

Martin, E.W. (1961) *The Tyranny of the Majority* (London: Pall Mall Press).

Matsuda, M.J. et al. (1993) *Words That Wound: Critical Race Theory, Assaultive Speech, And The First Amendment* (Boulder, CO: Westview).

McCullagh, D. (23 October 2002) 'Google Excluding Controversial Sites,' *CNET News*.

McGroarty, P. (10 July 2009) 'Germany Calls for Ban of Neo-Nazi Sites Abroad,' *The Sydney Morning Herald*, <http://news.smh.com.au/breaking-news-technology/germany-calls-for-ban-of-neonazi-sites-abroad-20090710-devv.html> (accessed on 20 April 2012).

McQuail, D. (2003) *Media Accountability and Freedom of Publication* (New York: Oxford University Press).

Meiklejohn, A. (1965) *Political Freedom* (NY: Oxford University Press).

Meiklejohn, A. (1966) 'Freedom of Speech,' in Peter Radcliff (ed.), *Limits of Liberty* (Belmont, CA: Wadsworth Publishing Co.), 19–26.

Method and Systems for Locating Geographical Locations of Online Users, <http://www.implu.com/patent_application/20080275978> (accessed on 20 April 2012).

Mosse, G.L. (1997) *Toward the Final Solution: A History of European Racism* (NY: Howard Fertig).

Nazi racism, <http://www.ushmm.org/outreach/en/article.php?ModuleId= 10007679> (accessed on 20 April 2012).

Newman, S.L. (2010) 'Should Hate Speech Be Allowed on the Internet? A Reply to Raphael Cohen-Almagor,' *Amsterdam Law Forum* 2(2), 119–23.

'Online Auction of Nazi items sparks debate issue: National laws on global Web' (25 July 2000), *San Jose Mercury News*.

Organisation for Economic Co-operation and Development, Directorate for Science, Technology and Industry, Committee for Information, Computer and Communications Policy (2006), *Working Party on the Information Economy* <http:// www.biac.org/members/iccp/mtg/2008-06-seoul-min/DSTI-ICCP-IE(2005)3-FINAL.pdf> (accessed on 20 April 2012).

Painter-Morland, M. (2011) *Business Ethics as Practice* (Cambridge: Cambridge University Press).

Piazza, P. (1 February 2001) 'Yahoo! must prevent French from accessing Nazi memorabilia auction sites,' *Security Management* 45: 38.

Price, M.E. and Verhulst, S.G. (2000) 'The Concept of Self-Regulation and the Internet,' in Jens Waltermann and Marcel Machill (eds.), *Protecting Our Children on the Internet: Towards a New Culture of Responsibility* (Gütersloh: Bertelsmann Foundation).

Public Order Act 1936 <http://www.legislation.gov.uk/ukpga/Edw8and1Geo6/1/6> (accessed on 20 April 2012).

Public Order Act 1986 <http://www.statutelaw.gov.uk/content.aspx?activeText DocId=2236942> (accessed on 20 April 2012).

Race Relations Act 1976 <http://www.legislation.gov.uk/uksi/2003/1626/contents/made> (accessed on 20 April 2012).

Race Relations (Amendment) Act 2000 <http://www.legislation.gov.uk/ukpga/2000/34/contents> (accessed on 20 April 2012).

Racism: An Overview, <http://www.ushmm.org/wlc/en/article.php?ModuleId= 10005184> (accessed on 20 April 2012).

Radin, D. (11 January 2001) 'Yahoo! Auction is right to ban Nazi goods,' *Pittsburgh Post-Gazette* (Pennsylvania), F3.

Ramasastry, A. (6 February 2003) 'Can Europe block racist Web sites from its borders?,' *CNN.com*.

Reidenberg, J.R. (2005) 'Technology and Internet Jurisdiction,' *Univ. of Penn. L. Rev.* 153, 1959, <http://papers.ssrn.com/sol3/papers.cfm?abstract_id=691501> (accessed on 20 April 2012).

Reuters (21 November 2000) 'French court tells Yahoo to block Nazi auction sites,' *Orlando Sentinel* (Florida), B1.

Reuters (22 November 2000), 'Yahoo! stock plunges to lowest level since'98,' *Orlando Sentinel* (Florida), B5.

Reuters (27 February 2002) 'Yahoo headed for trial in France,' *The New York Times*, C4.

Sadurski, W. (1999) *Freedom of Speech and Its Limits* (Dordrecht: Kluwer), <http://books.google.co.uk/books?id=4Ldb0cIbS7kC&pg=PA179> (accessed on 20 April 2012).

Schauer, F. (1982) *Free Speech: A Philosophical Enquiry* (Cambridge: Cambridge University Press).

Scheeres, J. (9 November 2002) 'European Outlaw Net Hate Speech,' *Wired News*.

Sereny, G. (1983) *Into That Darkness: An Examination of Conscience* (NY: Vintage Books).

Shapiro, M. (1966) *Freedom of Speech* (Englewood Cliffs, NJ: Prentice Hall).

Shea, C. (15 January 2006) 'Sovereignty in Cyberspace,' *The Boston Globe*, K4.

Smolla, R.A. (1993) *Free Speech in an Open Society* (London: Vintage).

Supperstone, M. (1981) *Brownlie's Law of Public Order and National Security* (London: Butterworths).

'The Internet's new borders' (11 August 2001) *The Economist*.

Thornburgh, D. and Lin, H.S. (eds.) (2002) *Youth, Pornography, and the Internet* (Washington, DC: National Academy Press).

Tsesis, A. (2002) *Destructive Messages: How Hate Speech Paves the Way For Harmful Social Movements* (NY: New York University Press).

Tsesis, A. (2002a) 'Prohibiting Incitement on the Internet,' *Virginia J. of Law and Technology* 7(2), 5, <http://www.vjolt.net/vol7/issue2/v7i2_a05-Tsesis.pdf> (accessed on 20 April 2012).

Tsesis, A. (2009) 'Dignity and Speech: The Regulation of Hate Speech in a Democracy,' *Wake Forest Law Review*, 44: 497–532.

Tung, J.C. Shih (1921) 'The Central Theme of Confucian Philosophy,' *China Review*, 1: 80–82. Online. Available at: <http://books.google.com/books?id=YYpIAAAAYAAJ&pg=PA81> (accessed Sept. 1, 2012).

Union des Etudiants Juifs de France, TGI Paris (20 November 2000), Ord. ref., J.C.P. 2000, Actu., 2219.

Vick, D.W. (2005) 'Regulating Hatred,' in Mathias Klang and Andrew Murray (ed.), *Human Rights in the Digital Age* (London: GlassHouse).

Vogel, D. (2005) *The Market for Virtue* (Washington, DC: Brookings Institution Press).

Waldron, J. (2010) 'Dignity and Defamation: The Visibility of Hate,' *Harvard Law Review* 123: 1596–657.

Werther, W.B. and Chandler, D.B. (2010) *Strategic Corporate Social Responsibility: Stakeholders in a Global Environment* (Los Angeles, CA: Sage).

Wistrich, R.S. (2010) *A Lethal Obsession: Anti-Semitism from Antiquity to the Global Jihad* (NY: Random House).

Wolverton, T. and Pelline, J. (2 January 2001) 'Yahoo! to charge auction fees, ban hate materials,' *CNet News.com* <http://news.com.com/2100-1017-250452.html?legacy=cnet> (accessed on 20 April 2012).

Yahoo! Inc. v. La Ligue Contre le Racisme Yahoo! Inc. (7 November 2001), 169 F. Supp. 2d 1181; 2001 US Dist. Lexis 18378.

Yahoo! Inc. v. L.I.C.R.A. and U.E.J.F., 169 F. Supp. 2d 1181 (N.D. Cal. 2001) (No. 00-21275).

Yahoo! Inc. v. LICRA and UEJF, 379 F 3d 1120 (9th Cir. 2004).

Yahoo! Inc. v. LICRA and UEJF, 433 F 3d 1199 (9th Cir. 2006) <http://ftp.resource.org/courts.gov/c/F3/433/433.F3d.1199.01-17424.html> (accessed on 20 April 2012).

'Yahoo! Ruling Exposes Risks of Being Global' (1 July 2000) *Internet World*.

9   Neutralizing the open Internet

Hannibal Travis[1]

Both sides impose tests of ideological purity. To some, unless their test is met, open Internet rules are "fake net neutrality." To others, unless their test is met, open internet rules are "a government takeover of the Internet."

For myself, I reject both extremes in favor of ... Internet freedom and openness and ... robust innovation and investment throughout the broadband ecosystem.

Julius Genachowski, Chairman of the FCC (FCC, 2010, 18,039)

Introduction

The Federal Communications Commission (FCC) handed a stunning victory to advocates of media reform in 2005 when it endorsed a robust theory of the First Amendment in the *Comcast* adjudication (FCC, 2008). It is a theory that moves away from the dark ages of selective deregulation of discriminatory corporate media and looks towards prioritizing media consumers' right to access diverse and antagonistic sources of information and opinion, rather than the right of large corporations to acquire and control ever-larger combinations of media infrastructure. This theory, if upheld, may herald a new era of attention to citizens' First Amendment interests in accessing and benefiting from regulated telecommunications facilities such as broadcast airwaves and cable networks.

This Chapter will begin with a brief history of telecommunications regulation, and turn to net neutrality activism, culminating in the law of Internet discrimination. The Communications Act of 1934 created the FCC for the precise purpose of making available, "so far as possible, to *all the people of the United States* a rapid, efficient, Nation-wide, and world-wide wire and radio communication service with adequate facilities at reasonable charges" by the mechanism of "centralizing authority" (Communications Act of 1934, Section 1). The 1934 Act made it unlawful for common carriers to discriminate unduly or unreasonably against any particular person or class (ibid., sections 201–202).

---

1 Portions of this chapter appeared previously in the article 'The FCC's New Theory of the First Amendment,' *Santa Clara Law Review*, 51 (2007): 417.

Common carriers were intended to be liable for damages to any person so discriminated against (ibid., section 206–207). The Telecommunications Act of 1996 restated many of these obligations, clarifying that although broadcasters are not common carriers, their "newscasts, news interviews, news documentaries, and on-the-spot coverage of news events," must be "in the public interest and … afford reasonable opportunity for the discussion of conflicting views on issues of public importance" (U.S. Code, title 47, section 315).

The FCC formally repealed this public-interest "fairness doctrine" in 1987, finding it to be inconsistent with the First Amendment rights of a corporate broadcaster (Baker, 1997, 971 n. 59; Syracuse Peace Council, 1987, 5054–5). As one FCC opinion issued early in President Ronald Reagan's second term stated:

> In *FCC v. League of Women Voters* the Court has recently reaffirmed that the constitutional permissibility of the fairness doctrine is predicated upon a factual presumption that the doctrine has the effect of enhancing the coverage of controversial issues available to the viewing and listening public. Indeed, the Court stated that it would be obligated to reevaluate the constitutionality of the doctrine if the [FCC] demonstrated the falsity of this assumption …
>
> By restricting the amount and type of controversial programming aired, a broadcaster minimizes the potentially substantial burdens … of the doctrine while remaining in compliance with the strict letter of its regulatory obligations. Therefore, … in net effect the fairness doctrine often discourages the presentation of controversial issue programming …
>
> The evidence of record in this proceeding, however, reflects that broadcasters are convinced that these costs [of responding to fairness doctrine complaints] can in fact be a significant inhibiting factor in the presentation of controversial issues.
>
> (FCC, 1987, 152, 161, 167)

The FCC predicted that the free market, by the mechanism of competition among broadcasters, would ensure the balanced presentation of controversial issues better than the fairness doctrine could. Cable television and print media would also compete with radio and television broadcasters to cover issues of public concern. Congress attempted to force the FCC to implement the fairness doctrine by law, but President Ronald Reagan vetoed the law (Ivins, 2003).

Net neutrality activism prior to 2008

As the FCC was deregulating the broadcast networks in a way that ensured widespread corporate censorship (Travis, 2011, 47–86), it was paradoxically constructing a free and uninhibited Internet through carefully targeted regulation of the cable, telephone, and broadband infrastructure providers. Unlike the broadcast airwaves, which lost full First Amendment protection by being subjected to FCC licensing unrestrained by the fairness doctrine, the Internet had free speech safeguards:

> In a society which relies more and more on electronic communications media as its primary conduit for expression, full support for First Amendment values requires extension of the common carrier principle to all of these new media ....
>
> A communications common carrier, such as a telephone company is required to provide its services on a non-discriminatory basis. It has no liability for the content of any transmission. A telephone company does not concern itself with the content of a phone call. Neither can it arbitrarily deny service to anyone. The common carrier's duties have evolved over hundreds of years in the common law and later statutory provisions. The rules governing their conduct can be roughly distilled in a few basic principles. Common carriers have a duty to:
>
> * provide services in a non-discriminatory manner at a fair price
> * interconnect with other carriers
> * provide adequate services.
>
> Given Congress' plan to build the [Internet] with services from privately-owned carriers, a legislatively-imposed duty of common carriage is necessary to protect free expression effectively. As Professor Eli Noam, a former New York State Public Utility Commissioner, explains:
>
> [C]ommon carriage is the practical analog to [the] First Amendment for electronic speech over privately-owned networks, where the First Amendment does not necessarily govern directly.
>
> (Kapor and Berman, 1991, 240–41; Kapor, 1992, 231–42)

The FCC's policy decisions ensured the rapid development and diversification of the Internet as a means of communication. Former FCC Chairman Reed Hundt has argued that due to the efforts of the FCC and Congress to mandate more telephone industry openness, there were soon 6,000 Internet service providers (ISPs) (Hundt, 2000, 193; Krause, 2000, A10; Charman, 2007). The number of Internet users in the United States rose from very few in 1989, to 63 million in 1999 (Walker, 1999), and to more than 245 million in 2012 (Miniwatts Marketing Group, 2012). Although it is difficult to segregate bloggers by geographic location, the number of blogs skyrocketed from fewer than a million in 2000, to 30 million in 2005, and to more than 100 million or even 500 million in 2011 (Travis, 2007, 1530).

The Internet's designers envisioned an ecosystem that had more content- and application-neutral information than proprietary networks or communications systems such as AT&T's telephone network or General Electric's broadcast network NBC. The design principle that crystallizes this commitment to neutrality is commonly referred to as the "end-to-end principle." It says that innovation and filtering should occur at the ends or the edges of the Internet, rather than in the connections or at a central hub (i.e., the AT&T or GE networks). This principle enjoyed the support of Vinton Cerf and Robert Kahn, who explained how an "internetwork protocol" could facilitate the sharing of information and computer resources between different networks operating on distinct protocols (Cerf and Kahn, 1974, 637). The principle was more fully articulated by Professor Jerome Saltzer of the computer science department at the Massachusetts Institute of Technology (MIT), who was a key player in the development of the Internet (Saltzer et al., 1984). The Internet was meant to operate as a "stupid network" with "dumb pipes" (Isenberg, 1997) just moving data along, without, in the words of a federal statute, "selection of the material by the service provider," or the "select[ion of] the recipients of the material except as an automatic response to the request of another person" (U.S. Code, title 17, section 512).

In the aftermath of 9/11, the Internet proved capable of fulfilling the high hopes that Internet pioneers Mitch Kapor, Tim Berners-Lee, and Jon Postel had for it. Kapor argued in 1991 that the Internet could be "open to diversity" and "safeguard the freedom of users" (Kapor, 1991). Berners-Lee, Postel, and other pioneers ensured in the early 1990s that nearly anyone could create a Web site, blog, multimedia communication, online store, or online profile (Google, 2010, 9). As a result of having more diverse and cross-referenced inputs, the Internet is frequently more reliable than the print or broadcast media. Web-based archives of news and opinion like Common Dreams or CounterPunch warned profusely in late 2002 and early 2003 that Iraq was being falsely blamed for the conspiracy to attack the United States on 9/11, which in fact had roots in Pakistan and Saudi Arabia (Common Dreams, 2003; CounterPunch, 2002). Contributors to such Web sites argued that Iraq's weapons subject to U.N. resolutions had been destroyed starting in 1991 by U.N. inspectors, and there was little to no evidence of ongoing production. Wikipedia contributors attempted to warn in 2002 and 2003 that the Iraq war would be a foreign policy and humanitarian disaster (Wikipedia, 2003b; 2003c). Wikipedia contributors in 2003 also warned about billions of dollars' worth of financial derivatives going unregulated and threatening financial disaster (Wikipedia, 2003a). Other Internet-based extremists warned as early as 1995 of an Internet bubble, and as early as 2003 of a housing bubble (Patterson, 2003; Shostak, 2003).

The decentralized, open, innovation-rich Internet seemed in the late 1990s to be at risk of increasing corporate control and management. A book published in 1999 suggested that AT&T was unwilling to allow an unfettered Internet to develop into a competitor to its voice or television services (Naughton, 1999, 106–7). AT&T had recently acquired Tele-Communications, Inc., the cable provider for San Francisco that would control that city's high-speed Internet access lines (Travis, 2011, 450). AT&T spent $100 billion buying up potential competitors in the cable and broadband industry between 1997 and 2000 alone (Martinson, 2000). In late 1998, America Online (AOL) and Time Warner announced the largest merger in history (Wolff, 1998). Questioned in Congress about its pending merger, AOL refused to commit to allowing other ISPs to reach consumers subscribing to the merged company's services (Lemley and Lessig, 2001, 928).

By 2004, it had become clear that efforts to deregulate the corporations that were acquiring ever-increasing control over the Internet were in high gear. By acquiring their competitors in the broadband industry, large corporations threatened to undermine the "dumb pipe" model of the Internet, replacing it with a corporate-filtered Internet. In 2002, the FCC approved Comcast's $51 billion acquisition of AT&T's cable and broadband assets, forming an Internet "giant" with unparalleled power over the network (Travis, 2011, 451). The company promptly raised the price of high-speed Internet access in places like St Paul, Minnesota by $11 to $58 per month (or $61 if a modem was leased), if customers opted out of a plan to subscribe to the basic cable service for $11 per month (Alexander, 2003, 1D). That same year, the FCC announced that it was releasing cable broadband services from the "common carrier" obligations that guaranteed an interconnected, interoperable Internet (FCC, 2002b). The FCC declared its intention to do the same with digital subscriber line (DSL) service (FCC, 2002a). It had previously "distinguished between the common carrier offering of basic transmission service, which provides a communications path for the movement of information, and the offering of enhanced services, which ... [consist] primarily of data processing services" (FCC, 2001). In 2004, the Supreme Court declined to recognize an obligation on the part of telecommunications network licensees to provide nondiscriminatory access to their competitors for purposes of interconnection (*Verizon Communications v. Trinko*, 2004, 410–11). The decision was a blow to efforts to roll back the increasingly rigid policy of telephone companies to refuse to offer broadband service without tying it to (increasingly obsolete) local telephone service (FCC, 2004; Kimmelman, 2005).

In 2005, all of these developments seemed to come to a head. In January, sources revealed to the press that AT&T and SBC were in talks to merge, a previously "unthinkable" step towards recreating the "sprawling AT&T telephone monopoly" broken up in the 1980s (Noguchi, 2005, E1). The FCC reported that most U.S. households had access to only one cable provider. Comcast was on its way to being the local cable provider (one commentator said "monopoly") in about four out of five of America's largest media markets (FCC, 2005a, 2828; Roth, 2009). In April, Comcast and Time Warner announced their acquisition of Adelphia Communications, which had 5.3 million subscribers, for $17.6 billion in cash and stock (Fabrikant, 2005, C4). Also in April, a Comcast subscriber sued Comcast for releasing her data to the Recording Industry Association of America, causing her to have to pay a $4,500 settlement (CNet, 2005). In June, the Supreme Court upheld the

FCC's 2002 decision to deregulate cable broadband (Brand X, 2005, 973–5). In August, the FCC relieved AT&T and other telephone-based broadband networks from many interconnection and nondiscrimination obligations that the 1934 and 1996 Acts imposed upon them (FCC, 2005b, 14,855, 14,862).

The FCC finally responded to a rising tide of consumer and industry demands for reinstituting basic nondiscrimination obligations on broadband providers. In August 2005, the FCC released a policy statement designed to preserve the Internet as "a forum for a true diversity of political discourse, unique opportunities for cultural development, and myriad avenues for intellectual activity" (FCC, 2005b, 14,987). The FCC adopted four net neutrality principles designed to guarantee that: (1) "consumers are entitled to access the lawful Internet content of their choice"; (2) "consumers are entitled to run applications and services of their choice, subject to the needs of law enforcement"; (3) "consumers are entitled to connect their choice of legal devices that do not harm the network"; and (4) "consumers are entitled to competition among network providers, application and service providers, and content providers." The FCC noted that the principles it adopted were not rules, and that they were "subject to [the requirements of] reasonable network management" (ibid., 14,987–8). It justified the principles as being necessary for the progress of advanced technology and the protection of First Amendment values (ibid., 13,040, 13,053).

Despite the FCC's new principles of net neutrality, activism for legislation in the area continued. Telecom mergers filled the news in late 2005. In October, the FCC approved Verizon's acquisition of MCI, which gave the company control over much of the Internet backbones and thus the power potentially to block traffic from competitors deemed a threat (FCC, 2005, 18,496; Werbach, 2008, 371–7), like public broadband networks or innovative commercial alternatives like FON or Google.[2] As the Verizon/MCI merger was under consideration by the FCC, the *Wall Street Journal* reported

---

2 Verizon controlled most telephone-based broadband networks, along with AT&T, by 2008 (Werbach, 2008, 371). It condemned entry by public providers such as cities or municipal utilities into the broadband delivery business. Neal Peirce, *City-Sponsored Wi-Fi's Wild Ride*, Seattle Times, Aug. 21, 2005, http://seattletimes.nwsource.com/html/opinion/2002446112_peirce21.html; Gavin Clarke, *Municipal WiFi is the New Hope for Net Neutrality – Thinker*, The Register (U.K.), Aug. 16, 2006, http://www.theregister.co.uk/2006/08/16/wifi_net_neutrality_lessig/. It also condemned FCC auctions of "open access" wireless spectrum that would permit the delivery of video, voice-over-Internet telephone calls, and mobile handsets that do not pass the approval process of Verizon and the other corporations with both wireline and wireless businesses. Tim Greene, *FCC Auction Could Mean More Flexible Broadband Wireless Services; Auction Rules Could Influence Who Wins the License*, Network World, July 20, 2007, at 14. Verizon called the auction "corporate welfare" for Google even though Google had to pay for the spectrum, ibid. Verizon also sought to kill the upstart broadband-sharing service FON. See Dan Frommer, *Hold the FON*, Forbes, Feb. 9, 2006, http://www.forbes.com/2006/02/08/google-ebay-verizon-cx_df_0209wifi.html.

that corporate owners of broadband infrastructure were purchasing software designed to "block ... Internet applications such as phone calls, video and photo downloads." BitTorrent, Skype, and YouTube were among the likely targets of this "crackdown" on the Internet (Grant and Drucker, 2005, A1). In November, the FCC voted to approve the AT&T/SBC merger (Mohammed, 2005, D5). This vote was followed by news reports about plans by AT&T and Comcast to charge Internet access fees and disallow access to popular applications and content, contributing to heightened public concern (Travis, 2011, 454). As one commentator described all of these developments in early 2006: "Combine ever-fewer broadband pipe providers with legislation designed to give them practically dictatorial powers over what is and isn't allowed on the Web," and you may "kill a lot of the Internet entrepreneurial fervor that's been bolstering a piece of America's (and probably to a greater extent India's) economy of late" (Rist, 2006).

In 2006, concerns within the Internet industry and the public about likely effects of Internet discrimination, gave rise to continued net neutrality activism. Google hired a key architect of the Internet's interoperable, non-proprietary structure to lobby Congress for net neutrality laws (Cerf, 2006). Jeffrey Cinton, Chairman and CEO of Vonage Holdings Corporation, the largest Internet telephone company in the United States, testified that Vonage could cut consumers' phone bills in half and provide innovative new choices to Internet users, but was increasingly being blocked by network providers who also sold landline telephone services (Citron, 2006). Representing 180 companies, the COMPTEL trade association warned that the Internet requires common carrier regulation of telephone and Internet backbone companies to thrive and that the ongoing efforts of broadband companies to limit the upstream bandwidth and broadband modems available was restricting competition and innovation (Comstock, 2006). Other testimony before Congress in 2006 cautioned that effective Department of Justice and FCC oversight was needed to prevent AT&T's acquisition of BellSouth from locking up much of the FCC-regulated wireless spectrum that could be used to develop an alternative wireless broadband system, namely, "Wi-Max" transmission, over the 2.3–2.5 GHz spectrum (much of which BellSouth bought in 1997), bands of which AT&T had acquired along with SBC's assets the previous year (Geiger, 2006; Rubin, 2006).

Such efforts won important concessions from the broadband infrastructure industry. The President of the United States Telecom Association promised that his member companies would not "block, impair, or degrade content" that was lawful and did not harm the network (McCormick, 2006). Similarly, the President of the National Cable & Telecommunications Association argued that there were no identified cases of discrimination against Internet content, such as Web sites or blogs, within his industry (McSlarrow, 2006).

Congress addressed the prospect of merged, deregulated broadband super-networks by attempting to draft its own net neutrality rules for network providers. The House Judiciary Committee voted 20–13 to pass the Internet

Freedom and Nondiscrimination Act of 2006, which would have given Internet users and infrastructure firms the right to sue broadband providers for discriminating against lawful content, impairing other firms' ability to interconnect, or offering enhanced quality of service to the super-networks' own information or services with the effect of prejudicing their competitors' or users' information or services (U.S. House of Representatives, 2006c). The committee noted that the diverse array of advocates for regulatory action by the FCC and/or Congress included Google, Intel, Microsoft, the Financial Services Roundtable, the American Association of Retired Persons, the Gun Owners of America, the Christian Coalition, National Religious Broadcasters, and others (U.S. House of Representatives, 2006b). The Senate Commerce Committee passed the Advanced Telecommunications and Opportunity Reform Act (ATORA) of 2006, which would have given the FCC the power to fine and enjoin efforts by broadband providers to prohibit Internet content because of the lawful views expressed therein, or to restrict any non-harmful voice application, software, search engine, or legal device of a subscriber's choosing; or to tie different services together (U.S. House of Representatives, 2006a). ATORA would have directed the FCC to report annually to Congress on developments in Internet access markets, including relationships between broadband service providers and online companies like Google and eBay, and how these trends "impact the free flow of information over the public Internet and the consumer experience using the public Internet." If the FCC discovered "significant problems," it would need to recommend steps to help users better "access lawful content and run Internet applications and services over the public Internet subject to the bandwidth purchased and the needs of law enforcement agencies" (ibid.).

The FCC theorizes net neutrality as free speech

In 2004, a new Internet protocol became famous by making it possible to download and view videos of the Indian Ocean tsunami disaster from many different perspectives (Krim, 2005, E1). The protocol, called BitTorrent, breaks large files into smaller pieces and incorporates error-checking so that it is possible to retrieve a single file from numerous different computers, even at several different times (FCC, 2008, 13,029–30). It also attempts to force downloaders to upload pieces to other users as one downloads pieces of a file (Taylor, 2007). Lacking a search engine, BitTorrent requires trackers to connect users and files, and several trackers were established for such purposes as multimedia file-sharing and open-source software development (FCC, 2008, 13,029–30; Travis, 2011, 459). BitTorrent began to be used in diverse contexts, including to distribute independent film, video blogs, and high-quality NASA images (FCC, 2008, 13,029–30; Travis, 2011, 459).

On November 1, 2007, the FCC received a complaint from two leading consumer groups, joined by several groups focused on freedom of expression and faculty on the cyberlaw programs of Harvard, Yale, and Stanford law schools (FCC, 2008, 13,032). That same month, BitTorrent-based online video site Vuze, Inc. filed a petition to establish a must-carry rule for broadband networks (ibid., 13,033). The FCC requested public comments and received more than 6,500 such comments (ibid.).

On August 1, 2008, the FCC concluded that it had jurisdiction to enforce its net neutrality principles against cable and DSL companies (ibid., 13,033).[3] It found Comcast's practice of interfering with peer-to-peer protocols, such as BitTorrent, was unreasonable and discriminatory due to the effects on media and video game companies that use the protocol, as well as multiple consumers (ibid., 13,051–2). It declined to find the practice to be a type of "reasonable network management," noting that the interference swept up homes consuming little bandwidth, failed to address the bandwidth-intensive use of other protocols, and was discriminatory against a protocol (ibid., 13,054–8).

Since the 1980s, the FCC had adopted what could be called a Chicago School theory of the First Amendment in abandoning the congressionally-mandated fairness doctrine. The FCC argued that despite extensive licensing of television broadcast networks by federal bureaucrats, and extraordinary barriers to entry by new networks such as Fox, UPN, or The WB (now The CW), the First Amendment could best be promoted by competition among cable, broadcast television, and radio (Travis, 2011, 460). The broadcasters, formerly a regulated public trust enjoying privileged access to the public airwaves and corridors of political power, became mere participants in the marketplace of ideas.

In 2008, however, the FCC returned to a First Amendment theory that characterized the fairness doctrine era of the 1950s and 1960s. The FCC cited the *Associated Press* antitrust case from 1945, a lodestar of advocates of limiting corporate control over public debate, for the principle that saving the open character of the Internet from restrictions on the content and software available on the network furthers First Amendment values and helps ensure a diverse and vigorous public debate (FCC, 2008, 13,040). The FCC evoked the language of Mitch Kapor and other Internet pioneers:

> Historically, "the innovation and explosive growth of the Internet [has been] directly linked to its particular architectural design." Thus, "variances from those standard protocols and practices damages the Internet

---

3 The FCC relied extensively on the Communications Decency Act, 47 U.S.C., 230, which Comcast characterized as mere prefatory language to the immunization of Internet service providers from tort liability for their users' speech, but which the FCC read as a mandate "to promote the continued development of the Internet" (FCC, 2008, 13,034 (citing 47 U.S.C., 230(b)(1)). The Act defines the FCC's jurisdiction over wire and broadcast communications to include "all instrumentalities, facilities, [and] apparatus" incidental to such communications. 47 U.S.C., 153(52). It also provides that the FCC may "make such rules and regulations, and issue such orders, not inconsistent with this chapter, as may be necessary in the execution of its functions." 47 U.S.C., 154(i).

as a whole," including the ability of entrepreneurs to enter the market with new Internet services. Contravention of these standard protocols and practices through discriminatory conduct thus erects barriers to entry that would not otherwise exist. Entrepreneurs are no longer able to design new services and technologies around known protocols and standards, but must spend considerable time and resources in an effort to accommodate Comcast's particular network management practices—a task made all the more difficult by the company's obfuscation regarding its actual practices. By exercising authority over this complaint, we are able to ensure that Comcast's actions do not inappropriately hinder entry by "entrepreneurs and other small businesses in the provision and ownership of telecommunications services and information services." In addition, by facilitating such entry, we also promote the Act's policies favoring "a diversity of media voices" and "technological advancement."

(ibid.)

Invoking the *Associated Press* case in particular, the FCC stated that the First Amendment ensures "the widest possible dissemination of information from diverse and antagonistic sources," rather than corporate interference with citizens' communications and speech (ibid., 2008, 13,053, quoting *Associated Press v. United States*, 1945, 20).

Net neutrality as censorship of the Internet?

The FCC's intervention into the BitTorrent/Comcast affair provoked a collision of First Amendment interests. On the side of regulation mandating net neutrality are the First Amendment interests of the public in sending and receiving countercultural, oppositional, and underground speech and communications, and in using new applications and Internet protocols along the way (ibid., 13,040, 13,053). On the side of the status quo prior to the order is the asserted interest of Comcast and its investors and employees in communicating messages they favor over "their" equipment, and to be free from any compulsion to carry speech or applications that they dislike or with which they disagree (Wong, 2011, 706–7). Broadband networks exercise two roles: that of an editor and publisher of a subset of all possible Internet communications, an editor that has a First Amendment right to be free of forced-carry obligations (Blevins, 2012, 374–7), and the role of a conduit for data that benefits from a series of common-law and statutory safe harbors that immunize it from defamation and privacy-tort liability as the "speaker" of all messages, images, and videos that flow across the global Internet (ibid., 365, 378).

Comcast initially challenged the FCC's action as in excess of its jurisdiction, rather than as a violation of the cable network's First Amendment rights (Comcast, 2009, 31). It emphasized the absence of any law or regulation prohibiting its conduct, pointing out that the FCC based its decision on enforcing what its Chairman announced as an unenforceable policy statement rather than a series of rules issued in compliance with the Administrative Procedure Act, 5 U.S.C., Section 551 *et seq.* (ibid., 17, 21–7, 36). It further claimed that there is no harm to consumer choice of content and applications, because it only slows certain protocols to prevent other consumers from experiencing a degraded Internet connection (ibid., 24). It also asserted the right to filter out infringing audio and video Net content on behalf of other media conglomerates (ibid., 54–5). Such "reasonable" Internet "management" prevents copyright infringement, it claimed (ibid.).

A related public relations campaign, on the other hand, emphasized Comcast's free speech rights. The "Hands Off the Internet" movement argued that the government should stay out of micromanaging Internet companies' relationships with their customers: "the Internet has flourished because government has not tried to regulate it" (Hands Off, 2008a). The movement's statement listed a series of companies and organizations sponsoring the press release, but did not list Comcast, and an investigation of the movement's former Members page reveals that one member is called NetCompetition.org, which includes AT&T, Comcast, and Time Warner Cable as members (Hands Off, 2008b).

So far, it has been the administrative rather than the constitutional argument that has torpedoed net neutrality. Hearing Comcast's appeal of the FCC's order in the matter involving BitTorrent, the United States Court of Appeals for the D.C. Circuit ruled that the FCC lacked the jurisdiction to issue the Comcast order, but the court did not address the First Amendment issue (*Comcast Corp. v. FCC*, 2010, 645). The court held that several statutory delegations of authority to the FCC to monitor and improve competition, including competition in providing "advanced telecommunications capability," efficient telecommunications networks, and wire and radio communication, did not give the FCC jurisdiction over the Internet (ibid., 648–60).

The FCC, some members of Congress, the Internet industry, and academic experts on telecommunications law did not view the FCC's 2010 defeat as precluding it from exercising the constitutional and statutory authority to preserve the Internet against private corporations' efforts to use state or federal licenses or powers to control Internet content. The FCC pointed to language in the court's opinion suggesting that Congress had granted it jurisdiction in 1996 to ensure that all Americans have access to "advanced telecommunications capability," and to "take immediate action" if they do not (FCC, 2012, *6–7, 10). The FCC and its Chairman, after the D.C. Circuit's opinion, reaffirmed that the FCC had the jurisdiction to enact a National Broadband Plan, which would include rules guaranteeing to Internet users their choice of lawful content, applications, and devices to the extent consistent with reasonable network management (FCC, 2010; Genachowski, 2010). Congressman Byron Dorgan remarked that "I hope the Federal Communications Commission takes action under its own authority because it has plenty of authority to respond to this [BitTorrent] decision" (Dorgan, 2010, S2275–S2287).

In late 2010, the FCC announced a new net neutrality framework (FCC, 2010), which entitled all users to enjoy the four principles released in 2008, and obligated all broadband providers to respect them, subject to reasonable network management (ibid., para. 92). The codified rules promptly drew fierce criticism from all sides of the debate (Wong, 2011, 691–5). The framework had the same basic legal foundation as the Comcast order that was rejected by the D.C. Circuit (ibid., 694–5). Moreover, it was riddled with "loopholes" that authorized cable and telephone companies to remove "unlawful" material from the Internet, even though it takes U.S. courts years of inquiry and often an appeal to define what is unlawful on even one Web site such as Google (ibid., 694–5, 707). For example, cases related to Napster were pending for more than four years, and those related to YouTube have been pending for more than five years, with no end in sight.

Within weeks of the new framework being issued, Verizon challenged it under the First Amendment (ibid., 696). Verizon made three principal arguments against its constitutionality. First, Verizon argued that net neutrality limits its "speech" (Verizon, 2012, 43). Second, Verizon claimed that net neutrality represents "forced speech," analogous to instances in which the government attempted to give victims of defamation in newspapers a "right of reply"[4] (ibid.). Third, Verizon cast itself as a victim of discrimination by the federal government against broadband providers and in favor of search engines (ibid., 48), which also have a "capacity to impact consumers' Internet experience" (Blevins, 2012, quoting Verizon Reply Comments, 2010, 112).

Resolving the conflict between net neutrality and freedom of speech

The problems with Verizon's arguments are best illustrated with a hypothetical. Imagine that a giant conglomerate formed by merging various companies (such as AOL Time Warner, Microsoft, or Apple) gained control over 90% of all media—newspapers, radio, television, and Internet access points. Imagine further that this behemoth desired to purchase or destroy the remaining 10% of independent media companies. If the United States or some other government blocked a proposed purchase, in which the excess profits earned in a 90% monopoly funded an effort to eliminate the remaining competition in the industry, would freedom of speech be violated? Or rather, would the more serious violation be continued federal enforcement of the contracts and FCC frequencies that made the 90% monopoly over

---

4 Such a statutory "right of reply" has been unconstitutional since *Miami Herald Publishing Co. v. Tornillo*, 418 U.S. 241 (1974). However, government-compelled corrective advertising is probably constitutional in the case of false advertising or misleading commercial speech. *Warner-Lambert Co. v. FTC*, 562 F. 2d 749, 756–61 (D.C. Cir. 1977).

the media possible? Obviously, the existence and potential growth of the conglomerate would be a far more serious threat to freedom of speech as a result of governmental regulation of the media marketplace than would the government's attempt to block a merger to 100% monopoly. Net neutrality regulation merely represents the insight that many customers already confront a 100% monopoly in their local wireline Internet access market, and that many others confront an oligopoly or other environment of inadequate competition, elevated prices, and substandard service. The FCC's prevention of anticompetitive activity in such a market promotes choice, in other words.

The FCC has articulated various theories to justify broadcast and Internet neutrality. In the *Comcast* case, it adopted a purposive theory of the First Amendment. In response to the claim that its net neutrality adjudication conflicted with Comcast's First Amendment right to be free of legislation or regulations abridging its freedom of speech, the FCC argued that net neutrality regulations "promote the dynamic benefits of an open and accessible Internet," protect speakers from interference with their Internet applications and communications, do not dictate the content of Internet communications or prevent Comcast or other companies from communicating with their customers or other persons or entities, and therefore advance "First Amendment values ..." (FCC, 2008, 13,053). It has also relied upon the identification by Congress of a "substantial ... First Amendment interest in promoting a diversity of views provided through *multiple technology media*" (ibid., 13,041).[5] Finally, it cited Supreme Court case law for the idea that the First Amendment supports limiting corporate restrictions on individual citizens' ability to enjoy "the widest possible dissemination of information from diverse and antagonistic sources" (ibid., 13,053, quoting *Associated Press*, 1945, 20).

Net neutrality may be necessary, as described above, to prevent large conglomerates from distorting public discourse according to their ideologies or preferences. It enhances the individual liberty interest in speaking and writing freely by preventing the government from acting in league with corporations to block politically disfavored or culturally unpopular viewpoints from enjoying access to the public. When communication is not subject to a censor or other "gatekeeper," the completeness and sophistication of public policy debates are enhanced (Jefferson, 1788). If the federal government backed a series of Internet access monopolies or duopolies controlled by AT&T or Verizon, the censorial power would be in the "Government over the people," rather than "in the people over the Government" as James Madison hoped (Madison, 1794, 934; 1800, 647–8). Madison recognized

---

5 This is a quotation, with emphasis in original, of the Cable Television Consumer Protection and Competition Act of 1992, Pub. L. 102-385, Section 2(a)(6), 106 Stat. 1460, 1461 (Oct. 5, 1992), *codified at* 47 U.S.C. Section 521 nt.

that the value of the right to vote "depends on the knowledge of the comparative merits and demerits of the candidates for public trust, and on the equal freedom, consequently, of examining and discussing these merits and demerits of the candidates respectively" (Madison, 1800).

Economic analysis may support net neutrality regulation for reasons analogous to those invoked by Madison and Jefferson. First, net neutrality regulation prevents markets from being distorted, a particular risk when companies enjoy monopoly power due to exclusive rights bestowed by government and/or restrictive contracts (Kaplow, 1984, 515). Second, it guarantees to innovative individuals and companies a minimum ability to access essential, partially government-financed infrastructure such as the high-speed Internet (FCC, 2008, 13,024; 2012, 3, 12–17, 77; Financial Services Roundtable, 2008; Google, 2010; Scott, 2008).

On the other hand, the "victims" of net neutrality rules suffer a mainly economic harm, which is outweighed by the harm discrimination inflicts on Internet users, competitors, and the public. Unlike a newspaper, which articulates a distinct point of view using no part of the public domain, such as the land alongside or under a roadway used for cable or telephone wires, Comcast and Verizon are "granted the free and exclusive use of a limited and valuable part of the public domain," which must be "burdened by enforceable public obligations" (*Office of Communication of the United Church of Christ v. FCC*, 1966, 1003). In return for being granted valuable public land rights, they are paid for the privilege of carrying Internet messages neutrally as a conduit (FCC, 2012, 76). Comcast and Verizon have repeatedly insisted to the federal courts and the Congress that they operate neutrally, as "conduits" for the speech of others or as being subject to "common carrier" regulation by the FCC, positions that a newspaper would never take (*Comcast Corp. v. FCC*, 2010, 647–8, Frieden, 2010, 36; United States Internet Service Provider Association, 2003; *Recording Industry Association of America v. Verizon*, 2003, 1237; Verizon, 2003). As the FCC pointed out in response to Verizon's arguments:

> [B]roadband providers obtain immunity from copyright violations and other liability for material distributed on their networks on the very ground that "they lack control over what end users transmit and receive." ... Thus, Verizon argued—and this Court agreed—that it is not subject to subpoena in a copyright infringement case because as a broadband provider it "act[s] as a mere conduit for the transmission of information sent by others." *Recording Indus. Ass'n v. Verizon Internet Servs., Inc.*, 351 F. 3d 1229, 1237 (D.C. Cir. 2003) ...
>
> Verizon has articulated no plausible claim of expressive activity in providing its end users access to their chosen Internet content. By delivering the information requested by its customers, Verizon is no different from a messenger delivering documents that contain speech ...
>
> To the extent Verizon wishes to exercise editorial discretion, it may host its own website on which it may disseminate any content of its choice.

Moreover, the Open Internet Rules apply only to "broadband Internet access service," which the Commission defined to mean a service that enables user access to all Internet endpoints ... Verizon is free to provide to its customers "a wide range of 'edited' services," such as "Best of the Web," that reflect Verizon's selection of Internet content.

(FCC, 2012, 69, 71)

While neutrality does little harm, non-neutrality is regarded as a serious threat to the freedoms that people actually exercise on a daily basis, according to most informed observers. One in eight Americans have only one wire-based high-speed Internet provider to choose from, while one in ten may eventually have one option but currently have none (Blevins, 2012, 381; FCC, 2010, 7, 37). Cable and telephone broadband providers proclaim their intention not to allow Google or YouTube equal access to high-speed access lines (Cerf, 2006; FCC, 2012, 73). Such a pay-to-play model for the Internet would have prevented YouTube from being created, or the next Facebook from becoming popular (FCC, 2012, 13; U.S. House of Representatives, 2006, 2). When media conglomerates gained ownership of both their means of distribution (television networks) and their sources of supply (television production), they refused to deal with independent television producers they had formerly allowed access to their networks (Franken, 2010). Today, broadband providers claim "sweeping rights" for themselves to "block, degrade, or favor" traffic going over the Internet (FCC, 2012, 15).

Commentators supportive of "free speech" challenges to net neutrality regulation have noted that if the FCC has jurisdiction to promote "neutrality," it might also promote decency or other lawful uses of the Internet as well, becoming a censor of a formerly free medium (Wong, 2011, 707). The problem with this argument (a variant of the slippery slope) is threefold. First, it was Comcast, not the FCC, that was blocking or slowing access to applications reliant on the BitTorrent protocol (FCC, 2008, 13,031–2), which is widely used to transmit and download indecent material. Second, the federal government already claims the authority to prosecute the sale of indecent or obscene material over the Internet, or sending it to minors, an authority which preceded in time and is unrelated to that of the FCC to implement net neutrality or other telecommunications regulations. Finally, in the event that the FCC moved from a content-neutral promotion of net neutrality to a content- or viewpoint-based policy of censorship, the U.S. courts' scrutiny of its actions would be much closer, and the policy would be unlikely to survive due to its chilling effect on speech (Kwall, 2006, 1989; Magarian, 2007, 199–203).

Conclusion

The FCC's activist stance in the BitTorrent matter prompted it to articulate a theory of the First Amendment that it had all but abandoned in deregulating the broadcast space. The FCC has explained that conduits like Comcast and Verizon transmit the speech of others, and enjoy lucrative benefits as a result of doing so, including protection from the liability of others' speech. Moreover, it has emphasized that unlimited corporate control over a mechanism for mass communication such as the Internet is incompatible with the equal access of all Americans, which the law guarantees.

Bibliography

Alexander, Steve, 'AT&T Broadband Raises Net-only Price,' *Star Tribune* (Minneapolis, MN), Jan. 16, 2003, p. 1D, http://www.highbeam.com/doc/1G1-96530228.html.

Associated Press v. United States, 326 U.S. 1 (1945).

Baker, C. Edwin, 'The Independent Significance of the Press Clause Under Existing Law,' *Hofstra Law Review*, 35: 955 (1997).

Blevins, John, 'The New Scarcity: A First Amendment Framework for Regulating Access,' *Tennessee Law Review*, 79: 353 (2012).

Cerf, Vinton G., Net Neutrality: Hearing Before the Senate Committee on Commerce, Science, & Transportation, 109th Cong. 7–9 (Feb. 7, 2006), http://frwebgate.access.gpo.gov/cgi-bin/getdoc.cgi?dbname=109_senate_hearings&docid=f:30115.pdf.

Cerf, Vinton G. and Kahn, Robert E., 'A Protocol for Packet Network Intercommunication,' IEEE *Transactions on Communications*, 22: 637 (1974).

Charman, Karen, 'Recasting the Web: Information Commons to Cash Cow,' *Extra!*, July/Aug. 2007, http://www.fair.org/extra/0207/open-access.html.

Citron, Jeffrey, Net Neutrality: Hearing Before the Senate Comm. on Commerce, Science, & Transportation, op. cit., 16–20.

CNet, *Comcast Sued for Disclosing Customer Info*, Reuters/CNET News.com, Apr. 15, 2005, http://74.125.93.132/search?q=cache:w0xd3Yz4E1gJ:www.mail-archive.com/isn@attrition.org/msg04135.html.

Comcast Corp. v. FCC, 600 F. 3d 642 (D.C. Cir. 2010).

Comcast, Petitioner's Brief, Comcast v. FCC, No. 08-1291 (D.C. Cir. filed July 27, 2009).

Common Dreams News Center Views Archive Feb. 2003, http://www.common-dreams.org/views03/february2003.htm (last visited Oct. 21, 2009).

Communications Act of 1934, chap. 652, § 1, 48 Stat. 1064, 1064 (1934).

Comstock, Earl, Net Neutrality: Hearing Before the Senate Comm. on Commerce, Science, & Transportation, 23–44.

CounterPunch Stories Archive, Aug.–Oct., 2002, http://web.archive.org/web/20021114224544/www.counterpunch.org/archive.html (last visited Oct. 21, 2009).

Dibadj, Reza, 'Toward Meaningful Cable Competition: Getting Beyond the Monopoly Morass,' 6 *N.Y.U. J. Legis. & Pub. Pol'y* 245 (2003)

Dorgan, Sen. Byron, 'Statement,' Congressional Record, 156:S2275-S2287 (2010).

Fabrikant, Geraldine, 'Time Warner and Comcast Seal Adelphia Purchase,' *The New York Times*, Apr. 22, 2005, p. C4. Online. Available at: <http://query.nytimes.com/gst/fullpage.html?res=9C00E0DF1431F931A15757C0A9639C8B63>.

FCC, Appellate Brief, *Verizon v. FCC*, United States Court of Appeals for the District of Columbia Circuit, 2012 WL 3962421.

FCC, Connecting America: The National Broadband Plan (2010). Online. Available at: <http://www.broadband.gov/download-plan>.

FCC, *In re* Appropriate Framework for Broadband Access to the Internet over Wireline Facilities (notice of proposed rulemaking), 17 F.C.C.R. 3019 (2002a).

FCC, *In re* Annual Assessment of the Status of Competition in the Market for Delivery of Video Programming, Eleventh Annual Report, 20 F.C.C.R. 2755 (2005a).

FCC, *In re* Appropriate Framework for Broadband Access to the Internet over Wireline Facilities, Report and Order and Notice of Proposed Rulemaking, 20 F.C.C.R. 14,853 (2005b).

FCC, *In re* Complaint of Syracuse Peace Council, 2 F.C.C.R. 5043 (1987) *rev'd on statutory grounds*, 867 F. 2d 654 (D.C. Cir. 1989).

FCC, *In re* Inquiry Concerning High-Speed Access to the Internet Over Cable and Other Facilities, Internet Over Cable Declaratory Ruling, Appropriate Regulatory Treatment for Broadband Access to the Internet Over Cable Facilities, 17 F.C.C.R. 4798 (2002b) (notice of proposed rulemaking)

FCC, *In re* Matter of Inquiry into Section 73.1910 of the Commission's Rules and Regulations Concerning the General Fairness Doctrine Obligations of Broadcast Licensees, 102 F.C.C. 2d 145 (1985).

FCC, *In re* Verizon Communications Inc. & MCI, Inc. Applications for Approval of Transfer of Control, 20 F.C.C.R. 18,433 (2005) (memorandum opinion and order).

FCC, *In re* Unbundled Access to Network Elements, Unbundled Network Elements Fact Report 2004, Review of Section 251 Unbundling Obligations of Incumbent Local Exchange Carriers, WC Docket No. 04-313, CC Docket No. 01-338, Oct. 2004.

FCC, *In re* Formal Complaint of Free Press and Public Knowledge Against Comcast, 23 F.C.C.R. 13,028 (2008) (memorandum opinion and order).

FCC, *In re* Policy & Rules Concerning the Interstate, Interexchange Marketplace, 16 F.C.C.R. 7418, 7419–20 (2001).

FCC, Preserving the Open Internet, 25 FCC Rcd. 17,905 (2010).

Financial Services Roundtable, Statement in Support of Net Neutrality, in U.S. House of Representatives (Ed.), H.R. Rep. No. 110-95, p. 51 (2008). Online. Available at: <http://www.gpo.gov/fdsys/pkg/CRPT-110hrpt95/html> (accessed Sept. 1, 2012).

Franken, Al, 'Net Neutrality Is Foremost Free Speech Issue of Our Time', CNN (Aug. 5, 2010), http://articles.cnn.com/2010-08-05/opinion/franken.net.neutrality_1_net-neutrality-television-networks-cable?_s=PM:OPINION.

Frieden, Rob, 'Invoking and Avoiding the First Amendment: How Internet Service Providers Leverage Their Status as Both Content Creators and Neutral Conduits,' *First Amendment Law Review* (2010), http://papers.ssrn.com/sol3/papers.cfm?abstract_id=1425138.

Geiger, James F., AT&T and BellSouth Merger: What Does It Mean For Consumers? Hearing Before the Subcommittee on Antitrust, Competition Policy and Consumer Rights of the S. Committee on the Judiciary, 109th Cong. 34–37 (2006), http://frwebgate.access.gpo.gov/cgi-bin/getdoc.cgi?dbname=109_senate_hearings&docid=f:29938.pdf.

Genachowski, Julius, The Third Way: A Narrowly Tailored Broadband Framework, Broadband.gov (May 6, 2010), http://www.broadband.gov/the-third-way-narrowly-tailored-broadband-framework-chairman-julius-genachowski.html (accessed Nov. 1, 2010).

Google Inc., Comments on Preserving the Open Internet, GN Docket No. 09-191, Broadband Industry Practices, WC Docket No. 07-52 (Jan. 14, 2010), http://fjallfoss.fcc.gov/ecfs/document/view?id=7020378767.

Grant, Peter and Drucker, Jesse, 'Phone, Cable Firms Rein in Consumers' Internet Use,' *Wall Street Journal*, Oct. 21, 2005, A1.

Hands Off (2008a), Statement on FCC Resolution of Comcast-BitTorrent Issue (Aug. 1, 2008). Online. http://www.handsoff.org/blog/page/3/ (accessed June 30, 2009).

Hands Off (2008b), Member Organizations (2009). Online. http://www.handsoff.org/blog/member-organizations/ (accessed June 30, 2009).

Hundt, Reed, *You Say You Want a Revolution: A Story of Information Age Politics* (New York: PublicAffairs, 2000).

Isenberg, David, 'Rise of the Stupid Network,' *Journal of the Hyperlinked Organization*, June 1997. Online. http://www.hyperorg.com/misc/stupidnet.html.

Ivins, Molly, 'Media Concentration is a Totalitarian Tool,' *Boulder Daily Camera*, Jan. 31, 2003. Online. http://www.commondreams.org/views03/0131-09.htm.

Jefferson, Thomas, 'Letter to Alexander Donald,' 1788, in *The Writings of Thomas Jefferson* Vol. 6 (1903–04), p. 425, http://etext.lib.virginia.edu/jefferson/quotations/jeffcont.htm.

Kaplow, L., 'The Patent-Antitrust Intersection: A Reappraisal,' *Harvard Law Review* 97: 1813–92 (1984).

Kapor, M., 'Building the Open Road: The NREN as Test-Bed for the National Public Network,' *Journal of Science, Education and Technology* 1: 231–42 (1992).

Kapor, Mitch and Berman, Jerry, 'Building the Open Road: The NREN as Test-Bed for the National Public Network,' Request for Comments 1259. Electronic Frontier Foundation. (Sept. 1991), http://w2.eff.org/Misc/Publications/Mitch_Kapor/nren_npn_nii_kapor_eff.rfc (accessed Sept. 15, 2012).

Kimmelman, Gene, SBC-AT&T and Verizon-MCI Mergers Remaking the Telecommunications Industry Part II: Hearing before Senate Judiciary Committee, 109th Cong. (2005). Online. http://judiciary.senate.gov/hearings/testimony.cfm?id=1465&wit_id=4176 (accessed Nov. 1, 2010).

Krause, Reinhardt, 'Former FCC Chief Hundt on Telecom Outlook,' *Investor's Business Daily*, Apr. 4, 2000, A10.

Krim, Jonathan, 'High-Tech Tension Over Illegal Uses,' *The Washington Post*, Feb. 22, 2005, E1.

Kwall, Roberta Rosenthal, 'Inspiration and Innovation: The Intrinsic Dimension of the Artistic Soul,' *Notre Dame Law Review*, 81: 1945 (2006).

Lemley Mark A. and Lessig, Lawrence, 'The End of End-to-End: Preserving the Architecture of the Internet in the Broadband Era,' *UCLA Law Review* 48: 925 (2001).

Madison, James, *Annals of Congress*, 4: 934 (1794).

Madison, James, 'Report on the Alien and Sedition Act (Jan. 17, 1800),' in Jack N. Rakove (Ed.), *James Madison: Writings* (1999).

Magarian, Gregory P., 'The Jurisprudence of Colliding First Amendment Interests: From the Dead End of Neutrality to the Open Road of Participation-Enhancing Review,' *Notre Dame Law Review*, 83: 185 (2007).

Martinson, Jane, 'AT&T Revamp Plan Wins Few Fans,' *The Guardian* (U.K.), Oct. 26, 2000, http://www.guardian.co.uk/business/2000/oct/26/8 (accessed Nov. 1, 2010).

McCormick, Jr., Walter B., Net Neutrality: Hearing Before the Senate Commerce on Commerce, Science, & Transportation, 14–19.

McSlarrow, Kyle, Net Neutrality: Hearing Before the Senate Comm. on Commerce, Science, & Transportation, 20–23.

Miniwatts Marketing Group, Internet World Stats – Usage and Population Statistics, <http://www.Internetworldstats.com/stats2.htm> (last accessed Aug. 1, 2012).

Mohammed, Arshad, 'FCC Approves Verizon, SBC Mergers', *Wash. Post*, Nov. 1, 2005, p. D5.

National Cable & Telecommunications Association v. Brand X Internet Services, 545 U.S. 967 (2005).

Naughton, John, *A Brief History of the Future: From Radio Days to Internet Years in a Lifetime* (New York: The Overlook Press, 1999).

NetCompetition, Members (2009). Online. http://netcompetition.org/index.php/go/about-us-members/ (accessed Sept. 9, 2009).

Noguchi, Yuki, 'AT&T-SBC Union Now Looks Possible,' *The Washington Post*, Jan. 28, 2005, E1.

Office of Communication of the United Church of Christ v. Federal Communications Comm., 359 F. 2d 994 (D.C. Cir. 1966).

Patterson, Scott, 'A Conversation with John Burns,' Smart Money (Apr. 2, 2003), http://www.smartmoney.com/investing/economy/a-conversation-with-john-burns-14132/ (accessed Nov. 1, 2010).

Rist, Oliver, 'Don't Neuter the Net', *InfoWorld*, Mar. 9, 2006, http://www.infoworld.com/d/security-central/dont-neuter-net-106.

Roth, Daniel, 'The Dark Lord of Broadband Tries to Fix Comcast's Image,' *Wired.com*, Jan. 19, 2009. Online. Available at: http://www.wired.com/techbiz/people/magazine/17-02/mf_brianroberts?currentPage=all.

Rubin, Jonathan L., AT&T and BellSouth Merger: What Does It Mean For Consumers? Hearing Before the Subcommittee on Antitrust, Competition Policy and Consumer Rights of the S. Committee on the Judiciary, 109th Cong. 38–48 (2006), http://frwebgate.access.gpo.gov/cgi-bin/getdoc.cgi?dbname=109_senate_hearings&docid=f:29938.pdf.

Saltzer J.H. et al., *End-to-End Arguments in System Design*, ACM *Transactions on Computer Systems*, 277 (1984), http://web.mit.edu/Saltzer/www/publications/endtoend/endtoend.pdf.

Scott, Ben, Statement on the Internet Freedom Preservation Act of 2008, http://archives.energycommerce.house.gov cmte_mtgs/110-ti-hrg.050608. Scott-testimony.pdf.

Shostak, Frank, Posting to Mises Daily, Mar. 4, 2003, Housing Bubble: Myth or Reality?. Online. http://mises.org/story/1177.

Taylor, Kelvyn, 'Closer Look at P2P Technology', *Personal Computer World* (July 5, 2007), http://www.businessgreen.com/personal-computer-world/features/2193584/closer-look-bittorrent?page=2 (accessed Nov. 1, 2010).

Travis, Hannibal, 'Of Blogs, eBooks, and Broadband: Access to Digital Media as a First Amendment Right,' *Hofstra Law Review* 35: 1519 (2007).

Travis, Hannibal, 'Postmodern Censorship of Pacifist Content on Television and the Internet,' *Notre Dame Journal of Law, Ethics, and Public Policy* 25: 47–86 (2011).

U.S. Code, title 17, section 512(a) (2006).

U.S. House of Representatives, Advanced Telecommunications and Opportunity Reform Act, H.R. 5252, 109th Cong. (2006a); H.R. Rep. No. 109-470 (2006b).

U.S. House of Representatives, House Report No. 109-541 (2006c).

U.S. House of Representatives, House Report No. 110-95 (2008).

U.S. House of Representatives, Internet Freedom and Nondiscrimination Act of 2006, H.R. 5417, 109th Cong. (2006).

United States Internet Service Provider Association in support of Verizon Internet Services, *Recording Industry Association of Am. v. Verizon Internet Service*, No. 03-MS-0040 (JDB) (D.D.C. Apr. 24, 2003), 2003 WL 22341287, http://www.eff.org/cases/riaa-vverizon-case-archive.

Verizon, Reply Brief for Petitioner, *Verizon Communications Inc. v. Law Offices of Curtis V. Trinko, LLP*, No. 02-682 (2003), 2003 WL 22068099.

Verizon Communications, Inc. v. Law Offices of Curtis V. Trinko, 540 U.S. 398 (2004).

Verizon & Verizon Wireless, Appellate Brief, *Verizon v. FCC*, No. 11-1355 (DC Cir. appeal filed July 3, 2012).

Verizon & Verizon Wireless, Comments on Preserving the Open Internet, GN Docket No 09-191 (Jan. 14, 2010).

Verizon & Verizon Wireless, Reply Comments on Preserving the Open Internet, GN Docket No. 09-191 (Apr. 26, 2010).

Walker, Leslie, '.Com-Live,' *The Washington Post*, July 29, 1999. Online. http://www.washingtonpost.com/wp-srv/business/talk/transcripts/walker/walker072999.htm.

Werbach, Kevin, 'The Centripetal Network: How the Internet Holds Itself Together, and the Forces Tearing It Apart,' *UC Davis Law Review*, 42: 343 (2008).

Wikipedia, (2003a) 'Derivatives (finance)', http://en.wikipedia.org/w/index.php?title=Derivative_(finance)&oldid=8952061.

Wikipedia (2003d), 'Governmental Positions on the Iraq War Prior to the 2003 Invasion of Iraq (Apr. 21, 2003),' http://en.wikipedia.org/w/ index.php?title=Governmental_positions_on_the_Iraq_War_prior_to_the_2003_invasion_of_Iraq&oldid=854580.

Wikipedia (2003b), 'Iraq Disarmament Crisis (Mar. 12, 2003),' http://en.wikipedia.org/w/index.php?title=Iraq_disarmament_crisis&oldid=743590.

Wikipedia (2003c), 'Opposition to the Iraq War (Apr. 11, 2003),' http://en.wikipedia.org/w/index.php?title=Opposition_to_the_Iraq_War&oldid=98495.

Wolff, Michael, 'You've Got Merger,' *New York Magazine*, Dec. 14, 1998, http://nymag.com/nymetro/news/media/columns/medialife/1642/.

Wong, Jennifer, 'Net Neutrality: Preparing for the Future,' *Journal of the National Association of the Administrative Law Judiciary*, 31: 669 (2011).

10 The "monster" that ate social networking?

Hannibal Travis

> The reason I've always believed Facebook will be a monster business over time is that it is gathering an unprecedented amount of personal information about me that I am only too happy to share (though I understand many are not).
> Columnist Chris O'Brien, *San Jose Mercury-News* (2012)

The birth of Facebook

In 2012, a debate erupted about the "nationalization" of Facebook as a bid to save user privacy. Philip Howard of the University of Washington argued in *Slate* (2012) that Facebook was a "monopoly" that offended most users' expectations of privacy, arbitrarily banned certain pages, and was complicit in tyrannical regimes' tracking of their opponents who use their real identities. Some business writers pilloried the idea as trusting a government that spies on its citizens without warrants to safeguard the anonymity and freedom from surveillance of Facebook users (Bercovici, 2012; Krayewski, 2012; Thierer, 2012). The debate (resulting in 25,000 Google results in a matter of days) suggested that Americans are concerned about the implications of Facebook for their freedom and privacy.

Facebook is describable as a map, list, or interface. As a map, it provides a guide to the territory of real-world and online networks of people, or social networks. As a list, it compiles groupings of people, groups of people, and profiles of such people and groups. And as an interface, it provides a Web- or mobile-based platform to view such lists, profiles, and related communications of memories, plans, and thoughts (Grimmelman, 2009, 1150). A social-networking site such as Facebook generally facilitates the creation and display of user profiles, and the sending and receipt of messages to and from other users, in centrifugally expanding affinity networks (Baron, 2010, 80).

Social networking became popular in the early 2000s as a way of forming relationships, finding jobs, and advertising products over the Internet (NewsInc., 2009). Some networks are now all but forgotten, like Friendster and Xanga (Levitt and Rosch, 2008, 12). Others, like Classmates.com, Evite, and MySpace, continue to enjoy some users, but few in comparison to Facebook. Dating sites such as Match.com and eHarmony, which remain popular, also permit social-networking and relationship-building.

In 2002, Divya Narendra and Cameron and Tyler Winklevoss began planning a Web site for Harvard students that would facilitate social networking on the model of Friendster, which was the "place to be" as social networking rose to prominence during the early 2000s (Hamilton, 2007). They hired Mark Zuckerberg to program their site, called Harvard Connection. They claimed in a later lawsuit that: "While assuring [them] in multiple meetings, calls, and emails that he was working diligently to complete the planned website for their partnership, Zuckerberg had decided to steal [their] creative ideas and business plan and to use them in a hastily completed and preemptively launched competitive website with different partners" (ConnectU, 2007, 3). Even worse, they argued that Zuckerberg copied the code for their Harvard Connection project (ibid., 16–17). In 2008, Facebook settled these lawsuits by agreeing to pay the founders of Harvard Connection $20 million in cash and $40 million in stock in 2008 (Winklevoss and Winklevoss, 2011, 1–4).

TheFacebook, as it was initially known, grew more quickly than Friendster, ranking just below MySpace in 2005 as the fastest-growing major platform for social networking online (Baron, 2010, 81). Expanding from colleges and universities to high schools in the fall of 2005, the site became accessible to the general public in the fall of 2006 (ibid.). By 2008, Facebook was one of the most popular social-networking sites in the world, attracting about 100 million users (Foreign Direct Investment, 2008). Facebook had about 150 million unique visitors per month in the summer of 2012. This made it the second-largest network of Web sites in the world, just behind Google (Burn-Murdoch, 2012). A userbase estimated at more than 900 million people uploaded billions of photos per month and created more than a billion "friendships" per month as of 2012 (Burroughs and Repicky, 2012).

Privacy implications of Facebook use

Facebook's legions of users are even more impressive because of the daunting disclosures of personal information that the site requires to become a member. Facebook asks not only for a name but also for an email address, gender, and birthday. If a potential user bothers to read Facebook's privacy policy, he or she might learn that Facebook treats names, photographs, gender, and social networks as public information (Facebook, 2012b). In addition, Facebook inquires into, but does not require disclosure of, "a vast array of personal information," making it "a treasure trove of evidence for government investigators." Categories of personal information solicited by the site's Web forms include tastes in books, movies, and music; educational and employment history; membership in clubs and associations; sexual orientation; daily activities, and political preferences (Semitsu, 2011, 301).

Facebook builds networks by the process of "Friending." Initiating a friend request to another user of Facebook generates an email inviting the user to respond on Facebook (Baron, 2010, 82–3). Friends may send Messages or Wall postings to one another. Such Facebook communication is less time-consuming than telephone or in-person conversations, and is seen as being more private than communicating by public bulletin board or Web site (ibid., 85). Facebook automatically generates communication among its members by (since the fall of 2006) sending News Feed updates about changes by a user's friends of their relationship status, favorites, likes, employment history, and other information (ibid., 85–6). After an outcry from some users, Facebook announced enhanced privacy settings and controls, which allowed News Feed to be disabled (Associated Press, 2006, B6; EPIC, 2012; Zuckerberg, 2006). As Anita Hamilton explained (2007), the News Feed helped Facebook become dominant by giving users an activity to perform on an ongoing basis, as opposed to the more "boring" Friendster.

In late 2006 and early 2007, Facebook released a series of interfaces to developers, which enabled applications to be written that exploit user data such as user profiles, events, photos, photo tags, albums, groups, and networks (Morin, 2007). Within three months, "Facebook ha[d] some 7,000 free add-on applications that let members do everything from monitor their stock portfolios to map anyplace they've ever visited to text friends' phones via the site" (Hamilton, 2007). Within a year, there were 24,000 applications in Facebook's directory of them, and 400,000 developers for Facebook (Gallagher, 2008). Facebook users currently visit Facebook application sites at a rate of more than six billion times per year (Matus, 2012). More than a million "websites and third-party applications allow users to interact through Facebook, even without actually visiting the Facebook site." Thus, persons and corporations may knowingly or unknowingly communicate information "'through' Facebook" without maintaining a profile there or visiting the Facebook.com domain (Semitsu, 2011, 301–2).

Facebook instructs its users that it may provide friend lists and other profile information to third parties such as Microsoft, as well as law enforcement when it thinks public safety is at issue (Facebook, 2012b). The service warns users that it may disclose information without permission, but with "notice, such as by telling you about it in [a data use] policy" (ibid.). An account may be deleted by a user, subject to account information remaining stored in backup copies and logs for 90 days (ibid.). In addition, users may restrict postings to their own eyes, friends, or custom-generated combinations of friends and networks (Facebook, 2012a). Similarly, a feature called "timeline visibility control" promises users the ability to decide whether updates, photos, or other content is available on his or her timeline of Facebook-visible life activity (Facebook, 2012c). Yet Facebook warns that a user's "friend list is always available to the games, applications and websites" that are used, as well as potentially in friends' timelines or in the searchable areas of Facebook (ibid.).

Finally, for some years now Facebook has warned that it cannot guarantee that unauthorized persons will not access and view users' information, or that the information will not be publicly available (Facebook, 2009). Moreover, it has updated its Privacy Help Centre to state that: "We may also share information when we have a good faith belief it is necessary to prevent fraud or other illegal activity," and that such sharing extends to "other companies, lawyers, courts or other government entities" (Facebook, 2012d). Facebook has, however, persuaded one court that its terms of use may create a reasonable expectation on the part of users as to the privacy of that data, misuse of which may be a crime.[1]

In 2009, Facebook announced the settlement of a class-action lawsuit brought on behalf of users of Facebook as of November 2007 (United States District Court for the Northern District of California, 2009). Facebook users received no compensation for the alleged privacy violations, which involved Facebook's Beacon program, a program which Facebook characterized as being "designed to allow users to share information with their selected friends about actions taken on affiliated, but third-party, websites" (ibid.; see also Tokson, 2011, 627–8). Remarking on the controversy surrounding Facebook and Beacon, among other violations of users' expectations as to the privacy and integrity of Facebook, James Grimmelman pointed out that Facebook's privacy policy promises that "'Facebook takes appropriate precautions to protect our users' information'" was a "beautiful irrelevancy" because most users would not read it and it would not protect their privacy in any event (Grimmelman, 2008, 1181). According to surveys, most Facebook users either did not read or grossly misunderstood Facebook's privacy policies; often, they misunderstood without reading (ibid., 1181–2). This is rational, as it would take at least 181 hours per year for a typical U.S. Internet user to read all relevant privacy policies, with a low likely return on that investment (McDonald and Cranor, 2008, 18). The opportunity cost of reading all of this boilerplate would exceed the benefit of Internet use to the typical user, and would cost the United States as a whole nearly a trillion dollars in lost time (ibid., 19).

---

1 In that case, Mark Zuckerberg's former business partners went on to lead a competing social network called ConnectU, which harvested the email addresses and other user data of Facebook's users. ConnectU argued that Facebook's unilateral terms of use did not make ConnectU's taking, copying, or using Facebook user data a crime or civil tort. The court responded, in part, that Facebook user data might be confidential information under California law given "the right of Facebook users to disclose their email addresses for selective purposes ...." *Facebook, Inc. v. ConnectU LLC*, 489 F. Supp.2d 1087, 1091 and n. 5 (N.D. Cal. 2007).

Is Facebook a natural monopoly?

The popularity of Facebook may be placing some of the core values of the Internet at risk, or so says a growing chorus of commentators and Internet pundits. As more and more people spend their Internet time on Facebook, the terms of use and privacy policies of one company take on tremendous importance. Combining information in one place about a person's appearance, habits, and desires may even lead to the victimization of the person, as in cases of kidnapping that have been linked to Facebook use (*Daily Advertiser*, 2012, 33; Del Bosque, 2012, 4; *Jakarta Globe*, 2010). In 2010, Facebook seemed poised to take over half of all Internet use in the United States, having grown from a very small site to claim one out of every four page views of a Web site in the United States (Dougherty, 2010). If, as Facebook's Chief Operating Officer Sheryl Sandberg predicted, the next generation of Internet users eschews email in favor of communicating by Facebook, the stakes in Facebook privacy battles will be elevated (Carr, 2010, 16).[2]

Is Facebook poised to monopolize social networking? Some journalists and scholars believe that it is. A spate of articles in 2010 observed that Facebook had achieved a "critical mass" of users that would be difficult to duplicate.[3] In 2011, Ruben Rodrigues argued that Facebook may represent "the rise of a single dominant player ... capable of exercising monopoly power," which may be oblivious to user appeals for greater privacy or friendlier terms of use.[4]

A comparison of MySpace to Facebook cuts both ways on the question of whether Facebook could build an enduring social-networking monopoly. On the one hand, some journalists argued after the decline of MySpace that Facebook enjoyed a virtual monopoly, having cornered the market on the real-identity "universal social network."[5] According to a CEO of a social media index fund, many social media firms "are the ultimate monopoly. The reason why we go to places like LinkedIn and Facebook is not necessarily

2 Austin Carr, 'Facebook: The Social Network,' Fast Company, Oct. 2010, p. 16.
3 Jonathan Sibum, 'St Mark Goes on Charm Offensive: After Visiting No 10 Last Week, Facebook Founder Mark Zuckerberg Is Now Off to Asia to Woo Advertisers as the Networking Site Seeks 1bn Users,' *The Sunday Telegraph* (UK), June 27, 2010. Available at: http://web2.westlaw.com (search for document "2010 WLNR 12941587"); Dan Whitcomb, 'Facebook's Road to Web Domination; Technology "Lock-in" Makes Site Tough to Unfriend,' Calgary Herald, Feb. 1, 2010, p. B8. Available at: http://web2.westlaw.com (search for document "2010 WLNR 26134160").
4 Ruben Rodrigues, 'Privacy on Social Networks: Norms, Markets, and Natural Monopoly,' in Saul Levmore and Martha C. Nussbaum (Eds.), *The Offensive Internet: Speech, Privacy, and Reputation*, Cambridge, MA: Harvard University Press, 2011, 237.
5 'Facebook: A Fistful of Dollars,' *The Economist*, Feb. 3, 2012, p. 51. Available at: http://web2.westlaw.com (search for document "2012 WLNR 2436701"); Rick Newman, 'Facebook's GM Problem,' *U.S. News & World Report*, May 17, 2012. Available at: <http://web2.westlaw.com> (search for document "2012 WLNR 10406984").

because they have the best technology but because our friends or business relationships are there, and replicating that is very, very difficult."[6] Google, for example, after investing tens of millions of dollars in creating a competing social network called Google Plus, attracted less than a hundredth of the minutes spent per user on its network in early 2012, compared with Facebook.[7]

On the other hand, Facebook rapidly overtook MySpace in the 2008–2011 period, even though Facebook was founded by students and MySpace had a contract to provide $900 million of advertising space to Google (Potter, 2012, 131). MySpace was much more dominant than Facebook between 2005 and 2007, enjoying visits from about 90% of all Internet users who used social-networking services in the fall of 2006 (*Liveuniverse v. MySpace*, 2007). Facebook's popularity could also fade, for millions of users have already switched from Friendster to MySpace or from MySpace to Facebook without hesitating or encountering much difficulty (Dumenco, 2011, 16). Facebook lost North American users at a rate of 400,000 per month in early 2012, as Twitter grew at a rate of more than five million users per month, worldwide (Miniwatts Marketing Group, 2012).[8] Surveys suggest that many users consider leaving Facebook (Barnes, 2011, 4). This echoes what the founder of the World Wide Web, Tim Berners-Lee, says that a colleague once told him about competing on the Internet: "It's amazing how quickly people on the internet can pick something up, but it's also amazing how quickly they can drop it" (Katz, 2012). Another observer argued that MySpace appeared to suffer a network effect in slow reverse: "When a social network passes out of favour [sic] in a small network, the large network suffers. The loose connections that held the wider network together start to disappear" (Waller, 2012, 1785).

Facebook is certainly dominant within the social-networking market, but it is not clear that it has monopoly power in the legal or economic senses of the concept. Facebook exploits a two-sided market, in which it attracts two types of users who find it useful—social networkers and advertisers—but generates revenue principally from the advertisers (Waller, 2012, 1785). In advertising, its main source of revenue, it is far from being a monopoly. Even in display advertising, courts and regulators in the United States and Europe would probably not categorize Facebook as having a monopoly (a dominant position, in Europe; ibid., 1781–2). In social networking as a

6 Quoted in Hung Tran, 'From Bull(et)s to Bears, There's an ETF for That,' *Money Management Executive*, June 18, 2012. Available at: <http://web2.westlaw.com> (search for document "2012 WLNR 12706198").

7 David Angotti, 'Google Plus: Average User Spends Only 3 Minutes Per Month!,' Search Engine Journal, Feb. 28, 2012. Available at: <http://www.searchenginejournal.com/google-plus-user-time-low/40726/>.

8 Twitter's figures are derived by dividing the difference between 100 million users in Sept. 2011 and 140 million users in April 2012, by seven months.

service offered free of charge to users, Facebook enjoyed about two-thirds of all visits to such sites in summer 2012 (Kallas, 2012). Measured in terms of minutes per user on average, Facebook is very dominant, with about 400 minutes per user compared to 24 for Twitter, 16 for Linkedin, and 12 for MySpace (Bullas, 2012).

There are at least two potential obstacles to Facebook becoming a dominant platform for Internet communication: Google and patent litigation. In 2010, Google perfected its prototypes of its own social network called Google+, with the +1 button taking the place of Facebook's "Like," and with arguably improved capabilities compared to Facebook for uploading photos and embedding videos (Helft and Hempel, 2011, 119–20). Google could advertise Google+ continuously on its network of sites such as Gmail, Google Search, and YouTube, sites which collectively had more unique users than Facebook in 2010 (ibid., 119, 124). The other challenge was posed by Yahoo! It has the third largest audience of any Internet network, with 66 million unique visitors per month. More importantly, it claims to own 1,000 patents relating to display advertising, Web sites, and social networking. Even worse for Facebook, Facebook's own patents cite Yahoo!'s as related prior art. Yahoo! owns patents on important innovations in online services, including in personalization, profiles, social media, messaging, news feeds, advertising display, click fraud, and privacy controls. Yahoo! argued that Facebook's infringement of its patents turned around "one of the worst performing Internet sites for advertising," in Facebook, to one with increasing click-through rates for Internet advertising, making them more profitable for advertisers and for Facebook itself (Yahoo!, 2012, paras. 25–8; see also Brodkin, 2012). Yahoo!'s suit was resolved with a settlement on terms in which Facebook promotes Yahoo! (Letzing, 2012).

Although the most significant threat on the patent front seems to have been resolved with a 2012 settlement with Yahoo!, the struggle with Google remains an issue. Facebook has certain decisive advantages over Google in the social networking space, however. Its "critical mass" of users makes it "immensely more valuable" to users than Google+, with the "number of users and the array of fine-grained information that users have posted [growing] on a scale vastly superior to its competitors and [representing] an important source of direct and indirect network effects for users, advertisers, application developers, and other service providers" (Waller, 2011, 1788). This advantage is reflected in users' average time spent on Facebook as opposed to Google+, with the latter used for roughly one minute for every 100 minutes of Facebook use (Bullas, 2012). Despite "integrating Plus into all aspects of [Google services] and the dominant position in search" that Google enjoys, Google+ has a very low market share (Kallas, 2012). More than a year after launching, it had fewer than one active user for every nine or ten Facebook users. Even more dramatically, Google+ "users spent just 3.3 minutes on Google+ in January [2012] compared to 7.5 hours for Facebook" (Wasserman, 2012).

With the Yahoo! patent litigation resolved and Google+ apparently struggling, the prospect exists that Facebook might patent or otherwise exclude competition in social networking. After buying 750 patents from computing giant IBM in 2012, Facebook claims to own Internet-related advertising, information "tagging," and social-networking patents which, if enforced, could put companies like Yahoo! virtually out of business by denying them 80% of their revenue (Perlroth, 2012, B4). A prominent patent judge has warned that such patents "raise significant First Amendment concerns by granting a private party the right to impose broad restrictions on the free flow of ideas and information over the Internet." He reasoned: "the concept of allowing users to control the content of their online communications is [too abstract to be patented] because free and unrestricted Internet communication has become a staple of contemporary life," and that it would be very troubling to allow any one company "to exert monopoly power over any online system that allows users to control the content of their own communications" (*MySpace v. GraphOn*, 2012, 1265). The majority of the court, and the court's actual ruling, disagreed, stating that there is no "brightline" test for what sort of technology is specific enough to be patentable, and found that such technology could be patented if it was sufficiently new or innovative to be patented, accounting for similar prior technology (ibid., 1259–62). Somewhat abstract social networking patents are proliferating rapidly.

Is Facebook a threat to privacy and freedom of speech online?

Fifty-four percent of Internet users told a survey released in 2008 that they were "uncomfortable with third parties collecting information about their online behavior" (Consumers Union, 2008). Yet Facebook's legal position has been that even when it discloses user communications to third parties not intended to receive them, the user does not suffer an "injury" (*In re Facebook Privacy Litigation*, 2012, 712–13). A court found, by contrast, that if Facebook sent "the contents of its users' communications [without user consent], [then] all of the users of [Facebook] suffered the same injury, which will necessarily mean that each individual Plaintiff will have demonstrated that he was injured" (ibid.). In a later opinion, the court explained that users suffer an invasion of a statutory right to restrict disclosure of their personal information (*Fraley v. Facebook*, 2011, 798).

Does a Facebook profile have economic value to its "owner," potentially giving rise to a claim akin to theft when Facebook uses it without permission? Yes, suggested a court on Facebook's home turf of Northern California. The court reviewed public announcements by Facebook's own Chief Executive Officer and Chief Operating Officer that product endorsements by Facebook friends are very valuable to Facebook's clients, the advertisers (ibid., 800). Mark Zuckerberg once said that "[n]othing influences people more than a recommendation from a trusted friend. A trusted referral influences people more than the best broadcast message. A trusted referral is the Holy Grail of advertising" (quoted in ibid.). Facebook's Chief Operating Officer Sheryl Sandberg also called a friend's Facebook recommendation "the Holy Grail of marketing," with advertisements branded with friend's names being much more memorable and likely to lead to purchases of whatever advertised. Even more controversially, the court ruled that Facebook may have acted "fraudulently" by amending its Terms of Use at some point to disclose that members may not always "opt out of Sponsored Stories" (ibid., 800, 806, 814). The standard for "fraud" is low in California, analyzed via a test for a reasonable likelihood of deception regardless of intent to deceive (ibid., 813). Facebook and the "Sponsored Stories" plaintiffs agreed to settle for $20 million, but the judge rejected this amount on the first attempt for an absence of evidence of its basis and fairness ("Judge Rejects Settlement," 2012, A5; see also Sengupta, 2012, 15).

On the other hand, a group of Facebook users have claimed that "Facebook's use of plaintiffs' names and likenesses can be seen as serving a commercial purpose, undertaken with at least the intent of achieving growth in Facebook's user base, thereby ultimately resulting in monetary gain for Facebook" (*Cohen v. Facebook*, 2011, 1–3). The court disagreed, finding that the users' names and likenesses may have had no commercial value, unlike celebrity names or images, for example. The same court noted that nothing in Facebook's terms of service indicate that users have consented for their names or profile pictures to be employed in endorsements or testimonials for products or services sold by Facebook's advertisers (*Cohen v. Facebook*, 2011, 1095). The Stored Communications Act, which applies to messages received from another Internet user and stored on one's Facebook "Wall" or other message center,[9] invokes a Web site's terms of service by referring to the "intended recipient" of a communication, and "consent" to divulge it (U.S. Code, 2011, title 18, section 2702(a)(1)–(b)(3)).

More recent developments give even greater cause for concern. One-third of U.S. employers surveyed have refused to hire prospective workers based on the content of their Facebook profiles, and three-quarters of employers scour such profiles before offering work (Associated Press, 2012). As noted above,

---

9 One court stated that "a Facebook wall posting or a MySpace comment … results in that post being stored for backup purposes" and governed by the Stored Communications Act. *Crispin v. Christian Audigier, Inc.*, 717 F. Supp. 2d 965, 989 (C.D. Cal. 2010). Another noted that the defendant was an "intended recipient" under "its privacy policy." *In re Am. Airlines, Inc.*, Privacy Litig., 370 F. Supp. 2d 552, 560–61 (N.D. Tex. 2005). Summarizing these cases, Steven Zansberg and Janna Fischer observe that "users' subjective expectation of privacy in information they post to a social media site does not necessarily coincide with courts' views that such information is entitled to no reasonable expectation of privacy because it is either available to the public or shared with a sufficiently large group." 'Privacy Expectations in Online Social Media—An Emerging Issue,' *Communications Lawyer*, 28: 1–30 (2011).

Facebook has proudly announced its intention to transmit user profile and communication records to law enforcement even without a subpoena or court order. At the same time, it claims that its employees should not have to testify about the reliability or susceptibility to tampering of the information it shares, because Facebook is "self-authenticating" (Facebook, 2012e).

Moreover, Facebook has endorsed legislation that would abolish existing privacy laws when it comes to "sharing of threat information" and "malicious activity in cyberspace" (Facebook, 2012f). Facebook already enjoys immunity from many common-law privacy lawsuits as a result of what some legal scholars call the efforts of an "activist judiciary" to expand Section 230(c)(1) of the CDA "to preclude all tort lawsuits against ISPs, websites, and search engines" (Rustad and Koenig, 2005, 371). The U.S. Chamber of Commerce, of which Facebook is a member, has argued that further immunity from federal laws protecting privacy were necessary to promote public-private cooperation:

> [B]usinesses need certainty that threat and vulnerability informa-
> tion voluntarily shared with the government would be provided safe
> harbor and not lead to frivolous lawsuits, would be exempt from
> public disclosure, and could not be used by officials to regulate other
> activities ....
>
> [Congress] has an opportunity to take a positive, nonregulatory step
> forward on cybersecurity—as regulations would divert businesses' focus
> from security to compliance—by removing legal roadblocks that prevent
> the private sector and government from sharing cyber threat information
> while protecting personal privacy.
>
> (American Bankers Association, 2012)

The American Civil Liberties Union condemned the new legislation as establishing "unprecedented powers to snoop through people's personal information—medical records, private emails, financial information—all without a warrant, proper oversight or limits" (ACLU, 2012). The law would define a threat to include misappropriation of intellectual property or personal information (U.S. House of Representatives, 2012), something that users of social media such as Facebook, Twitter, and YouTube are constantly accused of by major corporations seeking to protect their officers and brands from criticism, and their content from quotation or parody (Abrams, 2010; Twitter, 2012). According to Web programming consultants Lumin Consulting (2012), the law gives companies like Facebook unprecedented power to share user information with the government at no cost to Facebook, even as to probes lacking probable cause or that violate a user's reasonable expectation of privacy in online activity.

Public-private cooperation threatens user privacy not only by providing Facebook with legal immunity for invading privacy, but by mandates that Facebook build in a "back door" for government surveillance in "real time" of communications intended to be private. There is a precedent for this mandate dating to the mid-1990s, and applicable to telecommunications (as in telephone) companies as opposed to "information" companies like Facebook or Google (BeVier, 1999, 1120–21). Experts argued that such mandates provide "technical 'back doors' that make it easier for federal law enforcement agencies to execute wiretapping orders" (Downes, 2010, 565; Stanton, 2012, 24).

In April 2012, the British interior ministry, the Home Office, proposed pervasive scrutiny of Facebook messages even absent evidence that the senders and recipients had committed any crime. "The government hit a storm of criticism this month when it emerged that it was planning to allow GCHQ to monitor all communication on social media, Skype calls and email, as well as logging every site visited by internet users in Britain" (Katz, above 1). Web innovator Tim Berners-Lee warned that government would "know every detail" about its subjects, "more intimate details about their life than any person they talk to, because often people will confide in the internet as they find their way through medical websites ..." (ibid.). The following month, the Federal Bureau of Investigation urged Facebook, as well as Microsoft, Yahoo, and Google, to support or at least remain silent about a plan that social media firms "build backdoors for government surveillance" (Asian News International, 2012). Under the plan, any site or app that permits communication must link up to the "National Electronic Surveillance Strategy" to enable monitoring of the communications (ibid.).

Constitutional and statutory protections for Americans' privacy offer some cause for hope, however. The United States Supreme Court declared in 2010 that "text message communications are so pervasive that some persons may consider them to be essential means or necessary instruments for self-expression, even self-identification, a development which might strengthen the case for an expectation of privacy" under the Fourth Amendment to the U.S. Constitution (*City of Ontario v. Quon*, 2010, 2630). In the case of American Medical Response of Connecticut, which was the subject of negative comments by an employee on Facebook, who was then fired, the National Labor Relations Board (NLRB) declared that retaliation against an employee for criticizing her employer on Facebook is unlawful if the employer intends to discourage unionizing activity by means of such retaliation (*American Medical Response*, 2010). The Stored Communications Act also protected Facebook users from "privacy breaches which the Fourth Amendment does not address" in one California case (*Crispin v. Christian Audigier*, 2010, 971). Remarking on these cases, Peter Pizzi argues that: "The Electronic Communications Privacy Act (ECPA), Stored Communications Act (SCA), and National Labor Relations Act (NLRA), for example, serve as hurdles for an employer seeking to go directly to a repository of social media such as Facebook or Twitter to obtain social media activity of employees, even if that activity takes place on the employer's machines" (Pizzi, 2011).

Although some scholars suggest that Facebook messages may be doomed to lose Fourth Amendment protections from unreasonable searches and seizures (Semitsu, 2011, 296), this result is by no means inevitable. The "Third Party Doctrine," which might lead to this outcome, would analogize Facebook messages to bank records, which may not be private because they can be reviewed by employees doing the ordinary business of the bank (Tokson, 2011, 598). Yet "Internet users do not waive their privacy interests in content data stored online with a third party and disclosed to its automated systems; rather, available evidence suggests that they consider such stored information to remain wholly private" (ibid., 642). As Henderson and Tokson have argued, "Eleven states have rejected the Third Party Doctrine in some form on state constitutional grounds, and their courts have typically ruled that the police cannot obtain dialed phone numbers without a warrant" (ibid., 641; see also Henderson, 2005, 396–9). Based on these precedents, courts may well distinguish bank records from the content of Facebook communications or the records of when they were sent and by whom they were received, from bank records.

Some observers have looked to the U.S. Federal Trade Commission (FTC) for remedies to privacy violations on Facebook. The FTC has identified the following practices by Facebook as potentially unlawful or deceptive under federal trade law:

- In December 2009, Facebook changed its website so certain information that users may have designated as private—such as their Friends List—was made public. They didn't warn users that this change was coming, or get their approval in advance.
- Facebook represented that third-party apps that users' installed would have access only to user information that they needed to operate. In fact, the apps could access nearly all of users' personal data—data the apps didn't need.
- Facebook told users they could restrict sharing of data to limited audiences—for example with "Friends Only." In fact, selecting "Friends Only" did not prevent their information from being shared with third-party applications their friends used.
- Facebook had a "Verified Apps" program and claimed it certified the security of participating apps. It didn't.
- Facebook promised users that it would not share their personal information with advertisers. It did.
- Facebook claimed that when users deactivated or deleted their accounts, their photos and videos would be inaccessible. But Facebook allowed access to the content, even after users had deactivated or deleted their accounts.
- Facebook claimed that it complied with the U.S.-EU Safe Harbor Framework that governs data transfer between the U.S. and the European Union. It didn't. (FTC, 2011a)

In late 2011, the FTC announced an important settlement with Facebook of complaints the agency had received from the Electronic Privacy Information Center and other groups. The settlement would require Facebook to seek affirmative user consent to material changes in its privacy policies. It would also give the FTC oversight in the future over regular independent audits of Facebook's privacy policies and practices. Finally, it would prohibit misstatements concerning the privacy or security of information posted to Facebook (FTC, 2011b). The misrepresentation and independent-audit provisions mirrored those of an earlier settlement with Twitter.

Although the FTC trumpets that each violation of such a settlement may cost a company such as Facebook or Twitter up to $16,000, it would seem that the FTC has not stacked the fines across multiple users, as it arguably might need to do given the networks' scale; it fined Google only $25,000 for widespread privacy violations. Given that this was the outcome of Google's having allegedly "willfully and repeatedly violated Commission orders to produce certain information and documents," the deterrent effect of FTC orders is suspect (Adweek, 2012). Although the FTC issued a larger fine against Google for violating a prior settlement, as opposed to failing to produce documents, the fine represented less than a tenth of a percent of Google's annual revenue (Valentino-DeVries, 2012). Prior to the Google fine, Facebook settled a class-action lawsuit concerning "Beacon," a service that sent reports of users' non-Facebook Internet activity to their friends, for only $9.5 million, a rather small amount for a company with revenue of 68 times that (Grimmelman, 2008, 1147–8; Perez, 2007; Tokson, 2011, 627–8; TR Daily, 2011). The Ninth Circuit narrowly affirmed the settlement in 2012 (Goldman, 2012).

A more fundamental critique of the FTC as guardian of Facebook privacy is that the agency rarely, if ever, exercises the power to protect users from privacy policies and terms of use that they blithely "agree" to, after being denied any meaningful choice by standard-form policies.[10] As Declan McCullagh points out,

> Federal Trade Commission officials spent the day touting a new settlement with Facebook, with FTC Chairman Jon Leibowitz saying the company now will be "obligated" to keep its privacy promises.
>
> But in reality, the agreement is likely to have little, if any, actual impact on Facebook users.
>
> One reason is that Facebook won't have to roll back any changes to its default privacy settings, which have grown more permissive over the last

---

10 One court has suggested that Facebook users lack certain key federal privacy protection because under its privacy policy, Facebook is an intended recipient of communications among users. *In re Facebook Privacy Litigation*, 791 F. Supp. 2d 705, 714 (N. D. Cal. 2011) (construing 18 U.S.C. Section 2702(b)(3)).

few years. Photos, wall posts, and lists of friends were once visible by default only to people you were associated with; now the default settings include everyone on the Internet.

(McCullagh, 2011)

As noted above, most people do not read and understand the privacy policies on which the FTC places so much emphasis in its settlement with Facebook. Moreover, the independent privacy audits guaranteed by the agreement need not be made public, so Facebook's violations of its obligations under the policies, if any, may be very difficult for users to discover (EPIC, 2011).

Facebook versus government censorship

As with the issue of government surveillance, in which Facebook often appears in the role of intermediary and enforcer of governmental objectives to invade Internet users' privacy, in cases of government censorship of content, Facebook is often complicit out of the profit motive. For this reason, one author warns that despite America's "First Amendment tradition," freedom of speech is coming under the control of private companies more often than under control of the government. With Facebook acting as a gatekeeper due to private interests in some types of communications, private censorship may occur (Albanese, 2010, 24). Evgeny Morozov has argued that in the future, censorship will be customized just as sophisticated forms of advertising are, with user history and profiles being used to identify and restrict communications to dangerous users (Radio Free Europe, 2010). The breadth of information available to Facebook is suggested by a report that Facebook's mobile app informs users that Facebook may read or edit their text messages (Tsukayama, 2012). Web sites that tailor their content to users' actual or perceived identities and histories may colonize the formerly independent and universal Internet, as sites and apps turn to Facebook and Google services (Battelle, 2010; Radio Free Europe, 2010).

When Pakistan blocked Facebook on the basis that blasphemous content was available on it according to Pakistani telecommunications authorities, Facebook removed some of the blasphemous content (Agence France Presse, 2010). The Penal Code of Pakistan (1960) prohibits giving offense to religious texts or historical religious leaders (O'Dowd, 2010, 4–6). Facebook reassured the Pakistani director of telecommunications that such content would be restricted on its site (*The Dawn*, 2010). In June 2010, a Pakistani judge issued a ruling disallowing any Internet communications content contradictory to Islamic principles, including on email services (Eaton, 2010). Along with Saudi Arabia, Pakistan is part of a campaign to ban criticism of fundamentalist Sunni Muslim orthodoxy wherever it occurs, through the United Nations (Buhrer, 2003; United Nations, 2003). Despite complying with Pakistani law regarding giving offense to Muslims, Facebook has permitted entire groups to be formed which not only give offense to but incite violence against Pakistani

Christians, notably one dedicated to Mumtaz Qadri, the assassin of Pakistani Christian politician Salman Taseer, who was slain in 2011 for opposing Pakistan's blasphemy laws.[11] Facebook has also complied with an order of the Delhi High Court in India to remove material critical of, offensive to, or defamatory in the view of, Indian religious sects (domain-b, 2012). Outside of Asia, a series of recent petitions to Facebook seeking the removal of Holocaust-denying pages or groups may test the scope of freedom of expression in Western Europe and North America (Eglash, 2012, 22).

In other cases, Facebook has played a more benign role. Iran banned Facebook by 2009 after many Iranians looked to Facebook, as well as Twitter and YouTube, to communicate messages and organized protests surrounding the disputed re-election of Iran's president (McCullagh, 2009). At that time, Facebook was arguably precluded from providing commercial services to Iranian nationals pursuant to a ban on exports to Iran administered by the U.S. Treasury Department's Office of Foreign Assets Control (Lai, 2009). Facebook did not restrict Iranians from using its services during the critical months of the Green Movement opposing the 2009 election results, however (Luhr, 2009–2010, 500–16). It may be that the Office of Foreign Assets Control reassured Facebook that telecommunications or Internet services are not subject to the ban, or that Facebook was not pursued despite an arguable violation in favor of higher-value targets or to further U.S. foreign policy in the region. The arbitrariness of the entire export-restriction regime is highlighted by the fact that Saudi Arabia is not subject to it despite the country being a major source of terrorist financing (Danchin, 2002, 50, 59–61, 125). In removing sites such as Facebook from a list of restricted exports, the U.S. Office of Foreign Assets Control argued that sanctions on communications capabilities restrict "the universal right of free speech and information" (Luhr, 2009–2010, 501–20).

Similarly, Facebook was very prominent during the Arab Spring revolutions in Egypt, Tunisia, Libya, and Syria, as well as protest movements in India, Russia, and the United States (Cowi, 2011; Elder, 2011; *Hindustan Times*, 2011; Hsu, 2011, 2; Preston, 2011, A10; Timpane, 2011, A02). The government of Egypt, as well as other governments, shut down access to Facebook after it was used to convene a million-strong protest in Cairo, and

11 One fan page for the assassin has 1,400 "likes." Facebook, "Mumtaz Qadri," 2012. Available at: <http://www.facebook.com/pages/Mumtaz-Qadri/208083902556948>. Another calls the assassin the "new hero of Pakistan." Facebook, "The new hero of Pakistan Mumtaz Qadri," 2012. Available at: <http://www.facebook.com/pages/The-new-hero-of-Pakistan-Mumtaz-Qadri/164131403634412>. Another proclaims solidarity with the assassin. Facebook, "Mumtaz Qadri: we are with you," 2012. Available at: <http://www.facebook.com/pages/Mumtaz-Qadri-we-are-with-you/276050722413933>. See also, Issam Ahmed, "What Salman Taseer's Assassination Could Mean for Pakistan," *Christian Science Monitor*, Jan. 5, 2011. Available at: <http://web2.westlaw.com> (search for "2011 WLNR 272376").

invoked licensing agreements with Internet service providers to shut them down (Glanz and Markoff, 2011, A1). Scholars of Internet law and culture have long predicted that this sort of dynamic would gain in importance, as "many-to-many" communication democratized political discourse around the world (Godwin, 1994, 443; Unsworth, 1996).

The ultimate battle over the future of the Internet may involve the U.S. government struggling with Internet users on the terrain of Facebook. The National Security Agency and Domestic Communications Assistance Center are employing Internet experts to intercept billions of Internet communications and access many gigabytes of social networking data annually (*Business Insider*, 2012). For up to a decade, secret devices capable of downloading Internet communications without the permissions of their authors or recipients may have been operating in major cities in California and Washington State, where firms such as Google, Facebook, and Microsoft are based (*Hepting v. AT&T*, 2006, 988–92).

While defenders of such surveillance might argue that it is not an issue involving freedom of expression, but rather the Fourth Amendment or statutory interpretation, privacy is in fact closely linked with the practical ability of a human being to speak out without the chilling effect imposed by the fear of retaliation.[12] In the 1960s, the Supreme Court concluded that the interception of and the creation of dossiers containing citizens' political communications may dissuade Americans from engaging in vigorous advocacy of political ideals out of fear of retaliation from the state and its agents.[13] A desire to avoid classification by various bureaucracies as a "subversive" may deter Americans from joining or financing unpopular causes, including political ones (*Dombrowski v. Pfister*, 1965, 479). Journalists and attorneys who do research around the world and communicate with potentially dangerous individuals complain of being intimidated by growing surveillance of such research (*ACLU v. NSA*, 2006, 767). In addressing the impact of such spying on the political activities of Americans, one court reasoned that it imposes a "chilling effect on protected expression" and causes the loss of membership in political organizations, and that there is "'greater jeopardy to constitutionally protected speech'" when the government comes "'to view with suspicion those who most fervently dispute its policies'" (*ACLU v. NSA*, 2006, 767, quoting *U.S. v. U.S. District Court*, 1972, 313–14). Justice Samuel Alito has predicted that disclosure of Americans' political preferences will "become a

---

12 The traditions of the people of the United States establish a close link between expression and privacy. *U.S. v. U.S. District Court*, 407 U.S. 297, 313–14, 328–9 (1972); *Zweibon v. Mitchell*, 516 F. 2d 594, 618 (D.C. Cir. 1975) (en banc) (plurality opinion).

13 The cases arose out of the U.S. civil rights movement, a multi-decades long struggle which challenged comprehensive systems of spying on and disciplining members of both races in order to perpetuate racial and ethnic persecution, segregation, and the supremacy of the "white" race. *Bates v. City of Little Rock*, 361 U.S. 516 (1960); *Dombrowski v. Pfister*, 380 U.S. 479 (1965).

means of facilitating harassment that impermissibly chills the exercise of First Amendment rights ..." (*John Doe No. 1 v. Reed*, 010, 2825). Violating the anonymity and privacy of Internet communications "may inhibit free flow of information and create a chilling effect on the freedom of adults who wish to access lawful though perhaps controversial material" (*Southeast Booksellers v. McMaster*, 2005, 773). Unpopular causes are especially reliant on privacy to grow, and may be intimidated out of growing when it is trampled (*Black Panther Party v. Smith*, 1981, 1268). Thus, the identities and locations of protesters should receive a high degree of privacy protection (*International Action Center v. U.S.*, 2002, 3).

Conclusion

The operations of Facebook are intimately tied up with how millions of persons exercise their human rights to send and receive information, enjoy privacy from their governments, and connect with others for purposes of family life, maintaining health, improving the world, or pursuing the truth (Suthersanen, 2005, 107–8). Internet users are increasingly demanding that corporations and governments that assert control over their electronic communications also respect the fundamental rights to speak, write, be heard, and enjoy basic privacy protections (European Union, 2009).

Although it may be easy to switch to a different social network, many Internet users might not appreciate the severity of the threats to their privacy and freedom of speech until it is too late. The threat of a social-network monopoly in Facebook's hands, while still only an unproven possibility, may complicate the ability of Internet users to find other ways to communicate. If a person's friends, family, and co-workers constantly report the new developments in their lives on Facebook, is any other Web site really an effective alternative? When one must answer there is no real choice but to use Facebook, social networking may be in danger of seeing its possibilities and potential new uses restricted by one firm's dominance.

Bibliography

Abrams, David, YouTube Takes Down then Reinstates Video by Artist Using His Own Song, Chilling Effects Clearinghouse, Mar. 9, 2010. Available at: <https://www.chillingeffects.org/weather.cgi?WeatherID=631>.

ACLU, Oppose CISPA and Unfettered Access to Americans' Internet Activity, 2012. Available at: <https://www.aclu.org/secure/sem-oppose-cispa-and-unfettered-access-americans-internet-activity?ms=gad_SEM_MSN_Search-Cispa_Stop%20CISPA_CISPA%20what%20is_p_1285462989>.

ACLU v. NSA, 438 F. Supp. 2d 754 (E.D. Mich. 2006), reversed, 493 F. 3d 644 (6th Cir. 2007).

Adweek, FCC Fines Google $25,000, Adweek.com (Apr. 16, 2012). Online. http://www.adweek.com/news/technology/fcc-fines-google-impeding-investigation-139616.

Agence France Presse, 'Pakistan Court Blocks Facebook Over Mohammed Page,' Liveleak.com, May. 19, 2010. http://www.liveleak.com/view?i=7f1_1274306805 (accessed Dec. 1, 2011).

Albanese, Andrew Richard, 'The Game of Monopoly,' *Publishers Weekly*, Dec. 6, 2010, 24, 2010 PUBLRWKLY 24. Available at: <http://web2.westlaw.com> (search for "2010 WLNR 24394623").

American Bankers Association et al., Letter to House Speaker John Boehner and House Minority Leader Nancy Pelosi, Apr. 17, 2012. Online. http://intelligence.house.gov/sites/intelligence.house.gov/files/documents/MultiIndustryHouse CybersecurityBoehnerPelosi.pdf.

American Medical Response of Connecticut, Inc. and International Brotherhood of Teamsters, Local 443, Case No. 34-CA-12576 (N.L.R.B. region 34, Oct. 27, 2010), http://www.scribd.com/doc/41010696/American-Medical-Response-of-CT-NLRB-Nov-2010.

Asian News International, 'FBI Asks Internet Companies Help Its Proposed Wiretapping of Social Networking Sites,' Westlaw (May 5, 2012). Online. Available at: http://web2.westlaw.com (search for document "2012 WLNR 9479938").

Associated Press, 'Facebook Allows More Privacy Controls Amid Expansion,' Eugene Register-Guard, Oct. 1, 2006, B6.

Associated Press, 'Illinois Employers Barred from Asking Job Applicants to Hand Over Social Networking Passwords,' *The Washington Post*, Aug. 1, 2012. Available at: <http://www.washingtonpost.com/national/illinois-employers-barred-from-asking-job-applicants-to-hand-over-social-networking-passwords/2012/08/01/gJQA3VxrPX_story.html>.

Barnes, Rachel, 'Majority of Over-45s Consider Facebook Exit,' *Marketing*, June 22, 2011, 4.

Baron, Naomi S., *Always On: Language in an Online and Mobile World*, Oxford: Oxford University Press, 2010, p. 80.

Battelle, John, 'Identity and the Independent Web.' Battelle Media (Oct. 21, 2010). Available at: <http://battellemedia.com/archives/2010/10/identity_and_the_independent_web_.php>.

Bercovici, Jeff, 'Stupid Idea of the Day: Let's Nationalize Facebook!,' Forbes.com, Aug. 17, 2012, http://www.forbes.com/sites/jeffbercovici/2012/08/17/stupid-idea-of-the-day-lets-nationalize-facebook/2/.

R. BeVier, Lillian, 'The Communications Assistance for Law Enforcement Act of 1994: A Surprising Sequel to the Break Up of AT&T,' *Stanford Law Review* 51: 1049–121 (1999).

Black Panther Party v. Smith, 661 F. 2d 1243, 1268 (D.C. Cir. 1981).

Brodkin, Jon, Yahoo! IP Lawsuit: We Patented "Facebook's Entire Social Network Model," Ars Tehnica, Mar. 13 2012, http://arstechnica.com/tech-policy/2012/03/yahoo-patent-lawsuit-we-invented-facebooks-entire-social-network-model/.

Buhrer, Jean-Paul, UN Commission on Human Rights: Reporters Without Borders Calls for Drastic Overhaul of How the Commission Works, Nonviolent Radical Party Transnational & Transparty (2003). Online. <http://www.radicalparty.org/en/content/un-commission-human-rights-reporters-without-borders-calls-drastic-overhaul-how-commission-w>.

Bullas, Jeff, 6 Social Media Networks to Watch in 2012 [Plus Infographics], Jan. 3, 2012. Available at: <http://www.jeffbullas.com/2012/01/03/6-social-media-networks-to-watch-in-2012-plus-infographics/>.

Burn-Murdoch, John, 'US Web Statistics Released for May 2012: Which Sites Dominate, and Where Do We Go for Online News?,' Guardian.co.uk, June 22, 2012. Available at: http://web2.westlaw.com (search for document "2012 WLNR 13078861").

Burroughs, Allison & Heather B. Repicky, 'Reasonable Expectations of Privacy in the Digital Age,' Mondaq, July 16, 2012. Available at: http://web2.westlaw.com (search for document "2012 WLNR 14776344").

Business Insider, 'This New FBI Unit's Sole Mission Is to Spy on Americans' Cell Phone and Internet Usage,' Westlaw, May 25, 2012. Available at: <http://web2. westlaw.com> (search for "2012 WLNR 11072735").

Cassidy, John, 'Me Media: How Hanging Out on the Internet Became Big Business,' *The New Yorker*, May 15, 2006, p. 50.

City of Ontario v. Quon, 130 S. Ct 2619 (2010).

Cohen v. Facebook, Inc., No. C10–5282 RS, 2011 WL 5117164 (N.D. Cal. Oct. 27, 2011).

Cohen v. Facebook, Inc., 798 F. Supp. 2c 1090 (N.D. Cal. 2011).

ConnectU, Plaintiffs 'Consolidated Memorandum of Points and Authorities in Opposition to Defendants' Motions to Dismiss, Motion to Strike and Motion for Summary Judgment, *ConnectU, Inc. v. Facebook, Inc.*, 1:07-CV-10593 (D. Mass. Sept. 21, 2007), p. 3.

Consumers Union, 'Consumer Reports Poll: Americans Extremely Concerned About Internet Privacy,' ConsumersUnion.org (Sept. 25, 2008). Online. Available at: <http://www.consumersunion.org/pub/core_telecom_and_utilities/006189. html>.

Cowie, James, 'Egypt Leaves the Internet,' Renesys Blog (Jan. 28, 2011). Available at: <http://www.webcitation.org/5w51j0pga>.

Crispin v. Christian Audigier Inc., 717 F. Supp. 2d 965 (C.D. Cal. 2010) (quoting *Quon v. Arch Wireless Operating Co., Inc.*, 529 F. 3d 892 (9th Cir. 2008), *rev'd sub nom. City of Ontario v. Quon* (2010), 130 S. Ct 2619.

Daily Advertiser (Australia), The, 'A Man Who Created a Fake Facebook Account to Lure a Woman Released,' Aug. 4, 2012, p. 33, http://web2.westlaw.com (search for "2012 WLNR 16377204").

Danchin, Peter G., 'U.S. Unilateralism and the International Protection of Religious Freedom: The Multilateral Alternative,' *Columbia Journal of Transnational Law*, 41: 33 (2002).

Dawn, The, 'Court Lifts Facebook Ban,' *The Dawn*, June 1, 2010. Available at: <http://www.dawn.com/wps/wcm/connect/dawn-content-library/dawn/the-news-paper/front-page/court-lifts-facebook-ban-160>.

Del Bosque, Melissa, 'Tweeting the Disappeared,' *The Texas Observer*, May 7, 2012, 4.

domain-b, 'Google, Facebook Comply with Court Order to Remove Objectionable Content,' Westlaw (Feb. 6, 2012). Available at: <http://web2.westlaw.com> (search for "2012 WLNR 2579450").

Dombrowski v. Pfister, 380 U.S. 479 (1965).

Dougherty, Heather, Facebook.com Generates Nearly 1 in 4 Page Views in the US, Nov. 19, 2010. Available at: <http://weblogs.hitwise.com/heather-dough-erty/2010/11/facebookcom_generates_nearly_1_1.html>.

Downes, Larry, 'The Seven Deadly Sins of Title II Reclassification (NOI Remix),' PLI/ Pat 1030:555-565 (2010).

Dumenco, Simon, 'Five Reasons Google+ Is Exploding and Could Actually Hurt Facebook,' *Advertising Age*, July 25, 2011, 16. Available at: http://web2. westlaw.com (search for document "2011 WLNR 14949627").

Eaton, Kit, 'Pakistan Dials Its Islamic Net Censorship Up to 11, Shutters Yahoo! and Bing,' Fast Company, June 25, 2010. Available at: <http://www.fastcompany. com/1663977/censorship-pakistan-internet-islam>.

Eglash, Ruth, 'Power of the Online Petition,' *Jerusalem Post*, July 30, 2012, 22.

Elder, Miriam, 'Vladimir Putin Accuses Hillary Clinton of Encouraging Russian Protests,' *The Guardian*, Dec. 8, 2011. Available at: <http://www.guardian.co.uk/ world/2011/dec/08/vladimir-putin-hillary-clinton-russia>.

Electronic Privacy Information Center, 'EPIC – Social Networking Privacy.' Available at: <http://epic.org/privacy/socialnet/>.

Electronic Privacy Information Center, EPIC Comments In the Matter of Facebook, Inc., FTC File No. 0923184 (Dec. 27, 2011), 21. <http://epic.org/privacy/face-book/Facebook-FTC-Settlement-Comments-FINAL.pdf>.

European Union, Directive 2009/140/EC on a common regulatory framework for electronic communications and services, art. 1. Online. Available at: <http:// eur-lex.europa.eu/LexUriServ/LexUriServ.do?uri=CELEX:32009L0140:EN: NOT>.

Facebook (2012a), Choose Who You Share With – Facebook Help Center, 2012. Available at: <http://www.facebook.com/help/?page=119870658103124>.

Facebook (2012c), Data Use Policy (June 8, 2012), http://m.facebook.com/about/ privacy.

Facebook (2012b), Full Data Use Policy, 2012, http://www.facebook.com/full_data_ use_policy.

Facebook (2012e), Law Enforcement and Third-Party Matters, 2012. Available at: <http://www.facebook.com/help/?page=211462112226850>.

Facebook (2012f), Letter to House Intelligence Committee Chairman Rogers and Ranking Member Ruppersberger, Feb. 6, 2012. Available at: <http://intelligence. house.gov/sites/intelligence.house.gov/files/documents/FacebookHR3523.pdf>.

Facebook (2012d), Privacy Policy – Full Version, Oct. 29, 2009. Available at: <http://www.facebook.com/note.php?note_id=%20322194465300>, quoted in Dave Awl. *Facebook Me! A Guide to Socializing, Sharing, and Promoting on Facebook*, Pearson Education, 2010, http://books.google.com/books?id=mQEliT_03BUC& pg=PT142&lpg=PT142.

Foreign Direct Investment, 'Regions: Europe – Facebook sets up HQ in Dublin,' Dec. 19, 2008. Available at: http://web2.westlaw.com (search for document "2008 WLNR 24380353").

Fraley v. Facebook, Inc., 830 F. Supp. 2d 785 (N.D. Cal. 2011).

FTC (2011a), 'Facebook Settles FTC Charges That It Deceived Consumers By Failing To Keep Privacy Promises,' Nov. 29, 2011, http://ftc.gov/opa/2011/11/privacyset-tlement.shtm

FTC (2011b), 'FTC Accepts Final Settlement with Twitter for Failure to Safeguard Personal Information,' Federal Trade Commission Documents, Mar. 11, 2011, http://web2.westlaw.com (search "2011 WLNR 4890375").

Gallagher, Caithlin O'Farrell, f8 '08 Is Coming. … Facebook Developers Blog. June 12, 2008. Available at: <http://developers.facebook.com/blog/post/121/>.

Glanz, James & John Markoff, 'Egypt's Autocracy Found Internet's "Off" Switch,' *The New York Times*, Feb. 16, 2011, p. A1.

Godwin, Mike, 'Edited Comments Concerning Differentiating Action and Expression in a Virtual World,' Annual Survey of American Law 1994: 443.

Goldman, Eric, Split 9th Circuit Panel Approves Facebook Beacon Settlement – Lane v. Facebook. Technology and Marketing Blog (Sept. 21, 2012). Online. Available at: <http://blog.ericgoldman.org/archives/2012/09/split_9th_circu.htm>.

Grimmelman, James, 'Saving Facebook,' *Iowa Law Review*, 94: 1142 (2009).

Hamilton, Anita, 'Is Facebook Overrated?', *Time Mag.*, Nov 21, 2007. Online. Available at: <http://www.time.com/time/magazine/article/0,9171,1686825,00.html>.

Helft, Miguel & Jessi Hempel, 'Facebook vs. Google: The Battle for the Future of the Web,' *Fortune*, Nov. 21, 2011, 119–20.

Henderson, Stephen E., 'Learning from All Fifty States: How to Apply the Fourth Amendment and Its State Analogs to Protect Third Party Information from Unreasonable Search,' *Catholic University Law Review*, 55: 396–9 (2005).

Hepting v. AT&T Corp., 439 F. Supp. 2d 974 (N.D. Cal. 2006).

Hindustan Times, 'Anna Effect: Slacktivism Is Not Slack Anymore,' Westlaw (Aug. 21, 2011). Available at: <http://web2.westlaw.com> (search for "2011 WLNR 16573287").

Howard, Philip, 'Let's Nationalize Facebook,' *Slate*, Aug. 16, 2012, http://www.slate.com/articles/technology/future_tense/2012/08/facebook_should_be_nationalized_to_protect_user_rights_.html.

Hsu, Tiffany, 'Internet Restored in Egypt,' *Los Angeles Times*, Feb. 3, 2011, 2.

In re Facebook Privacy Litigation, 791 F. Supp. 2d 705 (N.D. Cal. 2011).

International Action Center v. U.S., 207 F.R.D. 1, 3 (D.D.C. 2002).

Jakarta Globe, 'Family Fears Missing Woman Was Kidnapped by Facebook Friend,' Feb. 16, 2010, http://www.thejakartaglobe.com/news/family-fears-missing-woman-was-kidnapped-by-facebook-friend/358954.

'Judge Rejects Deal in Facebook Ad Dispute; Terms of Settlement Questioned in Case Over Product Endorsements,' *The International Herald Tribune*, Aug. 20, 2012, p. 15, http://web2.westlaw.com (search for "2012 WLNR 17576406").

'Judge Rejects Settlement,' *Pittsburgh Post-Gazette*, Aug. 20, 2012, p. A5; Somini Sengupta,

John Doe No. 1 v. Reed, 130 S. Ct 2811, 2825 (2010).

Kallas, Priit, Top 10 Social Networking Sites by Market Share of Visits [May 2012], DreamGrow, Jan. 16, 2012. Available at: <http://www.dreamgrow.com/top-10-social-networking-sites-by-market-share-of-visits-may-2012/>.

Katz, I., 'Tim Berners-Lee urges government to stop the snooping bill,' *The Guardian* (U.K.), Apr. 17, 2012. http://www.guardian.co.uk/technology/2012/apr/17/tim-berners-lee-monitoring-internet.

Krayewski, Ed, Nationalize Facebook? Really?, Reason.com Hit & Run Blog, Aug. 17, 2012, http://reason.com/blog/2012/08/17/nationalize-facebook-really.

Lai, Eric, 'Should Facebook, Twitter Follow IM Providers and Block Access to U.S. "Enemies"?,' *Government IT/Computerworld*, June 10, 2009. Available at: <http://www.computerworld.com/s/article/9134233/Should_Facebook_Twitter_follow_IM_providers_and_block_access_to_U.S._enemies_>.

Letzing, John, 'Facebook, Yahoo Kiss and Make Up,' *Wall Street Journal*, July 6, 2012, http://online.wsj.com/article/SB10001424052702303684004577511132642631606.html.

Levitt, Carole & Mark Rosch, 'How Lawyers Can Mine A Social Network for Personal Information,' *Nevada Lawyer*, Mar. 2008, p. 12.

Liveuniverse, Inc. v. Myspace, Inc., No. CV 06-6994, 2007 WL 6865852 (C.D. Cal. June 04, 2007). Available at: <http://web2.westlaw.com>.

Luhr, Nadia L., 'Iran, Social Media, and U.S. Trade Sanctions: The First Amendment Implications of U.S. Foreign Policy,' *First Amendment Law Review*, 8: 500–16 (2009–2010).

Lumin Consulting, CISPA. 2012. Available at: <http://luminconsulting.com/cispa/>.

Matus, Jonathan, Growth and Mobile Apps, May 1, 2012. Available at: <http://developers.facebook.com/blog/post/2012/05/01/growth-and-mobile-apps/>.

McCullagh, Declan, 'Facebook's FTC Settlement Won't Change Much, If Anything,' CNet, Nov. 29, 2011, <http://news.cnet.com/8301-31921_3-57333398-281/facebooks-ftc-settlement-wont-change-much-if-anything/>.

McCullagh, Declan, 'Iranians Find Ways to Bypass Net Censors,' *CNet*, June 17, 2009, http://news.cnet.com/8301-13578_3-10267287-38.html?tag=mncol;txt

McDonald, Aleecia M. & Lorrie Faith Cranor, 'The Cost of Reading Privacy Policies,' *I/S: A Journal of Law and Policy for the Information Society*, 4: 18 (2008). Available at: <http://www.is-journal.org/>.

Morin, Dave. Facebook Platform Matures to Version 1.0, Feb. 8, 2007. Available at: <http://developers.facebook.com/blog/post/13/>

MySpace, Inc. v. GraphOn Corp., 672 F. 3d 1250 (Fed. Cir. 2012) (Mayer, J., dissenting).

NewsInc., 'KRI, WPO Join a Tribe,' Jan. 19, 2009. Online. Available at: http://web2.westlaw.com (search for document "2003 WLNR 17641988").

O'Brien, Chris, 'New Apps That Make Sharing Too Easy on Facebook Could Destroy It,' San Jose Mercury News, June 22, 2012. Available at: http://web2.westlaw.com (search for document "2012 WLNR 13043448").

O'Dowd, T. John, 'Pilate's Paramount Duty: Constitutional "Reasonableness" and the Restriction of Freedom of Speech and Assembly,' SSRN. 2010. Available at: <http://ssrn.com/abstract=1583181>

Ortutay, Barbara, 'AOL Plans to Sell 800 Patents to Microsoft for $1 Billion,' *USA Today*/Associated Press, Apr. 10, 2012, p. 1B, http://web2.westlaw.com (search for "2012 WLNR 7521612").

Pakistan Penal Code (Act 45 of 1960) Sections 295, 298.

Perez, Juan Carlos, 'Facebook's Beacon More Intrusive Than Previously Thought,' *PC World* (Nov. 30, 2007). Online. Available at: <http://www.pcworld.com/article/140182/facebooks_beacon_more_intrusive_than_previously_thought.htm>.

Perlroth, Nicole, 'Revamping at Yahoo to Focus on Its Media Properties and Customer Data,' *The New York Times*, Apr. 11, 2012, B4, http://web2.westlaw.com (search for "2012 WLNR 7597985").

Pizzi, Peter J., 'Addressing Security Concerns, and Responding to Recent IT Trends Where Cyber and Employment Law Intersect, Risks For Management Abound,' July 2011. Available at: <http://web2.westlaw.com (search for "2011 WL 3020563").

Potter, W. James, *Media Literacy*, London: Sage Publications, 2012.

Preston, Jennifer et al., 'Movement Began With Outrage and a Facebook Page That Gave It an Outlet,' *The New York Times*, Feb. 6, 2011, A10.

Radio Free Europe, 'The Future of Censorship,' Westlaw (Nov. 4, 2010). Available at: <http://web2.westlaw.com> (search for "2010 WLNR 22105845").

Rustad, Michael L. & Thomas H. Koenig, 'Rebooting Cybertort Law,' *Washington Law Review*, 80: 335–71 (2005).

Semitsu, J., 'From Facebook to Mug Shot: How the Dearth of Social Networking Privacy Rights Revolutionized Online Government Surveillance,' *Pace Law Review*, vol. 31 (2011): 291–381.

Southeast Booksellers Ass'n v. McMaster, 371 F. Supp. 2d 773 (D.S.C. 2005).

Stanton, Lynn, 'Legislative Measures to Address Spectrum Issues Seen as Likely to Follow Resolution of Disapproval,' *Telecommunications*, Feb. 25, 2012, p. 24.

Suthersanen, Uma, 'Towards an International Public Interest Rule? Human Rights and International Copyright Law,' in Jonathan Griffiths & Uma Suthersanen (Eds.), *Copyright and Free Speech: Comparative and International Analyses*. Oxford: Oxford University Press, 2005, pp. 107–51.

The Facebook v. Pacific Northwest Software, Case No. 08-16873 (9th Cir. Apr. 11, 2011). Online. <http://cdn.ca9.uscourts.gov/datastore/opinions/2011/04/11/08-16745.pdf> (last visited Dec. 1, 2012).

Thierer, Adam, '10 Reasons Why Nationalizing Facebook Would Be Ridiculous,' Forbes.com, Aug. 17, 2012, http://www.forbes.com/sites/adamthierer/2012/08/17/10-reasons-why-nationalizing-facebook-would-be-ridiculous/2/.

Timpane, John, 'Today's E-Protesters Live-stream to the Barricades,' *Philadelphia Inquirer*, Oct. 23, 2011, A02. Available at: <http://web2.westlaw.com> (search for "2011 WLNR 21744706")

Tokson, Matthew, 'Automation and the Fourth Amendment,' *Iowa Law Review*, 96: 627–8 (2011).

TR Daily, 'FTCs Proposed Settlement with Facebook Treads Path of Google Buzz Settlement,' Westlaw (Nov. 29, 2011), http://web2.westlaw.com (search for "2011 WLNR 24717825").

Tsukayama, Hayley, 'Facebook Denies Report It's Snooping Through Texts,' *The Washington Post*, Feb. 27, 2012. Available at: <http://www.washingtonpost.com/business/technology/facebook-denies-report-its-snooping-through-texts/2012/02/27/gIQAkGPydR_story.html>

Twitter, Twitter Blog: Twitter Transparency Report, July 2, 2012. Online. Available at: <http://blog.twitter.com/2012/07/twitter-transparency-report.html>

United Nations, 'Combating Defamation of Religions,' U.N. Doc. E/CN.4/Res/2003/4.

United States Court of Appeals for the Ninth Circuit (2011) *The Facebook v. Pacific Northwest Software*, Inc., Nos. 08-16745, Unofficial transcript of oral argument, Jan 11. http://wilta.files.wordpress.com/2011/04/the-facebook-inc-mark-zuckerberg-plaintiffs-and-apellees-divya-narenda-cameron.pdf.

Unsworth, John, 'Electronic Scholarship, or, Scholarly Publishing and the Public,' *Journal of Scholarly Publishing*, Oct. 1, 1996, http://web2.westlaw.com (search for "1996 WLNR 151484").

U.S. Code, title 18, section 2702.

U.S. House of Representatives, H.R. 3523 112th Congress, 1st Session, Section 1104(f) ("CISPA"), 2012. Available at: <http://www.docstoc.com/docs/118456990/CISPA-Full-Text>

U.S. District Court for the Northern District of California, Legal Notice of Proposed.

U.S District Court for the Northern District of California, Class Action Settlement, *Lane v. Facebook, Inc.*, Case No. 5:08-cv-03845 (N.D. Cal. preliminary approval granted Oct. 23, 2009).

Valentino-DeVries, Jennifer, 'Google to Pay $22.5 Million in FTC Settlement,' *Wall Street Journal*, Aug. 9, 2012, http://online.wsj.com/article/SB10000872396390443404004577579232818727246.html.

Wall Street Journal Abstracts, 'Facebook Ban Is Lifted After Site Removes Page,' Westlaw (June 8, 2010), A14, 6/7/10 WSJ-ABS A14. Available at: <http://web2.westlaw.com> (search for "2010 WLNR 11652450").

Wasserman, Todd, Google+ Grew 27% in March, Logged 61 Million Visits [STUDY], Mashable. Apr. 6, 2012. Online. Available at: <http://mashable.com/2012/04/06/google-plus-traffic-march/>.

Weber Waller, Spencer, 'Antitrust and Social Networking,' *North Carolina Law Review*, 90: 1785 (2012).

Winklevoss, Cameron, Tyler Winklevoss, and Divya Narendra, Appellants' Petition for Rehearing En Banc, *TheFaceBook, Inc. v. ConnectU, Inc.*, Nos. 07-16745, 08-16873, 09-15021, 07-01389 (9th Cir. petition for rehearing en banc filed Apr. 18, 2011), p. 4.

Wireless Operating Co., Inc., 529 F. 3d 892 (9th Cir. 2008).

Yahoo! Inc., Complaint, Yahoo! Inc. v. Facebook, Inc., No. 12-1212-CV (N.D. Cal. complaint filed Mar. 12, 2012).

Zuckerberg, Mark, An Open Letter from Mark Zuckerberg, Sept. 8, 2006. Online. Available at: <http://blog.facebook.com/blog.php?post=2208562130>.

Conclusion

Taking it down

Hannibal Travis[1]

Three sorts of findings emerge from the studies gathered in this volume.

First, the right of freedom of expression under the First Amendment should limit assertions of intellectual property rights against Internet critics or parodists of rights owners. As one court explained, the use of a trademark on the Internet may be "purely an exhibition of Free Speech, ... a type of public expression, no different in scope than a billboard or a pulpit," so that an Internet user "has a First Amendment right to express his opinion ..., and as long as his speech is not commercially misleading, the [law] cannot be summoned to prevent it." Similarly, the attempt to hold YouTube liable not only for specific infringing videos but for "red flags" of an infringing atmosphere in general threatens to restrict online video sites with copyright filters, in a bid to stave off massive liability. And with the march of patents into more abstract "method" claims, First Amendment analysis of patent issues is likely to become more refined, particularly in the social networking space.

Second, Internet communication is increasingly under threat from public-private collaboration to enforce private rights recognized under public law. Rights holders often press their claims against Internet users by pressuring intermediaries such as eBay or Google, with the effect that exclusive rights in ideas, phrases, symbols, and technologies may impede broader public availability and legitimate reuse of these creations of the mind. Courts have begun to realize that clear limitations on exclusive rights, limitations also known as the commons or the public domain, may do more to enhance the production and distribution of information than do some of the exclusive rights themselves. However, these insights may be mooted by direct negotiations between rights holders and online intermediaries concerning take-downs, account terminations, and automated filtering for lists of words, audiovisual clips, or infringing titles. These negotiations may impact a variety of societal aims related to public access to information, competition in the resale market, and freedom of expression. Likewise, norms of corporate social

---

1 Associate Professor of Law, Florida International University College of Law.

responsibility, recently invoked by the petitions to Facebook to get Holocaust-denying groups banned, highlight the power of private regulation. Taking down content may be a private step, but it has public consequences.

Third, privacy has a role to play in promoting the free and equal participation of Internet users in global communication and debate. The alleged privacy violations by Facebook prompted some users to sue, and commentators to complain of a convergence of social-networking platforms towards a single, relatively privacy-insensitive, network. Despite gaps in the law, and difficulties applying somewhat antiquated definitions to a new communicative order, courts have made progress in defining a minimal constitutional and statutory level of privacy for Facebook users. This level includes, among other things, a Fourth Amendment right to be protected from unreasonable searches and seizures of information stored by third parties, and a statutory right to be protected from the misleading advertising of privacy policies on social networks or other Web sites.

Future research in this area should be able to uncover rich new primary sources that may inform our understanding of how the regulation of the Internet operates in practice. Cases like *Tiffany v. eBay* and *Viacom v. YouTube* have made public excerpts from large repositories of emails and electronic documents relating to the enforcement of intellectual-property laws against Internet users. In the event that a class of all authors affected by Google Book Search is certified, despite Google's appeal of the certification issue to the Second Circuit, and full-blown discovery begins into Google's defenses of fair use and ownership issues, a path may become more clear as to how digital libraries can resolve copyright claims and mount fair use defenses. Matching up the evidence revealed in such cases against the revenues and profits of the industries that claim to suffer from Internet-enabled infringement may help us test such claims. Similarly, the regular federal audits of Facebook's privacy, and Federal Communications Commission inquiries into the progress towards giving all Americans access to advanced broadband networks, may shed light on how existing regulation of the Internet by means of courts and federal agencies is impacting Internet users. To date, Internet regulation has too often been based on an incomplete understanding of what technology makes possible, and of what the Internet's future holds.

Index